First Flight around the World by Helicopter

On September 1, 1982, Ross Perot Jr. and Jay Coburn left Dallas in the Bell 206L-1 LongRanger II *Spirit of Texas* in an attempt to be the first to fly around the world in a helicopter. On September 30, 29 days, 3 hours, and 8 minutes later, they landed in Dallas, completing their epic flight and capturing another first for the United States. During the flight, which covered 24,754 miles, they spent 246.5 hours in the air, an average of 9.5 hours per flight. The *Spirit of Texas* crossed 26 countries and 21 seas and oceans. Most of the flight was conducted at an altitude of 1,000 feet above the ground. One of the high points of the trip was the landing on the container ship *President McKinley*, in twelve-foot swells in the middle of the Pacific. Although neither Perot nor Coburn had landed on a ship before, they were successful on their first attempt.

R. PEROT

PILOT, ROSS PEROT JR.

At the time of the flight, Ross Perot Jr. was 23 years old and had about 500 hours of flight experience. A graduate of Vanderbilt University, Perot had been surprised to learn that no helicopter had flown around the world, and he was determined that a U.S. citizen should be the first to do so.

PILOT, JAY COBURN

A veteran helicopter pilot, Coburn served with distinction in the U.S. Army during the Vietnam War and had accumulated 3,500 hours of flying time before the trip. Ross Perot Jr. was introduced to helicopters with assistance from Jay. The two men had made a 122-hour helicopter flight to Alaska in 1981.

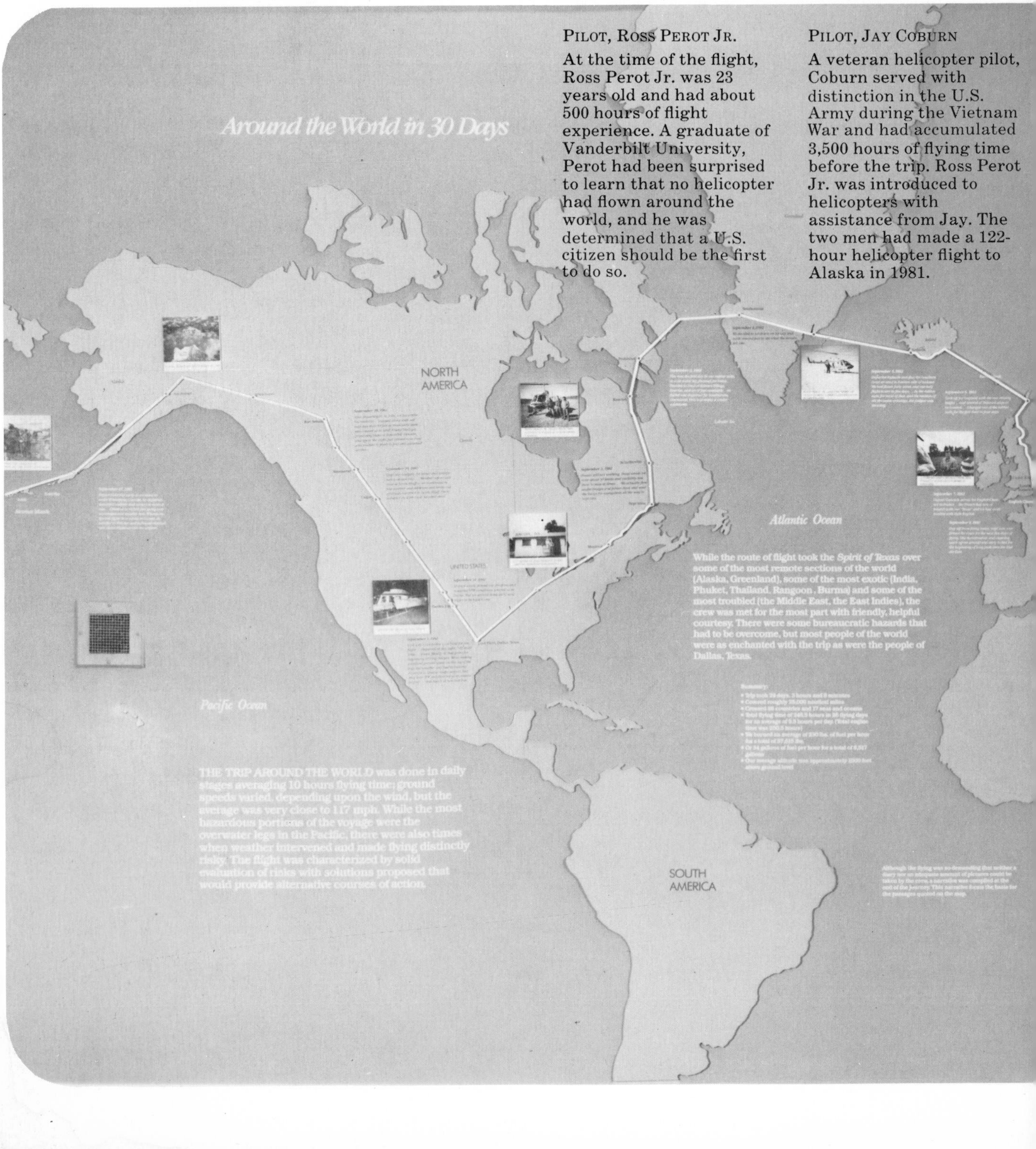
Around the World in 30 Days
NORTH AMERICA
Atlantic Ocean
While the route of flight took the Spirit of Texas over some of the most remote sections of the world (Alaska, Greenland), some of the most exotic (India, Phuket, Thailand, Rangoon, Burma) and some of the most troubled (the Middle East, the East Indies), the crew was met for the most part with friendly, helpful courtesy. There were some bureaucratic hazards that had to be overcome, but most people of the world were as enchanted with the trip as were the people of Dallas, Texas.
Pacific Ocean
THE TRIP AROUND THE WORLD was done in daily stages averaging 10 hours flying time; ground speeds varied, depending upon the wind, but the average was very close to 117 mph. While the most hazardous portions of the voyage were the overwater legs in the Pacific, there were also times when weather intervened and made flying distinctly risky. The flight was characterized by solid evaluation of risks with solutions proposed that would provide alternative courses of action.
SOUTH AMERICA

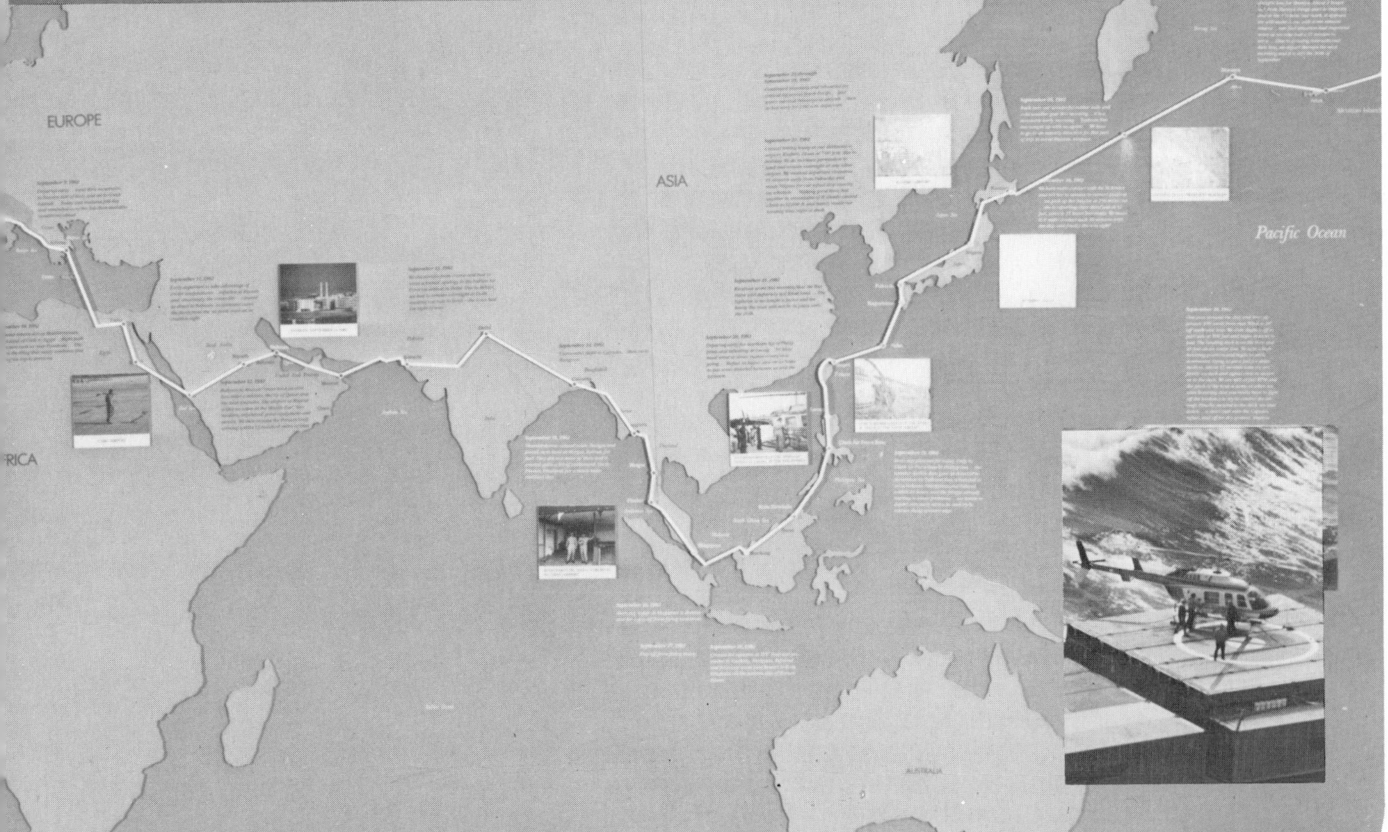
EUROPE
ASIA
Pacific Ocean

The Age of the Helicopter

VERTICAL FLIGHT

Edited by

Walter J. Boyne
Director, National Air and Space Museum

and

Donald S. Lopez
Deputy Director,
National Air and Space Museum

With contributions by

Ralph P. Alex
Edward S. Carter
William J. Crawford III
R. H. Jones
Charles H. Kaman
Edward F. Katzenberger
Bartram Kelley
Russell E. Lee
Charles Marchetti
Frank Piasecki
Dominick A. Pisano
R. W. Prouty
John J. Schneider
Sergei I. Sikorsky
John F. Ward
Steve Wartenberg
Arthur M. Young

Published for the
NATIONAL AIR AND SPACE MUSEUM
Smithsonian Institution
SMITHSONIAN INSTITUTION PRESS
Washington, D.C.
1984

Library of Congress Cataloging in Publication Data
Main entry under title:

Vertical flight.

Bibliography: p.
Supt. of Docs. no.: SI 9.2:F64
1. Helicopters—History. I. Boyne, Walter J., 1929– . II. Lopez, Donald S., 1923– .
TL716.V39 1984 629.133'352'09 84-600107
ISBN 0-87474-279-X

Designed by Gerard A. Valerio, Bookmark Studio

The paper in this book meets the guidelines for permanence and durability of the Committee on Production Guidelines for Book Longevity of the Council on Library Resources.

Contents

Preface

The history of any technology is best told by those pioneers who endured the hardships, blind alleys, and failures of the early days and emerged triumphant. Many of the articles in this book are first-person accounts by the pioneers who developed the helicopter. They take you through its growth from a vibrating, underpowered curiosity to the irreplaceable adjunct to aviation that it is today.

In 1942 the Sikorsky XR-4 was flown from the Sikorsky plant in Connecticut to Wright Field, Ohio, a distance of 761 miles, in five days. Forty years later, two young men from Texas flew a Bell LongRanger around the world, a distance of 24,754 miles, in just under thirty days, an average of more than 800 miles a day. Improvements of the same magnitude were made in speed, altitude, and payload (described by one pioneer in an early helicopter as "two oral messages") and in the critical area of reliability.

While today we accept the helicopter and its capabilities as part of our everyday life, this was not always the case. We hope you will find it rewarding to see not only where we have been but, more important, where we are going.

WALTER J. BOYNE, Director
National Air and Space Museum

DONALD S. LOPEZ, Deputy Director
National Air and Space Museum

Acknowledgments

The editors and authors wish to express their thanks to the following persons who assisted in the preparation of this volume. Helen McMahon, publications coordinator, ably directed the volume along its tortuous path to publication. Toni Thomas, special assistant to the deputy director, collected the photographs for the photo essay and maintained close liaison between the authors and the editors. Patricia Graboske initially edited the articles, organized the illustrations, and checked them for accuracy. Russell Lee, who prepared the chronology, helped her with the helicopter identifications and located many rare photographs in the NASM research files. Dorothy Cochrane provided photographs of Forest Service helicopters. Phil Edwards, chief reference librarian, assisted Dominick Pisano in the preparation of the bibliography. Susan Owen typed most of the articles into the word processor; Vivian Vines typed the remainder of them.

The National Air and Space Museum is grateful for the invaluable assistance provided by the American Helicopter Society in the preparation of this book. Steve Wartenberg of the American Helicopter Society, in addition to contributing an article, was most valuable as the principal link between the society and the National Air and Space Museum. Jane Ward provided invaluable assistance to Steve Wartenberg in the preparation of his article. John Zugschwert, executive director of the American Helicopter Society, and Leon Smith, vice president of Aerospatiale, Inc., arranged for the translation of Charles Marchetti's article from the original French.

Foreword

The American Helicopter Society was founded in 1943 in Bridgeport, Connecticut, by a small group of engineers who were interested in creating an organization that could serve as a forum for the discussion and dissemination of information on the helicopter. From this modest beginning, the American Helicopter Society has grown into an international organization with more than 5,700 individual members and 100 corporate members dedicated to the development and future of vertical flight technology and its application.

We at the American Helicopter Society are proud of the contributions we have made to the advancement of the helicopter. From its very beginning, the American Helicopter Society has dedicated itself to bringing together all segments of the industry to develop and plan for future generations of vertical flight technology. This book is being published in conjunction with the 40th Annual Forum of the American Helicopter Society, which represents forty years of advancement and service by the helicopter industry. During this period, the American Helicopter Society has sponsored a variety of meetings and programs that have brought together various segments of the industry and has published an array of magazines, journals, and proceedings about the latest advances in and future of the industry.

We pledge to continue our leadership and support of the helicopter industry and work toward the improvement of vertical flight technology and the services it can bring all mankind. The society is honored that the Smithsonian Institution's National Air and Space Museum has given us this opportunity to share with you the fascinating history of the helicopter and the pioneers who made it possible. We hope that you will find this book interesting and that you look toward the future of the helicopter with as much optimism as we do. The helicopter's time has come; it is serving all of us, every day, all over the world.

JOSEPH MALLEN, Chairman
American Helicopter Society

VERTICAL FLIGHT

STEVE WARTENBERG

Solving the Vertical Flight Puzzle: The Early History of the Helicopter

The development of the helicopter can be compared to the piecing together of a puzzle—a puzzle that took several thousand years to complete and the efforts and dedication of hundreds of brilliant, creative, and courageous pioneers. Like any puzzle, it was composed of thousands of pieces that had to be put together carefully and painstakingly, one by one. As each piece was put in place, a little more of the unknown was filled in and the helicopter moved inexorably closer to its destiny of flight.

The beginning of the vertical flight puzzle can be traced all the way back to the fourth century B.C., when the Chinese developed a flying top that was the first device of any kind to fly under its own power. These toys consisted of feathers mounted on top of a stick. The feathers were set at a slight angle so they would create a lifting force when spun, either by a string or by hand.

LEONARDO

In his now famous drawing of the lifting airscrew, or helix, Leonardo da Vinci proposed the first full-scale helicopter (see figure 1). In describing his drawing, Leonardo wrote, "I find that if this instrument with a screw be well made—that is to say, made of linen of which the pores be stopped up with starch—and be turned swiftly, the said screw will make its spiral in the air and it will rise high."[1]

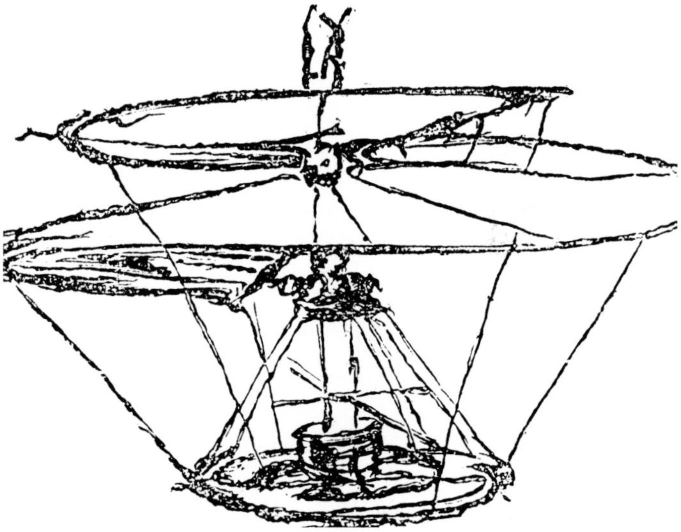

Figure 1.
Leonardo da Vinci's helix

LOMONOSOV

In the succeeding centuries many of the greatest minds addressed the concept of vertical flight, refining the idea of turning airscrews or rotors to provide lift. Jumping ahead to 1784, a Russian scientist named Mikhail V. Lomonosov built what is believed to be the first lifting airscrew model that was self-powered. His model was driven by a small spring motor and flew suspended from a string. He demonstrated it to the Russian Academy of Sciences, which wrote after the demonstration, "The honorable Advisor Lomonosov demonstrated his invention called 'Aerodynamic' to be used for the purpose of depressing the air by means of wings rotated horizontally in the opposite directions by the agency of a spring of the type used in clocks in order to lift the machine into the upper layers of the air."[2]

LAUNOY

Several other model helicopters were built and flown in Europe during the following decades, further demonstrating the feasibility of the concept. Another piece of the puzzle was added by a French naturalist named Launoy, who built a small model using two rotors that turned in opposite directions (see figure 2). This model thus addressed for the first time the problem of torque, in which the shaft of the rotor twisted or turned in the opposite direction from which the rotor spun. This was a problem that would continue to plague helicopter pioneers in succeeding years.

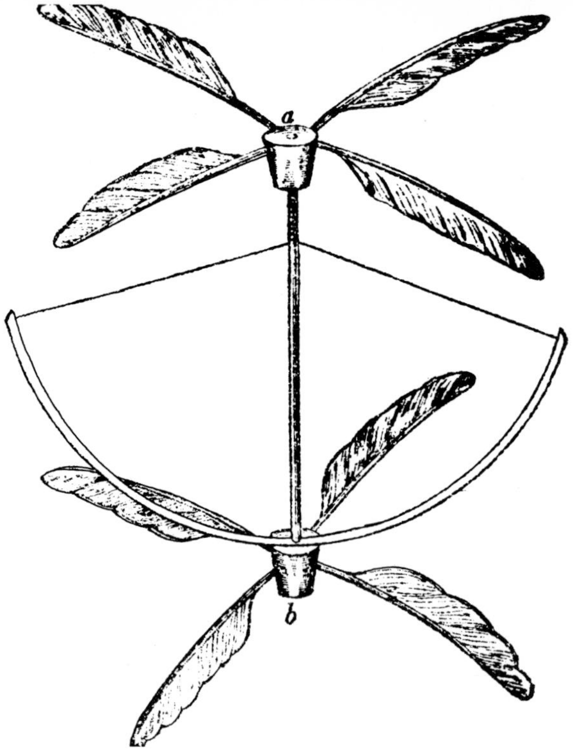

Figure 2.
Launoy's model, which addressed the problem of torque

Figure 3. Sir George Cayley's design for a full-scale helicopter

Cayley

In the early 1800s, an English scientist, Sir George Cayley, built several models that were capable of flight; during the 1840s he designed a full-scale helicopter (see figure 3). His aircraft used counterrotating rotors on either side of a canvas-covered fuselage, with an additional pair of pusher propellers at the rear of the aircraft to help with horizontal flight. In describing the rotor system of his helicopter, Cayley wrote, "The first [set of rotors] may be termed the elevating fliers to distinguish them from the two smaller ones, set at a very different angle with their axis and used for propelling the machine when the others are stationary. Both sets will be put into action gradually, or in any degree by friction plates."[3] Cayley's design, although it never left the drawing board because he recognized that a propulsion system powerful enough to turn his rotors did not exist, can be considered the first modern helicopter design. Several helicopters built in the twentieth century have used ideas first proposed by Cayley.

Forlanini

In 1878, Italian professor and inventor Enrico Forlanini built a small steam-powered helicopter model that flew to a height of forty feet, where it remained for twenty seconds. At the time, steam engines were much too heavy in proportion to the power they could produce to power a full-scale helicopter or even a model. Forlanini overcame this problem by forcing superheated steam into a small sphere slung underneath his model. The steam escaped slowly through cylinders to turn the rotors and lift the model.

Edison

In the 1880s, another famous inventor and scientist, Thomas Alva Edison, confronted the puzzle of vertical flight in the United States, only to be stopped by the lack of an adequate propulsion system. Edison set out initially to address the problem of measuring the lift of different types of rotors to arrive at the most efficient design. He mounted his experimental rotors on a vertical shaft powered by an electric motor, which was connected to weight-measuring scales. As the rotors turned, Edison could read how many pounds of lift the rotors produced. He soon realized that existing engines could create only 160 pounds of lift, regardless of the rotor design. Never having been one to let such problems stop him, Edison set out to design a more powerful engine; his engine experiments were not successful, however. As he described his efforts in his notes, "I used stock-ticker paper made into guncotton and fed the paper into the cylinder of the engine and exploded it with a spark. I got good results, but burned one of my men pretty badly and burned off some of my own hair and didn't get much further."[4]

Edison still believed in the helicopter, but he concluded that successful aircraft would not be built until an engine that weighed no more than forty-two to sixty-three ounces for each horsepower it produced could be developed.

As the twentieth century began, it seemed that the only thing delaying the development of a successful helicopter was a suitable propulsion system. During the early 1900s much more powerful gasoline engines were developed, engines that enabled the Wright brothers to make man's first powered flight in 1903. It seemed that successful helicopter flight was just around the corner, but as these early pioneers would soon find out, the development of propulsion systems was just one of the pieces in the puzzle. Most of the problems that would arise were not even imagined at the time, because the helicopter was still just a "paper" aircraft. Now, with more powerful engines being developed and produced, engineers were able to build helicopters that could fly and began to learn about all the other obstacles that would have to be overcome. The next forty years saw each of these problems addressed and solved by a number of noted engineers, through a wide variety of designs, throughout the world.

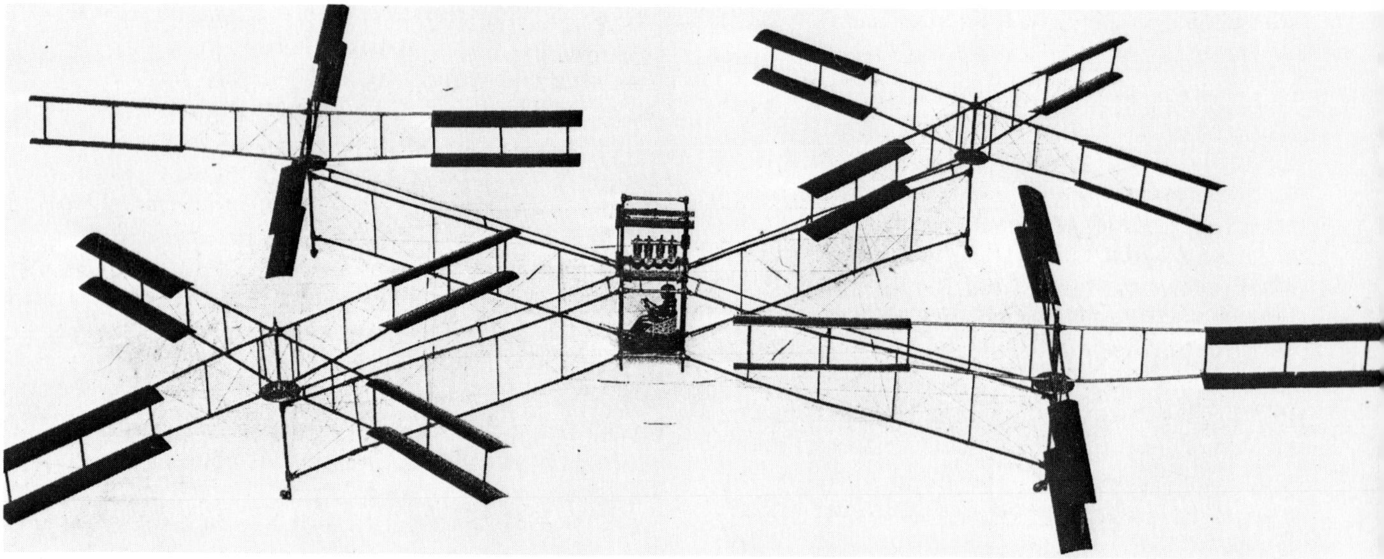

Figure 4.
The Breguet Gyroplane No. 1

Breguet

In 1907, helicopters developed in France by Louis Breguet and Paul Cornu took the first tentative, shaky hops into the air. On August 24, 1907, the *Gyroplane No. 1,* developed by Breguet, left the ground, held steady by four assistants to prevent any erratic movements or the possibility of a crash. The aircraft rose to a height of two feet and remained airborne for two minutes (see figure 4). In 1908 and 1909, Breguet built two more helicopters that flew, but each was beset by problems, including a lack of power and the lack of lightweight materials to reduce the overall weight of the aircraft. On July 22, 1908, one of Breguet's aircraft rose to a height of fifteen feet but, lacking enough control to land, it crashed. Breguet gave up his helicopter experiments to turn toward fixed-wing development, where he achieved great success, only to return to helicopter development in the 1930s.

Cornu

On November 13, 1907, Paul Cornu achieved the first true "free flight" of a helicopter when his aircraft rose to a height of one to five feet for twenty seconds. Cornu's aircraft had two rotors approximately twenty feet in diameter that were mounted one behind the other (see figure 5). His machine also had a means of propelling itself forward—two tilted wind vanes mounted under the main rotors that deflected the slipstream from the rotors backward and downward. The driving force of these wind vanes was weak, and they never functioned successfully.

Breguet's and Cornu's aircraft manifested similar problems—severe lack of control and stability in flight. These were problems that had never before been considered, but they would plague all the future development of the helicopter.

Sikorsky

In 1909 and 1910, a young Russian named Igor Sikorsky developed two helicopters. Although neither was successful, Sikorsky never lost his enthusiasm for the helicopter, and, like Breguet, he returned to helicopter development in the 1930s after a successful career in fixed-wing aircraft. Sikorsky explained the reasons for his early failures as follows:

> *The first machine achieved little results except mainly to teach me how things should not be*

done. This is a very important experience as every engineer knows. In 1910, I built the second helicopter which was lighter and had a total weight empty of about 400 pounds. The power was again 25 hp with two lifting propellers of 19 feet diameter, rotating in opposite directions, at 160 revolutions per minute, and this was sufficient to lift the machine off the ground without a man in it, however. While this was done, the machine had to be kept inside a sort of railing because she was unstable.

These two first attempts were very interesting and by the end of the second one, I learned enough to realize that my modest knowledge at the time and also limited financial resources would not permit bringing the helicopter to success in 1910 and, therefore, I shifted to airplanes.[5]

During the next thirty years Sikorsky gained the knowledge he lacked in 1910 and is considered by many to be the father of the modern helicopter.

Petroczy

During World War I, Lieutenant Stefan von Petroczy of the Austrian Army Balloon Corps constructed a vertical-lift machine that he hoped would replace the highly vulnerable captive observation balloon. Much of the experimental and technical work on the aircraft was done by the noted engineer Pro-

Figure 5.
Cornu's helicopter, which achieved the first true free flight

Figure 6.
Petroczy's helicopter with gasoline engines

fessor Theodor von Karman. Two types of aircraft were built, one, with an electrically driven motor, that was not successful, and one, with gasoline engines, that was much more successful. The aircraft consisted of a three-armed steel frame, each arm carrying an engine (see figure 6). Each of the three engines drove two counterrotating rotors through bevel gears. The observer's platform was mounted above the rotors. The aircraft was equipped with a parachute that could slow it down in the event of engine failure, and it was planned to equip the observer with a parachute as well.

The aircraft made several tethered test flights in 1916 without an observer, reaching an estimated height of 150 feet and remaining airborne for as long as an hour. In June 1916, the aircraft was destroyed during a test flight and the project was abandoned. Although the tests were not entirely successful, Professor von Karman stated that several valuable lessons had been learned, including something about the relation of the center of gravity to the position of the rotors.

DE BOTHEZAT

In 1921, the U.S. Army undertook its first important vertical flight program, under the direction of the Russian engineer George de Bothezat. Before starting the project, de Bothezat gave the army a summary of helicopter development up to that time, describing the technical advances that had been made and also displaying a little bit of his own character.

> *Actually we have all the necessary knowledge on hand in order to build a helicopter, and such an apparatus can be built, even with small expense, in a rather short time. Even no preliminary tests are necessary, so clear are all the relations that hold in this case. If the helicopter has not been realized until the present, it is only because those who have the facilities and possibilities to do it are usually ignorant on the subject. The usual helicopter inventor thinks that the entire problem is in securing the necessary lift. He concentrates all his attention on the last and because he is totally ignorant about blade screws, it is unable to even reach so far. If the building of helicopters would have been left to men of knowledge on the subject, it would have been long since realized.*[6]

With these strong words and high expectations, de Bothezat began to construct his aircraft in total secrecy in Dayton, Ohio, under the auspices of the U.S. Army Air Services (see figure 7). On December 18, 1922, the de Bothezat helicopter made its long-awaited first flight. As reported by the Army Air Service,

> *The four great propeller wings or screws began to rotate like giant pinwheels. The helpers then stood clear of the machine while the pilot gradually increased the speed of the motor. The propellers rotated faster and faster. . . . The movement seemed graceful and without the noise of friction in any part of the mechanism. She lifted herself lightly, an inch, two, three—up, up until she stood about three feet clear of the ground and remained at an altitude between two to six feet for one minute and forty-two seconds.*[7]

The aircraft made numerous flights during the following year, once lifting four persons. It had four six-blade rotors mounted at the end of four arms of steel and aluminum tubing. An attempt was made to increase stability by sloping the axes of the four rotors inward, so that imaginary lines drawn through the axes would meet at a point directly over the center of gravity of the aircraft.

Despite all the successful flights and the attempts at increased control, the army was not entirely satisfied with the de Bothezat helicopter. It was considered too complex and was not as stable as de Bothezat had claimed it would be. In a final evaluation, the U.S. Army stated, "It is believed that this type does not offer the best possibility for the future development on account, principally, of the unfavorable feature of (1) inherent dissymmetry, in case of mechanical failure, and (2) general mechanical complexity."[8] The report did conclude, however, that the de Bothezat helicopter "contributed a definite forward step in the helicopter progress in being a practical example of the proper method of design above mentioned and in being a helicopter which theoretically and practically has provision for more desired performance properties than any other existing machine."[9]

Berliner

In the United States, Emile Berliner, inventor of the Victor phonograph, experimented with helicopter designs as early as 1908. The culmination of his work came in the early 1920s, when several helicopters built according to his designs by Berliner and his son Henry flew with success. Like many other designers of the era, the Berliners chose to solve the torque problem by using counterrotating rotors. Their aircraft also featured a vertical rudder, with small horizontal vanes for control. Although the aircraft lacked stability, it did fly in 1920.

By 1922, the Berliners had drastically altered the design of their aircraft (see figure 8), using two separate rotors mounted on wings around a center fuselage. The engine was mounted in the nose of the helicopter and drove the rotors in opposite directions through shafts and gearing. A third propeller was mounted at the rear of the fuselage and could be controlled by the pilot to increase or decrease lift. The Berliners continued their experiments and made

Figure 7.
The de Bothezat helicopter

Figure 8. Berliner's helicopter

many alterations in their design during the next five years.

Eventually they were forced to abandon the effort when too many problems arose—the disc area of their rotors was too small to provide adequate lift, for example, the wing surfaces interfered with the rotors, and the aircraft lacked stability—that they could not solve.

Oehmichen

In France, Etienne Oehmichen, an engineer at the Peugeot motorcar and bicycle firm, began experimenting with helicopters in the early 1920s. After his initial, unsuccessful efforts he even tried using a large, gas-filled balloon atop his helicopter to provide additional lift. Finally, in 1922, Oehmichen succeeded in building a helicopter that flew without the aid of a balloon. This aircraft had four main rotors, each with two blades (see figure 9). It also had five small horizontal propellers with variable and reversible pitch, the purpose of which was to maintain the horizontal attitude of the aircraft in flight and to correct air disturbances. This aircraft made hundreds of flights, many of which lasted several minutes. On May 4, 1924, Oehmichen succeeded in flying the first one-kilometer closed-circuit course, winning the 90,000-franc prize offered by the Service Technique de L'Aéronautique. The following is Oehmichen's description of this historic flight:

> *I brought the apparatus back to the starting point of the prepared circuit, which was a triangular course of 1 km. marked out by stakes. The apparatus, oscillating between one and three meters, flew the first two sides of the triangle correctly, but the third corner stake was widely passed by, as at the same time the machine showed a certain sluggishness in turning. This brought me over a strip of deep ditches and small gullies, seeing which I gained altitude which allowed me to make my corner rapidly and get on course again.*
>
> *The last leg of the triangle was flown very rapidly at an elevation of one or two meters and with a slight turning to the left. The landing point, which was rather hard to see through the maze of tubes and wires, was pointed out to me by the men of my crew, one of whom, running along in front of the machine, showed me with outstretched arms the proper course. I soon passed him and a few seconds after I set the apparatus down a little less than 2 m. from the point of departure.*[10]

PESCARA

At the same time that Oehmichen was making his experiments, Spanish engineer Marquis Pateras Pescara was also developing a number of successful helicopter designs. Pescara's aircraft featured four-blade, biplane rotors, which operated from concentric transmission shafts (see figure 10). On April 18, 1924, Pescara made a flight of 736 meters, setting an official Fédération Aéronautique Internationale (FAI) world record for distance in a straight line, which beat Oehmichen's record of 525 meters, set only one day earlier.

One of the most important aspects of the Pescara helicopter was that it incorporated a feature that permitted the aircraft to land safely in the event of an engine failure. In such an instance, the rotors continued to turn freely and the pilot could control the pitch to provide lift. As the aircraft neared the ground, the pilot increased the pitch to use the remainder of the stored energy in the rotors and land softly. This was the beginning of autorotation, a safety feature unique to the helicopter.

In September 1923, Pescara tried to complete the first one-kilometer closed-circuit course, but the record would have to wait

Figure 9.
Oehmichen's helicopter, which completed the first one-kilometer, closed-circuit course by a helicopter

until the following year and Oehmichen's successful attempt. Pescara's attempt nearly ended in tragedy when his aircraft crashed from a height of three meters, with Pescara at the controls. The machine was severely damaged, but Pescara escaped with only minor injuries.

BRENNAN

In England, Louis Brennan conducted experiments from 1919 to 1926 at the Royal Aircraft Establishment in Farnborough. Brennan's aircraft had a single rotor of large diameter that was driven by airscrews at the tips of the two rotors. The first tethered flights took place in 1924 inside a hangar. Free flights began in 1925 and were concluded, after a crash, in 1926. Bob Graham, one of the test pilots, described the Brennan helicopters thus:

> *All flying controls including changing of the pitch for autorotation were by compressed air carried in the large diameter tubes forming the base of the main pyramid. We started with a two bladed rotor but had to add two vanes . . . to get improved stability. There was plenty of power available; in the shed [hangar] I carried four passengers with ease . . . but in free flight the aircraft was unstable and flying it was a balancing feat. Fully automatic gyroscopic controls were included in the design but unfortunately the Air Ministry insisted on flight trials before these controls were completed. Had we been allowed to install them before flight then in my opinion the results would have been very different.*[11]

BAUMHAUER

In the Netherlands, engineer A. G. von Baumhauer developed a helicopter that was one of the first to use a counterrotating tail rotor to compensate for the torque created by the main rotor. Baumhauer also developed a method to vary the blade angle of the rotor periodically to stabilize and control the machine, a system that is referred to today as a swash-plate system. Despite these advances, this helicopter was never really successful. On one occasion the aircraft rose to a height of several feet and hovered, but a crash shortly thereafter ended its flying days. Despite its failure, the Baumhauer helicopter was one of the first to use a single main rotor in conjunction with a tail rotor, thus providing much useful information on this configuration, which has now become the predominant design.

Figure 10.
Pescara's helicopter, which beat Oemichen's world record for distance in a straight line, set one day earlier

Figure 11.
The D'Ascanio helicopter, which had a system for feathering rotor blades

Asboth

As early as 1908, the Hungarian engineer Oscar von Asboth was working on ideas for vertical flight. During World War I he worked with Theodor von Karman on the Petroczy-Karman helicopter. Between 1928 and 1931, Asboth built and flew four different helicopters. The most successful was the fourth, which used counterrotating main rotors. Stability was achieved through the use of multiple hinged surfaces or vanes in the rotor slipstream. These air deflectors were operated by the pilot, who used standard aircraft controls.

D'Ascanio

On October 8, 1930, a helicopter built in Italy by Corridion D'Ascanio set three world records—altitude (59 feet), distance (1,180 yards), and endurance (eight minutes, forty-five seconds). The D'Ascanio helicopter was also notable because of its unique design, which included a system for feathering the rotor blades. It had two counterrotating main rotor blades (see figure 11). At the end of each blade was a tail elevator, which could be controlled by the pilot to change the angle

Figure 12.
Florine's tandem-rotor helicopter

or to feather the blades to control the aircraft. The tail elevators, as D'Ascanio called them, worked even if the engine failed. This aircraft provided valuable information on control and stability, but the overall complexity of its design was a drawback that ultimately prevented it from being completely successful.

Florine

In Belgium, Nicolas Florine began during the early 1930s to develop a radically different helicopter design: a tandem-rotor helicopter with the rotors located at the fore and aft ends of the fuselage (see figure 12). Even though the blades spun in the same direction, torque was counteracted in this configuration by tilting the axes of the rotors. Florine's helicopter first flew in April 1933; later the same year, it rose to a height of twenty feet and remained there for eight minutes. The tandem-rotor helicopter is a configuration that is used today for meeting the design requirements of many heavy-lift helicopters.

Breguet

More than twenty years after his initial helicopter experiments, Louis Breguet returned to the helicopter. This time, with the assistance of René Dorand, he was successful. The Breguet-Dorand helicopter, or *Gyroplane*, as they called it, flew so well that many consider it the first real helicopter (see figure 13).

The *Gyroplane* made its first flight on June 26, 1935, and underwent several more flight tests and design alterations during the next few months. Finally, on December 22, 1935, Breguet and Dorand were ready to show the world their helicopter. Before officials of the FAI, the aircraft flew at a speed of sixty-seven miles an hour, setting a world record. On September 26, 1936, it set an altitude record of 517 feet; on November 24 it set the closed-circuit course distance record with a flight of 27.4 miles.

Figure 13.
The Breguet Gyroplane

The *Gyroplane* had two four-blade rotors, mounted one above the other, that rotated in opposite directions. In a design feature unique for the time, Breguet mounted the rotor blades to the central hub by means of universal joints mounted on two orthogonal axes. This enabled each blade to adjust itself in flight, during each revolution, to the dynamic forces to which it was subjected. This system is today referred to as articulated rotor blades and is a method of providing stability and cyclic pitch control of the aircraft. This discovery added another piece to the helicopter puzzle.

Focke

Simultaneous with Breguet's developments was the work of Professor Henrich Focke in Germany. After a great deal of preliminary research and design, Focke developed a helicopter that broke all the existing world records and propelled the helicopter into a new age of success.

The first flight of the Focke-Achgelis Fa-61 took place on June 26, 1936, exactly one year after the first flight of the Breguet-Dorand *Gyroplane*. During the coming months, Focke made many improvements in his aircraft, and in May 1937, it made the world's first autorotational landing. In June,

Focke began to establish a series of world records, which included speed (77 miles an hour), altitude (8,000 feet), endurance (one hour and twenty minutes), and controlled flight over a closed-circuit course (50 miles).

There were many, foremost among them Asboth, who doubted the authenticity of Focke's accomplishments. Focke responded sharply to his doubters and to Asboth in particular. "Von Asboth thinks he can prove that such an altitude could not be reached by a pure helicopter, but only if the aircraft were piloted by an autogyro. . . . Now what Mr. von Asboth really thinks is that there are no good helicopters except those resulting from his own work."[12] But all Focke's records were verified by the FAI.

In February 1938, piloted by German aviatrix Hanna Reitsch, the Focke-Achgelis Fa-61 was flown inside a German sports arena. Reitsch amazed the spectators by lifting off vertically, hovering, then flying sideways, the length of the hall.

Focke's helicopter had two rotors, each having three articulated blades, one rotor mounted at the end of each of two wings that protruded from the sides of the fuselage. After a great deal of research, Focke decided on this configuration as the most practical to eliminate torque. Also, this method eliminated much of the vibration that was created by mounting the rotors one on top of the other.

The Final Pieces of the Puzzle

Nearly all the pieces of the puzzle were in place by the end of the 1930s, and it remained only for Igor Sikorsky, Arthur Young, and other pioneers to fit the final pieces in place, as will be seen in the succeeding chapters of this book. Problems such as the lack of power, stability, control, and torque had been overcome to a considerable extent by a number of engineers who made use of several design configurations.

The state of the helicopter is best summed up in the words of Professor Alexander Klemin, outstanding helicopter researcher and teacher, who wrote in 1938:

> *[Klemin] is thoroughly convinced that there is a splendid future for rotary-wing aircraft with no one type emerging supreme, and this conviction is based on the theoretical considerations . . . actual achievements recorded and the multiplicity of sound and novel ideas which are in the minds of exponents of rotary aircraft. It must be remembered that only a fraction of the time, energy and money which have been expended on the airplane have been given to the development of the [helicopter]. . . . Of course much difficult work lies ahead, but there is also a fascinating field of research ahead for the aerodynamicist, the structural man, the mechanical engineer. . . . No more interesting work in applied science is available today.*[13]

Steve Wartenberg is editor of *Vertiflite* magazine, the official publication of the American Helicopter Society. He has written many articles on the helicopter, including profiles of the principal manufacturers and leaders of the industry and reports on significant events.

1. Charles Gablehouse, *Helicopters and Autogiros* (Philadelphia and New York: J. B. Lippincott, rev. ed., 1969), p. 3.
2. Ibid.
3. Paul Lambermont and Anthony Pirie, *Helicopters and Autogyros of the World* (New York, A. S. Barnes, rev. ed., 1970), p. 5.
4. Frank Ross, Jr., *Flying Windmills* (New York: Lothrop, Lee & Shepard, 1953), p. 44.
5. Igor Sikorsky, "Commercial and Military Uses of Rotating Wing Aircraft," Proceedings of the Second Annual Rotating Wing Aircraft Meeting, Institute of the Aeronautical Sciences, 1939, p. 52.
6. George de Bothezat, *The Actual State of the Helicopter Problem*, Paper delivered to the War Department, Engineering Division, Air Service, McCook Field, Dayton, Ohio, April 22, 1921, pp. 2–3.
7. *The Slipstream*, publication of the Engineering Division, Air Service, McCook Field, Dayton, Ohio, (n.d., probably late 1922 or early 1923).
8. W. F. Gerhardt, *Report on the DeBothezat Helicopter*, War Department, Air Service, Engineering Division, McCook Field, Dayton, Ohio, January 29, 1924, p. 11.
9. Ibid.
10. Etienne Oehmichen, "First Helicopter to Fly a Circular Kilometer," *Aviation*, August 18, 1924, v. 17, pp. 888–89.
11. R. A. C. Brie, ed., *A History of British Rotorcraft 1866–1965*, Westland Helicopter Limited, 1968, p. 35.
12. Lambermont and Pirie, *Helicopters and Autogyros*, p. 92.
13. Alexander Klemin, "Principles of Rotary Aircraft," *Journal of the Franklin Institute*, vol. 227, no. 3 (March 1939), pp. 393–94.

RALPH P. ALEX

How Are You Fixed for Blades? The Saga of the Helicopter, Circa 1940–60

In April 1941 it was my good fortune to join Vought-Sikorsky Aircraft and have the rare privilege of becoming a member of a small, dedicated group of visionaries who forged ahead and built a successful helicopter "because we didn't know it couldn't be done." This group of twelve was led by Bob Labensky, long-time associate of Igor Sikorsky and chief of the test laboratory; Labensky and his assistant, Michael Buivid, built a rotor test rig to test rotor blades, rotor heads, and controls. Later they built the VS-300, a company-financed helicopter, to test various configurations such as single-rotor, one-, two- and three-blade main- and tail-rotor designs; one- and two-blade tail rotors; and one- and two-rotor longitudinal control designs.

Another member of the group was Ed Kottsieper, who had recently built a small, coaxial helicopter designed by George de Bothezat. This effort died aborning in the tie-down phase. De Bothezat delivered the first helicopter to the Army Signal Corps at McCook Field (later Wright Field) in Dayton, Ohio, in 1922. This machine was a quadrotor—that is, a four-rotor craft—which flew with a great thrashing, occasionally under the pilot's control. This first attempt was abandoned in 1924. During its test period it achieved a sustained flight of one minute, forty-four seconds, and at one time it lifted the pilot and four mechanics, unwilling passengers who were holding onto the structure to stabilize the craft.

It was Ed Kottsieper who urged me to come and join the helicopter group that was designing the XR-4 for the army. When I said that I knew nothing about helicopters, his answer was, "Neither does anyone else; we will be creating the textbooks and technology for rotary-wing aircraft."

Then there was Bill Hunt, senior designer, with autogiro experience, and Les Morris, who resigned his job as Connecticut Commissioner of Aeronautics to replace Igor Sikorsky as chief test pilot. Also in the helicopter group were Ray Coates, chief draftsman; Bill Kostuk, draftsman; Galy Lapin, secretary, who never forgot a birthday; Adolph Plenefisch, shop foreman, and Red Lubben, his assistant; Ed Walsh, crew chief; and several shop people.

Igor Sikorsky, then the engineering manager, Michael Gluhareff, chief engineer, and Serge Gluhareff, executive engineer, provided guidance and supervision. Igor Sikorsky contributed much to the design effort; his intuitive and innovative approaches had much to do with the success of the XR-4.

Performance analysis and aerodynamics inputs came from Igor Sikorsky and Alexander Nikolsky, an old associate of Sikorsky. Nikolsky left Sikorsky in 1942 to establish the Rotary Wing Aeronautics Department at Princeton University.

This cadre of ten engineering personnel was located in a small drafting room on the balcony of the S-44 flying boat hangar; the entrance was through an unmarked door next to one marked LADIES. Together with the several members of the shop crew, the group designed, built and delivered the XR-4.

Many respected aeronautical engineers had come to the analytical conclusion that it was a useless quest—that a rotorcraft was technically infeasible, and that while it might be easy to get it to fly, it would never become a useful vehicle. The predecessor of the helicopter, the autogiro, an impressive short takeoff and landing (STOL) machine in its day, was still being developed by the U.S. military with the addition of jump-takeoff capability to correct an important drawback, the lack of vertical flight capability.

The Birth of an Industry

The present helicopter industry actually began its cycle of successful development in 1938, when the Dorsey bill was presented in the House of Representatives, shortly afterward to become Public Law 787. This act authorized the expenditure of $2 million for research and development of rotary-wing aircraft. The following year, Public Law 61, passed by the Seventy-sixth Congress, appropriated $300,000 for the specific purpose of developing the helicopter.

Lieutenants H. Franklin Gregory and Victor R. Haugen, veteran autogiro pilots assigned to the Materiel Division, Wright Field, Dayton, Ohio, were given the task of searching for the proper helicopter. Government Circular Proposal 40-260 was prepared, and in response bids were received from several sources. An award was made to the Platt-LePage Aircraft Company of Eddystone, Pennsylvania, for the XR-1, a twin side-by-side rotor configuration that was already under construction using company funds. This helicopter was patterned after the Focke-Achgelis Fa-61, which was demonstrated successfully in Germany during the mid 1930s.

At about this time, Igor Sikorsky and his associates Michael Gluhareff and Bob Labensky were experimenting with a single-rotor helicopter at the Vought-Sikorsky Division of United Aircraft in Stratford, Connecticut. After several successful flight demonstrations to Gregory and Haugen, during which they flew the aircraft after only a few minutes of ground instruction from Sikorsky, they recommended that this configuration should also be procured. Although only $50,000 was left of the original appropriation, a decision to proceed was reached in December 1950, and a contract was awarded to Vought-Sikorsky to build the XR-4.

Sikorsky arranged a meeting with "our fathers who art in Hartford," the United Aircraft Board of Directors, to sell the parent company on accepting the remaining army money for rotary-wing development and subsidizing the rest of the cost. Raycroft Walsh, then vice-chairman, told me after his retirement that the board actually didn't believe that the helicopter had a future, but because of Mr. Sikorsky's enthusiasm and their high regard for his intuitive sense, the project was sanctioned. It should be noted that this was the first planned overrun, the prime difference being that the industry instead of the military made up the 300 percent deficit of $150,000.

The "Informal Proposal for an Army Two-Seater Service Observation-Trainer Helicopter" summarizes the required performance as follows:

> *This proposed Helicopter, to be known as the VS-316, shall be similar to the VS-300 Experimental Helicopter which was produced in 1939, gradually improved and which gave extremely promising results during tests conducted this summer.*
>
> *The proposed aircraft shall be a true helicopter with all lift and control being based on the action of the air on its rotating surfaces only. The machine shall be completely independent of speed for its lift and control. It shall be capable of rising vertically from small places surrounded by small obstacles; hover motionless over one spot for an indefinite period; travel forward at any speed from zero to about one hundred miles per hour, and travel backwards and sideways at a reduced speed. With these characteristics it shall be*

Figure 1.
VS-300 full cyclic-control tests. Connie Moeller, Sikorsky test pilot, is pleased.

possible to operate the aircraft from any place large enough to swing the rotors.

The proposed helicopter may be used and will be able to render valuable service under conditions which would not allow the use of existing types of aircraft.

As originally proposed to the army, the VS-316 had four rotors: a main rotor and two laterally displaced horizontal control rotors for longitudinal control, with lateral control obtained by differential pitch motion; the fourth control rotor was in the vertical plane for torque compensation and yaw or rudder action.

Halfway into the construction of the VS-316, the company's experimental VS-300 was modified by removing the two lateral control rotors, and cyclic pitch was added to the main rotor. It provided excellent lateral and longitudinal control (see figure 1). At that time, Gregory and Haugen flew it, and a decision was made to change the VS-316 to the new configuration, provided it did not delay the program. Within a few weeks the fuselage had been redesigned and modified and we were back on schedule.

On January 14, 1942, after several hours of ground and tie-down tests, the XR-4 made its first flight (see figure 2). Since there were no spares and no test program, all tests conducted were only to prove functional and operational adequacy. This approach was quite successful, because the helicopter was rarely down for maintenance and because the dynamic components were conservatively designed. When bevel-gear thrust bearings were accidentally installed backward, for example, only replacement of the bearings and regrinding and relapping of the gears were required to reinstall and continue with the flight tests.

A demonstration was conducted for the army and various representatives of the U.S. Coast Guard, the U.S. Navy, and the Royal Navy on April 20, 1942. That day the XR-4 flew to an altitude of 5,000 feet, carried a passenger, and demonstrated its helicopter attributes. To demonstrate its ability further, Sikorsky rappelled from the helicopter and I, its project engineer, climbed aboard

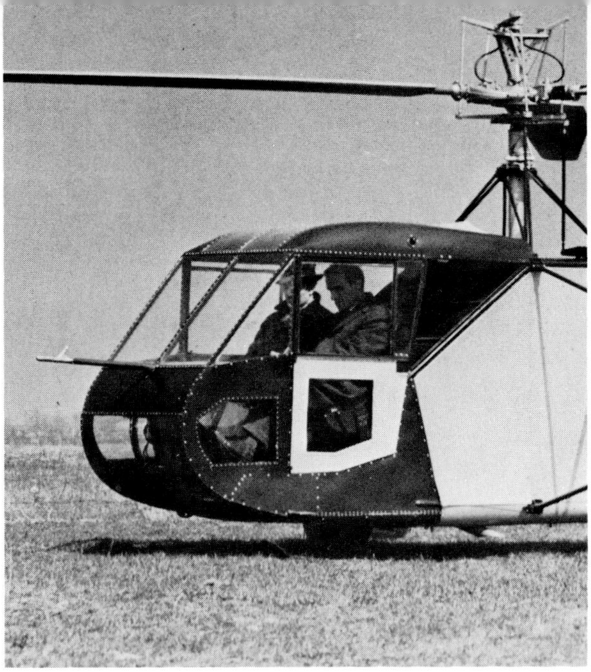

by rope ladder (see figure 3). A telegram was sent to Wright Field stating that the machine met contractual requirements and would be delivered to the army on or about May 1.

On May 14, 1942, the XR-4 began its 761-mile cross-country flight to Wright Field (see figure 4). Sixteen stops were made for

Figure 2.
The XR-4 ready for takeoff on its first flight in January 1942

Figure 3.
Ralph Alex climbs aboard the XR-4 (reverse rappelling) in May 1942.

Figure 4.
Project group before delivery of the XR-4, at Stratford, Connecticut. Front, left to right: *Ralph Alex; Michael Buivid, rotor design; Red Lubben, shop lead man; Bud Roosevelt, service department; Adolph Plenefisch, shop foreman;* rear, left to right: *Colonel Frank Gregory* (in cockpit), *Bob Labensky, chief; Serge Gluhareff, executive engineer; Ed Walsh, crew chief; Les Morris, chief test pilot.*

refueling. The longest leg, a distance of ninety-two miles, took an hour and fifty minutes against head winds. Having arrived safely at Wright Field (see figure 5), the aircraft was officially accepted by the U.S. Army Air Corps, on May 30, 1942, four months and twenty days after its first flight, fourteen months after award of the contract. Less than two months later, on July 24, 1942, the XR-4 had accumulated 100 hours of flight time in the test program. Two jump-takeoff autogiros, the XR-3 and YO-60, that were being developed during this period were

Figure 5.
Delivery of the XR-4 to Wright Field, Dayton, Ohio. Left to right: *Ed Walsh, Adolph Plenefisch, Igor Sikorsky, Orville Wright, Ralph Alex, Les Morris, Bob Labensky.*

quietly shelved after the successful delivery of the XR-4.

One visitor who came to see the first successful army helicopter was Orville Wright. During his several visits to the flight line, I tried to interest him in a flight in the XR-4, but he politely refused each time. Finally he told me that he couldn't accept a flight because he didn't believe the machine was practical. He gave me a copy of an article by Wilbur Wright from the *Dayton Herald*, January 15, 1909, in which Wilbur dismissed the concept. He wrote:

> *Like all novices, we began with the helicopter (in childhood) but soon saw that it had no future and dropped it. The Helicopter does with great labor only what the balloon does without labor, and is no more fitted than the balloon for rapid horizontal flight. If its engine stops it must fall with deathly violence for it can neither float like the balloon nor glide like the aeroplane. The helicopter is much easier to design than the aeroplane but it is worthless when done.*

On December 21, 1942, a contract for fifteen YR-4As was awarded to Sikorsky, and a short time later supplement number one, calling for fourteen additional helicopters (YR-4B), was added. The first of these machines was delivered to the army on July 3, 1943, and the remaining units were delivered to the navy, the Coast Guard, and the British after that; the last one was delivered on April 14, 1944.

Many demonstrations were made, including delivery of the mail and a landing on shipboard. It was also evaluated as a platform for dropping bombs and, later, depth charges for possible antisubmarine duty. Evaluation tests were conducted on the British freighter SS *Daghestan* in a convoy exercise crossing the Atlantic. Stretcher installations were made and an actual rescue mission was attempted on Anticosti Island at the mouth of the Saint Lawrence River. During this period cold-weather tests were started in Alaska.

Another contract was awarded on February 6, 1944, for 100 R-4B helicopters. The hundredth helicopter was delivered on September 7, 1944. On February 1, 1945, the U.S. Coast Guard demonstrated the first installation of a rescue hoist. On January 11, 1945, the first helicopter training school was opened at Sheppard Field, Wichita Falls, Texas, and in May 1945, seventeen helicopters flew in a group from Chanute Field, Illinois, to their new home, with fourteen R-4s and three R-6s participating.

The success of the XR-4 led to the design of the XR-5, which was twice the size of the XR-4 and carried twice the useful load. A contract for five helicopters was signed on December 21, 1942. The British were interested in the aircraft for convoy duty to combat the submarine menace. The first flight of the XR-5 was on August 18, 1943. An additional contract for 250 was received on February 26, 1944, and with 200 additional units added to the contract there were 455 on order. On V-J Day, 65 R-5s had been delivered. The rest of the order was canceled, as were almost all combat-priority aircraft.

The R-5 was the largest helicopter until then to be put into production. It was evaluated for many uses and missions—pipe laying, geodetic survey, photography, mapping, breaking of ice jams, calibration of radar, and forestry service. The R-5 established several world records: endurance of nine hours and fifty-seven minutes; distance in a closed circuit of 621.3 miles; speed for 1,000 kilometers of 66.6 mph.

Eight R-5As and R-5Ds were assigned to carry mail for the post office in the Los Angeles area—a six-day-a-week schedule, morning and afternoon, between twenty-nine post offices, requiring flight time of thirteen hours a day and 110 landings and takeoffs per day. A service was also set up to carry mail from the roof of the Los Angeles post office to the Lockheed Air Terminal. In October 1946, three Sikorsky R-5Ds initiated a service from the Chicago Municipal Airport to forty-one outlying towns. In addition, ten trips a day were scheduled from the Municipal Airport to the roof of the downtown Merchandise Mart. Later, several modified versions—the R-5D, E, F, G,

Figure 6.
R5-G U.S. Air Force rescue helicopter. The R5-G has fixed rigid amphibious floats, rescue hoist, two litter carries (one across cabin, the second aft of cabin), and payload of "several oral messages."

and H—were built for the navy and the air force.

The R-5G was outfitted as a search-and-rescue vehicle for the air force (see figure 6). It had cylindrical aluminum floats fitted with a quadricycle landing gear, a new hydraulic hoist, and two litter capsules installed laterally with enclosures projecting through the fuselage—one through the rear cabin section, and a second, called the "dead man's carry," aft of the engine. With all this equipment, its payload consisted of "several oral messages." With almost no operational capability, the R-5G was relegated to Sheppard Field, where it lived out its life as a trainer.

In early 1942, following the successful flights and demonstrations of the XR-4, mounting enthusiasm generated a requirement for an observation helicopter to succeed the R-4, which had fulfilled its purpose to prove that a helicopter was a practical and feasible concept and that with sufficient power and performance it could meet the requirements envisioned by the U.S. Army Air Corps, the U.S. Navy, and the British. Thus was the XR-6 born.

The main and tail rotors were the only components of the R-4 retained for this new helicopter. As project engineer, my task was to design the rest of the aircraft to incorporate the most advanced materials and technology then available and to keep the empty weight as low as possible and still have a rugged, producible machine with a respectable useful load.

The search for advanced materials led to extensive use of wrought magnesium and casting alloys, which were a third lighter than aluminum and had good structural properties and no critical aircraft applications on high-priority projects. The tail cone was constructed of 0.025 magnesium sheet with extruded magnesium stringers and 0.040 magnesium hot-formed frames. Fittings and bulkheads were magnesium castings. The landing gear cantilever strut was a tapered, roll-formed, magnesium sheet one-eighth inch thick, heli-arc welded, with the end fittings of cast magnesium. The internal inboard structure was of welded steel tube construction. A hydraulic dash pot cylinder with an internal rubber bumper for taxiing was designed. The main cabin was an autoclave-molded fiberglass built-up structure, as were the cabin doors. The main rotor and main transmission were also supported by a tapered, roll-formed, one-eighth-inch magnesium sheet monocoque, heli-arc-welded pylon, with the top and bottom attachments of 24ST extruded aluminum angle. The main transmission was a two-stage planetary with the planets rotating on silver-lead-indium bushings. These were replaced in the early stages of production by rolling-element needle bearings, to reduce the temperature of the transmission oil to acceptable limits so that the integrally cooled design could be maintained.

The main fuselage structure was a semi-monocoque aluminum floor beam; the center structure, in which the engine was mounted vertically and on the aft end of which was the magnesium tail cone, was of welded steel tubing. The main rotor transmission was also mounted on this structure. A steel-tube structure was chosen because it would give access to the engine and other accessories. The complete center section was cowled with panels made from an advanced cellulose composite consisting of kraft paper, impregnated with resin and cured in an autoclave. Because the cowlings were extremely light and easily damaged, several sets of spares per aircraft were procured so that if repairs could not be made easily replacements could be made immediately. The oil and fuel tanks were also constructed of welded magnesium. The three-pound, four-gallon oil tank proved to be serviceable, but the sixty-seven-gallon magnesium fuel tank lasted forty-five seconds during the slosh and vibration test at Wright Field. It was immediately replaced with an identical tank constructed of welded aluminum.

The XR-6 was to be powered with the Lycoming 225-hp engine, which ran into development problems and was never built. The aircraft was redesignated the XR-6A and the 245-hp Franklin 0-435-9 engine was substituted.

A joint army-navy contract for five aircraft was signed on April 30, 1943. The first flight was made on October 15 of the same year. Severe problems of control and vibration were encountered and required several months to correct. It took two pilots to handle the cyclic stick. One of the several improvements made in the YR-4 rotor head used on this model was the incorporation of tapered-roller thrust bearings of high capacity to replace the failure-prone face-roller thrust bearings. It took several months of intensive test and bearing modification to solve this problem. Problems with the centrifugal clutch (Rawson coupling) and the innovative main-rotor disc brake adapted from the first automotive disc brake were also solved during this period. An automotive silencer was installed to reduce internal and external noise, and with a fiberglass cabin the reduction in internal noise was substantial. Colonel Gregory wrote, "The R-6A cabin is so well soundproofed that there is only a steady purring noise and you can talk as if you were sitting side by side in a bus."

On March 1, 1944, five and a half months after first flight, the XR-6A, with Colonel Frank Gregory at the controls and me as passenger, took off for Washington, D.C., to demonstrate the helicopter to the army and navy at Washington National Airport. We encountered heavy snow as we approached Princeton, New Jersey, and decided to stop at Princeton University to show the aircraft to Professor Alexander Nikolsky, who had participated in the early development of the VS-300 and the XR-4A. While we were there, the professor suggested that since the temperature and humidity were ideal for icing

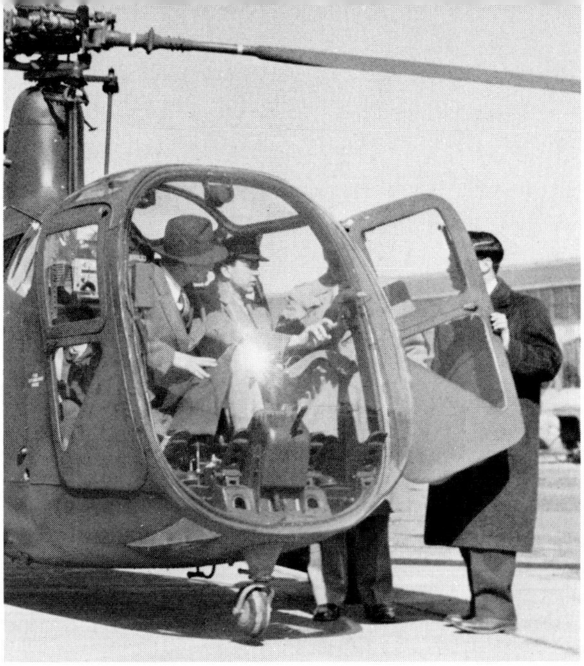

Figure 7.
Arrival of the XR-6A at Wright Field. Shown: *Ralph Alex, copilot; Col. Frank Gregory, pilot; Mandell Lenkowsky, Rotary Wing Branch.*

we should fly for a while and see whether we could pick up ice on the rotor blades. Nikolsky was quite disappointed when none accumulated, for he had expected to collect some data for his helicopter students.

We arrived in Washington that afternoon, to be met by a large, enthusiastic audience. Many demonstrations were given before the assembled brass. We arrived with litter capsules installed, and the surgeon general and his staff insisted on riding in the litters. Several flights were made with a passenger in the copilot's seat and two passengers in the litters, which was a substantial overload. With a good ground wind blowing and the ability to make a short running takeoff, and in spite of the substantial overload—for this was a two-place helicopter—the demonstrations were eminently successful.

Late in the afternoon Colonel Gregory, at a meeting with General Hap Arnold, was told that production of 900 R-6As was being ordered. General Arnold also stipulated that production of the aircraft not be given combat priority and that materials used must be noncritical and not interfere with the production of bombers, fighters, and other critical combat aircraft. The XR-6A met that requirement.

On March 2, 1944, with the litter capsules removed, Colonel Gregory and I left Washington and flew to Dayton, a distance of 387 miles. We flew at 5,000 feet, with head winds the first half of the flight. All the fuel was in the one sixty-seven-gallon main tank. We arrived over Springfield, Ohio, with the low-fuel warning light glowing bright red. Gregory wanted to look for a quick landing spot, but I convinced him that the twenty-minute warning was conservative, that we really had thirty minutes' flying time left and could make the remaining distance. We continued our flight at low altitude and made sure that at all times, if the engine quit, we would have a clear area for an autorotational landing.

When we arrived at Patterson Field, which is now part of Wright-Patterson Air Force Base, we had both used up all our courage, and Gregory decided that we would land at Patterson Field. We landed near a very large aircraft and were immediately surrounded by military police. The big airplane turned out to be the first B-29 delivered to the U.S. Army Air Force. The field had been closed for this event and it took some frantic explanations before we were allowed to refuel and fly to Wright Field a few miles beyond the highway (see figure 7). Our flight time was four hours and fifty-five minutes. A check of the remaining fuel during refueling revealed that we had less than two gallons left.

In the early months of 1943, the U.S. Army Air Force (AAF) had decided that the XR-6 would be successful and sent Sikorsky a contract for twenty-six YR-6As. The contract was refused because of critical production of the Navy F4U fighter at Vought in Stratford. The managers at Sikorsky thought that there would be a conflict, because production of the R-6A would drain skilled personnel from production of the F4U Corsair. The solution was an agreement reached with United Aircraft to license the production of the R-6A to the Kelvinator Division of Nash-Kelvinator, which was then a licensee of Pratt & Whitney, building Pratt & Whitney engines for all the services. Kelvinator was idle at its plant in Detroit, had many skilled workers available, and was experienced in production. In September 1943, contracts were awarded for 731 aircraft, including 36 for the navy. Engineering was to be furnished by Sikorsky with a team of Kelvinator engineers assigned to Sikorsky to produce aircraft from the drawings. The first YR-6A from Nash-Kelvinator was delivered to the army in October 1944. With production following the experimental program so closely, very little debugging had been done, and none was done on the production models. As expected, problems were encountered in operation of the aircraft. Even so, the R-6A was used for a considerable amount of flight training and flew many successful missions.

During the war shortages of aircraft parts such as AN fasteners and other standard parts were common. At Kelvinator, as in all high-production factories, the production line must not stop. The foreman is responsible for making substitutions, and when shortages were encountered, substitute parts were found at the local hardware store. Until quality control was established, it was sometimes said that Kelvinator was producing Kelvicopters and Refrigerotors. During this learning period, several incidents made it apparent that star washers under noncastellated nuts were not equivalent to elastic stop nuts or cotter-keyed nuts or safety wire.

Within three months after delivery of the first YR-6A, all twenty-six of the Y series of service test models had been delivered. In February 1944, delivery of the R-6A began. By September 1944, more than 200 had been delivered to the AAF. The production tooling of most of the components was a wonder to behold, especially for us in the aircraft industry. The complete production of 1,200 tail cones, main transmissions, fiberglass cabins, fuselage tub structures, and cowlings, which included spares, were completed at twice the monthly rate required by the contract.

In March 1944, several R-6As were delivered to Freeman Field, Rantoul, Illinois, to the new training command; two were delivered to the Air Force Tactical Air Center at Kissimmee, Florida; and several were assigned to the CBI (China-Burma-India) theater for rescue of downed pilots flying the "hump." They were assigned to Colonel Cochran's Raiders and actually rescued several pilots at altitudes up to 8,000 feet. It was an insurmountable task that was surmounted. The aircraft actually arrived in CBI in June 1945 and operated for several months. In May 1945, seventeen helicopters of the AAF Training Command, including three R-6s, participated in a mass flight from Chanute Field, Illinois, to Sheppard Field, Wichita Falls, Texas, their new training base.

As a consultant to the army's Air Technical Service Command, I arrived at Wright Field in early July 1945 to accompany an R-6A to Paricutin, Mexico, where it would take part in a volcano expedition. The National Research Council had commissioned the army to furnish a helicopter that could be based at an altitude of 7,200 feet and operate at 10,000 feet. It would investigate a new volcano that had begun in a farmer's field 7,000 feet above sea level and in a few years had grown to a cone a mile in diameter at the base and 1,800 feet high. It was the first new volcano to have been born in the time of man. A team of American volcanologists, the Mexican government, and Mexican volcanologists were to use the helicopter to examine the volcano at close range and to fly into the crater at times when it was quiet and not expected to erupt (see figure 8). Our primary mission was to study the performance of the R-6A under conditions of altitude, temperature, and turbulence similar to those encountered in the CBI theater. Also, Professor Gish of the University of Chicago was studying the violent electrical phenomena and thunder generated by the debris that poured out of the cone daily. More than sixty flights were flown during a period of two months (see figure 9).

Upon completion of this mission, we were invited by General Salinas, chief of the Mexican Army Air Force, to fly to Cuernavaca to demonstrate the R-6A to President Avila

Figure 8.
The R-6A hovering for test flight, waiting for volcano to quiet before flying over and into the crater for scientific study

Camacho. The arrangements were that we would be led by a Mexican AT-6 over the mountains, since the regional charts were considered inaccurate. Just north of Cuernavaca we lost the AT-6 and reverted to the inaccurate charts. The valley we were flying

Figure 9.
R-6A volcano expedition party, August 14, 1945. Left to right: *army mechanic; Professor Louis Graton, Harvard geologist; Igor I. Sikorsky, army project manager; U.S. AAF consultant, Captain George Colchagoff; Ralph Alex, pilot; Roy Beer, flight officer; army mechanic; army photographer; A. Bertram, Sikorsky photographer; Verne Short, army photographer.*

in showed 9,000 feet on the charts; our altimeter read more than 11,000 feet. The valley suddenly turned to the right and we were facing a headwall at least 2,000 feet high. With a remaining rate of climb of 200 to 300 feet a minute, our only choice was to make a 180-degree turn to fly back out of the valley. What had been a strong head wind was now a tail wind, and with our forty-miles-an-hour best-rate-of-climb speed now reduced to zero, we found ourselves descending at up to 3,000 feet a minute. Flight Officer Roy Beer saw a clear spot on the side of the mountain we hoped was big enough to provide rotor clearance in among the 100-foot evergreens for our touchdown. I handled the collective and throttle, Roy handled the cyclic, and between the two of us we made a perfect touchdown with the rate-of-climb indicator at the bottom at a rate of descent of 3,000 feet a minute. The right landing gear hit on a thirty-degree slope and broke off, the engine pulled out of its mounts and touched the ground, and the main blades came down through the tail cone and severed it. The altimeter registered 9,100 feet. This, our last test, demonstrated the excellent crashworthy design of the R-6A. No cabin or floor beam was deformed. We were intact. The fuel tank, although collapsed in its cradle, also remained intact.

In the meantime the AT-6 had searched for us and the pilot had concluded we had crashed in the heavy thunderstorm that descended on the area within five or ten minutes of our landing. The pilot went on to Mexico City and reported we had crashed. The consensus was that the crash in the trees at that altitude was unsurvivable, and no search was instituted. In Connecticut it was reported that we were dead.

After the storm a band of Tarascan Indians appeared and sat stoically around the helicopter with their rifles. During a frustrating attempt at communication we determined that they had notified a small Mexican town below us and that we would be turned over to the expected Mexican rescue party if they paid a suitable ransom.

The rescue team, lead by the mayor of Villa de Carbon, arrived a few hours later with two extra horses. While the party had excellent horses with silver-trimmed saddles and solid silver bridles and trappings, the two extra horses were bareback. It took little deduction to realize that they were expecting to bring back the bodies of the crew. Rope stirrups and a blanket were improvised for the pilot and me for the interminably long trek of about 30 kilometers down the steep mountainside to their town. The next day, we made a trip by jeep to Mexico City, where we were requested by the U.S. Embassy to bring the R-6A back to Mexico City in a face-saving exercise for the Mexican Army Air Force. When we returned to the crash site with a three-wheel trailer for the rescue operation, we found Mexican army mechanics already disassembling it. The disconnects provided for quick removal of blades, and components were largely ignored. The resultant damage was almost greater than that caused by the crash landing. A request was made by the Mexican government to General Phillips in Washington to rebuild the aircraft and proceed with the demonstration to the president, but the damage incurred in the disassembly was too great and the plan was abandoned. I returned to Sikorsky by commercial airline on V-J Day.

All combat-priority programs for fighters, bombers, transports, and helicopters were canceled almost immediately after V-J Day (see figure 10). The R-6A production line at Nash-Kelvinator was stopped, as was the production of R-5As at Sikorsky, which to that point had delivered 65 helicopters. Nash-Kelvinator had delivered 219 R-6As and had more than 200 additional helicopters completed and in production test flight before acceptance. These additional helicopters were built in August 1945.

As described earlier, most of the large components, including flight controls, electrical installations and harnesses, landing gear, rotor heads, blades and components of drive systems, cowlings, cabins, instrument panels, and engine packages, had been completed well in advance of the total program.

Figure 10.
R-5s on Sikorsky Flying Field 14 on V-J Day, when all contracts were cancelled

A powered moving assembly line resembling a Detroit automotive production line, with all parts lined up at the proper installation points, had been set up. Nash-Kelvinator estimated that the remaining 500 on order would have been completed and delivered within the next ninety days. During contract-cancellation negotiations for the undelivered 200-plus R-6As, the army decided to accept the aircraft. They were loaded on flat cars without any weather protection and shipped to Randolph Field, Texas, where they were stored in sheds, and several years later a plan was proposed to use them for spares, but the unprotected machines were finally scrapped because they had corroded and deteriorated to an unacceptable extent.

V-J Day signaled the end of an era of rapid progress in the development and acceptance of the helicopter as a military aircraft. With all production canceled abruptly, Nash-Kelvinator ceased to be a helicopter manufacturer and Sikorsky was required to reduce its engineering and manufacturing personnel by at least a third.

In summary, then, from the time of delivery of the XR-4, the first successful helicopter, to the military in May 1942 to the last delivery before V-J Day, September 2, 1945—a period of three years and four months—128 R-4s, 65 R-5s, and 219 R-6s were delivered to the army for use in military operations. This is a total of 412 helicopters; 205 additional R-6As were accepted and were placed in storage; thus, a total of 617 were built during that period. From December 1940 to September 1945, the XR-4, XR-5, and XR-6 were designed, built, and tested, then were redesigned and tested for production, and finally more than 600 of these helicopters were produced (see figure 11).

The Platt-LePage XR-1 was contracted for in July 1940; many control and vibration problems turned up in the second modified version, the XR-1A. Although these were finally overcome in January 1944, the test program was shelved a year later.

The Kellett XR-8, a synchropter—having two intermeshing rotors side by side—was contracted for by the army and flown in 1944. During the test program, the intermeshing rotors were instrumented so that lights on the instrument panel would indicate when the blades brushed or touched each other during maneuvers. The frequency of contact discouraged the pilots and the army. At about the same time a ten-place, much larger version with twin engines was built and was plagued with the same problems. The two aircraft, the XR-8 and XR-10, were finally retired.

Also during this period many military uses for the helicopter were proposed. The enthusiasm of the army knew no bounds. Among the uses demonstrated were the following:

- Dropping bombs and depth charges:

Bombs were dropped from the XR-4, XR-5, and XR-6 in tests for use against ground targets and ships.

Bomb racks were installed to carry 325-pound depth charges for use against submarines.

- Helicopters were towed by cargo aircraft, to extend the range of the helicopter significantly by using its autorotation features and to fly under power once it was released from the tow (see figure 12). During the last of many test flights in which the R-5 and R-6 were towed, the tow line was accidentally released from the C-47 tow aircraft. The line snapped back into the rotor of the R-5, causing loss of the main rotor and killing pilot Lieutenant Carter Harmon. The program was shelved, because the tests proved that during tow, the tow plane could not tow faster than the maximum speed of the helicopter, which was about 115 mph. The built-in head wind—the main rotor—prevented any great increase in range, since the tow aircraft was flying at its most undesirable and uneconomical speed.

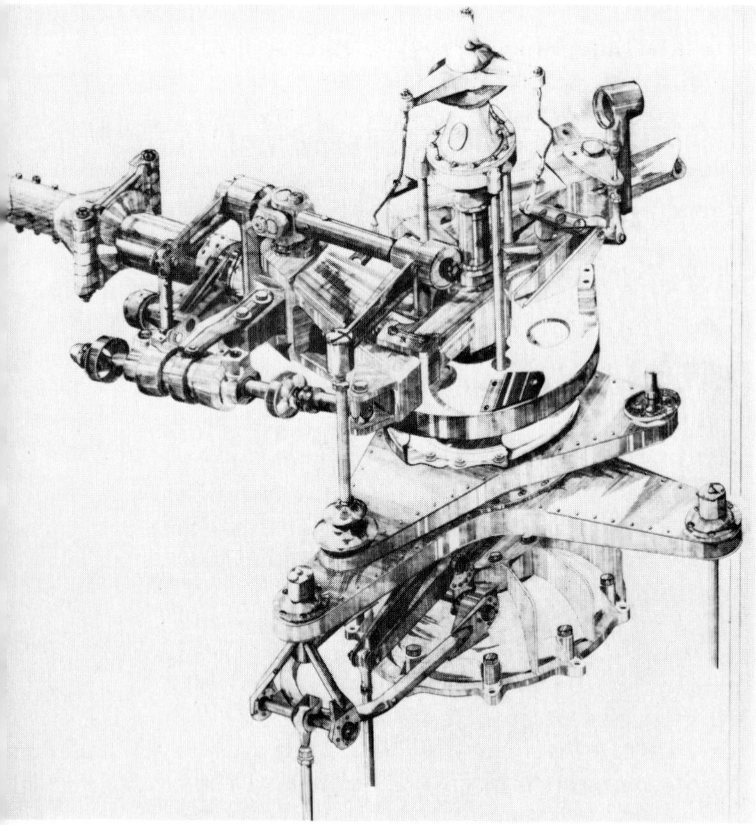

Figure 11.
XR-6A rotor head—isometric drawing. This is the same rotor head as on the XR-4; it has a concentric flapping Delta 3 hinge.

- Emergency medical rescue and evacuation was explored in Alaska and Canada, and several actual uses were demonstrated.

- The army made several planned demonstrations delivering the U.S. Mail from rooftop to airport in Los Angeles and Chicago. Many other extensive demonstrations were made during hundreds of flights.

- In July 1945, the army flew the R-6A on a mercy mission from Fortaleza to San Luis, Brazil, a distance of 430 miles, in five hours in standard configuration. This eclipsed the May 1944 record of 387 miles in four hours and fifty-five minutes set by Colonel Gregory flying from Washington, D.C., to Wright Field, Dayton, Ohio.

- An R-6A was used at Rockingham Park, New Hampshire, to take aerial photographs during a horse race to ensure the honesty of the race.

- In May 1943, several tests were made on the army transport *Bunker Hill* to evaluate the feasibility of operating from a small platform for use against the submarine menace, in both a patrol mission and a killer mission.

- Floats were installed and the ability of all helicopter models to operate off the water, on land, and on shipboard was demonstrated.

- The HNS-1, the navy version of the R-4B, was used to spray the Yale Bowl against armies of mosquitoes just before a concert. Attendance at the concert was seriously being jeopardized until the helicopter solved the problem.

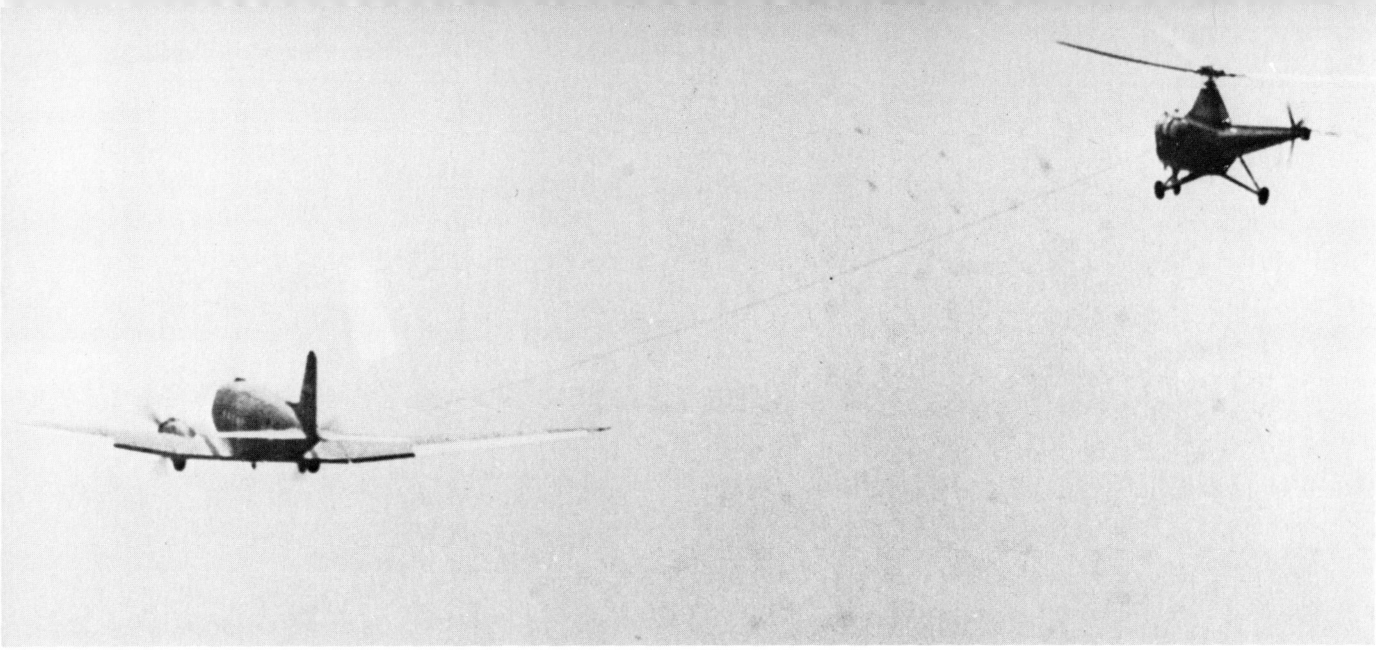

Figure 12.
The R-5 being towed by a C-47 to extend range. The helicopter flies in autorotation during tow and starts its engine when ready to release.

• An R-6A was reconfigured for the Coast Guard. The fuel tank was removed to make room for two additional passengers, a hydraulic rescue hoist was added, the forward cabin floor was redesigned to be substantially transparent for downward visibility, and the fuel tanks were mounted externally on each side of the center floor beam. The design was acceptable, but the reduction in performance because of the added weight was not.

• In January 1944, a Coast Guard YR-4A equipped with a hoist lowered a cargo of blood plasma to a U.S. Navy destroyer off New Jersey with 100 badly burned crewmen aboard who had been injured in an explosion aboard the ship.

• Lieutenant Carter Harmon air-delivered an R-4B into Burma over a 5,000-foot mountain range and rescued a downed pilot and crew, one by one, from an inaccessible rice paddy.

• The R-5A, with its 1,100-pound payload, participated in an engineering equipment demonstration at Colorado Springs. A rack was installed and loads of pipe were hauled and laid to simulate transfer of petroleum, oil, and lubricants. Pumps were also airlifted for the pipeline. Demonstrations in which army field wire was carried and paid out over trees and impossible terrain to provide rapid and secure communication were conducted.

• The YR-4A was used on U.S. Air Force repair depots floating off Okinawa to service the B-29s by delivering parts and personnel from ship to shore. The helicopter was vital in this operation, since small boats and barges were severely hampered by rough water in the open sea between the ship and the B-29 base.

In 1943, the Vought-Sikorsky Division of United Aircraft was separated into two independent divisions. Sikorsky Aircraft moved into a 500,000-square-foot plant in Bridgeport, Connecticut, to build helicopters, and Vought Aircraft remained in Stratford. Vought Aircraft later separated from United Aircraft and moved to Texas. The Bridgeport plant remained the home of Sikorsky until 1954, when a new plant was built in Stratford. This 830,000-square-foot plant was used only for manufacturing. Engineering, testing, and other services remained in Bridgeport. Then, in order to consolidate all operations at one location, an additional 500,000-square-foot building was added in 1958. More than 8,000 people were employed at Sikorsky at that time. The Bridgeport factory is still a part of Sikorsky and is used for overhaul of rotors, transmissions, and helicopters and also for the construction of the Sikorsky S-76A commercial helicopter.

Figure 13.
Coast Guard version of the HO3S-1. Close-up of helicopter stabilizer and inflatable emergency doughnut floats.

The Helicopter Industry Takes Off

After V-J Day, the helicopter industry grew at a phenomenal rate. Many small companies were formed during the postwar period to exploit the commercial and military markets. Among them was Frank Piasecki's company. Piasecki built and flew the PV-2, a single-rotor, two-place machine, in 1943. In 1945, with private funds, he began construction of a tandem-rotor aircraft. He convinced the navy that this configuration would be better suited to larger helicopters and that it would provide a solution to the center-of-gravity problem that severely handicapped the single-rotor types. The navy contracted for the ten-place HRP-1 and the fourteen-place HRP-2, a larger, semimonocoque version, for evaluation.

To keep the Sikorsky organization together after the massive cancellations at the end of World War II, the R-5A was redesigned and improved as a four-place machine, using company funds. The S-51, as it was designated, first flew on February 16, 1946. It was granted an FAA Approved Type Certificate H-2 on April 17, 1947, with a gross weight of 4,985 pounds. The first Type Certificate had been awarded to the Bell 47 several months earlier. The first demonstration of the S-51 to the navy was aboard the aircraft carrier *Franklin D. Roosevelt* during a Caribbean cruise. In the plane-guard role, flying alongside the carrier, it was ready to pick up pilots who crashed on takeoff, and it flew aft of the carrier to rescue pilots who didn't make the deck and crashed during landing. During the cruise, several aircraft crashed and the crews were spectacularly rescued by the S-51, piloted by Sikorsky chief test pilot Jim Viner. In one instance, the pilot of a Corsair was returned to the carrier less than two minutes after takeoff and ditching. In another instance, a crewman was blown overboard from a side elevator by the jet blast from an F9F fighter. Jimmy Viner saw this, picked him up at the stern of the carrier, and had him back on board before he was missed, surely saving him from drowning.

As a result of the demonstration the S-51

was designated the navy HO3S-1, and contracts were immediately placed for a small quantity. The air force also placed orders for the H-5D (S-51). Later the Coast Guard bought a small number (see figure 13). Through 1950, 161 units were delivered to the U.S. military. An additional fifty-three S-51s were sold for export and to commercial operators. Also, in 1946 Sikorsky entered into a licensing agreement for the S-51 with Westland Aircraft, in Yeovil, England. Variations of the S-51 were produced for the Royal Air Force, Royal Navy, and many civil and commercial users. It was used for rescue with two litter cases, one on each side; crop spraying and crop dusting; mail carrying; and airline operations. Later it was redesigned as the Widgeon, to carry four passengers and a pilot. This model carried two litter patients internally and a medical attendant. Other uses included transport of freight, transport of 1,000-pound external sling loads, police and forestry patrol, and, in an antisubmarine version, carrying sonar gear. A total of 152 units of the two models had been built by 1960.

In the United States, the S-51 also began charter and scheduled airline operation. In 1946, four were delivered to Helicopter Air Transport (HAT) of Philadelphia for use in the Camden, New Jersey, area. In January 1947, the G. Fox Department Store in Hartford, Connecticut, chartered three S-51s from HAT to celebrate its 100th anniversary by delivering purchases to customers in sixty-six towns in Connecticut over three separate routes. Also, demonstrations continued to be made to expedite delivery of the U.S. Mail.

By the end of 1947, Los Angeles Airways was flying five S-51s in the operation of the world's first official helicopter airmail route, a service that was initiated on October 1, 1947.

Fifteen S-51s were sold to the Argentine government in 1947, and on March 1, 1947, the first of three S-51s sold to the Royal Canadian Air Force was delivered.

Larry Bell, president of Bell Helicopter, became interested in the helicopter in 1942 and subsequently hired Arthur Young and Bart Kelley. Young had designed a two-blade see-saw rotor with a gyro stabilizing bar that provided the stability that had been lacking in other single-rotor helicopter designs. The company-funded Model 30 was built in 1943 and test flown, along with several other prototypes, for two years.

From it evolved the Model 47, which received the first FAA Type Certificate H-1 on March 8, 1946. Ten 47B helicopters were built that year for demonstration. The commercial market looked so promising that Larry Bell decided to build 500 of these machines without orders and sell them off the shelf. While there was some success in selling them to commercial operators for seismic work, crop spraying, power line patrol, and forestry surveillance, sales were disappointing, and more than 400 of these helicopters were put into storage and written off as a loss.

The sequel to this story is that in 1949, because of the Korean War, the army urgently required 300 observation-utility helicopters. The advanced Sikorsky S-52 was considered, but without production tooling, the delivery schedule could not be met. Larry Bell offered deliveries beginning in ninety days, all 340 helicopters to be delivered within a year. The only problem was to add the special requirements of the army to the 400 47Bs already built and in storage. Larry Bell's foresight was vindicated. Since the first Model 30 in 1943, Bell had produced 2,600 Model 47s through 1960, in many versions, for the army, the air force, the navy, the Marine Corps, and the Coast Guard and for delivery to many foreign countries and many commercial operators.

In 1946, the U.S. Navy conducted a design competition for a replacement of the S-51 (HO3S). They were looking for more lift and better performance and a five- to six-place machine. The Piasecki XHJP-1 tandem-rotor helicopter, powered by the Continental R-975, 550-hp engine, was selected. Because the configuration—overlapping and intermeshing rotors—was unconventional and untried, a backup program was also pro-

Figure 14.
The Hiller H-23, a two-place helicopter with Franklin 200-hp engine

cured, the Sikorsky XHJS-1 (S-53). The two machines were completed at about the same time, and a comparative evaluation was conducted at the Patuxent River Naval Air Test Center in Maryland. The Patuxent evaluation showed that with the same power plants, the same gross weights, and the same performance, there was little difference between the two machines. The deciding factor was that the Sikorsky XHJS-1 required ballast to accommodate changes in loading. This had also been a problem in the HO3S (S-51), since almost any mission involving rescue or transfer of personnel involved a large change in the center of gravity and repositioning of ballast. The end result was production of an aircraft designated HUP-1 by the navy.

During this period, the air force had canceled the last five H-5H rescue helicopters; a modification of the contract was issued to build the H-19, a ten-place helicopter powered with the Pratt & Whitney R-1340 engine to meet a requirement for a higher-performance, larger machine. This contract modification enabled the air force to acquire an advanced state-of-the-art helicopter without the long wait usually associated with funding approval and the formal competition requirement for a new machine.

As a result, the H-19 was designed, built, and delivered within a year of contract agreement. The first flight was in November 1949. With the adoption of the displaced flapping-hinge rotor pioneered on the S-52 in 1947, the H-19 now had an acceptable center-of-gravity range. The navy and air force liked the machine, and early orders were placed for the HO4S by the navy and for the H-19 by the air force. Deliveries began in 1950.

With the Piasecki HUP lagging behind in its program, the orders from the navy and air force to Sikorsky were steadily increased. Sikorsky delivered a small number in 1951 and 297 in 1952. It was the first antisubmarine helicopter to operate from shipboard and the first to be used in scheduled passenger service by Los Angeles Airways and New York Airways.

In July 1952, two H-19s of the U.S. Air Rescue Service were flown from Westover, Massachusetts, to their operating base in Manston, England, in nine stops across the North Atlantic without incident. The longest hop was the 670 miles between Goose Bay and Greenland.

The S-55 (H-19) received its FAA Type Certificate 1H-4 on March 25, 1952. A total of more than 1,250 were built.

The S-55 was licensed for production to Westland Aircraft in 1950. Four hundred seventeen were built through 1960. Naval versions were fitted with a tow hook to tow minesweeping gear.

In 1952, Sud Aviation in France was also licensed to produce the S-55. Eighty-seven were assembled from components and parts shipped from Sikorsky, and more than 150 were built. Later, the S-55 was licensed to Mitsubishi in Japan.

In 1942, Stanley Hiller, Jr., formed the Hiller Aircraft Company and proceeded to develop a coaxial helicopter, the XH-44, which was flown in 1944. In partnership with the Kaiser Corporation, he built a second coaxial helicopter, the X-235, supported by the navy, which was flown in 1948. He also developed a single-rotor configuration with an aerodynamic stabilizer bar that proved to be highly successful. Of the model 360, built in 1947, more than 1,100 were built for the army (H-23A, B, C, D) (see figure 14) and the navy (HTE-1 and -2). Many were delivered to operators in a number of countries.

I was assigned, in 1946, the task of designing a small, two-place commercial helicopter powered by the Franklin 178-hp engine. United Aircraft gave Sikorsky about a million dollars to build five experimental models. It was the first Sikorsky helicopter with all-metal blades—built around an extruded aluminum spar—and a displaced flapping-hinge rotor to eliminate the single-rotor flapping-hinge center-of-gravity problem. This feature was incorporated in all subsequent Sikorsky designs, as was the all-metal aluminum-spar blade. The first flight was on February 12, 1947. It was certificated by the FAA on February 25, 1948, Type Certificate H-3.

With a Franklin 245-hp engine installed, the helicopter, the S-52, was demonstrated to the army extensively at Fort Bragg. Tests of its ability to survive fighter attack by a P-51 were run. During these tests I flew as an observer. We survived very well by staying in the nap of the earth, using trees, a lake, and other natural objects as protective cover. The army project officer, Major John Rowan, told us between flights that the P-51 couldn't find us and requested that we climb to several hundred feet and allow the fighter to see us. That was a disaster. At times during his gun camera passes, the P-51 virtually came through the rotor. The gun camera pictures of the S-52 showed a lot during our exposed flight. When we were not in hiding we were a sitting duck. This issue is still not resolved. With its displaced flapping-hinge rotor, the S-52 had superb controllability, and much nap-of-the-earth flying was done.

In 1948, a high-altitude evaluation was conducted at 10,000 feet by the army at Leadville, Colorado. Later, three official world records were established: on April 27, 1949, the S-52-1, with a borrowed 0-425-1 army engine of 245 hp and Sikorsky test pilot Tommy Thompson, broke the world speed record held by the Fairey Rotodyne of England with a speed of 129.552 mph at Cleveland, Ohio; on May 6, 1949, the 100-kilometer closed-circuit course record was broken at 122.749 mph with Tommy Thompson as pilot and Ralph Alex as copilot; and on May 21, 1949, flown by Captain Hugh Gaddis, it climbed to 21,220 feet for a new record for altitude without payload (see figure 15). To demonstrate its positive control and maneuverability, it was filmed performing several loops below 300 feet.

In 1951, the army awarded Sikorsky a contract to modify the two-place S-52-1 to give it a four-place configuration, the YH-18A. Four service-test Y models were built and extensively tested. The aircraft, still retaining the 245-hp engine, was badly underpowered, and no further development of production was undertaken.

The Marine Corps needed the aircraft as a Medevac helicopter and contracted for eighty-seven of the HO5S-1 version to be powered with a new Franklin model 0-425-11 engine supercharged to 315 hp. Unfortunately, the new engine failed in its test program and the eighty-seven HO5S-1s were delivered with the same 245-hp engine used in the underpowered army YH-18A. In spite of the handicap of inadequate power, it saw extensive service in Korea with the marines in the observation squadron, VMO-6, at Ascom City. At the end of the Korean War, the Department of Defense estimated that more than 10,000 persons had been rescued by the Sikorsky HO5S-1 and HRS-1 and the Bell H-13.

Figure 15.
The S-52-1 visits the inner courtyard of the Pentagon. Tommy Thompson, pilot, and Ralph Alex.

The HO5S-1 was used as a trainer by the marines in New River, North Carolina. Colonel George Hollowell, commanding VMO-1, reported that his students had made more than 50,000 successful autorotation landings without damage to the machine or injuries to personnel. The exception was a landing in which one landing gear was broken off; the machine hovered and finally landed on hastily gathered mattresses. The HO5S was retired in the late 1950s.

Kaman Aircraft Corporation was formed in December 1945 by Charles H. Kaman to build the synchropter, a helicopter of a new configuration, with intermeshing rotors controlled by a servo-flap system that he had developed. In addition to achieving excellent controllability, he was eliminating the tail rotor. His first machine, the K-125, was built in 1946. In 1948, he built the K-190, and in 1949 the K-225. The navy became interested and an order was placed in 1950 for the K-240 (U.S. Navy HTK-1). Deliveries began in 1952. In 1950, Kaman won a design competition for a liaison helicopter for the navy. His winning design was a larger version of the HTK-1—the K-600 (HOK-1 navy, HUK-1 marines), which was accepted in April 1953. As the U.S. Air Force HH-43B, the Huskie, it was procured by the air force as a local crash-rescue and firefighter helicopter. One hundred sixteen were built. In 1961 this aircraft also established a world altitude record of 26,369 feet with a 1,000-kilogram payload and a world altitude record of 32,279 feet without payload.

McDonnell Aircraft Corporation, in St. Louis, Missouri, established a helicopter division in 1946, with C. Yakhartchenko as chief engineer. Its first project, undertaken for the U.S. Navy, was to complete the development of the XHJD-1 Whirlaway, a large, twin-engine, ten-place, side-by-side rotor design begun by Platt-LePage as a follow-on to the XR-1A. The configuration was extensively tested and later retired.

In 1949, the Hughes Aircraft Company, a division of Hughes Tool Company, acquired from Kellett Aircraft an army-sponsored test bed for development of a large cargo helicopter. It was to be a rotor-driven, pressure-tip jet system powered by two General Electric J-35 Turbojets, with a rotor diameter of 130 feet and gross weight of 50,000 pounds. After completion of ground tests, the army contracted with Hughes to build the XH-17 cargo-crane (see figure 16), and the first flight was in October 1952. On subsequent flights it carried a payload of 25,000 pounds. Problems of rotor-blade fatigue, noise, and high fuel consumption ended the project.

A company-funded small, two-place, single-main- and tail-rotor helicopter, Model 269A, was built in 1956, and five were bought by the U.S. Army for evaluation. The helicopter was adopted as a primary trainer, the TH-55A, and it is still in production for both the army and the navy. Several hundred have been built, many for commercial and private use, a sizable number for export.

In 1950, a competition for an air-rescue helicopter for the air force was conducted. Again Piasecki won the award, this time for the H-21 "Work Horse," which was a twelve- to twenty-place, tandem helicopter, powered with the Wright R-1820 1,425-hp engine, with a gross weight of 11,500 pounds. The army also ordered the H-21B and H-21C for transport of cargo and personnel with a 1,425-hp-rated R-1820 engine and fitted to carry twenty passengers or twelve litters. The first delivery was made to the air force in 1952 with a derated engine and a capacity for fourteen passengers or twelve litters. At the 1953 National Air Show, the H-21A set two new world records: standard 15–25-kilometer-course speed record of 146.75 mph and an altitude record of 22,210 feet.

At about the same time, the U.S. Air Force again issued a contract modification to Sikorsky, this time concerning the H-19 production helicopter, and reduced the quantity by five to obtain funds to build a backup for the Piasecki H-21. The upgrade of the H-19 became the Sikorsky H-34 (S-58), a 13,000-pound, four-blade, twenty-passenger machine using the same R-1820 engine. This helicopter was second best in the air force competition that was won by Piasecki. The H-34 was first flown in 1952, and the first delivery to the army was in March 1955 (see figure 17). Because of problems of vibration, control, and the drive system, the deliveries of the H-21 lagged again, as they had in the HUP and H-19 programs; the U.S. military increased their orders for the Sikorsky H-34A (army), the HSS-1 (navy) for antisubmarine warfare (ASW), and the HUS-1 (marines) (see figure 18). In 1956, with Cap-

Figure 16.
The Hughes XH-17 in 1952. A two-place helicopter with two GE J-35 turbojets. A 25,000-pound payload, as shown, was flown for a short period.

tains Claude Hargett and Ellis Hill as pilot and copilot, respectively, it established three closed-circuit-course world speed records in one flight: 100-kilometer closed-circuit course at 141.9 mph, 500 kilometers at 136 mph, and 1,000 kilometers (621 miles) at 132.6 mph. On this flight the auxiliary fuel tank was not filled. Conservative estimates of fuel requirements indicated that a weight reduction of 600 pounds was possible. Engine fuel consumption at full power caused the red light to come on during the last lap. By radio, Captain Hargett said he couldn't make it back to the Sikorsky plant, but he thought he could finish the course if he could land at the finish line after completing the last lap. When he landed at the finish line, the fuel remaining turned out to be enough for two or three minutes of operation. In the fall of 1957 it was tested as an armed helicopter equipped with forty 2.75-inch rockets, three .50-caliber machine guns, two 20-millimeter cannon, six .30-caliber machine guns, and two five-inch high-velocity aircraft rockets (HVAR). Within four years the army H-34s had amassed more than 110,000 flight hours. All the S-58s had flown a total of 220,000 hours by the end of 1958.

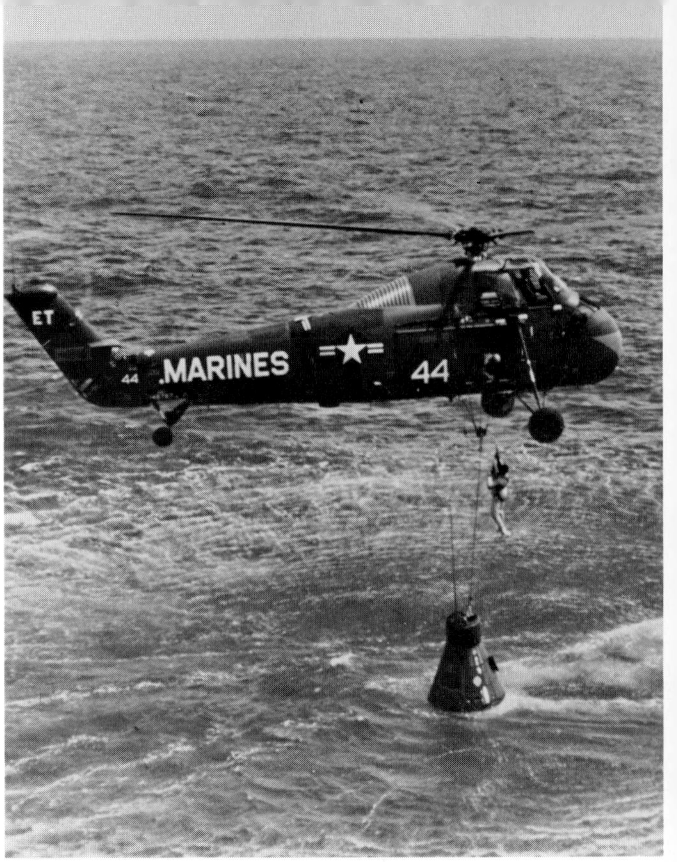

Figure 18.
The HUS-1 (H-34D) picking up astronauts

Figure 17.
The H-34 weapons test at Fort Benning, Georgia. The designation was changed to CH-34 in 1962.

On August 2, 1956, the S-58 received FAA Type Certificate 1H-11. It was used in scheduled airline service by New York Airways, by Los Angeles Airways, and later by Chicago Helicopter Airways. As the S-58T, with PT6 turbines, it is still used in scheduled passenger service by New York Helicopters.

The S-58 was also licensed to Westland Aircraft in 1956. It was re-engined with two Napier-Gazelle shaft turbines of 1,350 hp each, and later with two turbines of 1,600 hp each (Napier-Gazelle NGa22). A total of 348 were built for the Royal Navy for ASW, for the Royal Australian Navy, for the Iraqi Air Force, and for the Ghana Air Force. Another version was built for Bristow Helicopters and other commercial operators.

Later, Sud Aviation, in France, was licensed to build the S-58. A total of 185 were delivered to the French air force and navy and 5 to the Belgian armed forces. West Germany and Israel also operated several companies of H-34s and HUS-1s. More than 1,800 of this model were built altogether. As the VH-34 it was used to transport the President of the United States, many heads of state, and other visitors of the president.

In 1950, Piasecki also received a contract to build a large, general-purpose transport, the PV-15 (YH-16). This tandem machine was powered with two Pratt & Whitney R-2800 engines of 2,100 hp each. Its empty weight was 30,000 pounds, and it was configured to carry forty to fifty passengers, or a payload of five to six tons. The first flight was in November 1953. A year later, the YH-16A, a modification of the YH-16, with twin Allison YT-38-A3 turbines of greatly increased power, was lost when the test equipment severed the rear main rotor shaft during main-rotor strain-gauge tests. Its development was then canceled.

The navy conducted a design competition for a large assault helicopter transport with a three-ton payload for the Marine Corps. In early 1951, Sikorsky was chosen to build the S-56 (navy XHR2S-1), a thirty-six-place helicopter powered by two 2,100-hp Pratt & Whitney R-2800 engines, with a gross weight of 26,800 pounds and a five-blade rotor (see figure 19). It had a folding rear pylon and folding main rotor blades for carrier operation. The army joined the navy in development of the S-56 because it required an assault helicopter capable of carrying a three-ton payload. The army version, designated H-37A, incorporated several modifications, including the elimination of the complex automatic folding tail pylon and folding rotor blade. Deliveries to the army began in 1956.

The S-56 was first flown in 1953. During its construction, it grew in weight in several stages to 33,000 pounds. The result of this 25 percent increase in gross weight was an underpowered machine. The extra weight dictated an increase of 20–25 percent in rpm to reduce excessive rotor coning, which in turn increased the operation of the engine from 2,050 rpm to 2,500 rpm, thereby dramatically increasing wear and oil consumption. These deficiencies were responsible for the substantial reduction in the planned production quantity. Out of a total of several hundred required only 154 were built. General Bill Bunker, commanding general of the Aviation Systems Command (AVSCOM), contracted with Sikorsky to correct many of these deficiencies, and as the

Figure 19.
The S-56 (HR2S-1) navy assault transport, retrieving the HRS-2 from swamp after engine failure

H-37B, the S-56 was deployed to Vietnam in the early days of the conflict there. After its return from Vietnam, the H-37B was turned over to the National Guard and was soon retired.

Three world records were established by the H-37A in November 1956: maximum speed over a three-kilometer course, 162.7 mph; altitude with an 11,000-pound payload, 12,100 feet; greatest load carried to 2,000 meters (6,500 feet), 13,200 pounds.

Figure 20.
The YH-18B used for emergency medical service, fitted with two stretchers and with an attendant behind the pilot

Figure 21.
The XH-39, modifications of the YH-18B with an Artouste II 425-hp turbine

In 1951, the U.S. Army awarded Sikorsky a contract to install the French 280-hp Turbomeca Artouste I turbine in a Sikorsky YH-18A helicopter. During modification, the 425-hp Artouste II became available and the Artouste I was never installed.

The YH-18B was first flown on July 24, 1953 (see figure 20). During this conversion the decision was made to modify the YH-18B further into a prototype production four-place helicopter. The result was the XH-39 (S-59), which was first flown on June 1, 1954 (see figure 21). It had a four-blade displaced flapping-hinge rotor, now standard with all Sikorsky models, and a retracting landing gear.

The XH-39, with Warrant Officer Billy Wester as pilot, established a new three-kilometer world speed record of 156.009 mph on August 26, 1954, and on October 17, 1954, it established a new world altitude record of 24,521 feet (see figure 22). During flight it became apparent that the hot-weather power loss of 25 percent by the turbine—the Artouste II—dictated a larger engine. Since no American-built engine of higher horsepower was available at that time, the project was shelved. Sikorsky had also built the S-59, a company-funded model for the commercial market. It had completed tie-down tests for FAA Type Certification when it was also shelved because of lack of a suitable higher-powered American turbine.

With the advent of the shaft turbine in 1956 a new era began for the helicopter, which had been severely handicapped during the preceding fifteen years by the limited number of power-plant choices. Piston engines built for the airplane had many design compromises for the helicopter, the most important of which was lack of power for adequate performance. The Allison 250 (T-63), the Avco Lycoming T-53, and the General Electric T-58, developed for the army and navy, were the first of this new generation of power plants that were to lead to a significant advancement in the state of the art of the helicopter.

The first beneficiary of this new generation of turbine power plants was the Bell XH-40. In 1955 this helicopter won the U.S. Army competition for the development of a utility helicopter suitable for Medevac of front-line casualties, general utility use, and training. It was to be powered with the new 850-hp Lycoming T-53 turbines. The result of this development was the UH-1, the Huey, which became the mainstay of the army's helicopter inventory. The growth in performance and weight—7,200 pounds to 10,500 pounds—between the UH-1, delivered to the army in 1960, and the UH-1H of the 1980s, has been possible only because of the steady growth of the T-53 turbine—from 850 hp to 1,400 hp. More than 10,000 were built during a twenty-seven-year period.

In rapid succession the U.S. Air Force Kaman HH-43A, a local crash-rescue helicopter, was converted from a piston-powered machine to the HH-43B, powered with the Lycoming T-53-L-1A (derated to 720 hp) turboshaft engine. It went into production in 1959–60.

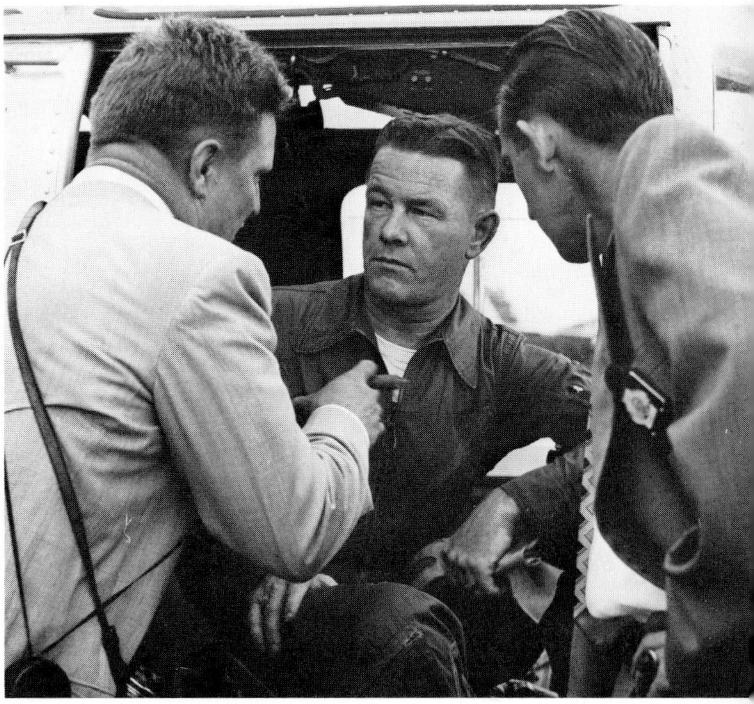

Figure 22.
The XH-39 with Flight Officer Billy Wester, at briefing before the attempt to set a world speed record

The army launched a competition for a new light observation helicopter (LOH) to be powered with the new army-sponsored Allison T-63 (model 250) turboshaft engine. The Bell OH-4, Hiller OH-5, and Hughes OH-6 competed through the flyoff. The winner was the Hughes OH-6, of which more than 1,200 were built. During the award of additional orders, Congress requested a new competition. Bell helicopter, with the OH-58, won with the lowest price, and the additional orders were for more than 2,000 helicopters. Bell also developed a commercial version of the OH-58 called the Jet Ranger (Model 206), which was highly successful and is still in production.

During this same period Vertol built the CH-46 for the marines, and Sikorsky built the S-61 (navy HSS-2), both powered with the 1,050-hp General Electric/Navy T-58 turboshaft and both twin-engined.

In 1959–60 Vertol also won the U.S. Air Force competition for a helicopter that would carry a two- to three-ton payload, the CH-47, powered with the T-55 Lycoming turboshaft engine. This helicopter, the standard light transport for the army, is still in production. During 1958, Sikorsky built the S-62, a company-funded project, using the proven S-55 (H-19) dynamic components, powered with a single General Electric T-58 turbine. The S-62A was used by San Francisco and Oakland Airlines to begin the first nonsubsidized scheduled airline. The Coast Guard adopted the HH-52A (S-62A) as the base for their helicopter fleet in 1962, and it is still in operation.

Highlights in the History of the Helicopter, 1940–60

There are three distinct phases in the development of the helicopter industry:

First Phase, 1939–43. This phase began with the dedicated small group at Sikorsky, motivated by Igor Sikorsky himself, who put in a minimum of two man-years per year of effort between 1939 and 1945. It continued with the enthusiasm and support of Majors H. F. Gregory and Vic Haugen of the U.S. Army, who risked their careers in promoting a rotary-wing concept that was pronounced worthless by academia and many of Gregory and Haugen's military peers.

Finally came the astounding feat of designing, building, and testing three different models—the Sikorsky XR-4, XR-5, and XR-6A—one twice the size of the other two—and building a total of more than 600 before V-J Day, September 2, 1945. There was no time for production tooling, extensive testing, or redesign of problem areas except in the case of the R-6A, which was built on a Detroit production line. But even without a test program for the experimental machines and with little time to improve production quality, the aircraft were reasonably successful in service. The R-6A was a prime example of the successful approach: Design the first experimental model for production because you will not get a chance to do it later. Using this approach, plan for simple tooling; build in at least 30–40 percent growth in the rotors, transmission, drive system, and power plant; and use "zero margin" in design areas only when it can be changed readily and in noncritical components and structures. Supervise the redesign for production in great detail to ensure that lessons learned from experience will not be ignored. High-risk design will always attract the best talent and the most attention and usually produces the fewest problems. When this approach doesn't work, an alternative must be available instantly. It certainly worked with the R-4, R-5, and R-6, which were put into operation and tested for extended periods without spares and in most instances completed their assigned missions.

Second Phase, 1945–53. During this phase the industry expanded with the formation of many new companies, such as Bell Aircraft Company, with Arthur Young; Piasecki Helicopter Company, with Frank Piasecki; Kaman Aircraft Corporation, with Charles H. Kaman; Hiller Helicopter Company, with Stanley Hiller; Hughes Helicopter; and many others, all of which, along with the established Kellett, Pitcairn, and G & A compa-

Figure 23.
Ralph Alex on visit to the Soviet Union in 1959, flanked by A. Kamov, coaxial designer, and M. Mil, single-rotor designer, at Tushino Aerodrome, Moscow

nies, were building prototypes that in most cases were successful and would become a part of the helicopter industry. There were more than fifty pioneers in this period; to name a few and their helicopter designs: Fred Landgraf with his side-by-side, rigid-rotor, all molded wood and plywood design; Kaiser Fleetwings single-rotor design; Platt-LePage side-by-side rotor design; Charles Siebel with his single-rotor American tip jet; Bendix coaxial, two-place and five-place; Brantly coaxial; and Doman single-rotor flexible spar design. I don't believe that any possible configuration was omitted. Most of the machines flew successfully but progressed little further than the prototype stage. The army did buy a small number of many configurations to do its own testing in an effort to gain varied experience in rotary-wing aircraft.

Third Phase, 1954–60. During this period the Piasecki tandem-rotor concept was sold to the services as the answer for the larger helicopter; that is, to enable a transition to a twice-size or larger machine without having to develop a new rotor blade and rotor system. Another advantage quoted was that it was more efficient, since it did not require a tail-rotor for antitorque correction, which Piasecki claimed saves 5–15 percent of the power, which can thus be converted to lift. The biggest advantage claimed still was the larger center-of-gravity range, which up to 1947 was an established fact. Piasecki won the next four competitions, in which Sikorsky was the loser.

The displaced flapping-hinge solution to the center-of-gravity problem of the Sikorsky S-52-1 was added to the S-51 (HO3S), with the result that backup contracts were awarded to Sikorsky for each of the Piasecki tandem-rotor projects. Because of vibration and other problems, Sikorsky was given production contracts in parallel with Piasecki and went on to garner the larger share of the production orders. The message seemed to be, lose the competition and collect the better part of the business.

At that time the S-52-1 also introduced the first all-metal, extruded-aluminum-spar rotor blades that were adopted for all Sikorsky projects. This was also a plus in competition. The later addition of the Sikorsky blade-inspection method of pressurizing the spar led to a quantum leap in reliability and acceptance by the pilots and an additional competitive advantage.

Bell, having developed its seesaw, gyro-stabilized two-blade rotor, had its day during this period and produced the greatest number of helicopters until 1960. Hiller, with its two-blade aerodynamic stabilizer bar, also became a larger producer. Hughes, with its flexible-strap rotor hub and unusual main rotor-shaft design, also came of age as a manufacturer of small helicopters during this time.

The Bell 204—the UH-1 "Huey" for the army—with the Lycoming turboshaft engine inaugurated the age of the gas turbine. Kaman's HH-43B synchropter also became a successful turboshaft-powered machine for the air force.

In summary, then, by 1960 the helicopter industry had become an important part of the transport sector. Its sales had surpassed $2.5 billion, of which more than $500 million was for commercial helicopters. More than 7,000 helicopters had been built—more than 1,200 for the air force, more than 1,800 for the navy, and more than 3,200 for the army. The scheduled airlines in the United States had nineteen helicopters in service in 1960—two S-51s, five S-55s, seven S-58s, and five S-44Bs. They carried almost half-a-million passengers, plus airmail and freight. Eight hundred eighty-two helicopters were being operated by 235 commercial operators and 50 flight schools. The operators had ordered 182 helicopters for delivery in 1961. Also in summary:

- In 1960, the industry exported 82 helicopters valued at $7.7 million.
- Employment at the end of 1960 was about 24,000, and the backlog amounted to more than $350 million.
- Several production helicopters had already been approved for 1,000-hour overhaul times.
- Helicopters with the capacity to carry twenty-five to thirty passengers were in production, and one had already received its FAA Type Certification.
- Operation by instrument flight rules (IFR) was now a reality.

Development of the Helicopter in the Soviet Union, 1950–59

In 1959, I attended the General Conference of the Fédération Aéronautique Internationale (FAI) in Moscow and met with prominent Russian helicopter designers (see figure 23). I flew the Mi-4, Mi-6 (see figure 24), Kamov 15, and Kamov 18.

Except for recent increases in size and payload, the current state of the art in Soviet helicopter design was achieved in a whirlwind period of development between 1950 and 1959. Russian designers such as Mil, Kamov, Yakovlev, Archangelsky, Tischenko, and others boldly pioneered many of the features not found on Western helicopters until the last ten years. Technical improvements in Soviet helicopters during this period include:

- Main- and tail-rotor liquid deicing equipment provided for on small helicopters and electric deicing capability to both rotors on large helicopters, using the 300–400-cycle AC electrical system.
- Deicing capability for engine inlets and windshields fitted as standard equipment.
- Use of radar altimeters standardized for precise measurement of altitude down to the foot, especially useful in low-visibility instrument flight.
- Long-range navigation equipment and single sideband radio used extensively.
- All models made capable of IFR operation.
- Manufacture of rotor heads, engine and transmission mounts, and other parts that

Figure 24.
The Mi-6, which set world speed record of 211.25 mph for the 100-kilometer closed-circuit course; notice the absence of a wing on this flight.

Figure 25.
The Kamov-26 twin-engine helicopter with fiberglass blades and 275-hp Shvetsov engines

Figure 26.
The Mi-1 single-rotor, three-blade helicopter with Shvetsov Ai-26W engine (575 hp), next to the Mi-6, single-rotor, five-blade helicopter with two Soloviev shaft turbines (4,635 hp)

are subjected to heavy loads switched from forgings to metal castings of greater strength.

- Engines derated to allow operation at 3,000 meters (9,900 feet), and high ambient temperatures where thin air significantly reduces the available power.
- Use of oxygen equipment standardized.
- Built-in connections, mounts, and fire-control hardware used on large helicopters for quick refit of weapons.
- Twin-engine turbine-powered helicopters introduced in the late 1950s.
- Self-refueling systems adapted to large helicopters for operation from remote areas without ground-based fuel pumps.

According to designers Mil and Kamov, the Soviet Union had built 3,000 helicopters by 1959, including several hundred Kamov K-15s and K-18s, some K-26s (see figure 25), and over 2,000 Mil Mi-1s (see figure 26) and Mi-4s.

In other chapters of this book the history of the helicopter industry will be traced from 1961 to the 1980s.

RALPH P. ALEX, or Mr. Helicopter, as he is widely known, started out in the fixed-wing industry. In 1941, he joined Vought-Sikorsky at Stratford, Connecticut, and was assigned to the XR-4 as a power plant and systems designer. At Sikorsky he progressed from project engineer to senior production engineer; from head, Production Components Design, to assistant chief, Aircraft Design and Development Branch; to chief, Marketing Research and Development. Mr. Alex is credited with many helicopter firsts. He was one of the founders of the American Helicopter Society in 1943, served as its first president, and was later elected again as its fifteenth president. In 1960, he became chairman of the board, the first to hold that office. He was awarded the Certificate of Merit in 1947 and was made an honorary fellow in 1964. In 1977, he was awarded the Dr. Alexander Klemin Award. He has written numerous articles on the helicopter, holds eight patents, lectures extensively on helicopters, and holds many posts on commissions and in associations. He has been president of the International Helicopter Commission of the Federation Aeronautique Internationale of Paris, France, since 1959 and was chief juror at the first, second, third, and fourth World Helicopter Championships. In February 1977, he was awarded the Yuri Gagarin Award by the U.S.S.R. Aero Club for his contribution to the international development of the helicopter. He was elected a fellow of the Society of Automotive Engineers in January 1983 and was re-elected Vice Chairman of the Council, ADPA, Washington, D.C., the same year. Mr. Alex retired from Sikorsky Aircraft in June 1977, after more than thirty-six years of service, and formed Ralph P. Alex & Associates, Inc. Since 1954, as an FAA Designated Engineering Representative for structures, power plant, systems and equipment he has been engaged in aircraft modification approval, STC programs, product liability, and aircraft accident analysis for insurers, and in consultation on advanced materials application and manufacturing technology.

Igor Sikorsky, with his second helicopter. Kiev, Russia, 1910.

SERGEI I. SIKORSKY

The Development of the VS-300

Igor Sikorsky once said, "the idea of a vehicle that could lift itself vertically from the ground and hover motionless in the air was probably born at the same time that man first dreamed of flying." Interestingly, all the early legends of flight have one characteristic in common: whether flying carpets, winged dragons, or magically propelled flying thrones, all these early vehicles were capable of vertical takeoff and landing. They didn't need runways. Igor Sikorsky was familiar with all these early legends of flight.

During his early childhood in Kiev, Russia, Igor Sikorsky read all the pioneering science fiction of Jules Verne, Hans Domenik, and others. He studied the sketches of Leonardo da Vinci, especially those in which Leonardo explored the concept of a flying machine. Though interested in all aspects of flight, he was particularly fascinated by the idea of the helicopter.

In 1909, Igor Sikorsky traveled to Paris, where he studied the earliest flying machines and became personally acquainted with a number of aeronautical pioneers. He discussed with them his dream of building a machine capable of taking off and landing vertically; the experts, however, all warned him against attempting to build a helicopter.

After purchasing a 15-hp Anzani engine in Paris, he returned to Russia. After some deliberation, he disregarded all the earlier advice. It was during the fall and winter of 1909–10 that Sikorsky built his first and second helicopters. Both were basically built in a coaxial configuration. Helicopter number one did not fly at all. Number two was nearly able to lift its own weight off the ground.

After some months of difficult work, Sikorsky realized that the available technology was insufficient. He postponed further research on the helicopter temporarily and turned to fixed-wing aircraft.

In the surprisingly short period of two years, he designed, built, and flew no fewer than six experimental aircraft. He also taught himself to fly during the brief hops that these aircraft made. None of the early machines survived very long, most having been destroyed in one accident or another. Igor Sikorsky seemed to lead a charmed life, however, and suffered no serious injuries during those two dramatic years. By late 1912, he was firmly established as one of Russia's leading engineers and pilots. The name of Sikorsky began to attract international attention when he built and flew the first four-engine aircraft in aviation history. The Grand, as it was called, made its first flight on May 13, 1913. It is an interesting fact that, for more than a year, Igor Sikorsky, the first four-engine pilot, was the only one in the world. It was only after an improved version of the same basic design was put into production in 1914 that he began to train other pilots on the machine.

Following the Communist Revolution of

Figure 1.
The original configuration of the VS-300 in late summer 1939. Only limited hops were attempted.

1917, Sikorsky emigrated to the United States. In the late 1920s and throughout the 1930s, Sikorsky Aircraft built a series of increasingly successful flying boats and amphibious craft. While still occupied with the flying boat, however, Igor Sikorsky was working constantly on the challenge of the helicopter. By early 1931 he was concentrating on the concept of a single main lifting rotor, with cyclic control, and a shaft-driven tail rotor. On June 27, 1931, he filed a patent describing a helicopter having a single main rotor with cyclic pitch control that used trailing edge flaps, or ailerons, on the main rotor blades.

In late 1938, Sikorsky approached the management of United Aircraft (later United Technologies) with the suggestion of building an experimental single-rotor helicopter. The proposal was based largely on his sketches and designs of the 1930s.

The proposal was initially greeted with some skepticism. Although a number of helicopters had been built and some had even flown, most scientists did not consider the helicopter a really practical idea. To compound the skepticism, the only helicopters to have shown any degree of success had multiple rotors. In 1938, Louis Breguet was already flying a coaxial machine that had established several world records, including a flight that lasted one hour and two minutes.

In Germany, Professor Henrich Focke had created the Fa-61, which advanced the world's endurance record to one hour and twenty minutes. On subsequent demonstrations in 1938, the helicopter had reached an altitude of 11,243 feet and made a cross-country flight covering a distance of 143 miles.

While these developments were being made in the helicopter, the autogiro, a craft which had a propeller for forward movement as well as a rotor for lift, remained a strong contender. The Spaniard Juan de la Cierva had designed and built the first successful autogiro in 1923, and the machine was developed steadily throughout the 1920s and 1930s. It was being built under license in a number of countries. Harold F. Pitcairn had secured the U.S. patent rights, which he had then sublicensed to a number of manufacturers. At one time or another in the late 1930s the Pitcairn Autogiro Company, the Kellett Autogiro Company, and the Buhl Manufacturing Company were all building varieties of the autogiro.

In conversations many years later, Sikorsky pointed out that the autogiro was the important missing link between the fixed-wing concept and the helicopter concept. Without a doubt, the technology of the rotor head and rotor blade, developed for the autogiro, was of significant use in the development of the helicopter.

At any rate, despite the prevailing opinion that "helicopters are almost impossibly difficult to design, and not really worth anything when completed," work began in the spring of 1939. The layout of the VS-300 was a single-rotor helicopter powered by a 65-hp Lycoming engine. A three-blade main rotor twenty-eight feet in diameter and a single-blade counterbalanced tail rotor were used in the earliest configuration. The gross weight was 1,092 pounds. In our research at Sikorsky Aircraft on the VS-300 we have found only four engineering drawings that describe the control system and rotor head. Most of the other details, such as fuselage and landing gear, were described verbally or simply sketched out. The main thrust was to build a light, simple test bed to demonstrate the concept. The machine was purposely designed to be easily modified. No attempt was made to streamline the VS-300 aerodynamically until very late in its career (see figure 1).

On September 14, 1939, Sikorsky made his first successful liftoff (see figure 2). During the rest of the autumn of 1939, he explored stability and control. Today, we strongly suspect that these first flights were also

Figure 2.
The first "hovering flight" of the VS-300, with Igor Sikorsky at the controls, September 14, 1939. The nose has been extended and a nose wheel added.

made with the cyclic control system misphased by at least 30 degrees. It seems that the 90-degree phase shift of the articulated rotor was not yet fully appreciated by Sikorsky and his small group of fellow researchers.

It must be noted that Sikorsky was also teaching himself to fly this new form of aircraft at the same time that he was flight-testing it. His own words describe it simply and accurately: "It was a wonderful chance to relive one's own life—to design and construct a new type of flying machine without really knowing how to do it, and then climb into the pilot's seat and try to fly it . . . without ever having flown a helicopter before!"

Concurrent with the early flights of the VS-300, in 1939 the U.S. Army Air Corps announced a competition for the design and manufacture of a rotary-wing aircraft to evaluate its military potential. Some seven companies submitted proposals. Five designs were improved autogiros, while Platt-LePage in Philadelphia proposed a twin-rotor, side-by-side helicopter, and Sikorsky proposed a slightly larger version of the single-rotor VS-300.

In December 1939, the VS-300 was severely damaged in the course of a training flight. While being repaired, it was extensively redesigned. The thin box beam carrying the tail rotor was replaced by a truss tail cone and now carried two horizontal rotors in addition to the antitorque tail rotor. The main rotor cyclic control was removed; only collective pitch control was retained. Fore and aft movement depended on increasing or decreasing the pitch of the horizontal tail rotors to tilt the aircraft in the desired direction. Differential pitch to the horizontal tail rotors produced a bank to the right or left (see figure 3).

On May 13, 1940, the VS-300 began to make a series of increasingly successful flights. Not only was the new configuration more stable, but it is evident that Sikorsky was gaining expertise as a helicopter pilot. In that same month, Sikorsky Aircraft submitted a new, last-minute proposal to the army. The configuration of this proposal followed that of the rebuilt VS-300, in that it showed a single main rotor and one vertical and two horizontal tail rotors (see figure 4).

On July 19, 1940, the U.S. Army Air Corps awarded a development contract to Platt-LePage. The air corps evaluation had concluded that the side-by-side rotor configuration showed the least technical risk.

By the end of July, the original 65-hp Lycoming engine was replaced with a 90-hp Franklin engine. The flight characteristics of the helicopter were slowly improving, as was the confidence factor of the test pilot, and several extended hovering flights of twenty minutes or more were logged.

Although the VS-300 hovered and flew sideward and backward rather well, anytime that forward flight reached twenty to twenty-five miles an hour, the VS-300 would become unstable and nearly uncontrollable. Technical attention was given to this problem, which was thought to be caused by the impact of main-rotor downwash on the horizontal tail rotors.

In midsummer 1940, the outriggers supporting the two horizontal tail rotors were extended outward and canted upward to raise the tail rotors away from the main-rotor downwash. This improved the forward flight characteristics somewhat, and speeds of twenty-five miles an hour were achieved before the aircraft became unstable. In addition, part of the cause of this instability was probably that the main rotor blade lead-lag movement was still being damped by rubber friction dampers alone. Contemporary photographs show that hydraulic dampers were in use but were mounted vertically in an effort to smooth out flapping movement.

On October 14, 1940, the VS-300 had its second serious crash when one of the horizontal tail rotor booms broke in flight, probably because of an earlier, very hard landing. The helicopter rolled over in the air and crashed sideways to the ground. Luckily, Sikorsky was not hurt; he stepped out of the wreckage, stood quietly for a minute or two, and is reported to have said, "I think we'll take her home now."

Figure 3.
First tethered flights of VS-300 following major redesign after December 1939 crash. The photograph was taken in February or March 1940. Notice the two horizontal rotors and one vertical tail rotor on new tail.

By November, the helicopter had been completely rebuilt. The tail outriggers were now straight, and the dihedral was reduced to zero. The tail rotor shafts had been lengthened to raise the two horizontal tail rotors even higher, and the vertical tail rotor was also raised.

In January 1941, flight testing of the VS-300 was resumed. The same month something encouraging happened: the U.S. Army Air Corps issued a contract to Sikorsky Aircraft to build a two-place observation helicopter to be powered by a 160-hp Warner engine. Like the VS-300 this helicopter would have a triple tail-rotor configuration. The army's designation for this machine was the XR-4.

In April, it was decided that it would be advantageous to establish an American helicopter record, so on April 15, 1941, Sikorsky lifted into the air and remained there for one hour, five minutes, fourteen and a half seconds. Since this endurance record was only fifteen minutes short of the international record held by the Fa-61, an oversized fuel tank was fitted to the VS-300 and arrangements were made to go for the world record. On May 6, Igor Sikorsky again lifted into the air, this time in front of a large group of officials, reporters, and cameramen. When he landed, one hour, thirty-two minutes, twenty-six seconds later, the VS-300 proudly held a new International Helicopter Endurance Record (see figure 4).

In mid June, an important decision was made. It was decided to return to the concept of full cyclic control for the main rotor. The second half of June was spent in sorting out a variety of control problems, and with the challenge of control precession finally solved, the machine began to fly with greater stability.

In August 1941, the VS-300 was further modified by replacing the two horizontal tail rotors with a single horizontal rotor on a tall pylon just ahead of the tail rotor. After some two hours of increasingly successful flight in the sesquitandem configuration had been logged, it was generally recognized that a significant breakthrough in control had been achieved.

In October 1941, the helicopter was grounded while another series of modifications in the tail rotors was made. A three-blade horizontal tail rotor was installed and flown. During October and November, flight tests of the helicopter continued and the log book begins to mention "ground rocking." It seems that the VS-300 was on the edge of ground resonance several times without the test pilot becoming aware of it. By the end of November 1941, however, all the control problems seem to have been resolved. The decision was then made to remove the horizontal tail rotor and return to full cyclic control of the main rotor and a single tail rotor for torque and rudder control.

On December 8, 1941, the day after Pearl Harbor, the VS-300 made the first flight in its final configuration. The flight log entries note fairly satisfactory control but a tendency to enter both ground and air resonance.

Then at the end of December, Sikorsky made the final breakthrough decision. He repositioned the oleo struts in a horizontal plane to damp the fore and aft movement of the main rotor blades. The first flights with this modification, made on December 31, 1941, showed a dramatic improvement in the flying characteristics. Meanwhile, all these changes were also being hastily engineered into the prototype XR-4, which was now rapidly nearing completion.

The XR-4 made its first flight on January 14, 1942. It is evident that Sikorsky was fairly confident of its technology, because six test flights were made by the XR-4 on that first day. Only three months later, the first public demonstration of the XR-4 was made. Not only had Sikorsky developed and tested a new configuration with the VS-300, he was also able to duplicate this in a significantly larger second-generation helicopter, which was ready to go into large-scale production.

Further evidence of the maturity of this new technology was given when the XR-4 departed on its delivery flight to Wright Field. When the XR-4 arrived on May 17, 1942, the five-day, 761-mile cross-country flight had broken practically all existing helicopter records. In those early days of World War II, however, military security prevented the publication of any details. After the aircraft was formally accepted, on May 30, the XR-4 immediately went into engineering evaluation tests and the first military pilots began their training.

During this time, a variety of rotor systems continued to be evaluated for the VS-300. Sikorsky continued to do much of the test flying himself, concentrating on exploration of the aerodynamic characteristics of a single-blade, counterbalanced main rotor.

A series of two-blade main rotors was also flown. These modifications did not improve the flight characteristics, however, and by late 1942 the VS-300 was refitted with the original three-blade main rotor as flight-testing was continued.

On December 21, 1942, Sikorsky received a cost-plus-fixed-fee contract for fifteen YR-4A helicopters; that same day the U.S. Army

signed a contract calling for five examples of a heavier helicopter to be designated the XR-5. In mid January 1943, the British government ordered 200 YR-4A helicopters and started negotiating for 600 additional machines.

Figure 4.
May 6, 1941—Igor Sikorsky waves a greeting from the VS-300 as it establishes a new world record for helicopters of 1 hour, 32 minutes, 26 seconds. The previous 1 hour, 20 minute record had been flown by the Focke-Achgelis Fa-61.

During the spring and summer of 1943, Sikorsky continued to evaluate minor refinements in the VS-300 that would then be incorporated into the design of the YR-4 helicopters, which were just beginning to enter mass production. In addition, a number of civil and military test pilots continued to make solo flights in the VS-300. Its log book carries the names of a number of aviation personalities in addition to that of Sikorsky. These include Colonel H. F. Gregory, of the U.S. Army Air Corps; D. D.

Figure 6.
October 6, 1943—Henry Ford and Igor Sikorsky with VS-300 helicopter at Ford Museum, Dearborn Village, Michigan. "She was a good ship . . . a sweet little ship."

"Jimmy" Viner and "Les" Morris, both to become pioneer helicopter test pilots; and Charles A. Lindbergh, who made a number of flights and who was an early and enthusiastic supporter of the helicopter.

The career of the VS-300 came to an honorable end on October 6, 1943, when the machine was donated to the Ford Museum at Dearborn, Michigan. On that day, after a brief flight demonstration by Les Morris, the helicopter was flown for the last time by Igor Sikorsky (see figure 5). He lifted into the air in front of a large crowd of dignitaries and several hundred invited guests. He hovered in the machine for a few minutes, then gently landed it and shut off the engine for the last time. Some who were there said that his eyes were a bit moist as he climbed out of the machine for the last time. He stood silent for a moment, then patted it affectionately. He turned to Henry Ford, who was standing near by, and said, "She was a good ship . . . a sweet little ship" (see figure 6).

Many years later, when all the changes and modifications had been researched and documented, I learned that the VS-300 had gone through eighteen major revisions, several hundred minor changes, and two major post-crash modifications.

All in all, the VS-300 logged 102 hours 35 minutes of flying time. During that period it proved the concept of the single-rotor configuration and quite literally sired a new industry.

Figure 5.
The last flight of the VS-300: October 6, 1943, with I. I. Sikorsky at the controls, at Ford Museum, Dearborn Village, Michigan, before the helicopter was put into the museum. Total aircraft time: 102 hours, 35 minutes.

SERGEI I. SIKORSKY, son of Igor Sikorsky, was born in New York City and grew up in Connecticut, watching the design and construction of the Sikorsky flying boats. He remembers visits to the Sikorsky home by the Lindbergh family, Jimmy Doolittle, Roscoe Turner, Eddie Rickenbacker and many other aviation personalities. During World War II, Mr. Sikorsky served with a joint U.S. Coast Guard–Navy Helicopter Development Squadron; he also participated in several of the earliest helicopter search-and-rescue missions. Following World War II, Mr. Sikorsky was graduated with a degree in fine arts from the University of Florence, Italy. He then joined United Aircraft (later United Technologies) and began a series of foreign assignments in Europe and the Far East, which lasted for some twenty years and concluded with coproduction of the Sikorsky CH-53G transport helicopter for the German armed forces. He is a member of numerous aviation associations, a guest lecturer at a number of European universities, and recipient of many awards, including the Italian Institute of Navigation medal, the Swedish Royal Aeronautical Society's Thulin Bronze Medal, and an honorary doctorate in aviation management from Embry-Riddle Aeronautical University.

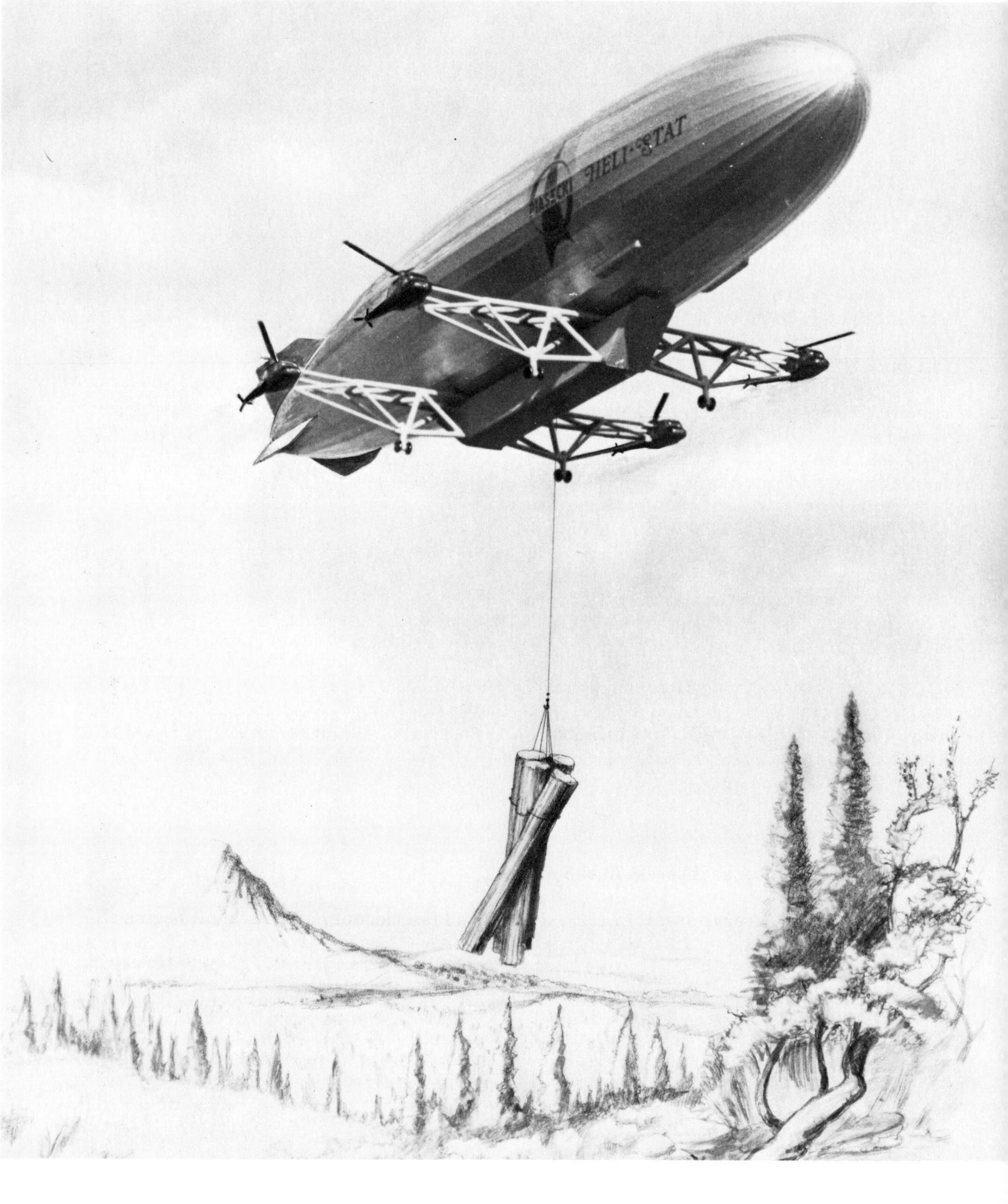
HELI-STAT

FRANK N. PIASECKI

The Piasecki Story of Vertical Lift

Vertical air lift began in 1783 with a hot-air balloon made by the Montgolfier brothers in France. One hundred twenty years later at Kitty Hawk, North Carolina, the Wright brothers flew the first successful powered airplane, thereby launching the development of an industry that has been responsible for many social, political, and economic changes throughout the world. Four years later, Louis Breguet of Paris built the first helicopter to lift a man.

This is a short history of the efforts and accomplishments of the Piasecki team in vertical airlift technology, depicting the aircraft that were designed, developed, produced, and flown in more than forty years of evolution and discovery.

The Beginning of Vertical Lift

World War I and intense interest in the airplane as a weapon delayed the development of the helicopter. After the war, in 1923, the autogiro was invented by Juan de la Cierva in Spain. Pitcairn and Kellett in the United States, the Autogiro Company of Great Britain, and Henrich Focke in Germany produced variations of this aircraft, with an unpowered wind-turned rotor capable of slow flight but without the ability to hover.

The helicopter, with a powered rotor, promised the ability to hover but presented greater technical problems than the autogiro. These early machines were not developed to the point of practical use, and many experts, including the Wright brothers, considered the helicopter too complicated ever to be successful. Despite the skepticism usually encountered by any new idea, a handful of designers were determined to make vertical takeoff and landing (VTOL) technology work.

Louis Breguet, in France, flew his second helicopter, a coaxial, over a nine-kilometer closed course. The four-rotor helicopter of the Russian engineer working in the United States, George de Bothezat, was flown in 1922, but the pilot declared it deficient in control. Focke, Wilford, Daland, LePage, Doblhoff, and others worked separately on methods to achieve VTOL. In 1939, Igor Sikorsky flew his VS-300, the first successful helicopter in the United States.

Model PV-2

The Piasecki story of vertical lift begins after these very early developments. A group of engineering students from the University of Pennsylvania organized the P-V Engineering Forum to design and build their own helicopter. Their first design to demonstrate advanced technology, the PV-1, featured an antitorque fan turned by control vanes in the exit area blowing air through the tail cone. They thought that the development time would be longer for the blow-

Figure 1.
The PV-2, with Frank Piasecki as the test pilot, was the second successful helicopter to fly in the United States.

ing system, so they decided to use a tail rotor for antitorque and yaw control.

The PV-2, a single-seat, single-rotor helicopter, was built as a technology demonstrator to prove several advanced concepts in the still undeveloped VTOL field (see figure 1). The machine featured the first dynamically balanced rotor blades, a rigid tail rotor with a tension-torsion, pitch-change system, an overhead stick, and a full cyclic and collective rotor pitch control. Its first flight took place on April 11, 1943. Frank Piasecki was the test pilot; having had only fourteen hours of previous flying time, in a fixed-wing airplane, he had taught himself to fly the PV-2 helicopter. On October 20, 1943, he demonstrated the machine's precise fingertip control characteristics in Washington, D.C., before military and commercial operators. The PV-2, now on display at the Smithsonian's National Air and Space Museum in Washington, D.C., was the second successful helicopter to fly in the United States.

Model XHRP-X

During World War II the U.S. Coast Guard had an urgent need for a means of rescuing personnel at sea from torpedoed ships along the East Coast. The navy said that the helicopter, to be useful in such rescue operations, would have to be able to carry 1,800 pounds of useful load; the navy was skeptical about building such a machine. The experience of the navy with autogiros showed that the empty-weight percentage of gross weight increased rapidly as rotor size increased—so much so, it was thought, that no helicopter could meet the useful-load requirement. The Coast Guard took the lead, and a contract was signed on New Year's Day 1944 for the first helicopter designed specifically to U.S. Navy and Coast Guard requirements, the XHRP-1.

The tandem configuration—rotors front and rear—was proposed as the most effective way to meet the design conditions of this helicopter that would be three times as large as any yet flying. Two rotors gave a low disc loading, yet allowed the blade spars to be within standard length of the materials available. In addition, the center-of-gravity range was increased significantly, negating the need for shifting ballast that was necessary in the single-rotor helicopters. Critics predicted that downwash from the front rotor in forward flight would cause severe rear-rotor turbulence, making the helicopter difficult to control.

Thirteen months later, Piasecki piloted the world's first successful tandem helicopter. Since a tail rotor was not needed to counter the main-rotor torque, more weight could be lifted with a given engine; this helicopter carried ten men.

The first tandem, the XHRP-X, nicknamed the "Dogship," was flown as a control demonstrator mock-up without its fabric cover and reached a speed of 90 mph (see figure 2). The predicted loss of control in forward flight never happened when the proper differential collective pitch was added to the longitudinal cyclic control. The 1,800-pound external loads—the world's first log lift—were lifted, first with two lines, then with one, and an autorotative test was conducted with the interconnecting shaft between the rotors disengaged.

This concept of a flying mockup, using the XHRP-X, permitted both rapid demonstration of its unique configuration and measurement of its flight and control characteristics; it was then possible to improve the design of the XHRP-1 prototype that followed.

Model HRP-1

Twenty production machines, designated the HRP-1, were purchased by the U.S. Navy. Nicknamed the "Flying Banana" because of the bend in the fuselage that provided rotor-blade clearance, the HRPs were found to be practical in many pioneering applica-

Figure 2.
The Piasecki XHRP-X Dogship, the world's first successful tandem-rotor helicopter

tions that today are standard military maneuvers, such as search and rescue (SAR), antisubmarine warfare (ASW), amphibious assault, heavy transport, and minesweeping.

Model HRP-2

The HRP-2, an improved version of the HRP-1 Rescuer, with an aerodynamically streamlined, all-metal fuselage, was built for the assault mission of the U.S. Marine Corps.

In the earlier tandems, the long distance from the cockpit to the landing gear and center of gravity caused some concern from the standpoint of piloting, so the original XHRP-X landing-gear design called for a caster about the main wheels to avoid skidding the tires off. Flight experience, however, showed that the pilot could hold the wheels motionless at touchdown for a vertical landing. The HRP-2 landing gear eliminated this feature, thereby making the aircraft more stable as well.

The pilot's position in the HRP-1 tandem was kept close to the center of gravity, because the center of a hover turn was not predictable; if it were at the center of gravity, the pilot would be at the end of a large turning radius. This meant reduced visibility for the pilot as he sat behind the forward rotor. From the flight experience of the HRP-1, however, it was learned that pilots always turned about their own centers, unless it was necessary to keep the center of gravity of the helicopter in a fixed position in relation to the ground, as in a log lift. In the HRP-2, therefore, the cockpit was put forward of the front rotor, with pilot and copilot placed side by side for better visibility and coordination.

This structure, lightly loaded in relation to its size and to similar airplane fuselages, required thinner skin to keep the weight down and also required thinner stiffener sections. A stretch-milling process, now common throughout the industry, was developed to make these parts.

Model XHJP-1

In 1945, the Navy Bureau of Aeronautics (BuAer) wrote requirements for a higher-performance utility-and-rescue helicopter to operate from aircraft carriers, battleships, and cruisers. The industrywide competition was won by Sikorsky, with the XHJS-1, and Piasecki, with the XHJP-1, in 1946.

The shipboard requirements, particularly those for the smallest carrier elevator—a forward elevator, Essex class—presented difficult rotor-folding problems if the helicopter was to be rapidly stored below deck. An overlapped rotor configuration previously designed by Piasecki for a more compact fuselage was ideally suited to fit these carrier elevators. The tips of two rotor blades of each of the three-blade rotors were placed at the corners of the smallest carrier elevator, leaving twenty-five feet between the rotor centers. Therefore, blade folding was not required and movement to the hangar deck below was expedited. The blades were foldable for the smaller cruiser elevators.

Models HUP-1 and 2

The HUP was a six-place, single-engine helicopter. The fuselage was all metal, of semimonocoque construction, and with conventional fixed landing gear. The HUP was powered by a Continental R-975-46 engine with a takeoff rating of 550 hp. The missions of the HUP were ship-based rescue, observation, and utility and transport of personnel and cargo.

The copilot's seat could be folded forward, and there was an electrically operated hatch door that lowered to permit a Stokes litter to be lifted directly into the cabin by a ceiling-mounted hoist. The engine and its mount, fan, cowling, oil system, and accessories were removable as a single unit through an overhead hatch in the rear fuselage. The HUP-2 was the first production helicopter to be equipped with an autopilot, which permitted flight under instrument flight rules (IFR) and hands-off flying, including hovering. A total of 339 HUP helicopters were delivered to the U.S. Army and Navy, and Royal Canadian Navy, and the French Navy.

Model H-21

To create the H-21, the forty-one-foot rotor of the HRP-2 was lengthened to forty-four feet and a 1,425-hp engine was installed, thereby increasing the gross lift to 14,700 pounds in the same configuration as the HRP-2 (see figure 3). The H-21A was designed as a high-altitude rescue helicopter for fourteen combat soldiers or twelve stretchers. Later the design was expanded—the H-21B/C—to lift twenty combat soldiers. The H-21 fixed tricycle landing gear had all-terrain alighting capability because of doughnut-shaped floats fitted around the wheels. Twin vertical fins were fitted at the tail. Several H-21Ds were made with two T-58 turboshaft engines, married to a common transfer case.

In 1953, the U.S. Air Force set two world records in the H-21: the record for speed, 146.7 mph, and the record for altitude, 22,110 feet. A U.S. Army H-21 made the first non-stop helicopter flight across the United States, refueling in flight, in thirty-seven hours.

The H-21 became the army's prime workhorse of the Vietnam War, pioneering an air-transport supply system that bypassed the road blockages that had had a stranglehold on the country. Various suites of weapons were fitted to the army H-21s, including two .50-caliber forward-firing machine guns, a rocket pack with 2.75-inch folding-fin rockets, and two .30-caliber flexible machine guns at the side doors.

Total production of the H-21 was 557 for the U.S. armed forces and 150 for use in West Germany, Canada, France, and other foreign countries.

Figure 3.
The H-21 transport helicopter, workhorse for the services

Figure 4.
The YH-16A Turbo Transporter, the world's first twin-turbine helicopter

Models H-16 and YH-16

The H-16 was developed in response to a U.S. Air Force requirement for a long-range rescue helicopter to pick up stranded bomber crews. The H-16 was the largest helicopter in the world in 1953, having a rotor 82 feet in diameter, a fuselage 134 feet long, and a gross weight of more than 32,000 pounds.

Initially, the YH-16 was powered with two Pratt & Whitney R-2180-11 radial engines, each in an engine room. The tandem-rotor design incorporated a large cargo hold and a rear ramp for three jeeps. The fuselage was designed with a flat bottom to permit snugging a container or other external payload, thus eliminating payload swing. A long landing gear with an external pod was built as an alternate for landing and takeoff. Various pods were designed for special functions, including a field operating room, an electronics center, and a mobile repair center. This feature was used on several subsequent aircraft, including the current Heavy Lift Helicopter (HLH), XH-62.

The three blades in each rotor were all aluminum alloy with step-taper-milled skins keeping a tolerance of ± 0.002 inch along their forty-one-foot length by a special process developed by Piasecki. The bonded blade was made in four pieces, with two outer skins, a honeycomb filler, and a leading-edge balance weight that was also a mechanical fastener of the leading edges.

The first flight of the YH-16 was made October 28, 1953. The slow turning speed of the rotors—125 rpm—almost made the blades visible in their rotation, and in-flight vibration was loping in character.

Because of its size, the H-16 was ideally suited for the existing turboshaft engine, the Allison T-38, but it was not a free-turbine engine and thus not ideally suited for multiturbine interconnection. Nevertheless, the advantages were great enough that the air force agreed to change to turbines, and a way of turning the two fixed-shaft turbines so that they would act in concert was developed. The same idea was later used in Air-Geep II.

The YH-16A became the world's first twin-turbine helicopter (see figure 4). It established an unofficial speed record of 166 mph in 1956. The improvement in performance and operations over previous helicopters was immediately evident, promising a great future for the machine. Hopes were dashed, however, by a tragic in-flight failure of a temporary instrumentation conduit, destroying the aircraft and killing two expert test pilots.

The New Company

In the late 1950s, Piasecki Helicopter Corporation had a greater backlog of orders than all other helicopter companies in the free world combined. Because of the rapid success of the company and the need for large capital inputs, many mergers were considered and investigated. Finally, the company was sold to the Boeing Airplane Company.

In 1955, Frank Piasecki and members of his original team left Piasecki Helicopter Corporation and started the Piasecki Aircraft Corporation (PiAC) to work on new VTOL aircraft designs. The design effort of the new company was concentrated on advanced VTOL configurations, continuing the exploratory work that had been done throughout the earlier periods of development of the helicopter. Heavier lift and higher speeds were the two primary goals.

Initially, heavy-lift studies were performed for the army. These studies included external carriage of a fifty-ton tank. A matrix of rotor-propulsion systems studied showed that multiple shaft-driven rotors were the optimum heavy-lift configuration for the near term, and the blade-mounted turbojet system (PA-1) was the potential configuration for the long term. The high development cost of the latter unfortunately precluded any further research effort.

By the mid 1950s, higher speeds were of growing interest to the U.S. Marine Corps for forward battle areas. A design study, wind-tunnel tests, and full-scale tests of components were made for BuAer for a vertical or short takeoff and landing (V/STOL) configuration using a vectored-flow ducted propeller in which the duct was of sufficient chord to provide the required wing area. A large instrumented test stand was built with a 1,200-hp piston engine for research on ducted propellers.

Model PA-2C

The PA-2C was designed to be a vertical-takeoff machine, capable of sustained, high-speed level flight and capable of operating from aircraft carriers, cruisers, destroyers, and unprepared landing sites. Called the Ring-Wing, it combined two ducted propellers that contained an integrated system of vanes to deflect the slipstream downward. Exit vanes were attached to the duct walls so that the thrust from the propeller could be directed over a 90-degree arc downward from the centerline of the aircraft in hover flight. In forward flight, the vanes would be straightened, allowing airflow directly aft for forward propulsion at high speeds. The airfoil area of the duct provided the wing lift.

The ducted propellers were interconnected with a shaft driving through a central mix box to which two T-58 turboshaft engines were attached. The turbine exhaust flow was used to provide part of the longitudinal and yaw control. For short takeoff and landing (STOL) missions, additional wing area was provided, attached to the outer diameter of the ducts; this also allowed a larger useful load. A full-scale Ring-Wing 7.5-foot propeller unit for ground testing and a one-fourth-scale model of the PA-2C aircraft for testing in the David Taylor Naval Ship Research and Development Center wind tunnel were built and were tested successfully.

Interest in VTOL aircraft for this Marine Corps mission subsided in the light of the short takeoff and landing distances being promised by STOL designers. Eventually the OV-1 Mohawk conventional short takeoff and landing (C/STOL) aircraft was selected.

Model PA-4

With the advent of the nuclear submarine, the navy increased its efforts to base heli-

Figure 5.
The PA-59K Flying Geep

copters aboard destroyers as a weapons-delivery system. Limitations of deck and storage space gave impetus to the idea of a drone. PiAC proposed to build such a craft—the Sea Bat—specifically designed for ease of control from shipboard radar and radio. To reduce the controller's need to "fly" the drone remotely, the drone-controlled system and rotor configuration were designed to allow the drone's center body to keep a constant azimuth heading regardless of the direction in which it was traveling. By using two pairs of tilting propellers with no cyclic control, but with dual differential collective control, the PA-4 was made omnidirectional. Its body was kept level by the vertical gyros and its heading constant by the yaw gyro. These signals went in twice to the differential pitch of each pair of rotors. For yaw, the combined tilt of the two pairs of rotors maintained a constant heading. Each pair was balanced in torque in all positions by turning in opposite directions.

The vehicle was not designed to carry a test or safety pilot during the tests, but a system of restraining cables was used to suspend it in the air safely above the ground. A vertical-shaft six-cylinder Lycoming engine was used, along with electronic controls made by PiAC. Flight tests, which were initiated in 1958, were proceeding so well that the machine was lowered closer to the ground on its tethered restraining cables for ease of adjustment of the controls.

A coaxial drone version of a single-seat helicopter was offered as an off-the-shelf solution by the competition; thus was the Destroyer Anti-Submarine Helicopter (DASH) program initiated.

Model PA-59K

Called the Flying Geep, Sky Car, or Air-Geep, the PA-59K was funded through an army contract for research on the concept as an observation platform, for light utility use, as a carrier of weapons, and as an ultimate answer to army nap-of-the-earth flight (see figure 5). The PA-59 could fly up to 75 mph over any terrain and was not dependent on ground effect, permitting flight between trees, buildings, and other obstacles, or it could hover, land, and travel as a ground vehicle on its three wheels. It derived vertical lift, propulsion, and control from two ducted horizontal rotors in tandem.

The 200-hp piston engines were mounted between the two rotor ducts. Differential collective pitch of the rotors provided longitudinal control, with lateral vanes in the duct to assist propulsion. Lateral cyclic pitch change of the rotors plus longitudinal vanes provided side force for control of lateral roll. These longitudinal vanes were also used to provide yaw control when moved differentially.

The pilot was placed on the starboard side of the vehicle to keep his collective pitch-control lever away from the open side of the machine. This placement also allowed the pilot to look down over his right arm and receive precise indications of the machine's motion in relation to near obstructions. The enclosed rotors made flight close to ground personnel feasible without danger of injury from rotors. The downwash was surprisingly different from that of the helicopter and gave the pilot clear local visibility in flying over sand, water, and snow, unlike the blinding recirculation characteristic of a helicopter rotor.

The Air-Geep was one of three winners of an army competition for an "invisible" aerial vehicle in nap-of-the-earth flight, the only one to reach field testing.

Model PA-59N

Substituting a gas turbine for the two piston engines and adding two inflatable floats enabled the Air-Geep to operate from the water. It was called the Sea-Geep (PA-59N) (see figure 6). Its compact size and weight made it ideal as a small ship-based SAR and ASW weapon carrier and for ship-to-ship transfer.

Figure 6.
The Sea-Geep, which proved the practicality of water-based operations

Experiments were conducted using various side shields to vary the patterns of water spray around the ducts and to increase lift within the ground effect without reducing lift out of ground effect. The spray pattern was negligible because spray was strongly forced away from the craft and not recirculated, allowing clean air to enter the ducts.

Landings aboard ship were safe and uncomplicated, because the rotating blades were enclosed in ducts, the float span was relatively wide, and the center of gravity of the vehicle was low. Landings alongside ships and on various deck areas were successful on the first attempt. Movies of the downwash flow over the water taken at the Philadelphia Navy Yard from a helicopter overhead and telephoto movies taken at the Patuxent River Naval Air Test Center of forward flights at various altitudes over the water recorded flow patterns that have been highly useful in VTOL downwash studies. Flights up to 220 feet above the water were recorded.

Experiments in at-sea rescue demonstrated the desirable features of the Sea-Geep. Its ease of pilotage, maximum compactness, low profile, and unique downwash characteristics gave impetus to further development.

Model PA-59H

Air-Geep II was powered by two turbines to provide one-engine-out safety and had a cant in the fuselage (see figure 7). Compactness in width, length, and height gave it mobility for operation on roadways, on ship decks, and in other confined areas that no other VTOL system possessed. The Air-Geep rotors were loaded higher than helicopter rotors and were thus not capable of autorotation. Multiple engines and zero-speed, zero-height ejection seats and parachutes were therefore used for safety.

The canted fuselage placed the rear duct at an in-flow turn angle smaller than that of the forward duct in forward flight. This

Figure 7.
The PiAC PA-59H Air-Geep II, which featured hydrostatic drive for ground travel

Figure 8.
The Piasecki 16H-1 compound helicopter

reduced the momentum drag caused by the sharp turn of the flow through the horizontal ducts.

The higher power and high fuel consumption of early turbines stimulated the idea of powering the wheels of the landing gear to extend range when not hindered by surface obstacles. A hydrostatic pump drive from one turbine to two hydrostatic motors mounted on the main wheel axles enabled the vehicle to move on the ground at 35 mph with substantially reduced fuel consumption.

The Air-Geeps could fire their weapons while remaining behind an obstruction. Only the weapon and sight had to be visible above the top of the structure. The helicopter, on the other hand, had to rise above the top of the obstruction to launch its weapons, which were mounted below the rotor plane, thus revealing the large rotor disc.

The ability of the machine to fly under trees, under overhanging obstructions, under bridges, and even inside buildings enabled the Air-Geep to operate within the nap of the earth and thus maintain its invisibility. The ducts of the Air-Geep, when in the hovering position, shielded the propellers so that the familiar flickering of the helicopter's rotor blades could not be seen visually or by radar, maintaining "stealth" in the battlefield. This capability may be important to the army in the design of future air vehicles.

Model 16H

A comprehensive market survey by PiAC of transportation needs, both in the helicopter market and the short-haul airplane market, revealed a large percentage of short-haul operations that were limited by the availability of airports and the surface distances from their end destinations. The 16H-1 was designed and built, both in twin- and single-turbine versions, to meet the needs of this commercial market (see figure 8). Other needs of the market, such as litter storage and hoist cable, were designed into the machine to broaden its sales base.

Figure 9.
The 16H-1A, which flew at speeds up to 225 mph

The 16H-1 combines the efficient vertical lift of the helicopter with the higher speed and maneuverability of fixed-wing aircraft by adding a wing to unload the rotor in forward flight and using a tail-mounted ducted propeller, the Ring-Tail, to provide forward thrust during high-speed operation. Directional and antitorque control during hover and slow flight were also accomplished by the Ring-Tail with moving vertical rudder vanes in the exit section. Thus, the main rotor was unloaded as speed increased, and rotor-blade stall and vibration problems of the conventional helicopter were greatly reduced. Powered by a PT6 shaft-turbine engine and limited to 400 shp, it logged a total of 185 flying hours, during which speeds as high as 170 mph were attained.

The advantages in operation and cost of the compound helicopter over conventional helicopters are still valid and represent a formula for the future.

The 16H-1 evoked interest throughout the military, but military needs for armaments and armor tripled the gross weight. Convinced that this was the best path for a new attack helicopter, the army launched a request for proposal for the Advanced Aerial Fire Support System (AAFSS) and for supporting technology programs.

In 1964, under army contract, PiAC modified the Pathfinder I (16H-1) to attain speeds of more than 200 mph. A General Electric T-58 shaft-turbine engine rated at 1,250 shp, a new drive system, a new propeller to absorb the increased power, and a forty-four-foot rotor (H-21) were added. In addition, the fuselage was lengthened to accommodate eight people. A three-blade Hartzell propeller hub was modified so that it would have a direct beta control from the 16H servo-control system.

The 16H-1A made its initial flight in November 1965 and logged more than 150 hours under the joint army-navy test program, including flight at forward speeds as high as 225 mph (see figure 9). It was highly maneuverable in forward flight and met the FAA requirements of sideward and backward flight up to a speed of 35 mph.

The end of the Vietnam War dried up the available funds for further development of the 16H series. Various existing helicopters were studied for the application of the developed techniques of the 16H series. Further improvements were designed for experimentation in advanced versions of the Ring-Tail.

The Ring-Tail antitorque, forward-propulsion, and integrated-control subassembly provided many advantages for the development of a compound helicopter. The 16H-1 was normally flown in level forward flight with the main rotor pitch reduced and with the cyclic pitch stick slightly forward. This gave the pilot the opportunity to autorotate immediately while reducing the propeller pitch to autorotation position. This was not time critical, although in a conventional helicopter it is, for conversion from power pitch to autorotative pitch is required in less than two seconds. In the 16H-1, the propeller would absorb the energy of the air flowing by and drive it back into the rotor, assisting in maintaining rotor speed while the pilot arranged the collective pitch of the rotor and the pitch of the propeller.

The protection offered by the shrouded duct minimized the danger of objects hitting the propeller when the aircraft was near the ground and prevented the propeller from hitting objects or people. The Army Safety Board declared the conventional helicopter tail rotor Public Enemy Number One because of the number of deaths and accidents it caused.

Today, the redundancy of control provided by the longitudinal trim vane in the exit flow of the duct provides a longitudinal trim force and a moment of control that can be used for emergency landings when longitudinal cyclic control of the rotor is inoperative. This longitudinal control moment is available not only in forward flight, but also in hovering and in autorotation, since the propeller is always pushing air across the vane. Helicopters that operate in populated areas are frequently criticized for the noise they make and complaints restrict their primary usefulness. The shrouded duct modulates the noise of the tail propeller and the wing unloads the rotor blades, reducing the usual "flup, flup" that is generated by the stall of conventional helicopter blades at high speeds and during approach maneuvers.

Maintaining a level attitude in the 16H without inclining forward with changes in speed as a conventional helicopter does is of real value for the orientation of the pilot, particularly at night or while flying on instruments. Marked improvements in reliability and maintainability are two significant advantages of the compound helicopter, in addition to the increases in performance and safety.

The 16H-3J/K was a later design that was to be powered by two PT6 turbines, which gave it a total of 1,500 shp. A maximum cruise speed of 195 mph was projected, its capacity was fifteen passengers, and its range was 480 statute miles.

PA-39 Series: Multiple Helicopter Heavy Lift Systems

Great efforts have been made to advance the lifting capacity of the helicopter, but as the capacity was successfully increased, the next stage became even more difficult. Since the 1950s, the army has hoped to lift its main battle tank, which now weighs more than sixty-two tons, by helicopter. Yet this goal is far from having been attained even in the new designs that are under construction.

In the West, the maximum vertical lift is fourteen tons by a commercial helicopter, the tandem-rotor CH-47 Chinook, and sixteen tons by a military helicopter, the triple-turbine single-rotor CH-53-E. The cost of designing a new helicopter for heavier lift has increased to the point that a high military priority will be required if the sixty-ton class is to be reached.

Quantum jumps in helicopter lift necessitate the design and testing of new rotor, transmission, and airframe systems. Thus, to design, build, and test an all-new heavy-lift helicopter would be tremendously expensive. Yet there are many military requirements as well as many commercial opportunities for a greater lift.

The idea of using several helicopters joined together to lift a common payload was born to meet this need. The multihelicopter heavy-lift system (MHHLS) with its rigid interconnections has been designed in a series of configurations using modified existing large helicopters to illustrate the feasibility of the design. The modifications can be designed so that the helicopters can be used singly when heavy lift is not required.

The MHHLS represents a large economic saving over a new heavy-lift helicopter. In all MHHLS configurations the controls are modified for one-pilot operation, and in some designs the drive systems are interconnected to allow transfer of power from one helicopter to another in case of an engine failure.

Figure 10.
Artist's rendering of the Piasecki Heli-Stat, showing logging capabilities for the U.S. Forest Service

PA-97 Series: The Heli-Stat Heavy Vertical Airlifter

In the search for economical means of providing greater vertical airlift in less time, other dynamic means of augmenting the vertical lift of the helicopter have been designed, from liquid rockets to jet engines, from ducted fans to propellers. The larger, lower-loaded rotor, however, has maintained its advantage.

Augmentation of lift with buoyant lift presented a unique opportunity to simplify lift production and further reduce cost. To keep the buoyancy in a central envelope, the rotors can be placed alongside the envelope to provide the moments of dynamic lift and control required to maneuver the large assembly. This large assembly is interconnected by a rigid structure to hold the rotors, their drive and power systems, and the aerostat.

Various proportions of lift can be obtained from the static and dynamic components of the hybrid lift system. The larger the displacement of the helium-filled envelope, the greater the total lift available, until the static lift is equal to the empty weight of the entire assembly. If the envelope is increased beyond that size, then ballast must be carried when no payload is attached, as it was by the early lighter-than-air airships.

The Heli-Stat is being built under an October 1980 contract with the U.S. Navy, financed by the Forest Service, to demonstrate the economic and ecological potential of heavy vertical airlifters in harvesting timber and other natural resources in difficult-to-reach terrain (see figure 10). By reducing the need for new road construction in inaccessible areas, the Heli-Stat can make new timber cuts more economical and eliminate destruction of the hill terrain of the forest for roads, drainage cuts, and bridges, thus leaving more acreage available for timber production.

The rapid development of timber-harvesting helicopters indicates increased opportunities for heavier vertical-lift systems, but the increasing costs of helicopters designed for larger loads have discouraged their development. The birth of the concept of a hybrid VTOL, marrying the dynamic lift of the helicopter rotor to the static lift of the lighter-than-air vehicle and, further, incorporating existing production helicopters, opens the way to reduction of harvesting costs.

The control systems of the four helicopters arranged about the static-lift aerostat are interconnected to a single pilot, allowing the differential collective pitch of the rotors to produce large moments of pitching, rolling, and yawing control to the entire assembly. In forward flight, the ruddervators attached to the tail of the blimp add their moments of pitching and yawing control to the combined helicopter control, thereby reducing turnaround time in shuttle-transport operations.

The twenty-four-ton payload of the Heli-Stat is designed to be lifted by external cables. In addition, the center body gondola can have an internal standard freight container eight by eight by forty feet lashed to its flat bottom; the same payload can be carried in the two decks of the gondola.

The static test program conducted under the direction of the Naval Air Development Center in Pennsylvania was completed late in December 1983, a milestone in preparation of the Heli-Stat for its flight tests. The key assembly of the Heli-Stat is the structural frame rigidly interconnecting four helicopters to an air-buoyant aerostat envelope and to the landing gear.

The rotor drive systems can be interconnected so that if the power unit driving one rotor fails, the power unit of the diagonally opposite rotor will take over, and symmetry of thrust about the center of gravity will be maintained. Lift by these two rotors is then reduced, while the other two diagonal rotors provide an increase in lift equal to the lost lift from the shut-down engine. The corresponding gross weight is then the maximum gross weight to hover one-engine-out.

Designed under FAA rules as a demonstrator vehicle, the Heli-Stat is a small versin of what is envisioned by the designers for the full potential of this type of craft. Future versions of the Heli-Stat should be able to lift payloads of more than 200 tons.

Frank Nicholas Piasecki was born in Philadelphia; he studied mechanical engineering at the Towne School of the University of Pennsylvania and in 1940 received the B.S. degree in aeronautical engineering from the Guggenheim School of Aeronautics of New York University. He has been influential as an aeronautical-mechanical engineer, pilot, and pioneer in the development of transport helicopters and vertical-lift aircraft. He is president of Piasecki Aircraft Corporation. In 1940, Mr. Piasecki founded and headed a research group that was incorporated in 1943 as the P-V Engineering Forum. He flew their first helicopter, the PV-2, the second helicopter to fly in America, on April 11, 1943. In 1946, the Forum became Piasecki Helicopter Corporation, which was later sold to Boeing Airplane Company and its name changed to the Vertol Division. Mr. Piasecki and his original founders formed the Piasecki Aircraft Corporation in 1955 to continue work on new VTOL aircraft designs. Mr. Piasecki is a member of numerous aviation associations and societies; he has been a guest lecturer and the recipient of many awards, including the Franklin Institute Philips H. Ward Jr. gold medal in 1979. In 1955, he was awarded an honorary Doctor of Aeronautical Engineering degree by New York University; in 1970, he was awarded a Doctor of Science degree from Alliance College, Cambridge Springs, Pennsylvania. In 1974, Mr. Piasecki was inducted into the Army Aviation Hall of Fame, Fort Rucker, Alabama, and received the Leonardo da Vinci award of the Navy Helicopter Association. He has written numerous technical papers and holds a number of patents. Mr. Piasecki is donor of the Dr. Alexander Klemin Award, given annually by the American Helicopter Society for outstanding work in the field of rotary-wing aeronautics.

NC 1H

ARTHUR M. YOUNG

The Making of a Helicopter

EDITED BY BARTRAM KELLEY

On the morning of September 3, 1941, I visited the Bell Aircraft Company in Buffalo, New York. In a suitcase I carried a model of a remote-control helicopter, the fruit of almost twelve years of research on the problem of vertical flight. My interest in the helicopter was first awakened in 1928. I had gone to Washington, D.C., to the Patent Office to evaluate various ideas for inventions that had come to me. I thought that if I could find some practical problem to work on for the next ten or fifteen years, I would be able to return to my study of philosophy and the theory of process later with a better grasp of the way things work.[1] The idea that impressed me was not suggested by the Patent Office, however. It was in a small book by Anton Flettner, the inventor of the boat propelled by rotating cylinders that had crossed the Atlantic in 1927.

Flettner's book showed a picture of a huge windmill with small propellers, themselves windmills, at the tips. The wind turned the big windmill, which in turn made the small propellers rotate at high speed, requiring small gears to transmit the power.

When I went to bed that night I saw Flettner's idea applied to a helicopter. A large rotor propelled by small propellers at the blade tips would not only not require heavy gearing, it would also solve the torque problem—that is, how to counteract the twist caused by the turning of the large rotor.

As I was to learn on my subsequent trips to libraries in Washington, Detroit, and other cities, many attempts to build helicopters had been made since the early 1900s. Leonardo da Vinci had of course made sketches, but he had not shown any way of correcting the torque. Furthermore, not until the coming of the automobile, with its internal combustion engine, was it possible to obtain engines sufficiently powerful and sufficiently light even to approach the requirements of vertical flight. Indeed, the smaller power requirements of the airplane were largely responsible for the fact that the airplane succeeded first. Certainly there were many more attempts to make helicopters than to make airplanes in those early days.

Among others, D'Ascanio and Isacco in Italy, Pescara in Spain, Karman and Petroczy in Austria, Berliner and Cooper-Hewitt in the United States, and Oemichen and Breguet in France, had made helicopters. Both Oemichen and Breguet succeeded on actual flights over a one-kilometer closed circuit, but at speeds of no more than six miles an hour. Not until 1937, some nine years after I began, did Henrich Focke, a German airplane designer, succeed in building a helicopter that was able to fly at an average speed of sixty-eight miles an hour. It was soon after this that Sikorsky, who had first attempted to build a helicopter in 1909 and had then become a successful designer of large airplanes, returned to the helicopter and achieved in 1938 the first truly successful experimental flights in the United States. By May 1942 a larger Sikorsky machine, the famous XR-4, was flown to Dayton, Ohio, for delivery to the U.S. Air Force.

But in 1928, despite advances in engine design, there were still no successful helicopters. In fact, there was no agreement as to what the design of a helicopter should be. Some used coaxial rotors—two rotors turning in opposite directions on the same shaft; some used side-by-side rotors; some had four lifting rotors. Oemichen made more than 1,000 flights in a machine with four lifting rotors and nine auxiliary propellers. One design even took the form of a maple seed. Also, as I learned later, Isacco designed a helicopter with a large single rotor turned by propellers and engines on the ends of the blades.

In any event, the helicopter was an interesting challenge in 1928, and I was intrigued by the possibility suggested by Flettner's design for a large windmill, of a single rotor with propellers at the tips.

I went back to Radnor, Pennsylvania, with the determination to test this idea. At a toy store I found rubber bands, carved wooden propellers, light strips of balsa wood, Japanese silk, and dope—lacquer—and soon had made a model helicopter, about six feet in diameter. It flew nicely, but only for short hops, indicating that a helicopter would require more power than an airplane (see figure 1).

For the next nine years I struggled with this design. During the first phase of the work, I developed the use of models powered by electric motors. During this period the most significant development was a whirling arm with which I could make accurate tests of propeller efficiency. I also built equipment to measure the lift and horsepower of the electric model and discovered the formulas to predict lift and horsepower for full scale.

I next undertook to build a larger machine. Since I had neither the facilities nor the money to build a full-scale model, I decided on an intermediate 20-hp machine, which I purposely made small in order to achieve high power density. Because this would increase the stresses to values even greater than would experiments with a full-scale model and would do so within a small compass, it would be an ideal test vehicle. I anticipated that I would fly it by remote control.

The stresses were even greater than I had anticipated. On the first test the propeller blades broke off. The stress induced by rotating the small propellers at 4,000 revo-

Figure 1.
Young's first model

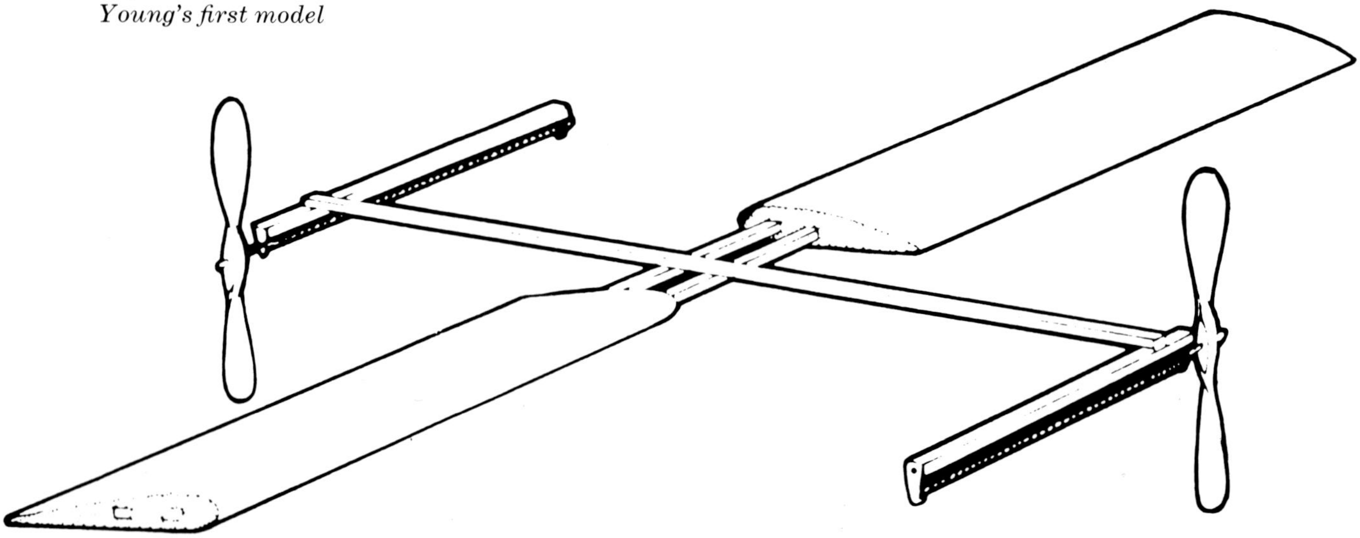

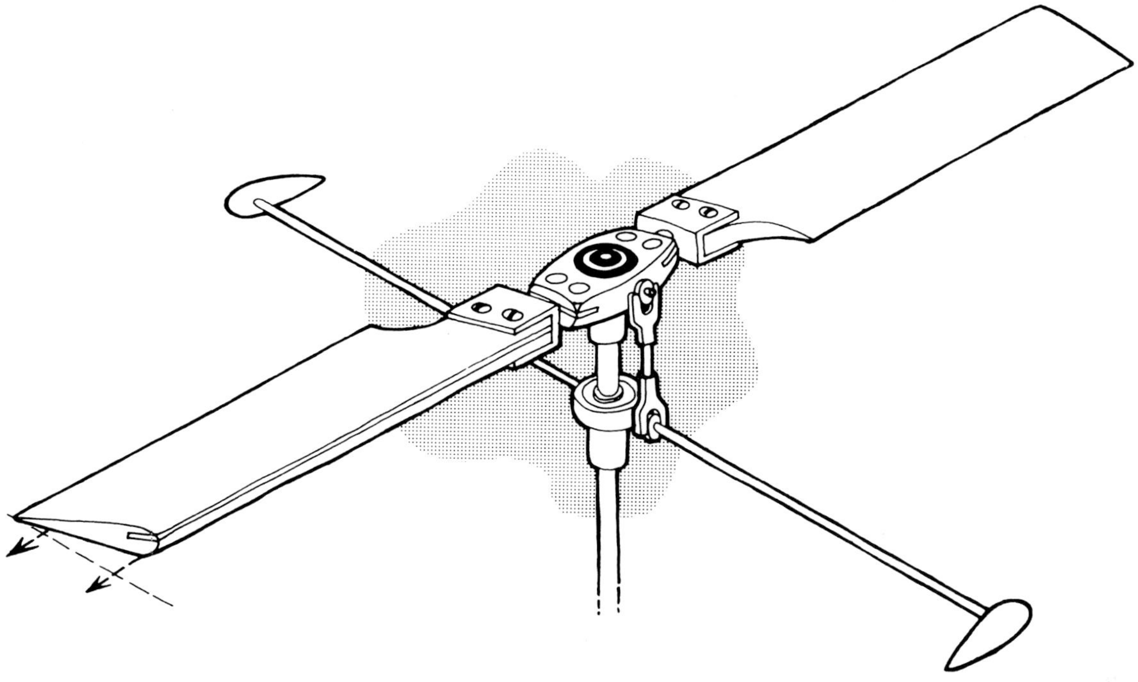

Figure 2.
As the stabilizer bar tilts it tilts the whole rotor, increasing the angle of one blade and decreasing the other, causing the rotor plane to track to a new position parallel to the bar. Conversely, if the mast tilts, the stabilizer bar, because of its inertia, remains in a horizontal plane, thus preventing the mast tilt from affecting the rotor, which continues to turn in a horizontal plane.

lutions per minute (rpm) and having to reverse the direction of their rotation at the same time as the big rotor turned 400 times per minute was too much.

I built stronger blades. The second time the whole shaft broke off and the machine destroyed itself.

A third time I rebuilt everything, using forged magnesium alloy blades and nickel vanadium steel shafts designed for maximum strength. This model held up. Next came the overspeed test, with lift wing blades at flat pitch—that is, generating no lift. This time the model blew up with a vengeance.

These explorations, in which I never even reached the question of flight, were time-consuming but gave me valuable experience, both in calculating stress and in redesigning and building parts. It was now 1938 and I had bought an old farm in Paoli. I rebuilt the barn into a shop and test area for model flights. I was beginning to think I should turn to a simpler configuration when I attended the first of the Rotating Wing Aircraft meetings organized by Burke Wilford. There I saw Sikorsky's film and was impressed with his argument for correcting the torque by means of a tail rotor.

I also heard a paper by Platt, in which he argued that a rotor with blades hinged to the mast would be stable in flight because the body could swing without tilting the rotor. This was the argument given in *Le Vol Vertical*, a French text on helicopters, but it was not until I heard it from Platt that I questioned it. Would the hinged rotor not follow the inclined mast? And was it stable in flight?

I went back to my shop and built a small electric model to test a hinged rotor. Tipping the mast with the rotor turning, I could see the rotor immediately "follow" the mast so that, despite the articulation, the rotor remained perpendicular to the mast. In flight it was definitely unstable, tipping as it took off and dashing in the direction of the tip, only to swing back and reverse direction. After several swings of increasing amplitude, it would upset.

The problems of obtaining a rotor system that would provide stable flight now took my attention. Since the hinged rotor, first proposed by Breguet in 1907, had been used by many pioneers, including the Frenchman Oemichen, whose work I admired especially, was it not possible that its unstable flight was responsible for their lack of success? Oemichen had finally attached a balloon to his helicopter, not for lift but for stability. Was it not likely that this factor had been responsible for some of the wrecks that had terminated earlier helicopter flights?

I could now put my mechanical skills to work. My long apprenticeship had taught me the virtue of simplicity, and, returning to small models, I could give my attention to principles, especially to stability. I could concentrate on flight. If the model were wrecked, I could rebuild it in a day or so and carry on. In this way I was able to speed the process of trial and error, and learn from my mistakes with a minimum investment of time. So after a half-dozen different rotor configurations, I hit upon the device of using a stabilizer bar linked directly to the rotor. In this way the rotor plane was controlled independent of the mast, which was attached to the rotor hub by a universal joint (see figure 2).

This configuration had superb stability; it could hover indefinitely without moving. It was no problem now to add remote control. With the remote control I could fly the model around a prescribed course in the interior of the old barn, or even fly it out the barn door and back again (see figure 3).

It was the description of this model, given by a friend to engineers at Bell Aircraft Company in Buffalo, that prompted them to invite me there to give a demonstration.

I visited the Bell Aircraft Company in September 1941. I unpacked the model and flew it in the factory, in the cramped space

Figure 3.
In early 1941, Young operates the famous remote control model outside his barn door. Remote capabilities were made possible by replacing the stabilizer bar with a flywheel which could be tilted by means of solenoids. When the time came to build a full-sized machine Young reverted to the original stabilizer bar, but added mixing levers to it so that both the bar and the pilot could directly control the rotor.

between the Airacobra pursuit planes, which filled most of the space in the factory.

By this time a number of engineers had gathered. We adjourned to the projection room, where I showed my film "Principles of Stability," which, beginning with an unstable model, demonstrated the flight of different types of rotors I had used, ending with the remote control model I had just flown in the plant.

Bell's patent attorney then informed me that Bell would like to make an arrangement. I was introduced to Larry Bell himself, whom I liked from the first. In November of that year we signed a contract, I to assign my helicopter patents to Bell and Bell to build two helicopters. I insisted on two in case the first should be wrecked. I asked whether my assistant, Bart Kelley, could come too and was told yes, if he could work for thirty-six dollars a week, a small sum even in those days.

Bart Kelley, whom I had known since boyhood, had worked with me on models in the summer of 1931. He had then disappeared, to return again one summer night in 1941, just at a time when I was able to use his help. He remained the rest of the summer, assisting me and teaching himself how helicopters were made. When I told him of Bell's offer, he accepted. Bart worked with me there and remained after I left, becoming vice-president in charge of engineering. He is now officially retired but is still active in the company.

Now that I had joined Bell I assumed that the organization would take over my responsibilities and build the two helicopters, but, as I gradually realized, nothing happened and nothing would happen. The company, already seething with wartime activity, working three shifts, and expanding all the time, hardly seemed to know of my existence, much less how to build helicopters. But I did not realize the extent of my predicament until after about two months of waiting. An engineer who had been assigned to me showed me the budget he was working on—$250,000. I thought that was fair enough, but to my consternation I found it was not to build two helicopters, as the contract had specified, but to *draw* two helicopters.

This was the normal procedure for airplanes, which required elaborate drawings to make the precisely curved metal panels of which body and wings consisted. This procedure would hardly suffice for designing something so complex as the helicopter, which involved all kinds of hitherto untried mechanisms. I wanted to build the helicopters first, using only working drawings, and get them to fly. Then, when we knew the requirements, we could make the drawings for the production prototype.

This awakened me to the fact that I would have to take action myself. I went to the head of production at the factory and explained my predicament. He spoke my language and understood the situation. He agreed to sign a budget that provided for *building* two helicopters for $250,000. Then he added a provision: "provided only that the engineering [drafting] department had nothing to do with it."

But even with the budget question set to rights, the problem remained. How to get something built? In my former life at Paoli, I could plan a model, go over to the barn, build the model, and fly it, but I had never even thought about full scale. How to begin? I went over to my temporary shop in the factory and mocked up an engine and, twenty feet away, a tail rotor. How would I ever fill the space between with actual machinery that would lift 2,000 pounds into the air? The problem seemed insurmountable. There was nothing to do but make everything six times model size. Drawings would be straightforward, but making the parts would require machinery and machinists. Assembly and flight would require space. We would have to have a plant of our own. Further, the project, small as it now was, was already split into office, model shop, and drafting room, each in a different location. It would be far better for coordination of the project to have it all in one place. Then, with a machine shop and space to build and fly helicopters, we would be in business.

I issued a memorandum stating the need for a plant of our own. When this brought no result I engaged a real estate company in Buffalo to look for a suitable place.

Things were now beginning to take shape. With the help of my shop in the factory, I was able to build a final model involving a control system that would be suited to pilot operation, since the remote control model system did not lend itself to operation by a pilot. The all-important gears were being made.

But still something was holding us back; funds were not released. At last I learned why. Larry Bell wanted to see a model demonstration of safe descent in case of engine failure. This would have been difficult to bring off in the available space, so I arranged a vertical wire and had the model climb up it some thirty feet to the ceiling, then cut the power and let it descend in autorotation. When it was ready, I went to the restaurant where Larry had lunch and told him it would be ready when he returned. I obtained two raw eggs from the chef. Back at the shop I placed one egg on the model and put it through the test. Unfortunately, the model climbed too fast and the egg bounced off when it hit the ceiling. Then Larry came. I was more careful this time. The model climbed to the ceiling, I cut the power, and it descended without breaking the egg. Larry was delighted.

After that, funds were released and the property we had found most suitable was leased. This was a garage on the outskirts of Buffalo, with open space behind it, a former Chrysler agency. The maintenance department set to work, surrounded it with a board fence painted Navy gray, floodlights, and an armed guard. I commented that this strategy only called attention to it, so the floodlights were removed and the guard was reduced to a single night watchman.

On June 23, 1942, we moved to the new location. Gardenville, as it came to be called, was ideal for our purpose. Behind the building proper was a good-sized yard where we would do the preliminary testing. Beyond that was an open meadow suitable for short flights. The building itself was divided into four parts: an office space with desks for me and my "brain trust"—Kelley, Tom Harriman, and Charlie Seibel; the secretary, Mary McCann; and later, the pilot, Floyd Carlson; the machine shop and assembly area, which occupied more than half the total space; the wood shop for making blades; and the drafting room, later referred to as the paper shop. What had been a display room for Chryslers was set aside as a model shop.

The helicopter project was now augmented by flight mechanics, body men, a welder, and two patternmakers for the wood shop, plus Tom Darner, the youth whom I had taught to make blades before I came to Bell. We were also fortunate in obtaining the services of three of the best tool makers from the Bell factory, who had somehow got wind of the operation and applied for transfer. The paper shop now included five men.

We could now get to work in earnest, and Model 30, our first helicopter, was under way. Draftsmen made drawings; machinists made masts, rotor hub, and control system; patternmakers made wooden blades—actually from a composite of steel-impregnated fir and balsa. The body men and the welder made the fuselage and landing gear. The riveted magnesium tail boom was made in the main plant from drawings.

About six months after arriving in Gardenville we had a helicopter ready to be wheeled out, with long legs of three-inch dural tubing, a thirty-two-foot rotor, and a 160-hp Franklin air-cooled engine. All dimensions were six times those of the model.

But Model 30, its Bell number, or *Genevieve,* as it was christened in December 1942, when we first took it out, was a bit cumbersome. To get it out the door, we had to remove the legs; then we wheeled it out on a dolly and pushed it up a ramp so that the legs could be replaced. By this time everyone was frozen stiff, as was the engine, which had the additional handicap that the huge rotor had to be pushed, for at this stage we had no clutch. A storage battery for starting was wheeled out on an express wagon,

but the starter was unequal to the task. My solution was simple: use two twelve-volt batteries. This did the trick, and I actually believe there was less strain on the motor as a result, because it turned over quickly and didn't draw as much current.

Since I was not a pilot—I had never even flown an airplane, much less a helicopter—my first hops were brief and erratic, six inches or a foot at most. I did not fly it long. We were assigned a regular pilot, Floyd Carlson, who is still with the company.

We now began to encounter the problems of helicopters that are not apparent until flight is attempted and that had caused the demise of many pioneers before us (see figure 4). I later learned that by 1943, 343 helicopter companies had failed.

A full explanation of these problems, which caused several crack-ups and required rebuilding and making changes in the design of the helicopter, would require going into a great deal of technical detail that would only tax the patience of the lay reader. Thanks to the flexibility of the Gardenville group, which could work in a coordinated way with a minimum of red tape, we were able to take these problems in stride, so that by July 1943 we had ship 1 flying well up to speeds in excess of seventy miles an hour (see figure 5). Then, because of an unsuitable landing gear, this ship was damaged on a power-off landing.

Figure 4.
Arthur Young in tethered flight trying out one of several different control systems. His left hand controls the pitch of the tail rotor. There is no main-rotor collective pitch. Engine power is controlled by a foot throttle.

Figure 5.
Model 30, ship 1, piloted by Floyd Carlson while Arthur Young looks on. The left hand controls the collective pitch of both main and tail rotors; the engine throttle is on the cyclic stick. This machine was damaged during test of autorotation landings and was later rebuilt as Ship 1A. It is now in the possession of the National Air and Space Museum of the Smithsonian Institution.

Figure 6.
Model 30, ship 2. The tubular structure near the rotor hub was invented by Floyd Carlson, who is at the controls. The purpose of the structure was to stiffen the rotor in the horizontal plane to avoid resonant vibrations at twice-per-rev.

Meanwhile ship 2, a streamlined two-passenger version, became our test vehicle. The first ship was rebuilt with a raised tail rotor and landing gear modified to permit the machine to remain in the nose-up position for the touchdown in power-off landings (see figure 6).

Then came the problem of engine wear, which plagued our early efforts. The cause was traced to gear wear, which was in turn corrected.

Next, we started giving rides to visitors, and the helicopter was tried out on rescue missions. Larry Bell had his ride. The time had come for the helicopter to make its debut. It was given a two-page spread in the Sunday paper, with the consequences that the road behind our shop, where until then no one had paid any attention to our test flights, was now blocked with spectators.

Then came a flight indoors in the Buffalo armory. The pilot, despite the glare of searchlights, maneuvered the ship slowly around under perfect control, ending by bringing the front wheel into my extended hand.

Later, on July 4, 1944, ship 1 was flying again and was demonstrated before a crowd of 5,000 in the Buffalo stadium.

At about this time Larry Bell, foreseeing the time when pursuit airplanes could no longer be sold, sent a contingent of engineers from the main engineering department to Gardenville to learn about helicopters. The plan was to design a large ship, Model 42, which, according to a market survey, would better meet demand. It was anticipated, for example, that helicopters would be used to carry passengers to airports.

Here began the problem that was later to become important, and which is the main theme of *The Bell Notes*,[2] a difference of philosophy. At Gardenville, we built things, tested them, modified them until they worked, and *then* made the drawings. The main engineering group made drawings, sent them to the plant, and only the project engineer ever saw the product fly. This was successful with the airplane, which did not involve unknowns; these had been ironed out in the forty years of development since the work of the Wright brothers. In retrospect, I can only suppose that Larry, who did indeed appreciate the problems and the Gardenville way of dealing with them, still felt that, the basics having been established, the main engineering department could do the job better. Besides, he had to think of the best interests of the company, which, with its thousands of employees, would be out of work when the war ended.

Meanwhile, we, the Gardenville group, were still not satisfied with ships 1 and 2 (see figure 7). In early 1945 we began work on ship 3, which was to incorporate the best elements of what we had found in our experience so far. A four-wheel landing gear that provided a better-behaved takeoff was designed. A different body shape, with instrument panel in the middle and almost no floor, gave unobstructed vertical vision, and later a bubble canopy, blown from heated plexiglas like a soap bubble, gave undistorted vision.

This ship, launched on April 20, 1945, was an immediate success. With room for two passengers, no body or windshield, and only a small instrument column between passenger and pilot, the pilot had an unobstructed view up and down. It was like sitting in a chair and flying about through space. Soon we added a makeshift plexiglas enclosure to protect the occupants from the elements, and we began to give rides to whoever came by—Governor Dewey and Mayor LaGuardia, for example (see figure 8). I recall the somewhat ludicrous sight of the latter, already short, stooping as he ran out under the rotor. Hundreds at the plant also had rides, which improved the morale, not only of our own group but of others who may have been depressed by the demise of the pursuit airplane.

Figure 7.
Vice President Harry S. Truman and Lawrence D. Bell pose after witnessing a demonstration of Model 30, ship 1A, the machine now in the custody of the National Air and Space Museum of the Smithsonian Institution.

Then came the great blow. Since we were now successful, we were to be transported back to the main plant. This had now been moved to Niagara Falls; it was the Wheatfield plant, built and owned by the U.S. government and located on the edge of a commodious airport.

Figure 8.
Governor Thomas E. Dewey of New York leaving Model 30, ship 3, after enjoying a ride. Floyd Carlson is at the controls. By this time several other pilots had been checked out in Model 30.

We were moved, machinery and all, June 24, exactly three years after we had moved to Gardenville. We were installed in a hangar, in which office, paper shop, wood shop, and model shop were partitioned off as before with plywood walls.

The most critical time had come; the drawings for Model 47, the production prototype, had to be made. The drafting department sent us more men, but they were not their best and made so many mistakes I recall saying to Bart that it would be better to buy the drawings from Sears Roebuck and fill in the dimensions ourselves. I really exerted myself to get every thing just right. Mast, hub, blade grips, bar control system, transmission with ground gears, all were redesigned to incorporate what our experience had taught us and to make it possible to use forgings and take advantage of mass production. What made it more difficult was that at this time Bart was sent to Germany to learn what could be learned there about helicopters.

But luck was with us, and on December 8, 1945, less than six months after our move to Wheatfield, the first Model 47 was rolled out, complete with bubble canopy. It was the first Bell ship, I was told, to be completed on schedule. We had even better lift than we expected, so even with two passengers, its performance was very good. I have a photograph of Model 47 hovering with seven people hanging onto it.

This ship (see figure 9) was one of ten made from production parts but assembled by our own crew in transition to the full production ship, which was to come off the assembly line. This ultimately turned out to be a fiasco; it took twice as long to assemble the craft on an assembly line.

It is important to mention that just before the launching of Model 47, anticipating that my task would be ended in about a year, shaken by the explosion of the atom bomb, and knowing that termination of my contract required a year's notice, I had written a letter to Larry to this effect. I recall writing the letter several times, ultimately making it perhaps too short and too abrupt.

Figure 9.
The first Model 47, NC-1H, which received civil certification on March 8, 1946. Note its similarity to Model 30, ship 3, and the addition of a free-blown plexiglas bubble enclosure.

This was disastrous; Larry interpreted it as quitting under fire, whereas I thought my job had been accomplished and that I could therefore step out.

As things worked out I stayed at Bell for two more years, getting the bugs out of production and, later, seeing Model 42 past its problems. But the main difficulty was with people. It was hard for the company hierarchy to learn new tricks, and three vice-presidents in succession were fired before Bart Kelley was eventually put in charge of engineering.

The Gardenville group remained dedicated throughout, and we continued to keep in touch, even when we had to go underground because some of those in management tried to break up the group. It was the loyalty and dedication of the Gardenville group and their successors, not the helicopter itself, that I think of as the main accomplishment, for it is not making a helicopter that counts; it is the process by which it is made, and this resides in people.

ARTHUR M. YOUNG, inventor of the Bell Helicopter, was graduated from Princeton University in 1927 with a degree in mathematics. During the 1930s, he engaged in private research on the helicopter and participated in early rotary-wing forums in Philadelphia. He demonstrated with the use of rubber-band-powered models that if a helicopter rotor was on the center of gravity the helicopter would be perfectly stable. In 1941, he assigned his patent to Bell Aircraft and worked with Bell to develop the production prototype. In 1952, he set up what is now called the Institute for the Study of Consciousness, located in Berkeley, California, and dedicated to the integration of scientific thought and the development of a science of interaction between mind and body. He is the author of *The Reflexive Universe, The Geometry of Meaning,* and *The Bell Notes.*

BARTRAM KELLEY, formerly senior vice-president—engineering of Bell Helicopter Textron, was born in Rosemont, Pennsylvania. After graduating from preparatory school in Kent, Connecticut, in 1928, he attended Harvard University, receiving the B.A. degree, and later, in 1934, the M.A. degree in physics. Having worked part time with Arthur Young, the inventor of the early Bell rotor system, Mr. Kelley went with Young to Bell as a development engineer in 1941. In 1948, two years after Bell was awarded the world's first commercial helicopter certificate, Mr. Kelley was named chief helicopter engineer. He became senior vice-president—engineering in 1971. He holds an active commercial helicopter pilot's license and has flown all helicopter models that Bell has built. Mr. Kelley is a member of the Society of Automotive Engineers and the American Institute of Aeronautics and Astronautics, he is a past president and honorary fellow of the American Helicopter Society, and he is a fellow of the Royal Aeronautical Society. He holds several patents in aeronautics and is the author of numerous publications, many of which form the basis for current work in rotary-wing engineering. Mr. Kelley provided the captions for the photographs that illustrate this paper.

1. That other research is described in my book *The Reflexive Universe: Evolution of Consciousness* (New York: Delacorte Press/Seymour Lawrence, 1976).

2. Arthur M. Young, *The Bell Notes: Journey from Physics to Metaphysics* (Mill Valley, California: Robert Briggs Associates, 1984).

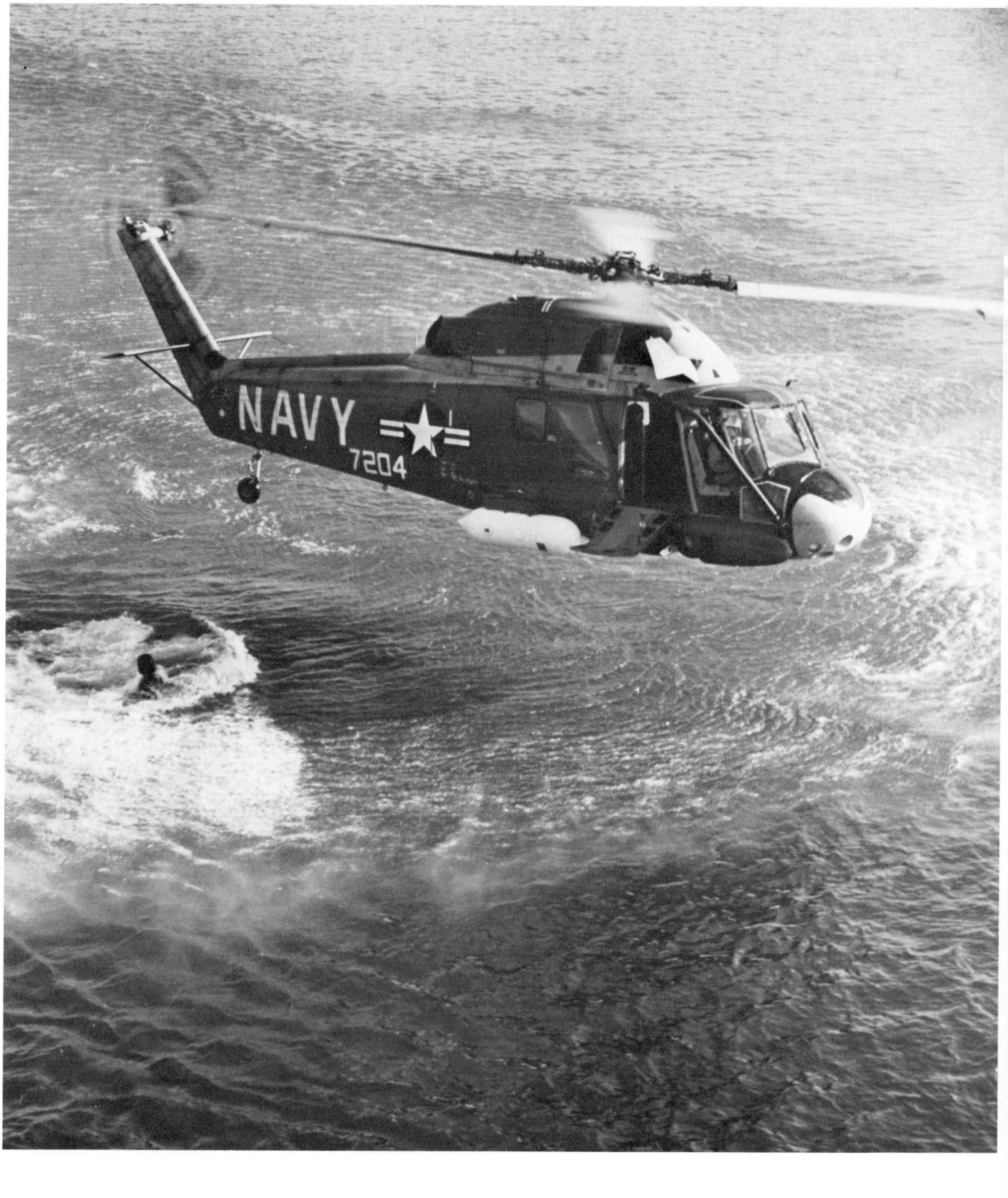
NAVY
7204

CHARLES H. KAMAN AND R. H. JONES

Evolution of the Helicopter

On a September afternoon in 1983, Secretary of the Navy John Lehman stepped from the cockpit of a new Kaman SH-2F helicopter and, shaking the hand of company chairman Charles H. Kaman, pronounced the aircraft "outstanding." "It's like a fine watch," Lehman told reporters at the Kaman Corporation headquarters in Bloomfield, Connecticut, following a test flight during which the secretary, himself a navy pilot, had personally flown the aircraft.

Delivery of the new helicopter signaled Kaman's continuing activity as a prime defense contractor and marked the first time in history that an American production line had been reopened to produce additional numbers of an existing military aircraft. That it was produced ahead of schedule and for less money than had been thought possible drew praise from Secretary Lehman, who told a gathering of more than 1,000 Kaman employees and dignitaries his advice to American leaders: "Don't sell American industry short. Don't sell American workers short."

Reopening the line was only the latest in a series of firsts for Kaman Aerospace. The company produced the world's first aerodynamic servo-controlled helicopter, the first turbine-powered and twin-turbine–powered helicopters, the first remote-controlled helicopter, and the distinctive twin intermeshing synchropter. Kaman set records in altitude and rate of climb and produced the world's largest rotor blade, a 150-foot, 25-ton composite blade for a wind energy project for the National Aeronautics and Space Administration (NASA).

The Early Years

This is the story of helicopter development at Kaman from the very beginning. It is a story of the determination and courage of men and women who succeeded in the shadow of incredible odds. It is a story of a great many dedicated and talented Americans who stayed on through good times and bad, often returning from other jobs in times of reexpanding employment, to make possible the diverse and strong Kaman Aerospace Corporation that exists today. It is more a human story than a corporate story, for its significance includes the evolution and realization of a spirit that people have come to recognize as the character of the entire family of Kaman companies.

It all started in the spring of 1943, when Charles H. Kaman stood in the marshlands of Stratford, Connecticut, to watch the first Sikorsky helicopter, the VS-300, hover and maneuver. Early helicopter flight was fraught with difficulty. Power was insufficient to provide a reasonable payload, instability made control and flight difficult and tedious, bearings were a major problem, and experience in mechanical design sufficient to ensure reasonable working life for components was lacking. The dynamic stress on parts and systems was incredible; there were serious questions about the potential usefulness of helicopters.

At the time, Mr. Kaman was employed at Hamilton Standard Division of United Aircraft Corporation. A former construction worker, then magna cum laude graduate of Catholic University in aeronautical engineering, Charles Kaman advanced quickly to the position of chief of aerodynamics for Hamilton's helicopter activities. There, despite long hours in a war economy, he started out on his own time to solve the early helicopter problems. To gain what material priorities he needed from the War Production Board, Kaman founded the Kaman Aircraft Laboratory and began the process of translating his drawings, ideas, and theoretical data into a working model of his radical new concept: aerodynamic servo flaps to achieve ease of control along with handling stability in flight. These principles were installed in an intermeshing rotor configuration to improve horsepower efficiency and lift.

Kaman gathered the engine and frame of a fifty-dollar 1933 Pontiac from a local junk yard, the rear end of an old Dodge truck with one axle mounted vertically, bathroom scales to verify lift, and a carefully selected spruce plank from a Hartford lumber dealer whose incredulous manager refused to believe that his $1.75 board would become a scale model of a new test blade for a helicopter. With these Charles Kaman assembled in his mother's basement and garage in West Hartford the rotor and rig that would prove his concept and ultimately set him on his own as the twenty-six-year-old founder of what would become one of the world's most important helicopter companies. When Erle Martin, manager of engineering at United Aircraft, buzzed Kaman's suburban driveway on his motorcycle one Saturday afternoon in 1945, his reaction to an impromptu but entirely successful demonstration of the scale model rotor and rig was, "Charlie, we have our inventor at United Aircraft and his name is Igor Sikorsky. We don't need another one." Remembering the occasion years later, Mr. Kaman recalled challenging Erle with, "If I weren't under contract [with United Aircraft and therefore unable to develop the concepts as my own business] I would give Sikorsky one hell of a run for their money." Mr. Martin released Kaman at once as he roared away on his cycle. In those seconds of confrontation and frustration, Kaman Aircraft Corporation became a reality. In giving up his job at Hamilton Standard Division, Kaman set out on the path he had long dreamed of following, and by the end of 1945, incorporation papers in hand, he had cast the die. From his unpublished memoirs, we have this account of Kaman's original test rig:

Leo Raessler, who was an old associate and long on electronics, rigged up a simple Baldwin SR-4 strain gauge wheatstone bridge circuit for us so that we could measure thrust and bending reactions at the rear of the rig and from this compute the amount of torque, power, and lift we were generating, and in time, how much control. It was time to replace the bathroom scales. In the beginning of these tests, we only had an rpm meter and that was me counting, but then the first time we started the full-scale rotor it only got to about 40 rpm or maybe 60 rpm before it went into such violent flutter as to scare us half to death (see figure 1). The blades weaved through an amplitude of four feet and it is truly amazing that they didn't just shed right off the rig. That first rotor had been designed with a flap in the front and a flap in the back, both mounted at about the 75 percent radius point to produce a lifting couple that in turn would twist the main rotor in pitch or blade angle. I had learned indeed how flexible helicopter blades were and how much of a problem this was. Since the early test rig days with the scale model, the main principle of the Kaman rotor was to use inherent rotor flexibility as its asset and let these external aerodynamic servo flaps position the main rotor to an angle that would produce adequate lift and control. In time, we would learn that so much torsion inertia added to the blade would drastically lower the natural torsion frequency and thus engage a mode of vibration known as unstable flutter. But then it was just blind reckoning to

Figure 1.
Charles H. Kaman and his test rig, 1945

figure out what to do. The first step was to remove the flap in the front, because that was an obvious move to stiffen the rotor aerodynamically and increase its frequency. That . . . moved us up to about 150–160 rpm. Then we added counter weights in the outer portion of the blade, which through the addition of centrifugal stiffness got us up to 190–200 rpm. By this time we had to break down and buy an automotive tachometer so that we could record or at least note the rpm from a meter.

Just before Kaman left United Aircraft, he stopped by to see Frank Caldwell, director of research and inventor of the controllable-pitch propeller. Frank was an extremely cordial, kindly person with bushy white eyebrows and a shock of white hair that had once been bright red.

On hearing of Kaman's plans for the new company, Caldwell was pensive and thoughtful. Fixing his pale, steely blue eyes on the young man, he finally said, "Charlie, you probably think that success depends on your ability as an engineer and how good your ideas are; well, that's not it. You can't do it without being a good engineer, but your success will depend upon your ability to continue to think and produce when you are beaten and crushed."

Armed with these words, which would give him courage time and again through the years, equipped with $5,000 worth of laboratory rigs and materials, and financed by two close friends who invested $1,000 cash each, Kaman Aircraft Corporation was begun. Charles Kaman established his office in the shower room of a World War II gymnasium at Bradley Field, north of Hartford. In that old wood-framed gymnasium, with snow blowing through cracks in the walls and a balky coal furnace trying to give up against the cold, Kaman's first experimental helicopter, the K-125, took shape in the hands of a few dedicated and excited young employees who worked in the fledgling venture seven days a week for shares of stock in the company and very little cash.

The K-125 was actually little more than an untethered test platform, yet the cheers of excitement that greeted it on its maiden flight January 15, 1947, carried more enthusiasm and emotion than any modern machine could hope to evoke. Investors, mainly New Enterprises of Boston, had been promised a January 15, 1947, flight; additional financing for the company depended upon it. The fact is, on that day the company was simply out of money, and no more would be forthcoming from the investors unless the aircraft flew. Tension was high. Here, in the words of the inventor, is a recollection of that eventful winter day:

I remember the day as if it were yesterday. Morning broke cold and dreary, grey and below freezing. It was raining, only the rain was turning to ice. My first thought was how we would ever get to Bradley Field; the roads glare ice, slippery. That was five A.M. By seven o'clock, we were somehow there. It was the deadline date set with the venture capital group: We simply had to fly.

But on this morning there were some technical problems. We have never been able to get the rotors on the K-125 up to speed. We tried a few times, but the clutch wouldn't engage properly and despite our persistence, it would grab and let go, grab and let go; the blades nearly ripped loose from their sockets as this occurred. The helicopter was a wild-looking thing with a bunch of angles and bare welded tubes, an engine, a transmission concocted out of some worm gears, and then one rotor that had been transplanted from the test rig along with another of opposite rotation. Thus, there were two rotors turning in opposite directions geared together so that they would intermesh. In fact, it was intermeshing helicopter. How we would ever get the rotors started, we didn't know; but we knew we had to fly that day! Our attention was so diverted with just getting the rotors turned up that somehow we hadn't quite figured out how we would get it to fly. Solve each problem in turn.

By nine o'clock, we had it outside slipping and sliding, and we spread ashes from the furnace to keep from falling down on the ice. We tried to rev it up again, but no luck. The clutch consisted of two concentric drums. The idea was when the engine came up to speed the clutch shoes would go out and engage the drum and with limited capacity would begin to accelerate the rotor. The second set of shoes was attached to the rotor side. This drum was on the engine side. As the rotor came up to speed, then the second set of shoes would engage the drum on the engine side. Incredible when one thinks about it. The design was originated at Worcester Polytech. They were very cooperative. In fact, they actually assisted me in the development of this clutch for the plane. So we called them, and their only suggestion was to change the size of springs that were holding the clutch shoes in place. We readily agreed, but we didn't have the material for the springs, and they did. One of the men was dispatched to drive to Worcester on that fateful morning to pick up a new set of shoes; somehow he got there and back. We had it all apart waiting for him. We put in the new shoes and their springs and tried it again about noontime. Despite our persistence, those blades nearly tore loose from the roots from the impact of the bang, bang, bang as the clutch would grab and release. It was unbelievable. By now, the sleet had turned a little bit more to rain and that was a relief; we were all drenched, cold to the bone, shivering. Back inside the gymnasium, no one knew what to do. We called Worcester again. Their best approximation was that we must have gone the wrong way. Let's try springs that are stiffer, rather than looser, they said. This time by four P.M. and with desperate haste, we were finally wheeling out the K-125. The ice had taken hold again as the temperature steadily slid down. It was absolutely bitter cold. There was a slight wind that had the cut of a razor and we were all ready to break down and cry. It is difficult to describe the emotion that men can experience when they are so close and yet so far. We tried again. Jack Rohr, former wartime test pilot for Sikorsky, was at the controls. This time, confidence in engineering began to seep back into our bones. The clutch held enough to accelerate the rotor, and as it accelerated, it gathered strength, took hold, and within a minute's time, the rotor was turning at a speed sufficient to provide lift. On this first rev up, the controls were not set for lift. It was strictly for ground run up. But the promise that we might fly was more than we could bear. Once we had successfully started the rotor, we shut it down and all went inside to warm up with coffee and tea. As as we walked in, we said, 'Don't tell the other guys, they'll get too excited.' So the handful trudged in thinking they could conceal the start from the others. Ridiculous! One look at our faces and the others knew. The hot drinks were never finished; after a few excited minutes, we were rushing back to see what lay ahead as control and lift were applied. We were really not greenhorns—I was a pretty experienced engineer. A lot of development had gone on in Kaman Aircraft to bring this rotor design from a mere conception to reality. And years before that, in the days of Hamilton Standard and United Aircraft and Sikorsky, working with tie downs, I had learned of conservative practice in early flights. A quick conference concluded that we should tie this plane down by the wheels, giving it enough freedom to lift maybe six inches before being restrained by the ropes. Stakes had already been put down, since optimistic youth does sometimes expect the best to happen. We took the plane to the site as dusk was falling, and with very heavy rope, proceeded to allow enough slack so that each wheel in turn could lift off a few inches, if that was to be.

On the second go around, we had a new problem. The blades had now accumulated ice from one end to the other. And now with the added weight on the rotor from the ice, the clutch was having real trouble again trying to get the increased inertia of this new rotor with ice up to speed. After a few excruciating tugs, grabbing and letting go, grabbing and letting go, we did manage to get there. It was as the grabs and let-gos came on that the ice shattered from the rotor, shedding and flying off in all directions. With that, the clutch held and the rotor came up to its 2,100 rpm on the engine side.

Lift control was applied. We had a man on each wheel. I remember it well. Jack applied the power, pulled up on the collective pitch lever, and the front wheel lifted. The two main wheels hadn't received quite enough lift as yet. Schuler, crouched down at the front wheel, didn't see that. He started screaming that it was off; it was off. But it wasn't. Jack lowered it down by relieving the pitch, talked it over, and now it was dark. It was bitter, bitter cold, we were frozen, but absolutely unaware of any physical feeling whatever. This would be the last try, so this was it. Having noticed the coning angle of the rotor, I elected to lower the pitch of all rotors by adjusting the servo flap so that we would get there with a little less collective pitch on board. This was done with flashlights. It was really quite dangerous when one stops to think about it. But then, at that time, who was thinking about anything but to fly. On the next try it worked [see figure 2].

Instead of being a sensational, dramatic, physical thing, it was in a way quiet. The rotors were turning; the engine was running; we had pitch on; it was vibrating. I looked at all three wheels, one at a time. The front wheel was off. The right wheel was off. The left wheel was off. We are flying! I looked down at Schuler and he had both hands under the front wheel and was scooping out the slush and ice to prove how high the wheel was off the ground. He was laughing, crying, hollering, and the others at the main wheels were doing the same thing. Jack Rohr, who was at the controls, was very, very tight with a grimace on his face. We stayed there for a couple of minutes and then he set it down. Was it true it had happened? Was it real? I said, 'Jack, you have got to do it again.' He did it again! It was not long thereafter that everybody was out there. Everybody in the company was out there and then it was over. The ice, the cold, had finally engulfed that very pitiful, sodden, and soaking bunch of gallant people. After the plane was put in and it was over, we broke down. I broke down. It was impossible to talk. For me, this was an experience to have once in my lifetime. The final surrender to the overwhelming feeling of having achieved virtually an impossible

Figure 2.
The Kaman K-125; first aircraft, 1947

event is an experience shared by very, very few. I had to be driven home. For the rest of that night, I could not speak. I could not eat. I could not sleep. It was well into the next day before the ability to resume normal life began to seep back into all of us.

Things moved right along after this. The pace accelerated. At the outset, the plane had a lot of vibration. It also had too much center-of-gravity displacement. We introduced lead-lag hinges as the first relief of the vibration and it helped a great deal. We introduced some balancing in the frame to stop from hitting the rotor flapping stops, and that took away some more. Little by little the plane was allowed to fly. It was here in the early spring of 1947 that the true realization of what had been achieved as a remarkable milestone began to be demonstrated in flight. Up to this point, it was sheer confidence and devotion, but when we began to notice the ease of control and the maneuverability and the agility of the plane, as Jack gradually moved it from spot to spot and entered into forward flight, we began to know, and boy it felt good!

As that year and the next unfolded, there was no money and there was no contract for aircraft. Company employees were *all* registered as stock sales representatives of a local brokerage house, and the company's most reliable source of funds for each week was Sunday barnstorming. Our K-190, a redesigned and improved version of the K-125 utility helicopter, would buzz the main road in the hands of Bill Murray, and dally just long enough that the curious would find their way to the Kaman laboratory. There, twenty to thirty flight demonstrations were conducted during the course of each Sunday while employees solicited potential investors. Large investors received photographs of themselves with the helicopter.

At the same time, potential commercial applications for the helicopter were being explored, and in April 1949, the K-190 was granted a Civil Aeronautics Authority (CAA) Type Certificate 1H-1 for commercial use. A short time later, the K-225, with a configuration similar to that of the K-190 but with a 225-hp engine, was also given a certificate by the CAA. The company produced a total of eleven helicopters of the K-225 configuration at the old wartime gymnasium at Bradley Field.

One K-225 was sold and delivered to Turkey, and another was sold to Mississippi State University for use in geological surveys. The remainder of the planes, however, were leased in 1949 for use in crop-dusting operations, as there were simply no military funds available in the wake of a war. The company managed to stay alive, living from hand to mouth.

The lease-versus-sell decision was a hard one for the cash-starved company to make, but it was a good one; crop dusting might not work out, and the company could not afford the problems that might arise with owners if it did not. Flying over the Adirondacks to control black flies that had discouraged tourists; over vegetable farms in Florida, North Carolina, and New York; over potato farms in Maine; and over tobacco farms in Connecticut, the helicopters were ideal in their ability to wash insecticides down to the very bottom leaves of a plant. Yet the clouds of dust and spray frequently impaired the vision of pilots, who were already imperiled by trees and power lines, which often ran right through a field of crops. Almost weekly, the beleaguered factory received back a plane that had crashed into a tree or was so corroded from harsh chemicals that it needed immediate attention. In a reincarnation of "The Dawn Patrol," the wrecked machines were rebuilt and sent back out time and again. Fortunately, no lives were lost; not even a bone was broken. But it was feast or famine. Growers called all at once—or not at all. This was not a good livelihood for Kaman Aircraft (see figure 3).

Efforts to interest the U.S. Navy in the servo flap and configuration had been recognized in May 1947, when the Bureau of Aeronautics awarded a small engineering contract to Kaman Aircraft Corporation to provide the National Advisory Committee for Aeronautics (NACA) with a rotor for evaluation. In 1948, a second navy engineering contract was awarded for evaluation of the synchropter configuration.

Figure 3.
The Kaman K-225 crop duster, 1949

Charles Kaman felt that he had to crack the military sales front. He made an appointment with Rear Admiral Alfred M. Pride, then Commander of the Navy Bureau of Aeronautics. We have these recollections of Mr. Kaman:

Mel Pride had one of those rare reputations in the navy. Long before I met him I had heard stories about his being the Air Officer on the staff of the Pacific Fleet that conceived the strike tactics that eventually prevailed against the Japanese in World War II. As Chief of Flight Testing in years gone by he had had the reputation of being unusually severe in his demand for perfection. He was known to give little quarter to contractors and to be absolutely rigid in his expectations of fulfillment of guarantees represented to him. Consequently, it was with some trepidation that I walked into that second floor office in the Old Navy building in Washington, D.C. Admiral Pride was military all the way, and he made me feel it instantly with his eyes.

"Well, Mr. Kaman, what do you seek of the Navy?"

I had planned what I would say, but under his stern gaze it all got revised into a single line "I'm here to tell you about my helicopter," I said. "I think it is a good one."

His face smiled a little and his eyes twinkled, as he said, "All right, go ahead."

And I did. Subsequently he agreed to come out and see it, and when he did he flew in it. The day he flew in it was the day Bill Murray took him over to Anacostia from Washington National Airport. He was going to meet some other admirals over there, and they were going to depart for some other place. We who stayed back across the Potomac at Washington National Airport saw the K-225 over at Anacostia zooming and doing pull ups and diving on the field and we knew that Bill had engaged the admiral. Later we learned that after doing the maneuvers with Mr. Murray, the admiral suggested that he give his friends an air show, which Bill Murray quickly proceeded to do. Admiral Pride actually had them close the airport briefly to enable the demonstration.

A week or two later when I went back to see Admiral Pride about his flight, he was quite stern with me. My intentions were to try to sell the navy a plane for their own flight evaluation. The fact is, crop dusting had expired and we were absolutely desperate. Unless something happened pretty quickly, the jig was up.

"Admiral Pride, I hope you were pleased with your flight."

"You have an interesting plane, Mr. Kaman, but I was disappointed to note that it has vibration just like the others. Can't you get rid of it?"

"Well, sir, our first priority was performance, stability, and ease of control. I feel we've made real strides on that side. Vibration . . . so there is more to be done tomorrow."

The Admiral said, "You bet there is. My years of flying just make me very concerned when I see any part of a flying machine shaking. It's bound to cause failure." I replied, "I certainly respect your opinions, sir, but helicopters have really just begun. Until we resolve the vibration problem, we will have to build them strong enough to take it and perhaps pay for extra maintenance along the way. I hope the facility of vertical flight and its potential attributes will justify the added cost."

"What are you planning to sell your planes for, Mr. Kaman, and to whom?"

"Today, I'd like to sell the navy a modified crop duster, K-225, for $25,000 and I would justify my asking you to buy it, CAA certified, on the basis of evaluating this new technology that we've created for its possible influence in future Navy considerations." I was hardly prepared for his reply.

"Mr. Kaman, why don't you give me a letter proposal including your price. I'll pass it down to have my experts look it over."

It was hard to put my foot all the way down as far as the floor in the outer office as I left.

The navy bought a K-225 for evaluation. I sold another to the Coast Guard to be used for training. We still needed a little more business so I went back and told Mel Pride that he simply had to have a backup in case they had an accident. After a while the navy concurred. It was those three orders that turned the tide and finally put Kaman Aircraft in business. My relationship with Admiral Pride developed into deep friendship and mutual respect, and on his retirement from the navy many tours of duty and years later, he became a director of the Kaman Corporation.

HOK/HTK

The late 1940s were lean times for the company. A layoff had reduced the work force to a mere handful, and with dreams of creating an everyman's helicopter for private individual use fading, the navy contracts—however meager and lean—were the breath of life.

As the technologies were developed, the navy turned with increasing frequency to the helicopter as the vehicle to meet the requirements of a mission. In 1949, the Marines needed an observation helicopter that could double as a rescue craft and general utility vehicle. Sikorsky and Bell submitted proposals for what people thought would be a two-way competition. But in the winter of 1949, snow having buried all thoughts of crop dusting, Charles Kaman, in long johns and a knitted cap, sat alone late into the night by the coal-oil stove in the shell of his half-finished house creating aerodynamic performance and stability aspects of the new Kaman craft, while Lew

Schuler, Jack Emerson, and others worked out the structural parameters. In contrast to the many millions an aircraft proposal costs today, Kaman's state-of-the-art proposal was conceived for a few thousand dollars. The proposal was submitted, and it generated considerable interest, yet tiny Kaman Corporation was not considered a military supplier, and this was to be a sizable procurement.

Meanwhile, in March of 1950, Kaman's K-225s were ready for evaluation. Bill Murray took the first to Patuxent River Naval Air Test Center (NATC) in Maryland for demonstrations and to train the navy pilots who would fly the aircraft. Confronted by a certain degree of official skepticism, Murray ascended before a large group of navy officers and performed an actual loop the loop—the first ever accomplished by a helicopter. The ability of the aircraft was clear, and Bill Murray was an instant hero; until his retirement twenty-five years later he served as president of Kaman's Aerospace subsidiary.

Although considerable time had already been invested in evaluation of the Sikorsky and Bell proposals for the observation helicopter, successful tests on the K-225s encouraged the navy to support the aerodynamic servo-controlled rotor and the synchropter configuration and to risk development of Kaman's design for the observation helicopter. Because of concern for the small company's ability to handle a fifty-aircraft program, the navy awarded Kaman's twenty-five employees working in a 10,000-square-foot factory a contract for four planes, to be designated HOK-1. The rest of the procurement was awarded to a competitor for a machine experts insisted could perform the mission.

There would be a gap between the delivery of the K-225 orders and the first HOK rollout—a potentially ruinous famine for the already lean company. Charles Kaman took his problem to the navy with every bit of energy he could muster, and in September 1950, he secured a navy contract for a production quantity of a helicopter to be designated HTK-1, to be used by the navy as a trainer helicopter. The HTK-1 was a refinement of the loop-flying K-225, with an enclosed fuselage. Work commenced immediately, and the first HTK-1 helicopter was completed in April 1951. Following structural and aerodynamic demonstrations at the Patuxent River NATC, a total of twenty-nine HTK-1 helicopters were built and delivered to the navy between 1951 and 1953. These aircraft were used all over the world as utility helicopters before finally assuming their intended function as training helicopters at Pensacola Naval Air Training Center, where they were in use until 1957. Experience gained from use of the HTK-1 in the Philippines and Okinawa led to the development of composite coatings for rotors that would withstand the monsoon in the Far East.

While the HTK-1s were being built, the work of designing the all-new HOK continued; it was the first helicopter designed to military specifications rather than to an inventor's conception of what could be done. It required an advance in technology, and the contract required extensive testing on the ground and in flight to prove that the rigid specifications had been met. The first flight test took place on April 21, 1953, and evaluations that followed drew respect from pilots and navy officials alike.

The Korean War highlighted the versatility of helicopters and their extreme usefulness to the armed forces. The need for observation helicopters grew, but the competitors' craft, ordered in the HO competition, proved disappointing: unable to hover in the heat of Korea, the underpowered aircraft required a runway for takeoff on hot days, and Kaman eventually produced the entire expanded requirement. Within eighteen months of that initial award to a company with 25 employees, Kaman had 750 workers in a new 155,000-square-foot factory, and Charles H. Kaman was awarded a lifetime honorary membership in the American Helicopter Society for his work as one of the principal aviation pioneers of the United States. In all, eighty-one model HOK-1 heli-

Figure 4.
The Kaman HOK production line, 1954, Bloomfield, Connecticut

copters and twenty-four utility-version HUK-1 helicopters were built between 1953 and 1958; these remained in service with units of the Marine Corps and the navy until 1964 (see figures 4 and 5).

Because of his reputation for innovation and his willingness to put aside preconceptions in favor of the customers' requirements, Kaman was eventually given the navy's toughest technology assignments and became one of the recognized leaders in technology.

An HTK-1 was flown as the world's first pilotless helicopter, or drone, controlled by radio from a remote station. Designated the HTK-1K, this program continued for several years, eventually leading to army use of aircraft as targets at White Sands proving ground for firings of the Hawk missile.

Another aircraft of the K-225 type was modified by installation of a Boeing turbine to create the world's first turbine-powered helicopter. In flight tests, pilot Bill Murray discovered the principle of droop compensation. As the helicopter ascended to higher altitudes, he found he needed to throttle the engine back to slow the rate of climb and keep from overspeeding the rotors. At 10,000 feet, with the throttle all the way back to idling speed, Murray radioed that the craft was still climbing. No adjustment of controls would stop the ascent and so, with the earth still falling away two miles below him,

Murray was forced to shut down the turbine. As Kaman and his coworkers watched, the speck in the sky began its powerless descent, autorotation of the twin synchropter blades providing what had become a Kaman trademark—a soft landing under no engine power. That aircraft is now on display at the Smithsonian's National Air and Space Museum (see figure 6).

Later, an HTK-1 was equipped with two Boeing 502-2 engines—the world's first twin gas-turbine installation (see figure 7).

Figure 5.
The Kaman HOK, produced from 1953 to 1958, in service until 1964

Figure 6.
The Kaman-225, produced from 1949 to 1950. This modified K-225 was the world's first turbine-powered helicopter and is now at the National Air and Space Museum of the Smithsonian Institution.

Figure 7.
The Kaman HTK-1, produced from 1951 to 1953, in service until 1957. This modified HTK-1 was the world's first twin-turbine helicopter.

HH-43

In 1956, an industrywide competition was held by the U.S. Air Force to determine the most suitable helicopter for a newly defined Local Crash Rescue Mission. The helicopter selected for this mission would maintain a condition of "ready alert" to proceed to a crash or rescue site with rescue personnel and equipment to suppress fires and effect a helicopter of the HOK-1/HUK-1 design and, after an intense competition, was selected as the winner. Accordingly, in 1957, Kaman was awarded prime contracts for air force model H-43 helicopters. Initial deliveries under these contracts in 1958 were H-43A helicopters, of the same basic configuration as the HOK-1/HUK-1 helicopters with equipment modifications for use in the crash rescue mission. A total of eighteen of these aircraft, powered with the Pratt & Whitney R-1340 reciprocating engines, were built between 1957 and 1959. Delivery of the last H-43A helicopter in July 1959 marked the end of production of piston-powered helicopters at Kaman Aircraft; at that point, the company became the first helicopter manufacturer to switch entirely to turbine power.

Most of the aircraft procured for the Air Force Local Crash Rescue procurement were model 43B helicopters, later designated HH-43B. While this helicopter was of the same general configuration as the H-43A, it was a completely redesigned aircraft, powered by a Lycoming T53-L-1B gas-turbine engine and fully qualified according to air force specifications. The initial delivery of this model was in 1958, and production continued uninterrupted for ten years. In 1964, modifications were incorporated in the design for installation of a T53-L-11A engine and for changes in internal arrangement, and the helicopter was redesignated HH-43F. A total of 202 of the HH-43B and 37 of the HH-43F helicopters were delivered between 1958 and 1968. The planes saw extensive rescue duty in Vietnam, where they were used to rescue thousands of flyers—more than 500 in 1967 alone—and they were noted for their fire-suppression duty in airfield disasters at fifty air bases in the United States and around the world. One of the last of this series was assigned to Andrews Air Force Base in Maryland, where it flew disaster cover at each takeoff and landing of the president's transport, Air Force 1. On its retirement in 1975, that helicopter was donated to the Bradley Air Museum in Windsor Locks, Connecticut, where it remains on permanent display.

Carrying a payload of 1,000 kilograms, an H-43B set an altitude record of 26,369 feet in 1961. Later that year, another H-43B climbed to 32,840 feet, an altitude of more than six miles. That same aircraft set world rate-of-climb records: 3,000 meters in two minutes and forty-two seconds (2:42), 6,000 meters in 6:49, and 9,000 meters in 14:12. In its era, the safety record of the H-43B, nicknamed the "Huskie," was the best ever established by a military aircraft, with an accident rate even lower than the U.S. Air

Force fixed-wing average. While Huskies were retired by the U.S. military in 1975, HH-43s remained in use through 1982 (see figure 8).

SH-2F

From the lessons of war came still more demanding design criteria. The navy of 1956 now needed a utility helicopter able to proceed 200 miles by night at sea in an ice storm, unaided by external means of navigation, land in the sea if necessary, pick up eleven persons from a hover, then proceed another 200 miles to another destination, still unaided by external means of communication. Nothing like it had ever been built. Rear Admiral William Schoech asked Kaman to meet him in Washington. There, Bill Schoech, assistant chief of the Navy Bureau of Aerodynamics (BuAer) for research and development, asked Kaman how much interested he was in the project, how realistic the specifications were, and whether, in his opinion, the project could be fulfilled. Kaman replied, "Bill, it is an exceedingly tall order. It can be done, but it will be extremely difficult and expensive."

The navy proceeded to hold the competition, and Kaman became a competitor, along with Sikorsky, Bell, and Vertol, in an intense four-way contest. Kaman actually submitted two proposals, one based on a synchropter configuration, the other on a single-rotor format.

Back in Washington to discuss HUK production with the BuAer officials, Kaman was standing in the doorway to leave when Rear Admiral Russell, chief of BuAer, said,

Figure 8.
The Kaman HH-43 Huskie, produced from 1958 to 1968, in service until the mid 1970s

"Charlie, we see you've submitted two proposals in the new utility helicopter competition. If you had a choice, which would you want?"

Kaman replied, "The single-rotor version."

"Why," asked Admiral Russell, "when the synchropter has been your trademark?"

"Because with the advent of the turbine, power is cheaper," Kaman answered, "and the single-rotor design requires less deck space, is more streamlined, and can go faster—an important criterion in a rescue mission."

Admiral Russell smiled, "Very interesting."

Early in 1957, the navy announced that Kaman had won the contract to produce the UH-2 Seasprite series of utility helicopters.

A full-scale, detailed mock-up of the HU2K-K was completed in the fall of 1957, and in June 1959, the first flight of the new helicopter was made at the Kaman flight test facility in Bloomfield, Connecticut. After completion of comprehensive demonstration tests at Patuxent River NATC, the first production delivery of a UH-2A helicopter—the navy's revised designation for HU2K-1—was accepted by the navy in December 1962. Deliveries of UH-2A and UH-2B, the two models differing only in electronic equipment, continued through 1965.

In the mid 1960s, a radically new procurement policy emerged whereby low cost was the principal criterion for the selection of military systems. The Navy UH-2 represented the highest level of helicopter technology of its era and was therefore expensive, just as Kaman had predicted. While the Kaman family of helicopters had helped save more than 20,000 lives in countless rescue missions, the navy could not answer the question, "How many lives will the navy be *unable* to save if it doesn't have this expensive procurement?" posed by Defense Secretary McNamara and his deputy, Enthoven. The Department of Defense stopped the program (see figure 9).

The navy later tried to use low-cost army helicopters for the mission, but in just a few months at sea those helicopters were badly corroded and unable to perform.

Figure 9.
The Kaman UH-2 Seasprite; various models were produced between 1962 and 1965. All existing modified to twin configurations, 1967–72. All existing modified to SH-2F configuration, 1970–82. The SH-2F line was reopened for new production in 1981.

Later, the army, under Secretary of the Army Cyrus Vance, undertook a thorough examination of the Kaman UH-2 helicopter as a possible gun platform in support of ground troops, along with other utility functions. After extensive evaluations, a decision was made to buy 220 of the planes in a procurement that received the approval of Congress in 1963. Five days after the assassination of President Kennedy and the succession of Lyndon B. Johnson to the presidency, the program for procuring UH-2s from Kaman was dropped in favor of purchasing Bell UH-1s from Bell in Texas.

These experiences could have destroyed the company. It was then that diversification efforts launched in the 1950s were accelerated, leading to a vastly stronger, balanced corporation in which business from the Pentagon represented less than 25 percent of annual sales. Since the corporation reflects on the people who shaped the destiny of the company, several of the real heroes were military men or civil servants of stature and foresight in the Pentagon who recognized the potential for reversal in government contracting principle and who urged just such diversification, providing insight and encouragement along the way. A patriot and a determined citizen, Kaman continued to see a place for his helicopter company in national defense and repositioned the company as a supplier of extreme-environment, high-stress components for other manufacturers' aircraft programs and pursued work on modification of existing UH-2s.

Between 1967 and 1972, all the UH-2A/B helicopters then in service, and a number of partially completed aircraft at the Kaman plant as well, were successfully modifed by Kaman to a twin-engine configuration, using two T-58-GE-8B turbine engines, and were redesignated UH-2C. Additional modifications to provide increased power and gross weight capabilities were later incorporated in the aircraft, to create models UH-2C (armored), UH-2D, and SH-2D. The U.S. Navy, in a continuing search to improve its antisubmarine warfare capabilities, decided in 1970 to convert its fleet of H-2 Seasprite helicopters from operation in its destroyer fleet with reactive weapons to the destruction of enemy submarines. Avionics mission equipment to detect, classify, and destroy submarines was incorporated in the successful helicopter, which, because of its small size, was ideal for operation as a single unit from navy destroyers. The designation of the LAMPS MARK-1 helicopter became SH-2F (see figure 10). Then, in April 1980, the navy requested that the SH-2F be brought back into production to provide aircraft for the empty decks of destroyers and frigates assigned to the antisubmarine warfare mission, leading to that exciting day in 1983 when Kaman employees gathered to hear Secretary of the Navy John Lehman's personal congratulations for a job well done.

Figure 10.
The Kaman SH-2F LAMPS in service

CHARLES H. KAMAN was born and raised in Washington, D.C. He was graduated magna cum laude from the Catholic University in Washington, D.C., where he earned the B.S. degree in aeronautical engineering. He worked on helicopter development at Hamilton (Standard) Propeller during World War II, but he resigned his position as chief of aerodynamics in 1945 to found his own aircraft company. He is founder and chairman of the Kaman Corporation, a widely diversified, Connecticut-based company. Mr. Kaman is a past president of the American Helicopter Society, past chairman of the Helicopter Council Aerospace Industries Association, and a charter member of the Aviation Hall of Fame. He is an honorary fellow of the American Institute of Aeronautics and Astronautics and a member of the National Academy of Engineering, and he holds the 1981 Dr. Alexander Klemin Award of the American Helicopter Society. Mr. Kaman is a present and past director, trustee, or incorporator of several corporations and public service organizations. He is a founder of the University of Hartford, a past trustee of Western New England College, and a former governor of the Catholic University.

RUSSELL H. JONES is a financial officer on the staff of the Kaman Corporation.

RESCUE

WALTER J. BOYNE AND DONALD S. LOPEZ

Uplifting Experiences: The Helpful Helicopters

In its relatively short career as a practical aircraft, the helicopter has become a very important, even vital, factor in many industries and activities. Countless people have been rescued and countless lives have been saved because of the unique capabilities of these marvelous machines. Helicopters have been used for missions and tasks that were not even dreamed of during their early years. As high power-to-weight ratio gas turbine engines, stronger and lighter materials, and advanced aerodynamic techniques were developed, the versatility of the helicopter increased significantly.

The reliability of the helicopter has improved to the point that it is used regularly to carry the president and other heads of state on short flights and airborne inspections. Also, the long overwater flights to offshore oil platforms—and even a flight around the world—can now be made by helicopter.

With its increased lifting capacity the helicopter has become invaluable as a crane in positioning heavy and unwieldy loads precisely in inaccessible locations as well as for carrying profitable loads of passengers.

Perhaps its most satisfying use is as a saver of lives; whether removing crewmen from a foundering vessel; rushing crash victims from the accident scene, above heavy traffic, to a trauma center; or lifting trapped tenants from the tops of burning buildings.

Here, then are action photographs of helicopters in some of their functions as servants of mankind.

Crewmen being rescued from a capsized ship by a Capital Helicopters Bell JetRanger (Rotor & Wing International)

Opposite page:
An 18,000-pound range tower being relocated at Edwards Air Force Base, California, by an Army Boeing Vertol CH-47 Chinook (U.S. Air Force)

Medevac version of a Hughes 500D being used by the California Highway Patrol for emergency transport of accident victims to trauma centers (Hughes Helicopters, Inc.)

A U.S. Air Force Kaman HH-43B Huskie suppressing a fire with downwash for rescue (Kaman Aerospace Corp.)

A U.S. Coast Guard Sikorsky HH-3F approaching a burning oil platform to check for survivors (U.S. Coast Guard)

A Boeing Vertol Model 234, operated by British Airways, landing on an oil rig in the North Sea (Boeing Vertol Company)

One of the presidential helicopters, a Sikorsky VH-3D Sea King, lifting off of the lawn of the White House (White House)

Ronald Reagan disembarking from a Bell 222 during his 1980 presidential campaign tour (Bell Helicopter Textron)

2
29

A Los Angeles Fire Department Bell JetRanger dropping fire-suppressant chemicals on a brush fire (Bell Helicopter Textron)

A 9,000-pound winch section of the drawworks being lowered to the oil drilling rig in the jungle near Arboletes, Colombia, by a Sikorsky S-64E Skycrane (United Technologies Sikorsky Aircraft)

A Japanese Maritime Safety Agency Bell JetRanger landing on an overturned tanker and rescuers cutting a hole in the ship's bottom to free trapped crewmen (Bell Helicopter Textron)

A Bell Model 47, equipped with spray bars, covering a wide swath while crop dusting (Rotor & Wing International)

A U.S. Coast Guard Sikorsky HH-3F hovering over a small boat while a sick passenger is winched aboard to be flown to a hospital (U.S. Coast Guard)

A Sud Aviation S.E. Alouette II dropping 160 gallons of water on a fire at the Aerial Tanker Demonstration sponsored by the U.S. Forest Service and the Maine, New Hampshire, and New York forestry departments (U.S. Forest Service)

A Hughes 500E, official helicopter of the Los Angeles 1984 Olympics, over the Los Angeles Coliseum. The helicopters will be used to ferry officials among the widely dispersed sites of the Olympic Games (Hughes Helicopters, Inc.)

A Sikorsky S-64 Skycrane descending over a river to refill its firefighting container with water (U.S. Dept. of the Interior)

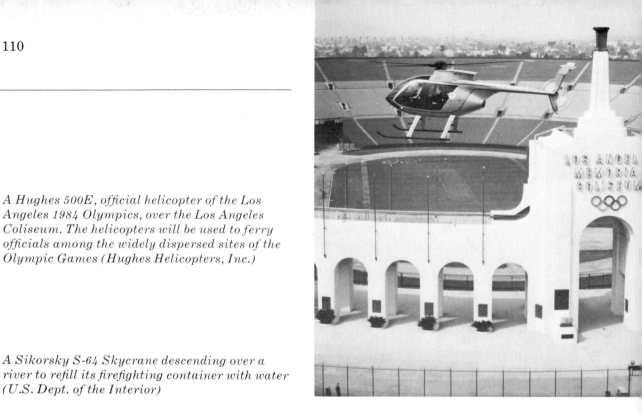

A Bell 212 dropping water on the 1980 fire on Rattlesnake Mountain near Cody, Wyoming (U.S. Dept. of the Interior)

A National Safety Council of Australia Hughes 500D ambulance carrying two divers to practice emergency jumps for sea search missions (Hughes Helicopter, Inc.)

This mockup of the interior of the air-ambulance-configured Aerospatiale SA 365N Dauphin 2 shows the swing-out litter racks and full cardiac emergency capability for each patient (Aerospatiale Helicopter Corporations)

A Hughes 300C, equipped with a complete electronic news gathering system, on a demonstration flight with a cameraman in the right seat (Hughes Helicopters, Inc.)

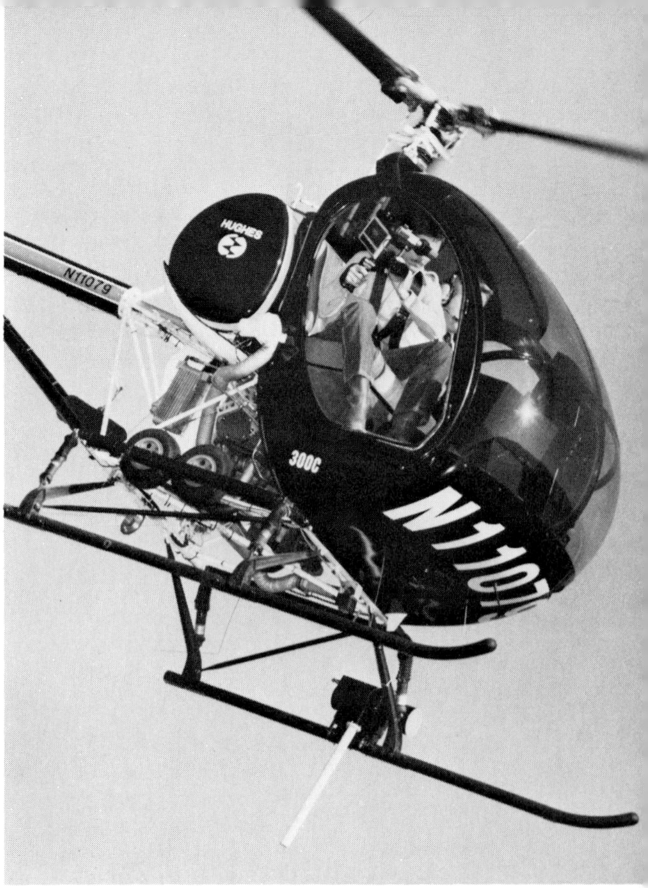

An MBB BO 195 Twin Jet II carrying a load of pipes in its pickup truck style cargo bed that allows it to carry material up to 15 feet long (MBB Helicopter Corporation)

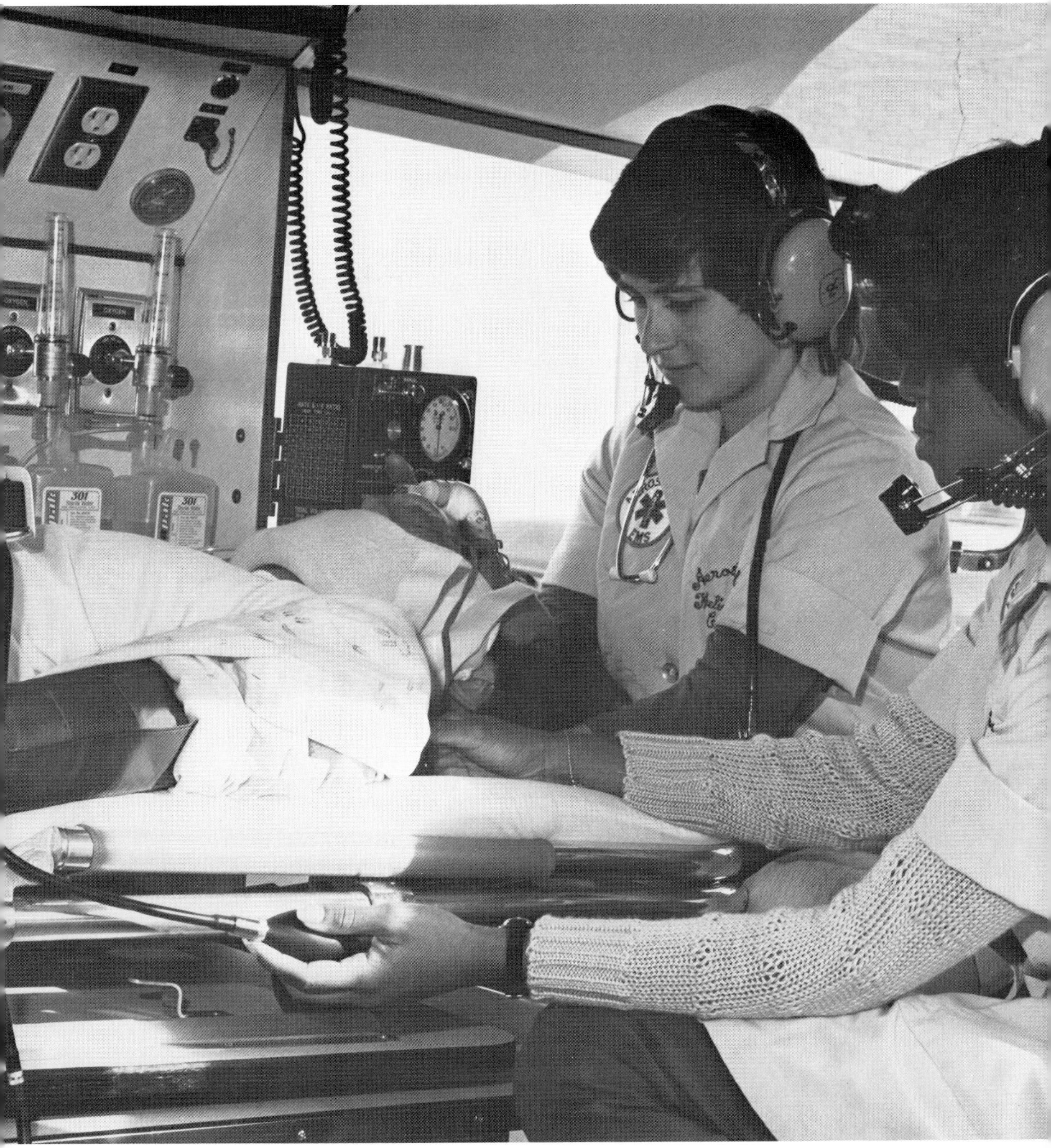

HUGHES

Exterior view of a Westland 30 used for the transport of commuters. (Westland Helicopters Ltd.)

Interior view of a Westland 30. The cabin has room for up to 17 passengers and there is a large baggage hold (Westland Helicopters Ltd.)

Opposite page:

A Hughes 500D delivering construction supplies to a remote site (Hughes Helicopters, Inc.)

WILLIAM J. CRAWFORD III

The Power to Lift Straight Up

Man has dreamed of flying since he first gazed into the sky and saw birds—from flitting hummingbirds to giant eagles—lifting from bushes, trees, and mountain peaks to soar majestically over his head. Historically, however, man's attempts at flight have been thwarted not so much by the inability to design an adequate airfoil as by the lack of technology to produce a source of power sufficient to sustain flight.

The most famous early efforts at flight were Leonardo da Vinci's quite sophisticated attempts in the 1480s to demonstrate, among his other achievements, what may have been the first helicopter—with a helix, or spiral screw—that is said to have flown as a model. Leonardo's power came from a simple clockwork mechanism, but the helix lacked the ability to stay aloft.

In the early 1800s, Sir George Cayley, often called "the father of aerial navigation," envisioned the use of the internal combustion engine to power not only aeroplanes, but rudimentary helicopters as well. Despite the significance of Cayley's contributions to aerial progress, he never succeeded in generating enough power to fly his helicopter. In 1842 another Englishman, W. H. Phillips, however, flew a model helicopter. Its unique characteristic was that it was powered by steam, which was produced by the combustion of charcoal, gypsum, and saltpeter. Using Hero's concept of jet propulsion from the first century A.D.—the Aeolipile—this British helicopter model flew because its blades rotated when steam was ejected from their tips.

Each of these milestone attempts at vertical flight shared a common drawback: lack of a source of propulsion sufficiently powerful to lift the weight of the vehicle and, ultimately, that of a human pilot.

Finally, on the sand dunes at Kill Devil Hill, Kitty Hawk, North Carolina, in 1903 the Wright brothers drastically altered the course of history. They demonstrated that, with adequate power, man could use aerodynamics to lift a heavier-than-air craft—and pilot—into the air.

Only five years later, in 1908, the Frenchman Louis Breguet designed and built his Gyroplane—half helicopter, half airplane. It rose to a height of thirty-three feet with power from an elementary internal combustion engine.

When his initial vertical lift efforts met with only limited success, Breguet turned to the development and flight of fixed-wing airplanes. The following year in Russia, however, the man generally considered the inventor of today's helicopter began serious experimentation. Igor Sikorsky's first helicopter was powered by a 25-hp Anzani engine, a development of a motorcycle engine specifically modified for use in the early airplanes of that day. To his disappointment, the engine was not sufficiently powerful to lift the craft. Sikorsky's second helicopter also used a single 25-hp Anzani engine. This model flew, lifting its own 400 pounds—but not a pilot—aloft. Although there were other serious technical problems, the power plant remained the limiting factor.

Twelve years later, in 1921, at McCook Field in Dayton, Ohio, the U.S. Army first took official notice of the potential for the helicopter and acted on it. A Russian immigrant, George de Bothezat, built and flew what Thomas Edison called "the first successful helicopter." The craft, powered by a 180-hp LeRhone engine, weighed 3,600 pounds. Although the army spent some $200,000 on the project, the U.S. Army Air Service could envision but little use for the unique vehicle, and the project was abandoned.

The progress of vertical lift during the late 1920s and 1930s was marked by the evolution of the autogiro. The combination fixed-wing and rotary-wing aircraft used conventional aircraft piston engines with power output up to 160 hp.

Piston Engine Power "Lifts" Helicopters

Four whose names are famous in aviation history—Louis Breguet in France, Igor Sikorsky in the United States, and Henrich Focke and Anton Flettner in Germany—were the first to recognize that with the advent of more powerful piston engines, rotary-wing aircraft could finally become practical vehicles for military as well as civil use.

Each of these successful modern-day helicopter innovators, despite widely varying design techniques, used a common source of power: the air-cooled reciprocating engine. The reason was simple. Air-cooled engines, requiring no radiators, fluid, or coolant pipes, were inherently lighter than water-cooled engines. Reduced engine weight contributed significantly to the weight-to-power equation for vertical lift. In addition, air-cooled engines were easier to repair and, in military use, were less vulnerable to ground fire.

Using surplus fixed-wing aircraft engines, Breguet was able to fly a helicopter in France in 1935. Progress was slow, however, and the project was discontinued in 1939, when French production efforts turned to conventional military fighters and bombers.

In Germany in 1936, the Focke-Achgelis Fa-61, powered by a nose-mounted 160-hp aircraft engine, was built. The Fa-61 is credited with being the world's first completely successful helicopter (see figure 1). Lindbergh called Focke's helicopter the most striking aeronautical development he had ever seen.

Demonstrations of the helicopter's capability included highly publicized flights by famed German aviatrix Hanna Reitsch inside Berlin's Deutschland-Halle sports arena. Following the Fa-61, an even more powerful helicopter, the Fa-223, was produced. Unprecedented power for the Fa-223 came from a 1,000-hp engine, which enabled the craft to carry as many as twelve people, fly at 115 miles an hour, and rise to altitudes of more than 23,000 feet.

In a late-1930s atmosphere of intense national competition and fever-pitch preparation for conflict, another German, Anton Flettner, developed and built the Fl-265 and later the smaller, lighter, Fl-282 Kolibri for the German navy. Recognizing the Kolibri's potential to do useful work in what was soon to be a wartime environment, the German navy ordered 1,000 of them.

Igor Sikorsky, following his emigration to the United States, developed and produced a series of successful fixed-wing aircraft for civil use. But his earlier interest in helicopters was revived when his aircraft company became a part of the giant United Aircraft and Transport Corporation, a development that enabled Sikorsky to concentrate on rotary-wing aircraft. By 1939 Sikorsky had designed and built his prototype VS-300, an assembly of metal tubing with the pilot sitting in the open in front of the helicopter's vertical 75-hp engine. Sikorsky was his own test pilot, preferring to shoulder the risks inherent in such a rudimentary, and essentially underpowered, vehicle himself. Fol-

Figure 1. Focke-Achgelis Fa-61

lowing the first cautious test flights in 1940, the U.S. Army Air Corps funded a larger, more powerful helicopter, the XR-4

In rapid succession even more powerful and successful piston-powered helicopters were developed, spurred by wartime requirements and innovation. In July 1940 a more advanced, sophisticated Sikorsky VS-300, powered by a 90-hp Lycoming piston engine, was flown; in 1943 the Sikorsky R-4, 170 hp of whose 185-hp engine was required merely to lift the R-4 and its total payload; in 1945 the Sikorsky S-55, the nose-mounted engine of which was linked to the rotor with a drive shaft that ran between the two seats in the cockpit; in 1949 the Bell 47G, with an engine exposed to the elements; and in 1952 the Piasecki H-21, with an aft-installed engine balancing a forward cabin load.

Piston power from increasingly sophisticated internal combustion aircraft engines served to demonstrate the practicality of the rotary-wing aircraft. Although the available piston engine power for helicopters increased more than sevenfold in the little more than a quarter of a century between the mid 1930s and the early 1950s, designers recognized that ultimate practical use of rotary-wing craft was limited solely by engine size, weight, and the total output of power that could be generated from the internal combustion engine.

Figure 2.
R. G. Standerwick and S. A. Moss with the General Electric Type B Turbosupercharger

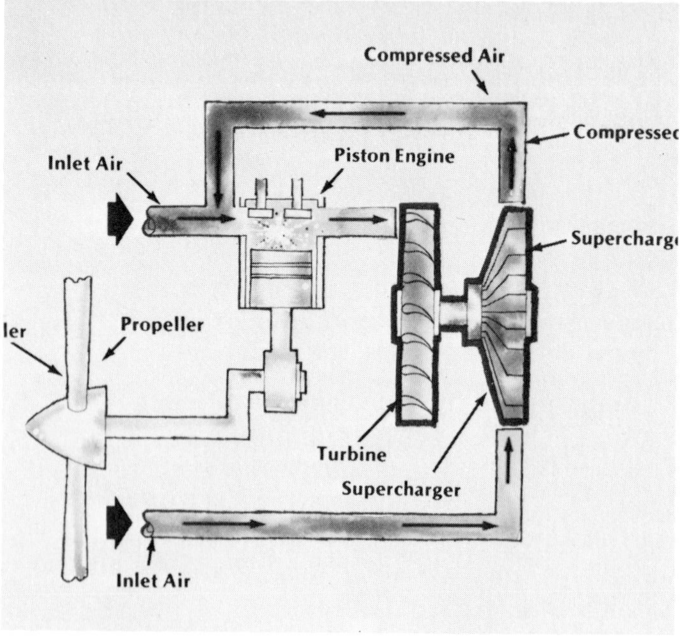

Figure 3.
Schematic of a Turbosupercharger

Turboshafts Transform the Helicopter

The Korean conflict had demonstrated vital applications of helicopters for a variety of logistical and tactical missions. Even with the advent of more powerful piston engines, however, the power plant continued to be the limiting factor. To produce additional power, larger, heavier piston engines were needed; they in turn required more space. Piston power, moreover, caused a problem inherent in all helicopters up to that time: vibration. Despite more powerful piston engines, helicopters still could carry only relatively small payloads.

The solution, for designers of an entirely new generation of helicopters, came from power plants conceived simultaneously during the 1930s in Great Britain and Germany. This development in propulsion that would change the entire course of aviation relied heavily on more than thirty years of experience with piston engine turbosuperchargers pioneered by Sanford Moss of General Electric as early as World War I (see figures 2 and 3).

The gas turbine engine, proved in military fighter and bomber aircraft during World War II and after, was soon to inaugurate the "jet age" of civil aircraft. This engine offered the combination of increased power and light weight. The principal limiting factor in the advancement of the helicopter—the power plant—had now been dramatically altered.

With the advent of the gas turbine—called "junior jets" in a 1955 front-page article in *The Wall Street Journal*—helicopters were finally ready to take off (see figure 4). The *Journal* noted that the "light, powerful engines were the key to faster, cheaper planes of tomorrow." Stating that the "tiny jet could outperform four motors on a DC-6," the *Wall Street Journal* subhead asked the question, "A spur to the helicopter?"

Gas turbines produced significantly more power per pound of engine weight than piston engines. Helicopter designers, however, were required to harness gas turbine power

THE WALL STREET JOURNAL.

SEPTEMBER 16, 1955 | Entered as Second Class Matter at the Post Office, New York, N.Y. | 10 CENTS in U.S. Territories and possessions

Junior Jets

Light, Powerful Engines Key to Faster, Cheaper Planes of Tomorrow

Tiny Jet Could Outperform Four Motors on DC-6; More Push Per Pound

A Spur to the Helicopter?

By Richard P. Cooke
Staff Reporter of THE WALL STREET JOURNAL

New York — A bevy of "little giant" jet engines are promising some startling aircraft advances within the next decade.

These junior size power plants, weighing roughly from 200 to 500 pounds, will deliver up to 10 times as much power as piston engines of the same weight. Mounted singly or in pairs, the little jets could power business planes or small-size commercial craft. Grouped in clusters they could drive faster military planes or more economical passenger airliners. Harnessed to shafts, little jets promise vastly improved helicopters. And the new engines may solve the power problems of fixed-wing aircraft that take off vertically.

A number of small but fairly heavy jet engine models have been built in Europe. Now, some U.S. manufacturers are rushing to fill a gap in U.S. technology, which has concentrated on big, super-powered jet engines. Engineers for such firms as General Electric, Fairchild Engine & Airplane Corp. and Lycoming division of Avco Manufacturing Corp. say they'll soon be building small size jets even more powerful than present French or British products.

Hovering Helicopter

The benefits of the smaller power plants aren't limited to whooshing straight-jet planes. G.E. and other engine makers are counting on a big helicopter market for the closely related gas turbine engine. "The helicopter market is all set up for turbines: what we have to do is produce engines to fill the need," says E.J. Woll, manager of engineering for General Electric's small aircraft engine department.

Helicopters spend much of their flying time with the throttle wide open for hovering or rising, explains Mr. Woll. Gas turbine engines run most efficiently at full speed; piston engines now powering whirlybirds are inefficient and subject to severe strain at full throttle. Futhermore, states Mr. Woll, the gas turbine runs cheapest at close to full speed, thus offering big opportunities for paring presently high cost of operating helicopters.

Helicopter designers also look for added safety from multiple small gas turbine engines. If one of the motors quits, the other could keep the craft in the air.

G.E. already is building a T-58 shaft turbine for Navy helicopters. Details of the 1,000-horsepower engine are restricted, as are the specifics of a lightweight straight jet of the 2,000 pound thrust class General Electric reportedly is building on Government contract.

Without talking details, Mr. Woll makes it clear that his company's present small jet work is just a starter. G.E. now has 4,000 employes at its River Works at Lynn, Mass., plant busy on "small" turbines, including both jets and shaft models. The Lynn plant has facilities for testing all the main components of jet or other turbine engines, indicating the company's stress on such development.

Utility 'Copter Engine

Lycoming started developing its XT-53 shaft turbine in 1952. The 770-horsepower engine will power a utility helicopter being built by Bell Aircraft Corp. The firm has a larger turbine engine under development for the Air Force but won't part with details of its expected performance.

Figure 4.
Significance of small jet engines recognized in 1955 Wall Street Journal *front-page article*

in a different way. The challenge was to capture the thrust of the baby gas turbine efficiently, through the use of a shaft geared from the turbine rotor to the helicopter rotor. The result was the turboshaft engine. Turboprops use a similar engine, but with a more direct power drive for the propeller.

Turboshafts offered unique advantages for helicopters (see figure 5). Because these rotary-wing aircraft hover at high power, a condition in which gas turbines run most efficiently, they were able to outperform piston engines significantly. The fewer operating parts and lighter weight of the turboshaft improved both the reliability of the engine and the performance of the helicopter. At only half the weight of an equivalent piston engine, a turboshaft engine was much smaller and thus permitted more flexible installation. Most significant, these characteristics enabled the helicopter to increase its payload.

Self-cooling turboshafts ran on less expensive kerosene. Because they operated with a single shaft connecting the compres-

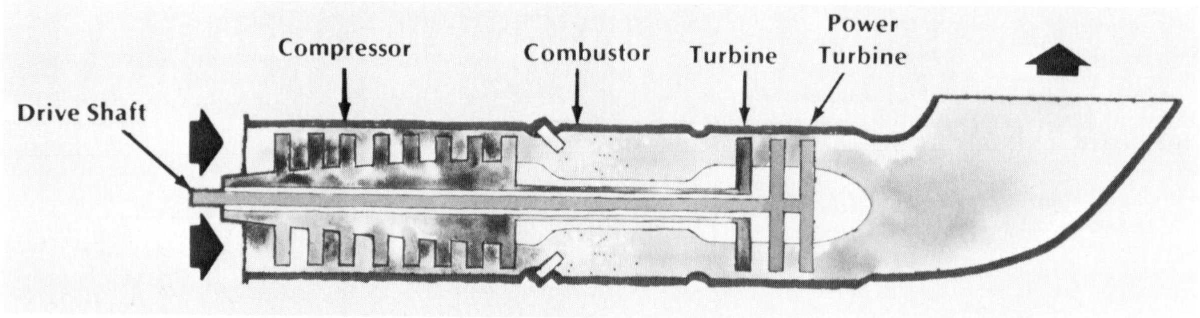

Figure 5. Schematic of a typical turboshaft engine

Figure 6. Boeing 502 gas turbine engine

sor with the turbine wheel, moreover, the engine operated essentially without vibration.

In 1951, the Kaman K-225, powered by a Boeing 502 turbine engine (see figure 6), made the first gas-turbine-powered helicopter flight in history. Three years later, a Kaman HTK-1, powered by two Boeing gas turbines, made the world's first twin gas turbine helicopter flight. The Boeing turbine produced 190 shaft horsepower (shp). In the Kaman HTK-1, a synchropter, the single piston engine was replaced by two turbines, producing a total of 380 hp, but they weighed no more than the single 240-hp piston engine of the HTK-1.

Carrying on a tradition of helicopter pioneering that had begun with Breguet, helicopter development in France provided a giant stride for rotary-wing advancement with the SNCA-S.E. 3130 Alouette II, which made its first flight in March 1955, the world's

Figure 7.
Five years after the Artouste II, the Astazou IIA engine powered the Sud Aviation SA 318, a new version of the Alouette II

first turbocopter to be produced in quantity. The Alouette was powered by a 400-hp Turbomeca Artouste II running at a speed of 35,000 rpm, geared down to produce a rotor speed of only 350 rpm (see figure 7). This helicopter continued to be produced until 1975.

American engine manufacturers whose principal thrust was centered on gas turbine engines—General Electric, Allison Division of General Motors, Lycoming, and the Canadian subsidiary of Pratt & Whitney—quickly became the primary developers and producers of turboshaft engines, which were to provide power for an entirely new generation of helicopters.

Gas turbine technology was also being advanced internationally by companies such as Bristol-Siddeley and Rolls-Royce of England and by Fiat of Italy. Russia developed a spectrum of helicopters, including the world's largest, the Mi-12, which is capable of lifting a payload of 55,000 pounds (see figure 8). It is powered by four 6,500-hp turboshaft engines.

The Lycoming T53 (see figure 9) provided the power for the famous Bell UH-1 Huey, the U.S. Army workhorse in the Vietnam War. More than 17,000 turboshaft engines were produced for the UH-1, ranging in output from 860 shp to 1,485 shp, thus attesting to the design versatility and popularity of this power plant. In 1960, Lycoming delivered its first 2,200-shp T55 engine for the Boeing Vertol CH-47 Chinook helicopter.

The Allison Division of General Motors began testing a 250-hp gas turbine engine in 1958. It became the T63 turboshaft for light observation helicopters and a host of small civil rotorcraft.

The PT6 family of small gas turbines built by Pratt & Whitney of Canada was introduced in 1964 (see figure 10). The unique PT6-T Twin-Pac, with two engines operating through a combining gearbox, is used widely in utility helicopters and military attack helicopters as well as for executive transport and in commercial operations with heavy lift assignments. The PT6 family ranges from 1,020 shp to 1,875 shp.

General Electric's experience with the turbine engine dates from the company's

Figure 8. Russian Mi-12 helicopter

Figure 9. Lycoming T53 turboshaft engine

work with gas turbines, which began around the turn of the century. The GE turbosupercharger, first used on a World War I Liberty engine, helped pioneer achievements in aviation during more than seven decades, including the first "over the weather" flight in a TWA Northrop Gamma in 1937. This extensive experience contributed directly to the selection of GE to produce the first American turbojet, the I-A. Two I-As powered the first U.S. jet aircraft, the Bell XP-59, in 1942. GE had already had extensive experience with direct power derived from a gas turbine for land-based applications. The company developed and ran the world's first turboprop, the TG100, in 1943.

In 1952, the U.S. Air Force called on industry to submit proposals for a 600-shp gas turbine engine for helicopters. The contract was awarded to Lycoming; General

Electric studies and work on the development of this engine, however, provided a foundation for the evolution of an entire family of GE gas turbine power for helicopters.

GE was awarded a contract by the U.S. Navy in 1953 for development of what was then an 800-shp turboshaft engine. Recognizing that navy specifications for what became known as the XT58 would not meet service requirements, GE found itself in the unique position of telling the navy it really needed a more powerful engine, but one that weighed less than the one originally specified. The resultant new T58 produced 1,050 shp and weighed only 250 pounds (see figure 11).

The T58's power-to-weight ratio of 4.2 to 1 was dramatic evidence of the advance in propulsion as a result of turboshaft development. Piston engines that powered early airplanes and helicopters weighed more than their horsepower output. A Gnome engine, for example, weighed 170 pounds and produced 45 to 47 hp; the famous World War I Liberty engine produced 420 hp and had what was considered an "unrivaled" weight-to-power ratio of "only" 2.1 to 1. Turboshafts reversed that ratio; the T58 produced more than four times its weight in power.

The T58 was first tested successfully in 1955. Two T58s were installed in a Sikorsky HSS-1 (S-58), replacing one piston engine. This turbocopter made its first flight in February 1957.

Recognizing the potential for gas-turbine-powered helicopters, Sikorsky proposed an entirely new airframe designed around the T58. It became the HSS-2 and, in commercial operation, the S-61.

The T58 provided a benchmark against which all other helicopter gas turbine power plants were measured. Throughout the thirty-year history of its development and production the basic engine design of the T58 has been modified continually to meet a variety of helicopter turboshaft applications. First developed at 1,050 shp, the engine has included models ranging up to 1,870 shp.

Even with these important improve-

Figure 10.
Pratt & Whitney Aircraft of Canada's PT6-T Twin-Pac®

Figure 11.
General Electric T58 turboshaft engine

ments in power, the weight of the T58 engine has increased only from 250 pounds to 443 pounds, which is an almost classic demonstration of the unique advantage of gas turbine power for both small and large helicopters. During this power-to-weight evolution, the specific fuel consumption (the ratio of fuel consumed to engine power produced) of the T58 has been reduced nearly 20 percent.

The commercial counterpart of the T58, the CT58, became the first U.S. gas turbine authorized for commercial helicopter use when it was awarded an FAA Type Certificate in July 1959.

By the end of 1983, total military and commercial flight hours of the T58 engine had exceeded 17 million. This average of more than 2 million service hours a year is strong testimony of the durability and reliability of gas turbine power for helicopters.

During the late 1950s General Electric, on the solid foundation provided by the success of the T58, began to develop in collaboration with the U.S. Navy a larger, more powerful turboshaft engine that could also be used as a turboprop for fixed-wing aircraft.

Seeing that two engine models were required, each derived from a common core engine, the company began concurrent development of both a turboshaft and a turboprop engine in the 3,000-shp class. In contrast to the objectives of earlier gas turbines that called for a single engine to meet a specific application, General Electric's aim for the design of this engine was to provide a single power plant to serve the requirements of a wide range of aircraft—helicopter and fixed-wing as well as vertical or short takeoff and landing (V/STOL) aircraft. Of particular significance was a specific criterion for fuel consumption significantly lower than that of the T58.

Figure 12.
General Electric T700 turboshaft engine

From this development study came the T64. As a result of General Electric's multipurpose design objectives, the T64 powers not only the Sikorsky H-53 family of helicopters, but also provides turboprop propulsion for several U.S. and international short takeoff and landing (STOL) aircraft as well as conventional fixed-wing aircraft.

From its original 3,000-shp class, newer models of the T64 produce 4,855 shp. Even with this substantial increase in engine power, the specific fuel consumption and engine weight of the T64 have been reduced through the use of advanced technology.

With flight experience that already exceeds 5 million hours, the T64 turboshaft-turboprop engine and its offspring will be operating well into the next century.

In the late 1960s, as a result of its experience in Vietnam, the U.S. Army saw a need for a new generation of helicopters and engines. Recognizing the fact that engine development paces the aircraft, the army in 1967 initiated a competitive prototype engine program for a new lightweight, low-fuel-consumption, low-maintenance turboshaft engine.

A U.S. Army contract was awarded competitively to GE in 1972 for a radical new helicopter engine design calling for reduced fuel consumption; less need for spare parts—and spare engines; significantly better maintenance time in the field, including faster removal and replacement of accessories; and a shorter time between periodic maintenance and engine removals. Army specifications called for the world's tough-

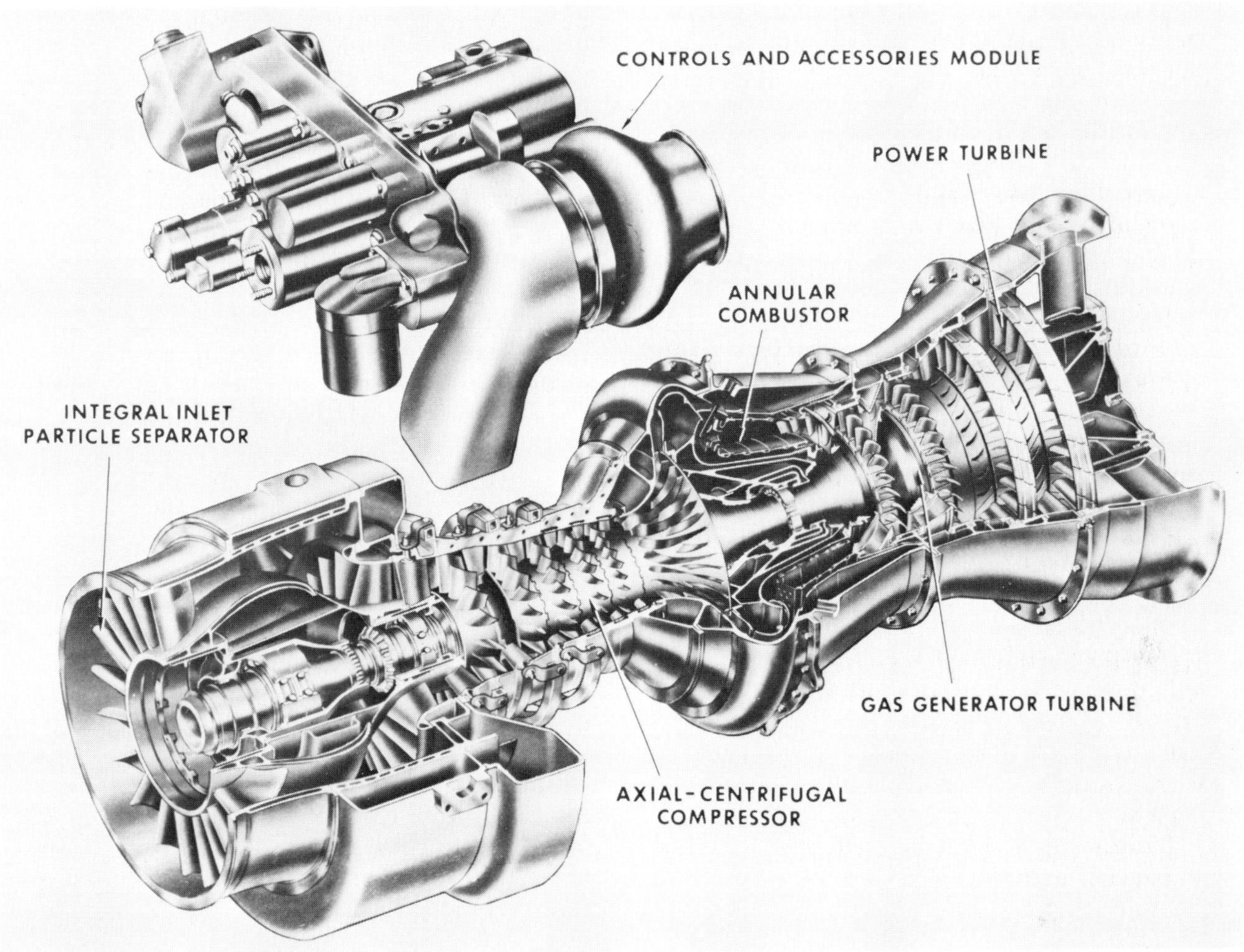

Figure 13.
Trimetric projection of the T700 turboshaft engine

est, most cost-effective helicopter engine. The engine was designated the T700 (see figure 12). Ultimately, it was selected to power the Sikorsky UH-60A, Hughes AH-64, Bell AH-1T+, Sikorsky SH-60B, Sikorsky HH-60D, and several international aircraft.

This next-generation turboshaft engine, which weighs 425 to 434 pounds, is in the 1,500- to 2,500-shp class (see figure 13). Specific fuel consumption of the lighter, less complex, but more reliable engine is even lower than that of its pioneering predecessors, the T58 and T64.

Mean time between engine failures of the T700 is a fourfold improvement over previous generations of helicopter engines. Maintenance requirements for this advanced power plant are 75 percent less than first- and second-generation helicopter engines.

Testimony of the acceptance and reliability of third-generation turboshaft helicopter engines came in late 1983, when GE was awarded a contract for 1,554 T700 engines.

The T700 designed for military application provided a logical course of development of a commercial derivative—the CT7, which was certified by both British and U.S. civil aviation authorities. In the early 1980s the CT7 was selected to power the Bell 214ST and Westland 30-200 civil helicopters.

The military T700 and civil CT7 provide prime examples of the rapid evolution of gas turbine power for modern helicopters. At the heart of present criteria for engine design are sharply reduced fuel consumption, lower maintenance requirements, and reduced weight. Only ten common tools, for example, are required for line maintenance of the T700 gas turbine helicopter engine (see figure 14); maintenance costs have been reduced 45 percent.

Of greatest significance to the increasing use of helicopters as practical aircraft for an array of civil and military tasks are the significant improvements that have been made in the reliability and durability of turboshafts. Engine maintenance and life expectancy no longer restrict the cost-effectiveness of the helicopter.

New Challenges of V/STOL Flight

The helicopter is a true vertical takeoff and landing (VTOL) aircraft. With the advent of gas turbines for helicopters, however, and their higher power-to-weight ratios, aircraft designers began to study variations of more conventional, fixed-wing aircraft for V/STOL designs.

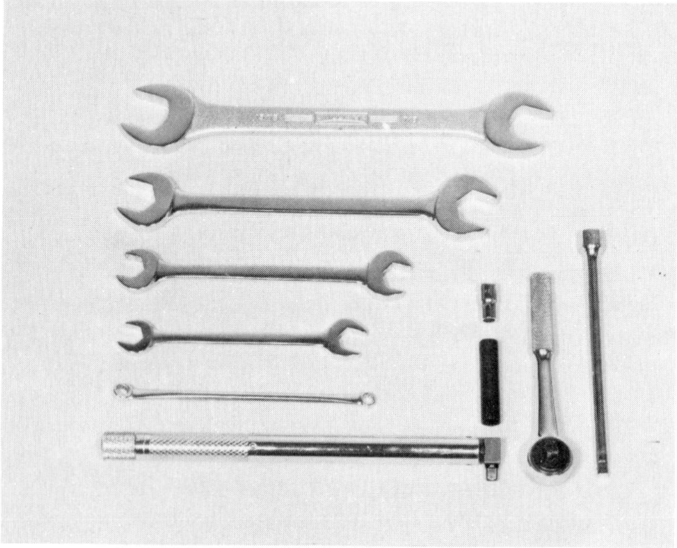

Figure 14.
T700 turboshaft engine tool kit

General Electric has participated extensively in the development of V/STOL aircraft, ranging from the company's own research, development, and production of the fan-in-wing concept in the Ryan XV-5A VTOL tactical research aircraft to the Vought XC-142 tilt-wing transport, the Bell X-22A VTOL research aircraft, and such STOL airplanes as the de Havilland Buffalo, the Fiat G.222, and the Shin Meiwa Boundary Layer Control flying boat. The XV-5A used the discharge from twin GE J85 turbojets to turn large fans in each wing and lift this fixed-wing aircraft off the ground vertically. After takeoff, engine thrust was rotated to the rear by a diverter valve for conventional jet flight.

One military aircraft has successfully—even dramatically—demonstrated the tactical advantages of VTOL aircraft in addition to their excellent maneuverability: the British Aerospace Harrier in service with the British Royal Air Force and the U.S. Marine Corps as the AV-8B. The exhaust nozzles of the Harrier's Rolls-Royce Pegasus engine are vectored down for vertical takeoff or landing and for conventional flight swiveled to the rear. The nozzles can even be rotated forward to act as brakes during maneuvers and actually to "back up" the aircraft while hovering.

After decades of V/STOL engine development and experimentation with alternate airframe approaches to vertical lift, Bell Helicopter, the National Aeronautics and Space Administration (NASA), and the U.S. Army successfully demonstrated a tilt-rotor aircraft that provides the efficient vertical lift and hover characteristics of the helicopter—in combination with the cruise and range capabilities of fixed-wing aircraft. The capability demonstrated by the XV-15 craft will be incorporated into the Joint Services Vertical Lift aircraft (JVX) now under development for a full range of military missions in the near future. Initial versions of the JVX, powered by T64 engines, use the full range of V/STOL engine features, including high power-to-weight ratios and multiattitude capability.

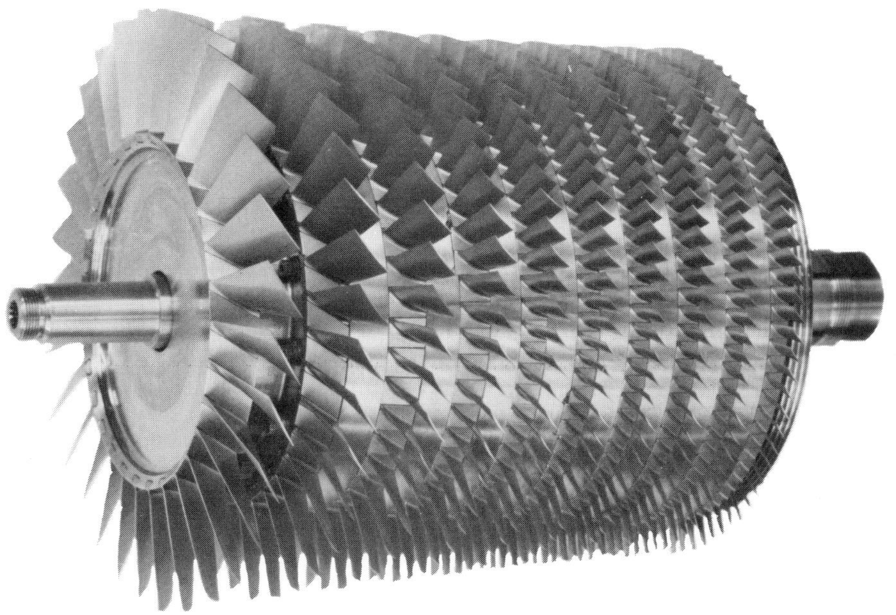

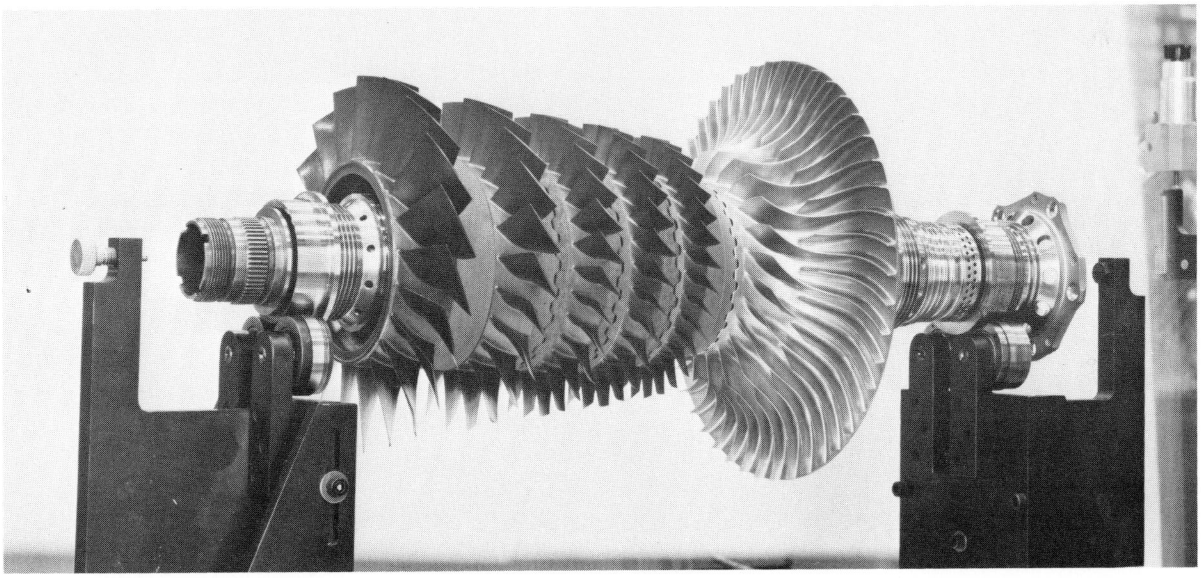

Figure 15.
Compressor comparison: T58 versus T700

Designed specifically for vertical operation, the T64 was in operation for more than 5,000 flight hours in the Vought Tri-Service tilt-wing XC-142 V/STOL aircraft during the late 1960s. The thirty-eight-engine, five-aircraft program demonstrated the suitability of the T64 for multimode operation, including conventional flight, transition to vertical operation, and full vertical operation.

Despite extensive design and development efforts with V/STOL conventional-wing aircraft during the past several decades, the helicopter remains the most successful, reliable, and durable pure vertical takeoff aircraft and is capable of meeting a wide range of requirements in civil and military aviation.

Figure 16.
General Electric GE27 Modern Technology Demonstrator Engine mockup

The Future of Turboshaft Power

Turboshaft engine power for helicopters has evolved through three generations. With the rapid advancement of aircraft gas turbine power during the past thirty years, these three generations have been roughly a decade apart. General Electric's T58 is representative of the first generation, the T64 of the second, and the T700 of the third.

The trend in turboshaft technology has been, and will continue to be during the immediate future, toward higher engine compressor pressure ratios (the ratio of compression of air within the engine to air entering the inlet) and higher turbine temperatures, to achieve even greater engine efficiency. This efficiency is being realized by progressive increases in engine temperatures made possible by advances in metallurgy and manufacturing that are matched by the ability of engine designers to increase the compression of air substantially as it moves through the engine. The result is more powerful, yet more efficient, engines.

Continuing technological advances provide new materials and new manufacturing techniques. These advances permit higher parts-stress levels and higher loading for each compressor stage, enabling designers to achieve higher pressure ratios with even fewer compressor stages (see figure 15). The five-stage axial, one-stage centrifugal, T700 compressor, for example, contains only 130 airfoils yet achieves a pressure ratio of 17 to 1. The earlier ten-stage T58 compressor contains 634 airfoils and achieves a pressure ratio of 8 to 1.

New materials and manufacturing techniques enable designers of turbines to achieve higher turbine temperatures, which increase engine power without increasing size or weight. Turbine inlet temperature in the third-generation T700 engine is 2,300° Fahrenheit; in the first generation T58, it was 1,800° Fahrenheit, yet comparable engine components are smaller, simpler, and lighter in weight.

Through the years, designers and producers of engines have striven for maximum power output with minimum fuel consumption. This was evident in General Electric's first- and second-generation turboshaft engines, the T58 and T64. In the design of

General Electric's third-generation T700 engine, however, in an effort to meet the customer's needs equal emphasis was placed on maintainability, reliability, and life-cycle cost. As a result, the T700 today operates with 75 percent less maintenance and 30 percent lower fuel consumption than earlier-generation engines, and is four times as reliable.

For fourth-generation engines, designers anticipate compressor pressure ratios beyond 20 to 1, to be achieved with still fewer compressor stages. This advanced development in technology, ironically, will also reduce the total number of engine parts. A second-generation turboshaft engine, for example, had more than 10,000 parts. The T700 has fewer than 5,000. The next generation may have fewer than 4,000 parts. With each significant reduction in the number of parts the costs of both maintenance and original procurement are reduced. With greater internal efficiency, engine operating costs will also be reduced.

To put the matter simply, fourth-generation helicopter engines should be more efficient, have a higher power-to-weight ratio, be simpler, and cost less to maintain, and throughout the service life of the engine, the total life-cycle cost of the turboshaft should be reduced. As is true of other articles, such as calculators, computers, watches, radios, and word processors, that embody advanced modern technology, the result of each forward step in helicopter power is lower cost per shaft-horsepower output throughout the life cycle.

In the United States, the Department of Defense early in 1983 established requirements for a Modern Technology Demonstrator Engine (MTDE). This demonstrator engine program is expected to last nearly four years. Its objective is a turboshaft-turboprop engine in the 5,000-shp class, a horsepower-to-weight ratio of 6.5, and 15 to 30 percent better specific fuel consumption than existing engines. At General Electric the engine proposed for MTDE is designated the GE27 (see figure 16). It is a fourth-generation engine that offers a careful balance of high performance, low weight, high reliability, low maintenance, and low acquisition costs. These MTDE characteristics combine to provide power-plant criteria for turboshaft-turboprop engines through the balance of this century and well into the next.

The Power to Lift Straight Up

Like aviation itself, the evolution of helicopters—and the power plants required to lift payloads straight up, cover short, medium, or even long distances, hover over a selected spot, and return safely—have made incredible strides in less than eighty years since the rudimentary attempts of the early twentieth century.

For Leonardo, Cayley, Breguet, and de Bothezat—and even Focke, Flettner, Kaman, and Sikorsky—power to lift a helicopter off the ground with a profitable payload was a limiting factor. The gas turbine, in the form of the turboshaft engine, eliminated that impediment. With turboshaft power the helicopter—civil or military—now performs useful work at a reasonable cost.

In little more than three quarters of a century man has achieved a centuries-old dream.

William J. Crawford III was graduated from the Massachusetts Institute of Technology with the B.S. degree in mechanical engineering. He holds the M.A. degree in automotive engineering from Chrysler Institute and is an Honorary Fellow of the American Helicopter Society. Mr. Crawford is vice president and general manager of the Engine Projects Division of General Electric's Aircraft Engine Business Group. He has overall product responsibility for the majority of GE's small military and commercial aircraft production engines. Mr. Crawford is widely recognized for his leadership of GE's turboshaft and turboprop projects during most of the last decade. He directed the highly successful development of the 1,700-shaft-horsepower-class T700 family, which is in full-scale production for advanced military and commercial helicopters. Mr. Crawford's earlier experience at General Electric includes full responsibility for small-engine testing, facilities, and instrumentation; development and flight test; airframe-engine installation compatibility; and domestic and overseas applications of configuration management.

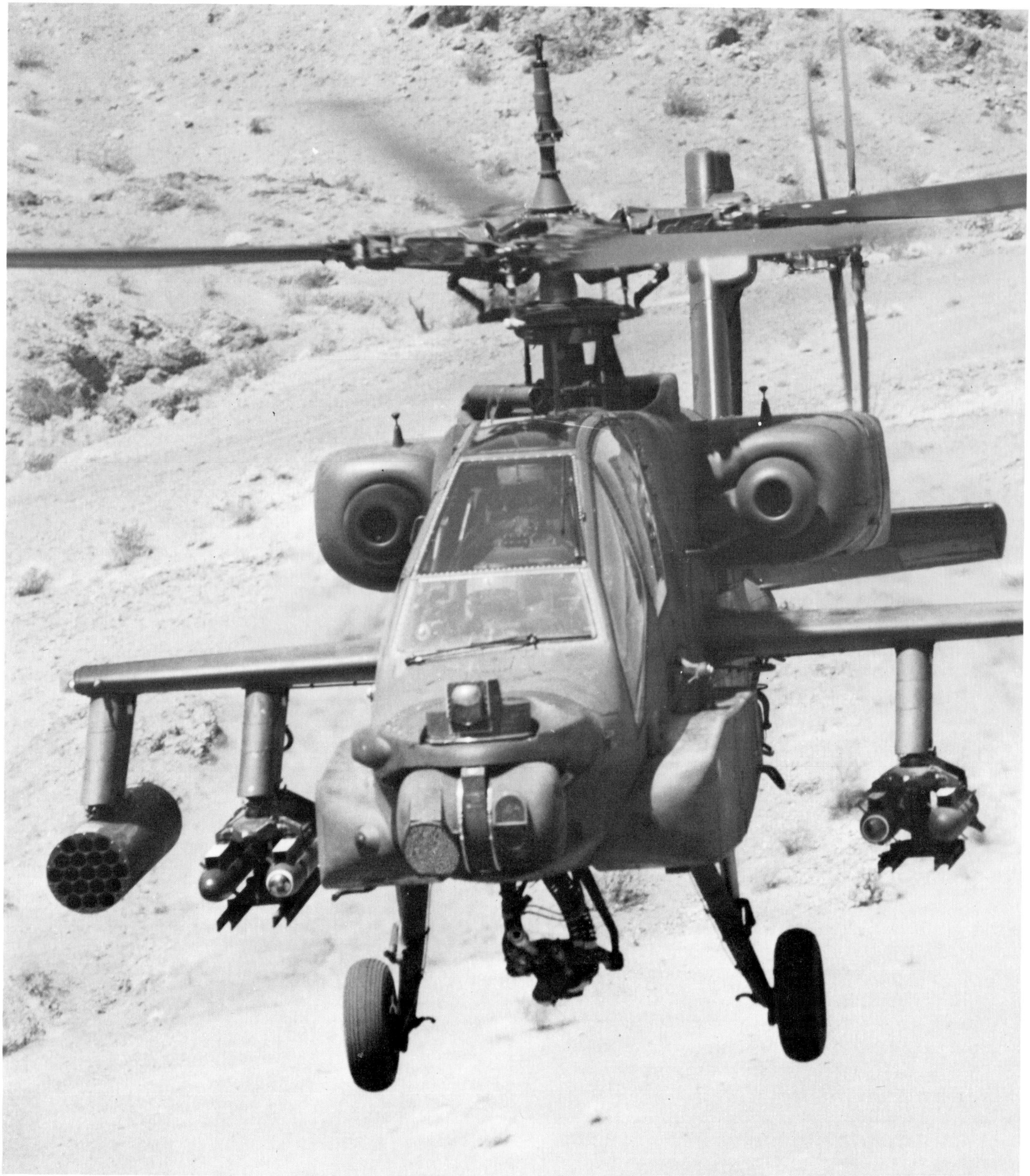

R. W. PROUTY

Attack Helicopters

It was not long after helicopters began to be shot at in combat that aviators started to improvise defensive shoot-back-to-keep-their-heads-down capabilities. This was first done with hand-held weapons, but normal evolution brought the development of weapons that the pilot could fire by aiming the helicopter. The French began this development in their battles with Algerian rebels in the 1950s.

Once the defensive capability had been provided, it was only logical to see the possibilities of using these wonderfully maneuverable aircraft for supporting ground forces, for escorting troop helicopters, and for independent attack missions—first with helicopters that had been designed for other purposes, later with helicopters whose narrow, streamlined fuselage configuration clearly identified them as attack helicopters. This is not to say that attack versions of wide-body helicopters have not been developed and used, only that they are not the subject of this discussion.

Modifications

In the United States, the development of the attack helicopter has had two purposes, one for escort and for soft-target suppression, as in jungle warfare in Southeast Asia, the other to establish the capability to find and to destroy heavy armor such as tanks, for which the most likely theater of operation was Europe. The first purpose was satisfied by quickly modifying existing helicopters into suitable attack configurations; the second is being met by developing entirely new helicopters with advanced characteristics.

Figure 1.
The Bell Sioux Scout, the forerunner of narrow-bodied attack helicopters

The Sioux Scout. The first example of a helicopter modified for an attack mission was the Bell Sioux Scout, a redesigned Model 47 with a 260-hp piston engine (see figure 1).

The Scout was built as a test bed to study a need then beginning to be recognized in Vietnam. For this helicopter, first flown in 1963, several innovations were developed that became standard features on many subsequent attack helicopters. A two-man crew sat in tandem in a narrow fuselage, each man thus having the best possible field of view. The copilot-gunner was in front and the pilot behind and above him. A movable turret-mounted machine gun was mounted in the nose. The copilot-gunner aimed the gun through a turret control by means of a telescopic sight. The gunner's turret control was located where a cyclic stick would normally be, but since he was sometimes expected to serve as copilot, he was given a short cyclic stick located to his right as a side-arm controller. By using a twisting motion of the hand, he could also use this as a directional control. This eliminated the need for rudder pedals, but pilots had trouble controlling direction precisely with this system, which has not since been used by Bell Helicopters.

The Cobra. With the Sioux Scout experience behind them, Bell embarked on a similar program as a private venture by modifying their much more powerful UH-1B, nicknamed the "Huey." The heart of the helicopter—the rotors, the engine, and the drive system—was saved, and a thin fuselage was designed around it. The design work was begun in early 1965 and the first flight was made the following September.

The original speed goal was 175 knots. To achieve this, the first prototype was built with a retractable skid landing gear (see figure 2). On later versions, however, the standard fixed skid gear of the Huey was used. This decision was made because although the retractable gear had less drag than the fixed gear and did increase airspeed, the offsetting weight-to-performance penalty was too great. An additional drag-reduction feature was the elimination of the rotor-mounted stabilizer bar that had been a feature of all previous Bell designs. Instead, a stability and control augmentation system (SCAS), consisting of a "black box" with gyros and solid-state electronics, was used to achieve even better handling qualities.

The right aircraft at the right time, it was ordered into production the following year as the AH-1—the attack version of the UH-

Figure 2.
The prototype of the Bell Huey Cobra, which had retracting landing gear and was the first Bell helicopter to dispense with rotor-mounted stabilizer bar

1, or Huey Cobra. The U.S. Army ordered a total of 529 the first year, and by August 1967 the AH-1G Cobra was in action in Vietnam (see figure 3).

The U.S. Marine Corps procured and used a few AH-1Gs, but as an army aircraft it lacked two important features for amphibious operations: twin-engine reliability for operation over water and a rotor brake to keep the rotor from windmilling when tied down to the deck of a ship. These deficiencies were remedied in the AH-1J Sea Cobra with 1,290-hp Pratt & Whitney T400 twinpac engines and with a rotor brake (see figure 4). The marines began taking delivery of this design in 1969.

During the early 1970s, Bell built two testbed Model 309 King Cobras—one single-engine Cobra and one twin-engine Cobra—for increased payload and higher performance. The King Cobra was evaluated by both the army and the marines and became the forerunner of the Marine AH-1T.

Figure 3.
The AH-1G Cobra, which saw action in Vietnam

Figure 4.
The Bell AH-1J, a twin-engine Cobra built for the marines

Throughout the 1970s, improved armament and systems were developed and incorporated by modification of existing models and creation of new production Cobra models, such as:

Model	*Armament or system*
AH-1Q	Tube-launched, optically tracked, wire-guided (TOW) missile system
AH-1S Mod	TOW missile system
AH-1S Production	Flat glass canopy
AH-1T	20-millimeter turret
AH-1S ECAS	20-millimeter turret and rocket-management system
AH-1S Modernized	Fire-control computer, airborne laser tracker, laser range finder, air data system, and doppler navigation
AH-1T TOW	TOW missile system

Figure 5.
The AH-1T twin-engine Cobra firing wire-guided antitank missiles

The modern Cobra can carry up to 3,303 pounds of expendable armament distributed between guided antiarmor missiles, unguided rockets, and ammunition for either a 20-millimeter cannon or a 7.62-millimeter (.30 caliber) machine gun. The power plant of the latest single-engine version, the AH-1S, is a ship-rated 1,290-hp Lycoming T53-L-703 turboshaft engine. The twin-engine AH-1T has a twin-pac Pratt & Whitney T400-WV-402 with a total of 1,970 hp (see figure 5).

Since the beginning of production, more than 1,800 Cobras have been built; as a result of continual improvements, both the aforementioned distinct single- and twin-engine models are available. They are now in operation, not only by the U.S. Army, the Marine Corps, and the National Guard but also by military organizations in Greece, Israel, Japan, and Spain.

Improvements in the performance, armament, systems, pilot workload, and power of the Cobra are continually being tested and developed today. A few of these are the cockpit missile control system, AH-1J Hellfire missile, AH-1T/700 with ship-rated 2,032 hp, AH-1T Hellfire, and Sidewinder missile system.

The First Blackhawk

The obvious need for attack helicopters during the Vietnam conflict encouraged Sikorsky to try to duplicate the Bell Huey Cobra program by modifying an existing cargo helicopter. For a prototype, Sikorsky Aircraft combined the rotors and drive system of their S-61 with an airframe consisting of a new fuselage and a generous wing to help the rotor in maneuvers and to carry external stores. The wing included dive brakes, which could be used to decelerate quickly or to assist in going into autorotation at high speed. Power was supplied by two General Electric T-58 turboshaft engines rated at 1,500 hp. The fuselage, while narrower than that of the S-61, could still carry eight fully equipped soldiers. The resultant design was designated the S-67 Blackhawk (see figure

6). Design work was begun in August 1969 and the first flight was made just a year later. During the next four years the aircraft demonstrated its capabilities, in the process setting an official speed record of 192 knots. It was one of the first helicopters to do loops, rolls, and "split Ss" as part of routine flight demonstrations. Sikorsky obtained several government contracts to evaluate specific S-67 features, but customers were not attracted. The effort ended with the crash of the prototype in 1974. The program was over, but the name Blackhawk was saved for use on a later Sikorsky helicopter, the army's H-60 utility transport.

Figure 6.
The first Sikorsky Blackhawk, which used the dynamic components from the S-61

The Tank Busters

The year 1962 saw both the beginning of American involvement in Vietnam and the army's Howze Board report recommending that the army acquire more transport helicopters to increase troop mobility and that an attack helicopter be developed to provide close-in support and antitank capabilities. For the latter, the army staff recommended procuring an interim attack helicopter, such as the Bell Sioux Scout, based on an existing off-the-shelf design. The Secretary of the Army, however, rejected this approach and directed the staff to lift its sights to a more advanced system. Thus in 1964, a request for proposal was issued for an Advanced Aerial Fire Support System (AAFSS). Besides seeking out and destroying enemy tanks, it was expected to provide armed escort for the army's Boeing Vertol Chinooks, while making quick sorties from the line of flight, and to clear landing zones of opposition. To do this effectively, the aircraft required performance characteristics on the remote edge of the state of the art. A dash speed of 220 knots, which at that time had been achieved only by jet-assisted compound helicopters, was the most critical. A second requirement was for a hover ability out of ground effect at 6,000 feet at a temperature of 95° Fahrenheit, which was expected to cover the worst possible combinations of altitude and temperature that the aircraft would see in worldwide operation. The third requirement was for a ferry range of 2,100 nautical miles, which would allow the aircraft to fly from California to Hawaii—the longest overwater flight envisioned in a wartime situation.

A crew of two was to handle both the flying and the weapons, which consisted of TOW antitank missiles, a 30-millimeter fast-firing cannon with a wide field of fire, and a 40-millimeter grenade launcher that was to be interchangeable with a 7.62-millimeter machine gun. The army also specified that the aircraft should have only a single engine—a decision based on an evaluation of the trade-off between cost and safety at the time. The army saw the airframe as only part of the AAFSS. The service also had ambitious plans for large advances in fire control, navigation, communications, and even automatic terrain following.

The Cheyenne. The request went out to 148 organizations, 12 of which responded with preliminary designs. From these, two companies were chosen to continue with contracted design studies. One was Lockheed and the other Sikorsky, which had proposed a winged helicopter with a powerful tail rotor that could pivot 90 degrees to serve as a pusher propeller. The design studies took six months. Each company then made a proposal to develop its concept by building and testing ten developmental prototypes. Lockheed won, and the AH-56 Cheyenne program was officially under way in November 1965. Because of aerodynamic limits on helicopter rotors, the 220-knot speed goal was too high for a conventional helicopter, so the AH-56 was designed as a compound helicopter. This means simply that it was

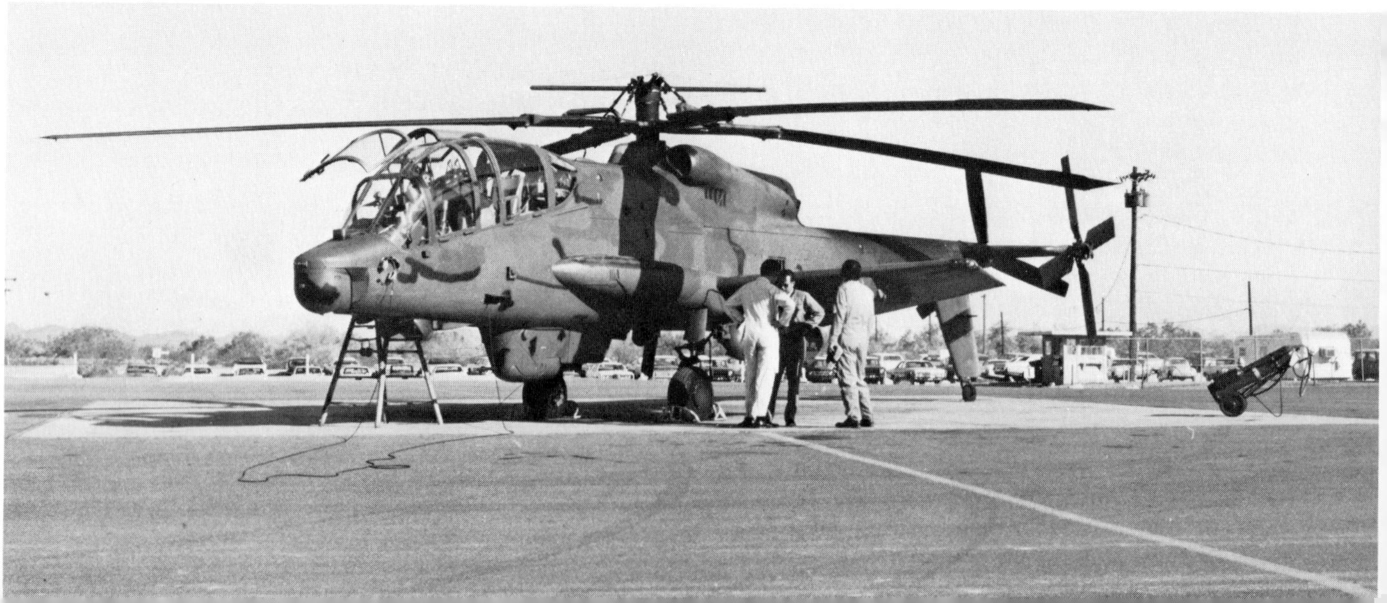

Figure 7.
The Lockheed Cheyenne being prepared for a test flight

an airplane with a wing and propeller to which an effective lifting device—the rotor—had been added for flight at hover and low speeds. At high speed, the wing and propeller provided the necessary lift and propulsion force, and the main rotor, essentially excused from its function in performance, was used in conjunction with the tail rotor to provide pitch, roll, and yaw control and to replace the elevator, aileron, and rudder found on conventional airplanes (see figure 7).

Lockheed had entered the helicopter field only a few years before, with a radical concept involving the combination of a hingeless rotor and a rotor-mounted control gyro, which gave excellent flying qualitites on two small helicopter designs. It was primarily this radical concept that attracted the attention of the AAFSS Source Selection Board of the army. On the Cheyenne, however, two years of flight tests showed that the rotor-mounted control gyro, while working well on small helicopters, could not be used satisfactorily on this larger machine. The technical problems were eventually solved by moving the gyro to an interior location. With this change, the Cheyenne demonstrated level flight to 215 knots, a dive speed of 245 knots, and high-speed maneuvers, including pull-ups to 2.6 g's and push-overs to −0.2 g's. By November 1970 a successful flight test had been completed, but in the meantime political, financial, and military considerations had combined to create an unhealthy climate for the Cheyenne. At the same time, for various reasons, the army was already contemplating a new set of requirements for a helicopter to undertake its attack mission.

The most dramatic change was a new concept of the role of the attack helicopter in combat. On the basis of its experience in Vietnam, the service decided that high speed was not essential. For this reason, the 145-knot cruise-speed capability of a conventional helicopter was deemed sufficient and became the new cruise-speed requirement. Also, since the ability to survive combat was now a primary consideration, the doctrine

Figure 8.
The AH-56 lining up to fire rockets at a target at the Yuma Proving Grounds in Arizona

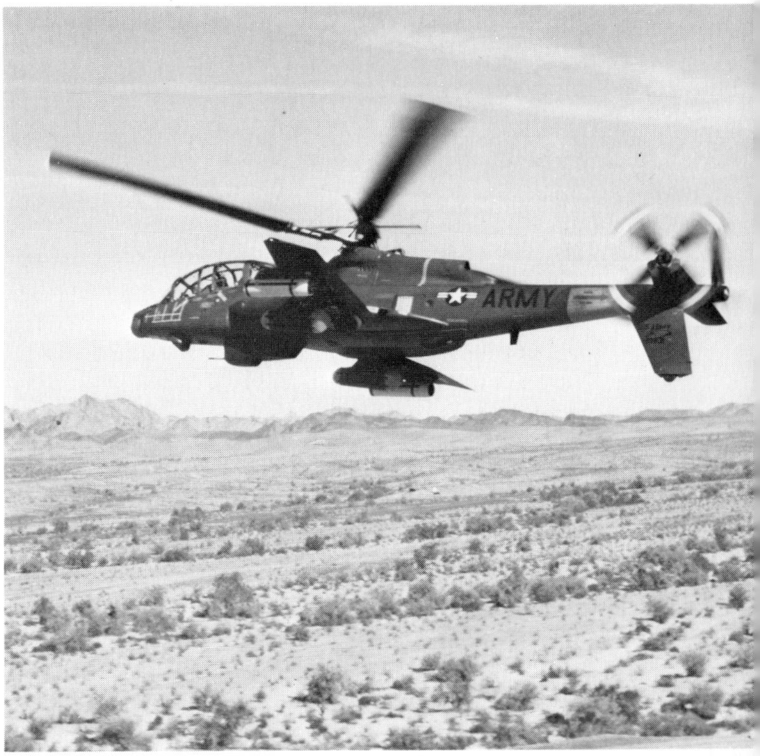

that two engines were better than one was accepted.

When Lockheed heard of the new ground rules, it proposed a propellerless Cheyenne—but it was too late. The army had decided to start from scratch with the Advanced Attack Helicopter (AAH). The competition began in 1973, and although Lockheed submitted a proposal, the two development contracts went to Bell and to Hughes.

The remaining Cheyennes were either scrapped or sent to museums. One is on display at the Army Transportation Museum of Fort Eustis, Virginia, and another is at the Army Aviation Museum at Fort Rucker, Alabama.

The Apache. The Hughes AH-64 and the Bell AH-63 were designed to meet the army's requirements for its AAH. The primary mission of the AAH was to find and destroy tanks by means of as many as sixteen guided

Figure 9.
The AH-63, Bell's entry into the army's Advanced Attack Helicopter competition

missiles. Neither bad weather nor darkness was to detract from the mission capability. In addition to its complement of guided missiles, the AAH was to have a turret-mounted rapid-fire 30-millimeter cannon for targets less well armored than tanks and the ability to carry up to seventy-six 2.75-inch folding-fin unguided rockets (see figure 8). A limitation on the size of the AAH was that two of them were to be transportable in a C-141 with a nine-foot ceiling in its cargo compartment.

Three performance goals represented a relaxation from those for which the Cheyenne had been designed: a cruise speed of 145 knots instead of a dash speed of 220; a hot-day hover altitude of 4,000 feet instead of 6,000, although a power margin for vertical climb was also required for the AAH; and a ferry range of 800 nautical miles instead of 2,100.

On the other hand, the potential for survival in combat was to be improved with two engines instead of one, with all components designed in such a way that minimum damage would be done by a 23-millimeter shell and no single 12.7-millimeter (50-caliber) round could cause enough damage to prevent continued safe flying. In the case of a crash, the crew was to be able to survive a vertical impact of forty-two feet per second, or twenty-nine miles an hour.

While both of the candidate helicopters were designed to meet the same requirements, their physical appearance, reflecting the design philosophies of Bell and Hughes at the time, was quite different. Bell used two-blade main and tail rotors as they had on the Huey series (see figure 9) while Hughes put four blades on each. Bell used a tricycle landing gear with a nose wheel, while the Hughes design had a tail wheel. Bell mounted the machine-gun turret in the nose with the sight on the belly while Hughes reversed the placement. In each aircraft the crew was seated in tandem, but Bell chose to put the pilot in the front seat instead of the rear as they had in their Huey Cobras and as their Hughes competitor had.

A significant difference that could not be determined by looking at the two designs was the approach to the development—and later to the production. Bell relied on their own extensive manufacturing experience and capability to make most of the components themselves. Hughes, on the other hand, chose to do the preliminary design of the components but to team with firms of proven expertise in the various fields for the necessary development testing and building. In the process, Hughes acted as the responsible integrator of systems and the assembler.

Each company built a ground test vehicle

(GTV) for testing the drive and control systems and two flight-test aircraft. The first Bell flight ship was lost in a landing accident, so the ground-test vehicle was converted to take its place.

The army accepted all four flight prototypes and tested them extensively for four months at its test site at Edwards Air Force Base in the California desert. In December 1976, the army declared the Hughes AH-64 to be the winner. Even as a loser, the Bell AH-63 served a useful purpose. One was used in a controlled crash test to demonstrate that helicopter designers could indeed make a crash at forty-two feet per second survivable.

As the winner, the AH-64 was ordered into phase two, in which three more test aircraft were built for development of the airframe and its associated systems. At this time the army changed the primary weapon from the wire-guided TOW missile to the laser-guided Hellfire. The goal of the phase two development contract was to integrate all the necessary systems into the helicopter before ordering it into production. The AH-64 airframe was nearly in its final form except for some details that were changed as problems came to light in flight tests. Two changes, obvious to even casual observers, were made: the main rotor blade tips were swept back and the horizontal stabilizer was changed from a fixed surface on top of the fin to a movable surface at the bottom. The first change was prompted by higher-than-anticipated blade loads at high speed caused by operation of the advancing tip at high Mach numbers. Sweeping the tip relieved this aerodynamic problem just as sweeping the wings on a jet aircraft allows it to fly faster.

Figure 10.
Flight test of the AH-64 showed that the "T-Tail" produced problems in flying qualities and dynamics.

Figure 11.
Replacing the T-Tail with this movable "stabilizer" was a successful fix.

The horizontal stabilizer was changed from a T-Tail to a stabilator configuration to minimize an unfavorable interference between the main rotor downwash and the surface, which had been causing high dynamic loads in forward flight (see figures 10 and 11).

A bigger task than modifying the airframe was the integration of the sophisti-

Figure 12.
The Hughes Apache with rockets, guided missiles, and a 30-millimeter gun

cated avionic systems for fire control, navigation, night vision, and communications. As in many modern military aircraft, the investment in these systems is considerably more than in the basic airframe that carries them to where they are to be used.

Of these systems, by far the most sophisticated is that which provides "visionics." It is contained in the nose turret and consists of two primary assemblies: The target acquisition and designation sight (TADS) and the pilot's night vision sensor (PNVS). The TADS is used to find the target at any degree of visibility. To do this, it has an array of sensors that includes direct-view optics, forward-looking infrared (FLIR), and television with zoom capability. In addition, the TADS includes the laser equipment for range finding and for illuminating a target for the laser-seeking Hellfire missile.

The PNVS turret is mounted on the top of the TADS turret but can move with complete independence. It contains a FLIR system that can project on a tiny television screen attached to the pilot's helmet (see figure 12). As the pilot turns his head, he can make the PNVS turret look in the same direction he is looking. By sensing very small differences in temperature of objects in its field of view and translating these differences to images on the television screen, the PNVS system makes nap-of-the-earth flight possible on the darkest night as well as during the brightest day. The helmet-mounted sight can also be used to aim the 30-millimeter gun automatically in any direction in which the pilot can see.

The TADS-PNVS is built by Martin Marietta and is supplied to Hughes for installation on the AH-64 as government-furnished equipment. The selection of Martin Marietta was the result of a separate army competition entered by several electronically competent organizations. Of all those that submitted proposals the army chose

Northrop and Martin Marietta to build prototypes, which were then tested in a fly-off on the AH-64.

Another important government-furnished system is the General Electric T700-GE-701 turboshaft engine, of which two are used. Each is rated at 1,510 hp for continuous running, 1,694 hp for thirty minutes, and 1,723 hp for two and a half minutes. The last is an automatic contingency rating, which is used only after the failure of one engine, to permit the other to shoulder the load.

During the phase two program, extensive tests of the helicopter and of all the systems using the GTV and the five flight aircraft were made. Both Hughes and army pilots and engineers participated in these tests, which included many hours of high-power running on the drive system, blade-deicing tests in the middle of a Minnesota winter, air-conditioning tests in the middle of an Arizona summer, live firing of all the weapons, night and bad-weather flying, and two months of remote base operation with maintenance done exclusively by army personnel.

The Apache can carry 3,327 pounds of expendable armament in various combinations of Hellfire laser-guided missiles, 2.75-inch folding-fin rockets, or 30-millimeter gun ammunition. It can dive to nearly 200 knots and do maneuvers from 3.5 g's up to −0.5 g's down.

Fulfillment of the phase two development contract in 1982 led to the award of a production contract for eleven helicopters in the first year's purchase. At that time the helicopter was given its Indian name, the Apache. To produce these and subsequent aircraft efficiently, the army and Hughes agreed that a new factory was needed, since the Culver City plant was busy making the Model 500 civil helicopters and did not have enough extra capacity to set up a modern assembly line for the Apache. A site at Mesa, a suburb of Phoenix, Arizona, was chosen and a new plant was built. The first production airframe structure was delivered by Ryan Teledyne, its builder, in March 1983, and the first flight was made the following January. For the second year of production, 48 aircraft have been authorized, for the third year 112. The army plans to procure a minimum of 515 aircraft. If we are lucky, none of these will ever fire a shot in anger.

Figure 13.
The Russian Mil Mi-24A Hind

The Hind. If the Apache is ever used, it might find itself in competition or even in direct combat with the Russian Mil Hind in its D or E variation (see figure 13). This helicopter went into operation as an assault aircraft in about 1980 and has seen extensive use in Afghanistan. It is a relatively large helicopter weighing about 22,000 pounds. One reason for this size is that it is configured to carry eight to ten fully equipped soldiers in addition to its armament. It is technically advanced, with five fiberglass main rotor blades and a retractable landing gear.

RAY PROUTY has worked as a helicopter aerodynamicist since 1952 at several American helicopter companies, including Sikorsky, Bell, Lockheed, and Hughes. Besides his technical interests, he has always been fascinated with the history of rotary-wing aircraft, and he has written several magazine articles on the subject. He served as the first chairman of the Historical Committee of the American Helicopter Society.

SE 3160
N°001
F-ZWVQ

CHARLES MARCHETTI

Helicopter Development in Europe, 1940–80

TRANSLATED FROM THE FRENCH BY JACK LOWELL NIXON

Before going into the matter of the development and rise of helicopters after 1940, it is well to remember that before World War II, certain European pioneers had already made important contributions to the budding technique of rotary-wing aircraft. In 1907 two Frenchmen, Louis Breguet and Paul Cornu, built the first prototypes. Later, other researchers constructed and tested helicopters with rotor configurations ranging from single rotors to multirotors, including lateral, coaxial, and tandem rotors. Of all these experimental helicopters, the following made history:

- A one-kilometer flight on a closed-circuit course, made by Oemichen in France, in 1924.
- Flights varying in altitude from 158 meters to 3,427 meters, made by Breguet-Dorand in France in 1936 and by Focke-Achgelis in Germany in 1939.
- Flights at speeds higher than 100 kilometers an hour, made by Breguet-Dorand in France in 1936, by Focke-Wulf in Germany in 1937, and by Weir Limited in England in 1939.

Rotary-wing technology was thus well established in Europe. Nevertheless, considering the difficulties encountered with helicopter prototypes, French and English manufacturers preferred a simpler aircraft, the Cierva autogiro, which had already made more significant progress and which they now mass-produced.

In 1939, when war was declared, Germany expanded its helicopter studies. In 1940, however, the war put a stop to the research in occupied countries. Aside from a few limited studies, England likewise abandoned helicopters to give priority to the production of airplanes.

Following this brief historical review, the period 1940–80 can be dealt with by dividing it into five subperiods, as follows:

1940–45—German helicopters
1945–52—The first postwar flights
1952–59—A good start
1959–68—European advances
1968–80—Modernization

German Helicopters, 1940–45

In northern Germany in 1940 the Focke-Achgelis Company, founded in 1937, had two types of helicopters: the Fa 61 and the Fa 266. Both were equipped with two lateral rotors. The first was a single-seat aircraft that had already made numerous flights. The second, designed for transporting several persons or cargo of equivalent weight over distances of 200 to 400 kilometers, was undergoing ground tests.

As soon as the war began, the Focke-Achgelis company was charged with adapting its Fa 266 prototype to military needs. Without delay two prototypes, designated Fa 223, were constructed and were tested between

1940 and 1942. These aircraft, each having a total weight of 4,300 kilograms, were equipped with Bramo engines of about 1,000 hp and had dual-control cockpits in front with good visibility. As soon as possible they were tried out for military use, flying over the various regions of Germany and being tested in the French Alps. Twenty aircraft were constructed, and mass production of 400 aircraft was planned in 1944. Bombing by the Allies destroyed most of the factories, and, at the same time, the efforts of the Focke-Achgelis Company.

At the end of the war, only three aircraft remained, two of which were salvaged by the Allies. One of these was flown across the channel to England.

Throughout this period, the technicians were continually rushed and did not always have sufficient time for the careful fine-tuning of the designs of aircraft already scheduled for mass production. In the final analysis, the technical and industrial development that had been planned never took place.

Credit is due the Focke team for some outstanding unconfirmed performances—a climb to 7,782 meters, a flight of more than three hours' duration, a speed of 200 kilometers an hour—and especially for having accumulated some significant theoretical data that were gradually refined through tests of all kinds.

Figure 1.
The Flettner Fl 282

During this same period, the Focke-Achgelis company undertook many other projects, including the surveillance autogiro Fa 330, designed to be towed by submarine. This small aircraft was remarkable in its simplicity, but its usefulness remained limited.

Among the other concepts that were under study were a lateral two-rotor flying crane of high gross weight and a convertible aircraft with forward-tilting rotors.

While the Focke-Achgelis team was improving helicopter technology in Germany, other German engineers, led by Anton Flettner in Berlin, were designing aircraft with meshed rotors, the two most successful of which were the Fl 265 and the Fl 282 (see figure 1). The German navy experimented with them and gave its approval to construction of twenty-four models of the Fl 282 two-seat aircraft in prototype series, followed by mass production of 1,000 models.

After this success, the Flettner team was given instructions to develop more powerful aircraft capable of transporting more than twenty fully equipped soldiers. Neither the production of the Fl 282 nor of this new aircraft could be carried out before the war ended.

During this period, helicopter construction was also going on in Austria, which had been annexed by Germany. In Vienna, the Wiener Neustadt aeronautics factory had authorized an engineer named Doblhoff and his team to construct a light helicopter driven by blade-tip jet propulsion. The first prototype, WN 342, made its first flight at the end of 1943 (see figure 2). The results encouraged the team to construct improved, more powerful prototypes. The originality of the design lay in its elimination of transmission mechanisms and the antitorque rotor, which was not needed. The ending of the war halted tests on the fourth and last prototype, the first tests of which as a helicopter seemed promising; they might have been even more promising had the craft been given the form

Figure 2.
The Doblhoff WN 342, the first helicopter to be powered by rotor-blade tip-jets

of a combined helicopter and autogiro, as had been planned from the beginning.

Doblhoff deserves credit for having been the originator of this jet propulsion design, which subsequently aroused the enthusiasm of numerous inventors.

In the spring of 1945, the cessation of hostilities brought great upheavals in Europe. Studies, construction, and tests came to an end in Germany and Austria, while in countries such as France and England work on autogiros and, in a few instances, helicopter plans was resumed. The technicians of Focke, Flettner, and Doblhoff were disbanded, and, like their aircraft, were for the most part taken over by the Allies—England, France, and the United States.

Without doubt, the teams in Germany, supported by military authorities, had advanced the design of helicopters. Their Fa 223 and Fl 282 aircraft were the first European aircraft to be put out in prototype series. Only the ending of the war had halted their mass production. For the same reason, construction of planned new prototypes, on which studies were already well advanced, was stopped as well.

The First Postwar Flights, 1945–52

This period can be divided into three more or less concurrent phases:

- Evaluation of German technique,
- The search for a national solution, and
- Taking American expansion into account.

Evaluation of the German Technique

In France, la Société Nationale de Construction Aéronautique du Sud-Est (SNCASE) opened its doors to Focke and some of his engineers—a total of twelve persons. The company was given instructions to modify and improve the Focke-Achgelis Fa 223 design, in anticipation of potential large-scale production. The redesigned aircraft was called the SE 3000 (see figure 3). At the same time, the technicians were ordered to construct a flying one-seat scale

Figure 3.
The SE 3000, a redesigned Fa 223

model equipped with a French Mathis 100-hp engine, an Fa 61 rotor of German origin, and two small rotors located on a V-shaped tail unit.

The small SE 3101 helicopter, flown in June 1948, was the first helicopter to be flown in France after the end of the war. The SE 3000 aircraft was not flown until October 1948. At the time of both the ground tests and the in-flight tests, adjustments were difficult to make. Breakdowns and mishaps occurred incessantly, and the improvements made were not sufficient to avoid further problems.

The SE 3000 lateral two-rotor design led to satisfactory forward flight without too much instability or vibration. On the other hand, during hovering and approach or forward flight near the ground the instability of the aircraft became obvious. A complete autorotation landing was achieved, but it did not satisfy the pilot. In view of the scant good results achieved after long months of effort, the company withdrew its financial support after the official acceptance of the third aircraft.

As for the small SE 3101 aircraft, it suffered from insufficient engine power (see figure 4). After some reduction in weight, it was flown by test pilot Jean Boulet in several flights that showed the existence of problems in stability and control. In spite of the technicians' tireless efforts, the problems could not be corrected satisfactorily. Work on the aircraft was therefore stopped in 1950 after twenty hours of flight time. By that date, the Focke team had been gone from France for three years.

During the same period, la Société Nationale de Construction Aéronautique du Sud-Ouest (SNCASO) became interested in the Doblhoff technique. The engineers quickly designed and constructed three prototypes having blades equipped with burners, the Ariel I and II, with piston engines, and the Ariel III, with a turbine, which made their first flights in 1949, 1950, and 1951, respectively. Because of the difficulty of adjusting the burners in continuous operation and the high rate of fuel consumption, the team of technicians then turned toward the construction of a combination aircraft with turbines, named Farfadet, which was capable of taking off in helicopter fashion and flying forward as an autogiro. Following an initial flight in 1953, helicopter-autogiro transitions were undertaken and continued without serious problems. Tests on the whole seemed promising, until several turbine problems developed. These mishaps were particularly ill-timed, inasmuch as necessary financing for going ahead with the work became unavailable. Work on the Farfadet aircraft was then stopped.

England also took an interest in German achievements. At the end of the war, the Focke-Achgelis Fa 223 helicopter that had crossed the Channel was transported to Farnborough. Tests were begun immediately, but they stopped abruptly, when the aircraft was destroyed during a takeoff following a technical failure.

Some time later, in 1950, the Fairey Aviation Company decided to study the Doblhoff technique for blade-end jet-propulsion helicopters. The company built a small, light, two-seat, turbine aircraft, the Fairey Ultralight, which was equipped with rudimentary blades having burners at their ends. This aircraft was designed for use by the British army in liaison and observation work. Following a number of modifications, relating in particular to the overhead control stick, several successful demonstrations were made. Despite these results, the authorities stopped its development in favor of the light, engine-powered helicopter named Skeeter, which had been developed by the Cierva Autogiro Company.

After all this testing of designs conceived during World War II, it seemed clear to both the English and the French that such designs could not be developed satisfactorily, to say nothing of their practicality.

The Search for a National Solution

Beginning in 1945, French and English government officials had fortunately decided to promote new helicopter concepts. Thus it was that the French government allocated funds to the principal aeronautical companies to design and build rotary-wing aircraft.

- The Société Nationale de Construction Aéronautique du Centre (SNCAC) planned three NC 2001 prototypes with two two-blade meshed rotors, the performances of which were supposed to surpass those of all existing aircraft of the period.

Figure 4.
The SE 3101, the first helicopter to fly in France after the end of World War II

- The Breguet Company launched into the construction of a helicopter with two three-blade coaxial rotors, the Breguet model III.
- The Société Nationale de Construction Aéronautique du Nord (SNCAN) produced two small aircraft, the N 1700 and N 1710, each with a single two-blade rotor, the hub of which was mounted on a pivoting frame so that cyclic pitch change of the rotor would not induce a pitch change in the fuselage. Antitorque was provided by an axial propeller blowing on movable flaps.
- SNCASE made its first light helicopter, the SE 3110, which was equipped with a three-blade rotor and a V-shaped double back rotor derived from the SE 3101 scale model.

Almost all these aircraft were flown during 1948, 1949, and 1950, but none could pass beyond the preliminary testing stage. They were all destroyed either on the ground or in flight near the ground. These results were disconcerting, to say the least. The SNCAC, Breguet, and SNCAN companies then decided to halt expenditures and abandon helicopters. The group of engineers from SNCAC left the company and continued helicopter research on their own, founding the Giravions Durand Company, which specialized in simulators and theoretical helicopter design studies. When the company

Figure 5.
The Girodyne, developed by the Fairey Aviation Company

took the risk of building an original two-blade aircraft, the wide blades of which were driven by low pressure from air blown by a double-flow turboreactor, it was unsuccessful, and the project was dropped in 1952.

After all this, only SNCASE and SNCASO remained competitive in 1950 to try, with limited design staff, to find more valid technical alternatives.

Development of prototypes in England went more or less the same way. The Cierva, Bristol, Westland, and Fairey companies decided it was necessary for them to go into helicopters.

- The Cierva company, well-known specialist in autogiros, quickly constructed three aircraft:

  The W 9—a light, single-rotor aircraft, the originality of which stemmed from its antitorque design, in which a mixture of exhaust gas and fresh air was ejected through the tail boom to obtain the desired lateral force. Its first flight was in mid 1946.

  The W 14—the Skeeter, a light, two-seat model that included a three-blade rotor and a small tail rotor placed high up on the back. Its first flight was in late 1948.

  The W 11—the Air Horse, which had a large capacity for the period, equipped with a three-blade rotor in back. Its first flight was in late 1948. It had a single engine and, toward the back of its large cabin, two steerable vertical fins.

The small W 9 and the large W 11 were quickly abandoned, one because of its insufficient power and antitorque, the other because of an accident that occurred in 1950. Only the W 14 Skeeter succeeded in making some headway. One hundred more or less successful military aircraft were produced.

- The Fairey Aviation Company, before taking an interest in blade-end jet-propulsion helicopters, designed and built in 1945 a helicopter-autogiro combination named Girodyne, a five-seat version (see figure 5). Equipped with a three-blade rotor, it provided antitorque through a variable-pitch propeller laterally located on a wing stub. In forward flight this propeller made it possible to fly the craft as an autogiro.

Not long after its first flight, in late 1947, the Girodyne in mid 1948 set the official speed record, reaching a speed of 200 kilometers an hour. Unfortunately during testing the aircraft crashed and was destroyed.

- The Bristol Aeroplane Company was more successful, constructing from 1945 onward the Bristol Type 171 helicopter Sycamore (see figure 6). This aircraft, weighing 2,500 kilograms and planned as a five-seat model, included mechanical transmissions that drove a three-blade rotor and an elevated back rotor. The rotor hub, conceived by an engineer named Hafner, with its spider-support control, was original. After its first flight, in mid 1947, and at the end of the main tests, the Sycamore went into production and 200 models were turned out. It thus became the first functional European helicopter.

- The Westland company was intensely involved in constructing Sikorsky helicopters under license. The company did design work on several heavy helicopters, one of which, the Westminster, equipped with an S-56 American rotor head, was used for experiments. This aircraft did not give rise to any further development because in 1959–60 the Westland company joined forces with the rotary-wing activities of the English firms Saunders-Roe, Bristol, and Fairey.

Taking American Expansion into Account

Manufacturers and technicians soon became aware of American helicopter development, which had been initiated before World War II by Igor Sikorsky. During the war, Sikorsky produced the first series of successful helicopters, which were soon followed by ever more efficient designs.

In 1945, the Bell Aircraft Corporation likewise presented to the Europeans its light, two-blade, mechanically driven helicopters perfected by pioneers Arthur Young and Bartram Kelley. Then the names of Frank Piasecki, Stanley Hiller, and Charles H. Kaman and their strongly impressive output came to the notice of Bristol.

It was only natural, considering the work accomplished, for the attention of the French to be drawn to the lateral two-rotor models built in America, such as those of Platt-Le Page and McDonnell, which were comparable to the SE 3000 and the blade-end jet-propulsion aircraft made by McDonnell and other builders, comparable also to those of SNCASO.

SNCASE, which had discontinued its two-rotor SE 3000, had the satisfaction of finding that American factories had likewise abandoned their lateral two-rotor models. As for blade-end jet-propulsion aircraft, the results achieved in the United States stimulated SNCASO to go ahead with this particular technique.

On the whole, the Europeans realized that the work done by the Americans was clearly superior to that done using German wartime technique and to the only faintly fruitful experiments of the French and the English. Quite understandably, manufacturers sought out American firms to enter into licensing agreements with them.

The Westland company was the first to obtain a Sikorsky license for the S-51 aircraft, then for the S-55. SNCASE, spurred on by events in Algeria, likewise began negotiations with Sikorsky in 1950, acquiring a license for the S-55 in 1952 and for the S-58 in 1956. Sales and maintenance contracts were signed by other French firms for Bell, Hiller, and Piasecki aircraft. The Italian firm Agusta joined the movement by buying the Bell license in 1952. European engineers could not help rejoicing at the sight of different helicopters developing on their soil and finding a valid source of dialogue among users, who promptly became enthusiastic about the outstanding potential of the helicopter.

The situation at the end of this eight-year postwar span can be summed up quite simply:

- Follow-up on work done beyond the Rhine was disappointing. What had been an acceptable innovative technique during the war was no longer that in peace time. Major improvements were required.

- The first European concepts brought further failures. Only the Fairey and Bristol mechanically driven, single-rotor helicopters made successful breakthroughs in England.

Figure 6.
The Bristol Type 171 Sycamore, the first post–World War II helicopter to be built in Great Britain

- The American products, five to ten years more advanced, dominated the market, prompting Europeans to enter into licensing agreements.

A Good Start, 1952–59

The many disappointments that they suffered taught great patience and caution to the small number of engineers still involved in helicopter research. These few were both determined and forced to succeed. All of them dreamed of success for their new prototypes that would erase the failures of the past.

So it was that a new range of helicopter prototypes came into being. Some of them led to the technical, industrial, and commercial development that had long been expected.

The new period was characterized by

- the end of faltering, and
- the arrival of turbine helicopters, favoring French success and the breakthrough of the mechanical, single-rotor helicopter.

The End of Faltering

France. The two principal Sociétés Nationales de Constructions Aéronautiques, SNCASO and SNCASE, remained in the race in 1950. One moved toward improvement of the jet helicopter, the other toward the mechanically driven, three-blade, single-rotor design.

This different choice by the two companies put their two technical teams in competition with each other. The comparison of rotors driven mechanically or by jet gave rise to many controversies concerning the advantages and disadvantages of each design. Obviously each company upheld its own views.

During the same period, curiously enough, another controversy arose, one that pitted the single-rotor design of Sikorsky against the tandem two-rotor version of Piasecki. It reached polemic proportions when government officials ordered both types of aircraft from the United States for operation in Algeria.

While indirectly involved in this disagreement, the heads of the design divisions had but one objective, that of coming up with a good design and building new prototypes of light helicopters weighing less than 800 kilograms empty.

The objective thus stated produced very little enthusiasm among military users already supplied with foreign aircraft of this type. Common sense and the limitation of the available funds automatically eliminated any more ambitious alternative.

In 1951, the services put out a program chart outlining an ultralight helicopter for use in observation work with and without a pilot on board. After the review of the proposals, preference was given to the design proposed by SNCASO, a small, rudimentary aircraft equipped with a jet rotor.

SNCASO quickly built the two SO 1220 prototypes, in which the ramjet-driven blades initially planned were replaced with blades driven by compressed air supplied by a Palouste air generator from the Turbomeca Company. The first flight took place January 2, 1953. After adjustments and improvements, spectacular flight demonstrations of the aircraft, made possible by the considerable inertia of its enlarged two-blade rotor and by its powerful air generator, were given. The forerunner of the Djinn two-seat model had been born.

For their part, the engineers of SNCASE were authorized to reconstruct the principal units salvaged from their latest prototype, which had had an accident, to use them in a new, deliberately simple and inexpensive model. Without hesitation they eliminated the accumulation of component parts of the two small rotors assembled on the V-shaped tail unit. A simple, antitorque rotor, less sensitive to the airflow from the main rotor and more efficient during slow-speed maneuvering, did the job.

Soon the two new SE 3120 three-seat prototypes, subsequently named Alouette I, were ready for testing on the Parisian field of Buc (see figure 7). Each aircraft was equipped with a vertical-axis Salmson piston engine to drive the three-blade rotor.

Figure 7.
The Sud-Est SE 3120, named the Alouette I

Following the first flights in 1951, adjustments were made slowly and meticulously, not only to avoid any further serious incident, but also to ensure the proper operation on the three-blade rotor of the gyroscopic stabilization system that was designed to facilitate piloting. Little by little flight time accumulated, until mid 1953, when the outstanding test pilot Jean Boulet flew the Alouette 1,252 kilometers to beat the world record for distance covered on a closed-circuit course. The success of the endurance flights and the success of several demonstrations caused the general management of SNCASE to decide in favor of mass production of the Alouette I.

At the same time, in the environs of Paris, a little-known engineer named Cantinieau made news by building two light helicopters with the help of a few friends. One was a one-seat model, C 100, the other a two-seat model, MC 101, containing an articulated engine-rotor assembly located above the pilot. As soon as the first flights were considered satisfactory, both aircraft were transferred to Spain, where they disappeared, much the same as did the offshoot aircraft built on the spot in the outskirts of Madrid, the AC 11, AC 12, and AC 14, or under license in France, the AC 13. During the 1960s, Cantinieau's design projects and testing gradually came to an end.

England. Unlike the French companies, the Fairey, Percival, and Bristol firms chose to build helicopters of higher gross weight, which were more satisfactory for military purposes. Fairey and Percival set out to build jet helicopters, and Bristol aimed toward the mechanical tandem two-rotor type.

The Fairey Company, after stopping development of its small Fairey Ultralight, put all its effort into developing a combination jet helicopter-autogiro, a design that SNCASO had tried earlier on its Farfadet. The new aircraft, named Rotodyne and equipped with a four-blade rotor and two Eland turboprops, was supposed to transport thirty-five to forty persons at speeds greater than 200 kilometers an hour.

The first flight, made in late 1957, was quickly followed by the transition to the autogiro flight phase. Despite the criticism made at the time concerning the inadequacy of control in yawing, the performance of the Rotodyne proved to be excellent. It was the first aircraft to go more than 300 kilometers an hour and to attract the interest of large airlines. The latter proposed that Fairey build an improved Rotodyne capable of transporting sixty to sixty-five passengers. Since the minimum of twenty-five orders was not forthcoming, the whole project was dropped, and in 1962 Fairey abandoned jet helicopter technology.

Percival Aircraft Ltd. made only a brief appearance in the helicopter field. After having participated in the contest for a small two-seater of the Fairey Ultralight type, the firm in 1950 launched into the design of the P 74 prototype, with blade-end air jet. This aircraft, equipped with two generators, underwent some ground testing, but problems with control prevented its ever taking off.

The Bristol Aeroplane Company, encouraged by the success achieved with its single-

Figure 8.
The Bristol Type 173 Belvedere, the first European tandem two-rotor helicopter

rotor helicopter Sycamore, decided to build the Bristol Type 173 helicopter Belvedere, which was the first European tandem two-rotor helicopter (see figure 8). This prototype, with a total weight of 4,800 kilograms, could transport fourteen passengers at speeds of 200 kilometers an hour or more. It took off for the first time early in 1952. The tests demonstrated the need for improvements, and the chief engineer, Hafner, introduced in succession the 173 Mark II version, characterized by a horizontal tail unit equipped with vertical fins in place of the initial V form, then the 173 Mark III version, equipped with a four-blade rotor and a new V-shaped tail unit. The Bristol company did its utmost to obtain, with the Bristol Type 191, an order for around fifty aircraft from the Royal Navy and, with the Bristol Type 192 concept, a civilian order for a small number of aircraft for British European Airways.

The failure of these military and civilian orders to materialize ruined the company's hopes. Bristol ended its helicopter work, and the Westland company took over its helicopter activities.

The New Generation of Turbine Helicopters

As soon as the gas turbine engine appeared, all heads of design departments felt compelled to look into its possible use in and adaptation to the helicopter.

Beginning in 1951, the American firms of Kaman, Bell, and Sikorsky proceeded to assemble one or two turbines on an experimental aircraft derived from their current production. The tests were limited, but the most thoroughly examined and successful were those of the engineer Ralph Alex, then with the Sikorsky firm, with the turbine-powered S-52, which in 1954 set world records for speed and altitude. In Europe it was SNCASO which, in 1950, for the first time in the world, installed in its jet three-seat model, Ariel III, the prototype turbine Artouste, made by the Turbomeca Company, to drive the compressor that supplied the air to be ejected at blade ends. This aircraft was flown in April 1951.

SNCASE also, beginning in 1950, kept abreast of the progress made by the Turbomeca Company in the construction of turbines capable of driving a propeller or a rotor. It was thanks to the dynamic president of the Turbomeca Company and his competent engineers that the first turbine helicopters were successful, both in France and on the Sikorsky S-52.

The advent of turbines to replace piston engines led to success in France and the breakthrough in Europe of the mechanically driven single-rotor helicopter.

French Success

At SNCASO the excellent results obtained with the two SO 1220 one-seat prototypes led the chief engineer, Morain, to construct immediately the offshoot two-seat SO 1221 helicopter Djinn, which made its first flight late in 1953 (see figure 9). It was equipped with a Palouste air generator. The reduction of noise, thanks to the elimination of blade-end burners, the good altitude performance, and the total absence of the danger zone near the ground caused the new aircraft to be highly regarded. The design was still not final when the company launched into prototype production of 25 aircraft and obtained a mass-production order for 150 models for French or foreign civilian and military needs.

French certification of the Djinn series was acquired in 1957, and by mid 1958 American certification had been received. To the credit of this helicopter, attention must be called to the outstanding altitude performance achieved in 1957 by J. Dabos, with an unconfirmed 8,458-meter world record in all categories, and the fact that this was the first certified jet helicopter to be mass-produced.

As the improvement of mechanically driven helicopters continued, the advantages of the Djinn two-seat model diminished. By way of comparison, users pointed out the disadvantages of the design, namely poor performance of the pneumatic drive, high fuel consumption, inadequate control during yawing, and a forward speed of only 120 kilometers an hour. The prospects of the Djinn were decidedly jeopardized when the several improvements proposed for the model were rejected. As a consequence, prototypes of significant gross weight were never constructed.

It was at this time—early 1957—that the Morain team of SNCASO and that of SNCASE were merged under the name of Sud-Aviation. At SNCASE the engineers' mission, assigned them by the services, was to equip Alouette I with a turbine and plan the subsequent mass production of this turbine-powered helicopter.

For the chief engineer, the author of this narrative, it seemed obvious that the future of helicopters could not be secured by Alouette I with turbines or with piston engines. A completely new turbine helicopter was indeed required, but on the condition that it be

- competitive, but superior in performance to existing light helicopters;
- in a favorable commercial market, that of five-seat aircraft;
- designed around the turbine to benefit as much as possible from its advantages; and
- basic in design and uncomplicated, making it capable of being disassembled into its principal subunits to facilitate production, maintenance, and sales.

Figure 9.
The Djinn two-seat helicopter, designed by Sud-Ouest

It was not easy to meet these conditions in an atmosphere in which other matters were considered more important. The secret of the success of the prototype called Alouette II lay in its good design and its ease of construction. In March 1955, scarcely a year after the first drawings had been made, the first five-seat, single-rotor prototype took off in Paris with Jean Boulet as pilot.

During the first phase, the engineers were concerned to proceed as far as possible by systematic testing of the critical assemblies of the prototype, such as the integral-wheel turbine, the mechanics of the engines, and the blades. Cooperation with the Turbomeca engineers was essential for testing and ensuring the proper functioning of the turbine speed regulator designed to simplify helicopter piloting by eliminating the classic pitch-throttle control. In spite of difficulties encountered in manufacturing and the laboratory testing of certain units such as blades and mechanical components, the work was finished by the deadlines that had been set. Scarcely three months after the first flight, the pilot, Jean Boulet, set the world altitude record in all categories, reaching 8,209 meters.

After that memorable date, the development phases of Alouette II moved along according to the schedule well known to builders of rotary-wing aircraft. The next phase consisted of accumulating a maximum of flight hours and tests of the prototypes, to determine the flight parameters and necessary adjustments and improvements accurately. During this same phase, the technicians were eager to freeze the Alouette II design so that production of it could be started by mid 1955.

It was at this time that the technical directors had to listen to and disprove with great patience criticism leveled against the use of the integral-wheel turbine, called a stationary turbine, on helicopters. According to specialists absorbed in their theories and calculations, only a turbine with unconnected wheels, called a free turbine, was appropriate for a rotary-wing aircraft. Conclusive tests obtained with the Artouste II turbine on the Alouette II demonstrated the absurdity of their exceedingly inflexible and absolute judgments.

This period turned out to be beneficial to the French development under way, because many foreign builders decided to wait for free turbines to become available on the market.

The third phase consisted of designing, building, and rapidly testing the special, quickly adaptable equipment on the aircraft of the line to meet the urgent needs of users operating both on shore and at sea in diverse atmospheric conditions. The first production helicopter was delivered in the spring of 1956, and about thirty more followed during the year. The technicians soon noted the often legitimate observations and complaints of the early military users. Improvements were made on operational equipment that completed the definition of the Alouette II line.

The purpose of the fourth phase was to secure certification of the aircraft by civil authorities. The French certificate of airworthiness for the world's first mechanical turbine helicopter was delivered to the new Sud-Aviation Company in May 1957. American certification was obtained at the beginning of 1958, on the basis of the specifications of the Federal Aviation Administration, which the authorized American delegate in France, R. Meyersburg, had explained to the engineers.

After four years of work, the development of Alouette II had become a reality. The performance of the aircraft exceeded that of aircraft in the same category, and the huge rush of purchase orders that followed the demonstrations that were required in France and abroad gave the best proof of all of the long-awaited success.

The production series carried out in the developing helicopter industry allowed the experimental aircraft to be used to test modifications worked out on the job, to broaden theoretical knowledge, and to prepare for the future. Thus it was that successive improved versions of Alouette II came into being. Several aircraft were equipped with more powerful Artouste II turbines, then with an Astazou turbine, more efficient and more fuel-economical. Thus overall weight and performance continued to improve.

Three special Alouette II helicopters were also tested. The first, the SE 3140, was equipped with a Turbomeca free-turbine engine. It enabled the engineers to broaden their knowledge of this type of turbine, planned for helicopters of greater useful load. The second was specially modified to be flown by remote control from the ground. It went through a few tests, which demonstrated that this version was premature. The third special Alouette II was entirely streamlined, with assistance from designer Raymond Loewy. It went through numerous tests, ultimately catching the attention of several customers who were interested in both its good performance and its elegant form and very comfortable interior. In spite of a significant number of potential orders, it was not produced in large numbers because a production version of it would have required some reworking of the drawings, causing additional work that would have overburdened the technicians.

At the end of 1959, the overall balance sheet for the Alouette II showed 333 aircraft delivered out of 490 ordered. Thus the development of the turbine helicopter was on the right path.

The Breakthrough of the Mechanically Driven Single-Rotor Helicopter

The advent of the turbine helicopter, brilliantly demonstrated in Europe by the Alouette II, also brought about the breakthrough of the technique of the single-rotor aircraft equipped with an antitorque rotor, a design with which the great American pioneer Sikorsky had been highly successful. The production and sale of single-rotor Bell aircraft by the Agusta company in Italy and the achievements of the Westland company in England emphasized this tendency, which was followed by Sud-Aviation in France, with its production of Sikorsky aircraft under licensing agreements.

The various jet helicopters, despite the good performance that some of them, such as the Djinn and the Rotodyne, achieved, gradually faded away. The multirotor designs, especially that of the tandem two-rotor, the advantages of which had been made clear by the Bristol Aeroplane Company with its Belvedere, were likewise discontinued.

Only single-rotor helicopters continued to hold their own on the European market. Most of them were still equipped with piston engines, but they soon gave way to the new single rotors equipped with turbines. One of the consequences of this evolution was the regrouping in Europe of the teams of helicopter specialists within a single firm such as Westland in England, Sud-Aviation in France, and Agusta in Italy.

Nevertheless, some companies or individuals continued with their own research. As a result, a certain number of prototypes, none of which ever achieved memorable results, were built. Among these the following deserve mention:

- The jet helicopters: Fiat 7002 in Italy, the light jet helicopters in Germany by Dornier and VFW, the helicopter equipped with blade-end ramjets by engineer Drees in Holland.
- The German mechanical helicopters of Focke/Borgward and Wagner, among which some were single-rotor models equipped with two antitorque propellers, while others were coaxial, two-rotor models.

To summarize, this seven-year phase made obvious:

- Mastery of the helicopter technique by the Europeans.
- The French breakthrough, thanks to turbine helicopters.
- The success of the mechanically driven single-rotor design.
- The regrouping of helicopter resources in England, France, and Italy.

European Advances, 1959–68

English and French engineers had shown that the period of technical faltering was over and that the mechanically driven, single-rotor turbine helicopter was a good, practical type. Helicopter companies therefore deemed it urgent that they take advantage of this proven technology to establish their own helicopter industry.

The national advance needed to take one of the following directions:

- Adoption of American developments under licensing agreements.
- Use of turbine power in the French manner.
- Development through technical continuity.

Although the progress made during the preceding years had been considerable, helicopter technology was still quite young. An engineer could still put forth new ideas to improve his prototypes. Such was the state of the progress and advance of helicopters.

Taking Over American Developments under Licensing Agreements

France. The Sud-Aviation Company, having been asked by the government to manufacture under license the Sikorsky S-55 and S-58 aircraft equipped with piston engines, made every effort to meet military needs quickly. The company did not sign any agreement to make the new Sikorsky S-61 and S-62 turbine helicopters, which were the logical descendants of the preceding aircraft.

On the other hand, the design engineers began to work on the two-turbine model by equipping one of the aircraft of the S-58 line with two Bastan turbines by Turbomeca, more powerful than the Wright Cyclone 1,525-hp piston engine. Flight tests of the Bi-Bastan S-58, the first two-turbine European helicopter, were begun in October 1962. Since the services did not adopt this new idea for the S-58 aircraft in use, the company ended the tests.

England. After the end of World War II the Westland company built the range of helicopters designed by Sikorsky. Under a licensing agreement it "anglicized" the products to turn out in succession the Widgeon, derived from the S-51; the Whirlwind, derived from the S-55; and the Wessex, derived from the S-58. On one of the Whirlwind aircraft, Westland experimented with an English turbine; after that it equipped the Wessex models with Napier turbines. The switch to turbine power for this medium-weight helicopter was a success.

Italy. The Agusta company, closely linked by contract with the American Bell Helicopter Corporation, adapted the turbine to its line of products at a later date. Agusta waited until the Bell 204 had come out to broach the matter of turbine helicopters. It was only some time later that the company worked out some original designs to show its technical capabilities in helicopter development.

Germany. The VFW-Fokker company obtained a license for the Sikorsky CH-53G heavy turbine helicopter in response to a request of the aviation branch of the army. The company provided for the assembly and manufacture of 112 aircraft, but did no design work on this occasion. The Weser Company of Bremen likewise experimented for a long time with the seventeen-ton Sikorsky Skycrane S-64 helicopters.

Turbinizing in the French Manner

The spirit of emulation caused by the success of the French Alouette II helicopter encouraged other European countries to develop helicopters to fill the same technical and commercial need.

England. The Saunders-Roe company, soon integrated into the Westland company, used the Blackburn/Turbomeca turbine with a power of 400 hp, equivalent to that of the Artouste, to power the Scout prototypes, which were flown in 1958. Westland improved this aircraft, making from it the sea version,

Figure 10.
A Royal Navy Wasp, built by Westland

the Wasp (see figure 10). For mass production of the Scout and the Wasp, the prototype having been judged underpowered, the original turbine was replaced by a Nimbus turbine of about 1,000 hp made by Bristol-Siddeley.

The single-rotor Scout had five to six seats and was equipped with a skid landing gear. It went into service in 1960. The Wasp, made for the Royal Navy, was equipped with special landing gear having four swiveling wheels designed to facilitate maneuvers and landings on the decks of ships. The Wasp was the first light helicopter to have a folding back pylon to make it easier to store aboard ship.

These creations gave rise to an important series of military aircraft used in England and in the Middle East.

Germany. The Merckle firm, near Stuttgart, decided in 1957 to design, with the help of an outside group of engineers and supported by the German armed services, an SM-67 three-blade, single-rotor aircraft equipped with the Turbomeca Artouste II turbine. In form it closely resembled the Alouette II.

The first prototype made its first flight late in 1959 but was destroyed because of ground resonance. The need to remedy this phenomenon caused delays in the testing of the two prototypes that followed. In 1961, results that looked favorable had been achieved. Nevertheless, work was stopped, because the government, aware of the technical lag behind French development, was inclined to purchase Alouette II models made by Sud-Aviation.

After that, helicopter design services were centered in Munich in the Bölkow Company, which already had to its credit the construction of some original prototypes such as the BO 102 Heli-Trainer, the BO 103 single-blade helicopter, the design for Derschmitt special articulations, and a test-bed for a crane-helicopter rotor with a twenty-ton payload. In 1962, it set as its objective the design and construction of a light, classical, single-rotor helicopter in response to the program established by the government for military and civilian needs. The engineers built three prototypes, the first of which was destroyed on the ground, while the other two took off in February and December 1967 and quickly accumulated flight hours.

The Bölkow technical innovations on the latter two attracted the attention of all

Figure 11.
The Bölkow BO 105

technicians. The highlights of the design were plastic fiber blades, a nonarticulated rotor hub, and two-turbine power.

After a normal testing period after which several improvements were made, the B 105 design took the lead, because of its good performance and overall flight qualities (see figure 11). This aircraft enabled German industry to participate in European advances in helicopter design.

Development through Technical Continuity

Any engineer aware of the problems in building and modifying a helicopter followed the example of the Americans' methodical development. The range of Sikorsky helicopters of gradually increasing weights, going from the S-51 to the S-62 by way of the S-55s and S-58s, demonstrated the technical continuity followed by their brilliant creator. The licensed companies recognized this continuity as beneficial to them.

France. Everything remained to be done in this field after the success of the Alouette II. The chief engineer, Marchetti, was strongly convinced of the need for gradual development through follow-up on prototype concepts. Beyond standard improvements on the models of the Alouette II line, two constructions seemed to him to take priority.

The first prototype derived was the seven-seat Alouette III (see figure 12). Streamlined, designed and manufactured with company funds, and equipped with a three-blade rotor eleven meters in diameter, it had a total weight of 2,100 kilograms and surpassed the performance of the Alouette II in every kind of flight. To emphasize this achievement further and increase flight safety, the chief engineer fiercely defended the good power reserve available thanks to the installation of the new 870-hp Turbomeca Artouste III turbine.

The Alouette III made its first flight in February 1959, and soon, without any trouble at all, Jean Boulet landed it, fully loaded, on top of Mont Blanc. In November 1960, on the occasion of a presentation in India, he landed with a passenger and 250 kilograms of cargo in the Himalayas at an altitude of 6,004 meters. At that time, this was an unprecedented feat.

The superiority of the Alouette III was demonstrated when the first French military orders were awarded to the company. In 1963, the order book called for more than 150 aircraft, and, like the Alouette II, the Alouette III attracted the attention of several foreign countries. India and Romania obtained licenses for it and continued production beyond 1980. Several improved versions emerged from the production chain.

Thanks to the Alouette III and Alouette II, Sud-Aviation soon became the leader in the European helicopter industry. The balance sheet spoke for itself: In 1975, 1,305 Alouette II aircraft had been built, and in 1980, production of the Alouette III in France and abroad was more than 1,900 aircraft.

The second design, with much promise for the future, was the SE 3150, which combined the simplicity of the Alouette II airframe and the power plant of the Alouette III. The desired objective was to obtain high-altitude performance, making it possible to

Figure 12.
The Alouette III, a seven-seat derivative of the Alouette II

transport cargo to places that until then had been inaccessible.

Thanks to this aircraft, Jean Boulet, in France, set the world record for helicopter altitude in all categories, reaching an altitude of 10,984 meters in June 1958, only three years after the flight of the Alouette II.

Despite their excellent performance, the two SE 3150 prototypes did not lead to further development at the time, for the simple reason that putting them into production was likely to upset the sale and the progress of the Alouette III, which had reached the testing stage.

In 1968, this design was entirely reworked, improved, and adapted to the objective identified ten years earlier. The new prototype, called SA 315 Lama, was flown in March 1969. Once again the chief pilot, Jean Boulet, went for the altitude record, which he had held since June 1958, and he raised it to 12,442 meters in June 1972. The Lama was put into production, and by 1980 about 300 aircraft had already been marketed, further enhancing the success of the Alouette design.

The advance achieved by the Sud-Aviation engineers could not end with this single family of aircraft. Design of a medium-sized helicopter was in order. Well before the Alouette III came out, several projects had been suggested. They were all for two-turbine models with a total weight varying between five and six tons. None of them was accepted. The military users, especially the French navy, demanded a helicopter of much higher gross weight for their operational needs.

The jump from a two-ton aircraft of the Alouette III type to a prototype of eight to ten tons was a large one. An aircraft with a weight somewhere in between would have suited the engineers better. Faced with the new program planned and financed, the design office proposed the single-rotor SE 3200 Frelon, driven by three turbines. In response to naval technical requirements, its storage space was reduced as much as possible.

After extensive work on design and manufacture, the first prototype took off in June

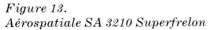

Figure 13.
Aérospatiale SA 3210 Superfrelon

1959. It was the first three-turbine helicopter in the world to reach the stage of tests and presentations. Before final adjustments had been completed, the official program was changed in favor of even higher gross weight, from eleven to twelve tons, allowing the transport of thirty persons. Thus it was that the SA 3210 Superfrelon replaced the SA 3200 Frelon (see figure 13).

To build this heavy helicopter, Sud-Aviation asked for the Sikorsky company's cooperation in equipping the airframe with a rotor hub with six blades that could be folded by remote control.

The first of two prototypes took off in December 1962. In July 1963, the Superfrelon was to surpass the world speed record by reaching 350 kilometers an hour on a course of fifteen to twenty-five kilometers.

After delivery of the first production series aircraft to the navy, commercial marketing of the aircraft required modification of some factors such as the passenger transport and air operations.

In 1980, about a hundred aircraft had been delivered. During the same period, the Italian firm Agusta, on instructions from its government, began the manufacture of a three-turbine, single-rotor prototype, a competitor for the Superfrelon, known as the AZ 101. This helicopter had a brief testing career and was not mass produced.

In France in 1960, while the Frelon was undergoing adjustments, Sud-Aviation learned that the army was becoming increasingly interested in a tactical transport helicopter configured for twelve fully equipped soldiers. The design for a medium-sized, six-ton helicopter was thus returned to the agenda, and old projects were reviewed and improved. In 1962, the Puma design was born and was proposed to the armed services. Pursuant to the cooperation agreement signed between the French and English governments, Sud-Aviation and the Westland company got together to go ahead with the Puma aircraft program designed for the French Army and the Royal Air Force.

Sud-Aviation was the prime contractor and, with engineer Legrand as technical head, proposed the Puma in the form of a four-blade, single-rotor helicopter with a total weight of 6,400 kilograms, equipped with two Turbomeca Turmo III turbines. The prototype made its first flight in April 1965. After meticulous final adjustments, deliveries were begun at the beginning of 1969.

Under the name SA 330 Puma, mass production was continued by the Aérospatiale Company, which had replaced Sud-Aviation. In all, 685 aircraft were constructed, not counting the aircraft built under licensing agreements in Romania and Indonesia.

The whole of this eleven-year period can be summarized as follows:

- The general spread of helicopters equipped with turbines, from the light helicopter to the heavy one, with the adoption of the free turbine for the latter type.
- The advance of French helicopter technique, which made it possible to add an international dimension to French industry.
- The start-up of German industry in the turbine helicopter field.
- A growing demand for helicopters throughout the world for both civil and military needs.

Modernization, 1968–80

Having arrived belatedly in the development of the helicopter, European engineers realized that they must build and make available increasingly efficient aircraft that were also more rational and polished in design. Also on the agenda were simplification of maintenance, improvements in safety, and easy piloting. Engine mechanics and manufacturers of equipment and machinery were duly brought into the effort to make the new designs a success.

The modernization stage was to reveal

- The use of new products and materials.
- A reassessment of helicopters of the preceding generation.
- The advance of two-turbine helicopters.

Use of New Products and Materials

Engine mechanics quickly made available to helicopter designers advanced turbines that were more powerful, compact, and lightweight and of which the hourly fuel consumption rates had been considerably reduced.

France. Turbomeca integral-wheel, or stationary, turbines continued to be used in single-engine aircraft. For two-engine helicopters on the other hand, free turbines were received more favorably, because of the ease with which they could be coupled, checked, and adjusted. Recommended from the start by American builders, the free turbine soon took over the market. It was not going to remain in the background.

The advent of products such as elastomers especially conceived for engineers responsible for designing rotor heads was a great success. After numerous preliminary tests in the United States, the time came when it was possible to resolve complex problems caused by bearings and joints of rotor hubs. The different functions of the latter could be resolved by a single, well-designed part called an elastomer bearing. This solution did not necessarily eliminate the flexible blades, which in themselves also represented a significant technical advance.

In 1960, the German Bölkow Company was the first in Europe to manufacture fiberglass blades, thereby advancing this highly desirable technology. Other helicopter builders followed suit, and soon, both in America and Europe, fiberglass and composite materials appeared that facilitated the manufacture of blades that were accurate in weight and shape and of fail-safe structures and subassemblies that were not subject to corrosion. Starting with these same products, the engineers succeeded in creating main rotor hubs characterized by the basic advantages of simplicity, lightness, and high fatigue strength.

The development of helicopters also called for increasing the quantity, weight, and volume of equipment placed on board so that users could carry out assignments under greatly varying conditions. The suppliers of equipment made their contribution to the modernization that was in process with the delivery of accessories and electrical, electronic, or hydraulic subassemblies that were as modern and reliable as possible.

Actually, new products and materials were even more numerous. Their use by design engineers compelled companies to develop immediately means of designing, building, and testing them. Modernization could not help but benefit the customer at the end of the line waiting for delivery of his flight-ready aircraft.

Reassessment of Helicopters of the Preceding Generation

From the European point of view, this reassessment of the preceding generation mainly concerned France, whose Alouette II and Alouette III had been produced in great numbers.

To prolong their success in the respective commercial markets, improvement and modernization were urgent and vital in view of the competition. Sud-Aviation, having become the Aérospatiale Company (SNIAS) in 1970, showed its dynamism by succes-

Figure 14.
The Aérospatiale Gazelle

sively producing three new single-turbine helicopters, the Gazelle, the Ecureuil, and the Dauphin. The Gazelle was a modernized version of the Alouette II (see figure 14).

The factory mass-produced this aircraft under the designations SA 340, SA 341, and SA 342; they were derived one from the other by the installation of increasingly powerful Turbomeca/Astazou integral-wheel turbines. The 600-hp engine of the SA 340 was replaced in the SA 342 Gazelle by an 880-hp engine, which allowed the weight to be increased to 1,900 kilograms. The trim fuselage of the Gazelle made it possible in May 1971 to reach a speed of 307 kilometers an hour over a three-kilometer course.

In addition to the airframe, the Gazelle incorporated two important innovations—accurate and efficient fiberglass blades and the Fenestron. The latter included the antitorque propeller within the vertical fin and had the basic advantages of avoiding accidents caused by the classic tail rotor, which was dangerous for ground personnel.

The first flight having been made in April 1967, when the Gazelle was still equipped with a classic back rotor, Jean Boulet took off with the Fenestron-equipped prototype in April 1968. After obtaining its certificate of airworthiness, this new, five-seat, high-performance helicopter was the first to be certified for flight by instrument flight rule (IFR) with only one pilot on board. In 1980, mass production was in the neighborhood of 1,000 aircraft. After analysis of the civil market, the authorities thought it time to design, following the Alouette II and the Gazelle, a new prototype of a light helicopter of the same kind, but even more competitive, by virtue of increased simplicity and a drop in the cost of manufacture and operation.

With a total weight of 1,950 kilograms, the single-rotor, six-seat AS 350 Ecureuil was equipped with a skid-type landing gear, fiberglass blades, and a classic two-blade rotor in back (see figure 15). The chief innovation on this prototype consisted of the installation of a hub of a composite material called Starflex. The great simplicity of the design made it possible to eliminate many parts included in previous rotor hubs. It was and still is highly valued. More than a modification of the Alouette II and the Gazelle, the Ecureuil became an avant-garde design.

The first AS 350 C prototype, equipped with an American LTS Lycoming 101 turbine, took off in June 1974. The two AS 350 B prototypes with Turbomeca/Ariel turbines made their first flights in February 1975. Mass production was undertaken by Aérospatiale in southern France jointly with its American branch, Aérospatiale Helicopter Corporation, located in Texas.

The large number of American orders added to those of other countries produced, in 1980, a rapidly growing trade balance sheet of 700 aircraft.

The reassessment study of the Alouette III gave rise to the ten-seat, single-rotor prototype, the SA 360 Dauphin, equipped with a 1,050-hp Astazou turbine. With pleasing lines like those of the Gazelle, the aircraft made its first flight in June 1972. A year later it won three world records for speed in the light-helicopter category. On a three-kilometer course it reached a speed of 312 kilometers an hour.

After improvements, the Dauphin was certified and produced in small quantities before being converted into a two-turbine helicopter.

The Advance of Two-turbine Helicopters

After 1970, users showed a preference for two-turbine helicopters, for many reasons. Flight over the ocean and continuing flight in case of turbine failure were considered priorities. Having two engines made it possible, furthermore, to plan new kinds of mission, such as flights over urban zones.

Germany. The Bölkow Company, now Messerschmitt-Bölkow-Blohm GmbH (MBB), had certainly taken this direction in designing the light, four-blade BO 105 helicopter equipped with two turbines, first of German make, then American.

After the prototypes, the company started work on several preseries aircraft, which enabled MBB to make technical, functional, and commercial tests. Then the company delivered the first assembly-line aircraft equipped with two Allison 250 turbines. In 1972, the added power of the latter made it possible to increase the total weight to 2,300 kilograms. American certification was acquired in April 1971.

Innovations such as nonjointed rotors and fiberglass blades, in addition to the fact of its two engines, ensured the success of this light helicopter. Its good performance and remarkable flight qualities were valued by customers in several countries.

To expand the market, the engineers designed and began to produce several variations on the basic design. Pilots tested successively

Figure 15.
The AS 350 Ecureuil, an avant-garde design

- The BO 105 HGH, equipped with small wings, which reached a speed of 400 kilometers an hour.
- The BO 106, with a wider cabin.
- The BO 105 CBS, with a longer fuselage (see figure 16).

In 1974, the German army accepted the BO 105 PAH, which was designed for antitank fighting. This ensured the success of the engineers and the company, which then became the main helicopter company in Germany, with nearly 1,000 aircraft on order in 1980.

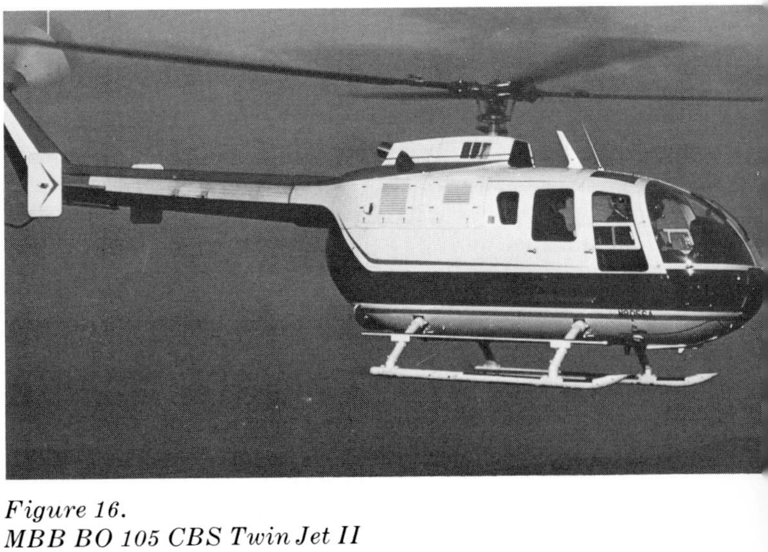

Figure 16.
MBB BO 105 CBS Twin Jet II

Figure 17.
The Agusta A 109 Hirundo

To increase its technical potential and its presence in the helicopter market, the MBB company in June 1977 concluded an agreement with Kawasaki of Japan to build jointly an aircraft with eight to ten seats, the BK 117, equipped with four blades and two Lycoming 650-hp turbines. The flight of the first prototype was made in June 1979 in Germany. It was to be followed in 1980 by large-scale production of the new design.

Italy. The Agusta company, already having produced, under license, several thousand helicopters essentially of the Bell type, decided to design and build a light helicopter of its own. The outgrowth of the design work was the A 109 Hirundo, a single-rotor helicopter equipped with four blades and two Allison 250 turbines (see figure 17).

After an accident on the ground in 1971 with the first prototype, tests were resumed in January 1973 on the second prototype. Results in flight were satisfactory and made it possible to obtain, in January 1976, the American certificate of airworthiness for a total weight of 2,600 kilograms.

Potential customers welcomed the Hirundo, which had an eight-seat cabin with ample room and good visibility. Its good performance, its good flight qualities, and particularly its lack of noise were noted.

Having produced 250 models of it, the company proceeded with the sale of this first attractive helicopter of Italian design in 1980. At the same time the Agusta company was continuing its work on derived aircraft, such as the A 109 Tow and the A 129.

France. To meet the demand, the helicopter directors of Aérospatiale decided to transform the Dauphin SA 360 quickly into a two-turbine helicopter. The resultant Dauphin AS365C prototype was equipped with a slightly enlarged rotor, new plastic blades, a new three-wheel landing gear with a retractable front wheel, and larger fuel tanks (see figure 18). Finally, new Turbomeca/Ariel turbines replaced the Astazou turbines so that performance could be further increased. This new, much improved SA 365 N version made it possible to cover the Paris–London route at 321 kilometers an hour.

The success of this two-turbine Dauphin was confirmed by an order from the U.S. Coast Guard and by the purchase of a manufacturing license by the People's Republic of China. By the end of 1980, more than 100 aircraft were in production.

As they had the Dauphin—and for the same technical and commercial reasons—

the engineers went back to the single-turbine Ecureuil version to transform it into a two-turbine craft. Named AS 355 Ecureuil in France and Twinstar in the United States, the prototype, equipped with two Lycoming turbines, was flown for the first time in September 1979.

Certified in October 1980, the new light, two-turbine helicopter, which took advantage of all the remarkable innovations of its single-turbine predecessor, made it possible to bring in substantial orders in 1980, thus achieving a commercial breakthrough.

In turn, the SA 330 Puma was reassessed, and successive improvements were made, the greatest of which made it possible in 1976 to bring its total weight up from 6.4 tons to 7.4 tons, thanks to the installation of new fiberglass blades. Then, with the AS 332 Super-Puma design, the engineers further increased the performance and operational capabilities. Having an overall weight of 7.8 tons and equipped with two new Turbomeca/Makila 1,700-hp turbines, the Super-Puma responded better to the needs expressed by civil users, especially in the offshore area. By 1980, it was well into mass production. For Aérospatiale, the two-turbine models, Ecureuil/Twinstar, Dauphin S 365 N, and Super-Puma AS 332, con-

Figure 18.
The SA 360 Dauphin two-turbine model

Figure 19.
The WG 13 Lynx, built by Westland and Aérospatiale

stituted the world's most modern helicopter threesome.

England. Development of two-turbine helicopters proceeded in England as in the rest of Europe. Within the framework of Franco-English cooperation, the Westland company became prime contractor for building a prototype of about 4,500 kilograms, in design located somewhere between the Dauphin and the Puma. The new helicopter, named WG 13 Lynx, was introduced in the form of a single-rotor aircraft equipped with four blades and two 900-hp Rolls-Royce turbines (see figure 19). Testing of the prototype began in March 1971. After systematic adjustments and tests on the first aircraft, the first of the Lynx line was put into production in 1978.

Not only was the Lynx adapted to the needs of the English and French navies, it also embodied an important design innovation in the semirigid rotor head that gave the aircraft a desirable controllability and maneuverability.

In 1980, several hundred of the Lynx were sold. Since all these helicopters were intended primarily to meet military needs, the Westland company thought it best to develop a civil version of the Lynx at the same time.

The new WG 30 aircraft, which used the mechanical assemblies of the military Lynx, was increased in total weight to 5,400 kilograms, following enlargement of the passenger cabin and an increase in the diameter of the rotor (see figure 20). Thanks to the 1,100 hp of its two Rolls-Royce turbines, the aircraft was able to fly at a cruising speed of 250 kilometers an hour. The prototype made its first flight in April 1978, and in 1980 its certification and mass production were under way.

This recent period of development shows

- Growth in the number of prototype and mass-production aircraft designed in Europe in response to the needs of users.
- Intensified, original modernization of helicopters, with a marked tendency toward two-turbine versions.
- Blossoming of national design work, with a decrease in the number of aircraft produced under licensing agreements.
- Dominance achieved by the French accompanied by an advantageous penetration of the world market.
- Strengthening of European and international cooperation.

Figure 20.
The Westland WG 30

Conclusion

Helicopter development in Europe during the period between 1940 and 1980 can be summarized briefly as follows:

- Development was difficult during the early years. A small number of engineers had a great deal of tenacity and patience in mastering the special technique of rotary-wing aircraft. Fortunately, the faltering and disappointments were followed by the great joy experienced at the time of the first flights and the first operations.
- A decisive stage was cleared, thanks to the design and breakthrough of light turbine helicopters, which took the lead because of their many desirable features and brilliant performance. Their success made it possible not merely to reduce the lag of European design and technology but to build a competitive helicopter industry.
- The flowering of European technique was favored by concentration of means and efforts exclusively on the single-rotor, turbomechanically driven model. It was emphasized by the building of a broad range of turbine helicopters of light and medium gross weight. To respond to the growing demands of the market, all the wheels of industry were put into action to improve and modernize these aircraft for the benefit of users and the entire world.

In conclusion, if faith can move mountains, as the Bible would have it, the faith of European engineers has enabled them, during these forty years of development, to rise above the mountains thanks to their helicopters.

CHARLES MARCHETTI, an aeronautical civil engineer, was born in Lorraine, France. As chief engineer in 1947 and then as the helicopter division general manager of Aérospatiale, he was involved in the construction of the post–World War II French helicopters. In 1954, he created and developed the French turbine helicopters. Then in 1964, he built the first French hovercraft. As president of his own research company, he developed new vertical concepts, such as flying platforms and light helicopters. Besides various French and foreign distinctions, he received in 1969 the Dr. Alexander Klemin Award for notable achievement in the advancement of rotary-wing aeronautics.

JOHN J. SCHNEIDER

Rotary-Wing V/STOL: Development of the Tilt Rotor

Historically, the rotary-wing vertical or short takeoff and landing (V/STOL) concept is as ancient as the earliest thoughts on airplane design. The Chinese top, dating from about 400 B.C., seems to be the earliest known embodiment of it. Though the term V/STOL is of relatively recent origin, Leonardo da Vinci dreamed of and designed his "aerial screw" 500 years ago. It was not until the nineteenth century, however, that the idea of flight really exploded, a direct result of the development of mechanical power—first steam, then gasoline. The earliest gasoline engines really got started with the development of the Otto Cycle in Germany in 1876, preparing the way for the engines developed there by Otto's assistant Gottlieb Daimler and by Karl Benz.

During the nineteenth century, many dreamers conceived a variety of both vertical-lift aircraft and winged airplanes. About 1843, Sir George Cayley conceived a design that had both rotors for hovering and propellers for cruise flight—probably the earliest precursor of the twentieth-century V/STOL test beds. During the nineteenth century, early gliding enthusiasts and airship experimenters were risking their necks to discover the secrets of the birds. By 1896, Otto Lilienthal had made more than 2,000 glides, and Henri Giffard flew his steam-powered airship in 1852. The net result of all this activity was the dawn of powered flight with the beginning of the twentieth century.

Successful development of the airplane was kicked off by Orville and Wilbur Wright on December 17, 1903, followed by all the familiar airplanes, autogiros, and helicopters. Incidentally, the Wrights were originally inspired by the concept of the helicopter for vertical flight. In about 1880, when Wilbur was eleven years of age and Orville was seven, their father gave them one of the latest toys—the rubber-band-powered helicopter invented by the Frenchman Alphonse Penaud. This stimulated their interest in flying. Wilbur tried building larger and larger models—finding that they did not fly well, because their rubber-band power was never adequate. They gave up at the time, and their interest in flying remained passive until 1896, when, triggered by the death of the German gliding pioneer Otto Lilienthal in a crash on August 10, it became intense. Wilbur did not live to see a successful helicopter; Orville finally became a reluctant convert, however, when Igor Sikorsky's pilot, Les Morris, flew the XR-4 out to Wright Field in 1942.

Another development, that of Emile and Henry Berliner in the 1920s, embodied the rudiments of a vertical takeoff and landing (VTOL) craft—even though what they were developing was a helicopter. This aircraft had tilting rotors on the wings and a pitch control rotor aft, near the tail.

Figure 1 is a glossary of V/STOL aircraft

V/STOL AIRCRAFT GLOSSARY

Hover	· Stationary flight at a given height with little horizontal movement with respect to air currents.
VTOL	· Vertical Take-Off and Landing. The capability to take off and land with zero ground roll (i.e., hover).
STOL	· Short Take-Off and Landing. The capability to take off and land with a steep gradient climb and descent with a short ground roll.
V/STOL	· Combined VTOL and STOL. The capability to accomplish VTOL at a specified weight and STOL at higher weights.
Rotor V/STOL	· A V/STOL aircraft whose vertical lift capability is provided by a hinged or hingeless helicopter rotor of relatively low disk loading (typically 15 psf or less).
Propeller V/STOL	· A V/STOL aircraft whose vertical lift capability is provided by a typical airplane propeller of moderately high disk loading (in the range of 35 to 75 psf).
Ducted Fan V/STOL	· A V/STOL aircraft whose vertical lift capability is provided by a shrouded fan (or propeller) of moderate to high disk loading (in the range of 50 to 350 psf).
Turbofan/Turbojet V/STOL	· A V/STOL aircraft whose vertical lift capability is provided by turbojet or turbofan engines of very high disk loading (typically from 800 to 2000 psf).
Lift Engine	· A turbojet or turbofan engine used only during the vertical lifting/transition modes.
Cruise Engine	· A turbojet or turbofan entine used only during the forward-flight mode.
Helicopter	· An aircraft whose vertical lift and propulsive thrust is provided by the same rotor(s).
Compound Helicopter	· A helicopter derivative wherein lift and thrust in the high-speed mode is provided by other systems such as wings, propellers, turbojets, etc.
Composite Aircraft	· A term for rotor V/STOL aircraft.
Convertiplane	· A term for aircraft capable of converting from helicopter-type flight to high-speed airplane-type flight.
Nap-of-the-Earth	· Constant-altitude terrain-following type flight.

Figure 1.
V/STOL aircraft glossary

terminology along with several other definitions related to vertical lift. Although helicopters technically fit the V/STOL definition, they are generally excluded; in practice a V/STOL craft is capable of much higher speeds and has more of the qualities of an airplane, along with its vertical-lift capability. The V/STOL aircraft differs from conventional airplanes in two essential respects:

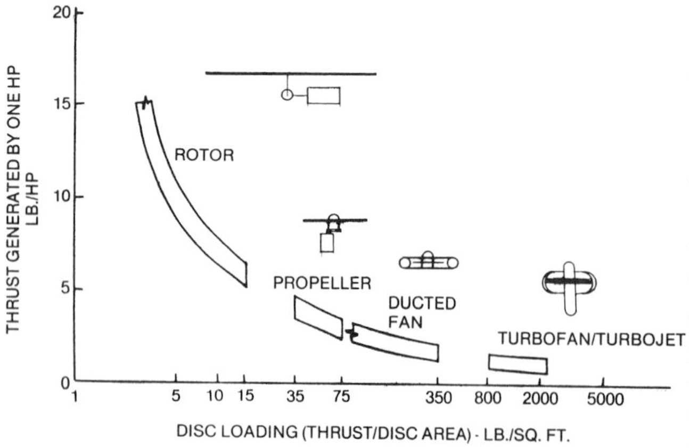

Figure 2.
Four methods for vertical lift

thrust in the vertical lifting mode must exceed the operating weight by some margin, and the craft must be capable of controlling pitch, yaw, and roll without the benefit of any aerodynamic forces that are the result of its speed.

Probably the most difficult problem to be solved—even today—is the provision of the lifting thrust in an economical and fuel-efficient manner. This thrust requirement—three to ten times as large as that of a typical airplane—was the factor that delayed the development of the helicopter and the V/STOL by some thirty to forty years. The search for economical methods of converting horsepower to thrust has led to the development of the V/STOL in four categories of thrust generation, as shown in figure 2. The thrust generated by one horsepower decreases in proportion to the size—that is, the disc area—of the generator, varying from the highest—the rotor—progressively lower to the propeller, the ducted fan, and the turbofan and turbojet.

In each of these categories there are generally four methods for converting the system from the vertical thrusting mode to the horizontal cruising flight mode (see figure 3). Within this simple four-by-four matrix, an endless variety of concepts is possible with the use of different methods of generation, different methods of thrust conversion, or redirection, and variations in hover control.

The simplest method of conversion or redirection of the thrust vector is that of tilting the aircraft, a method typically used in the conventional helicopter, in which a modest 5 to 10 degrees of tilting provides the necessary redirection of the thrust. Other, higher-speed concepts have relied on 90 degrees of tilting—the so-called tail-sitters. Rather than tilting the aircraft 90 degrees, others have tilted only the thrusting system. The tilt rotor tilts only the rotors, usually on the wing tips, while the tilt wing tilts the wing and the propellers, usually mounted midspan; tilting ducted fans and turbofans are similar in concept. A simplified approach to thrust tilting is the vec-

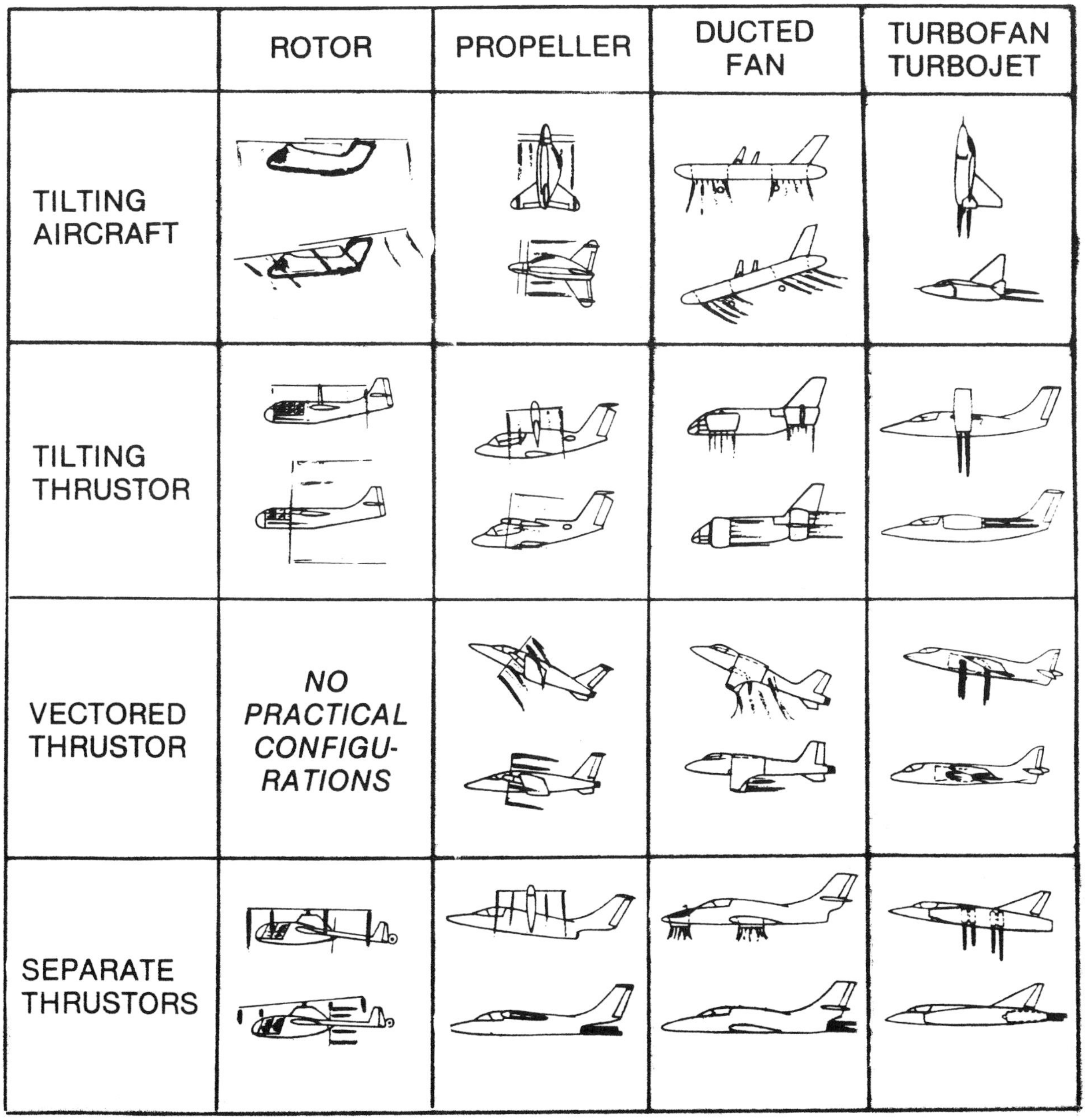

Figure 3.
Matrix of thrust redirection methods

tored-thrust method, wherein wing flaps, vane cascades, or nozzle-swiveling systems change the thrust vector 90 degrees or more. Separate thrusters have a long history, going back to the designs of Cayley, in 1843; they are typified in the compound helicopter, wherein the rotor is used for vertical thrust while lift in cruise is provided by a wing, and cruise thrust may be provided by either propellers or fans. In other categories, lift engines may be shut down in cruise with turbojets or turbofans providing cruise thrust.

Performance of V/STOLs generally follows the trend of disc loading—the higher

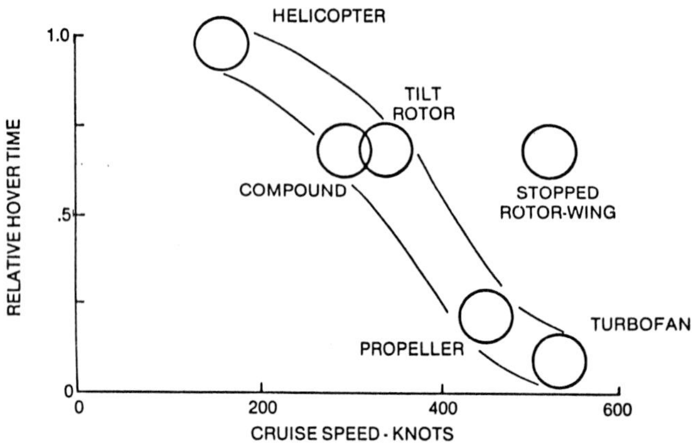

Figure 4.
Performance of V/STOLs

the disc loading, the higher the speed and range capability. Conversely, the relative hover time available decreases with higher disc loadings. Figure 4 illustrates this trend. Most of the V/STOL concepts based on rotor-lift systems, however, were specifically designed to avoid the loss in hover time by either tilting the rotor to become a propeller, stopping the rotor, or flying as a compound helicopter with a slowed rotor.

Why V/STOL? Obviously, by definition, a V/STOL can hover! From hover, the V/STOL can land in an area only slightly larger than its dimensions; from hover, the V/STOL can perform useful tasks such as rescuing personnel by means of hoist systems, picking up cargo loads on cables, maneuvering around obstacles, climbing over terrain—a nearly endless list of services that may be generally impossible for other vehicles.

While the airplane is an efficient, economical vehicle for transportation over moderate to long distances, its need to operate from rather large airports reduces its attractiveness for short-range operations. Conversely, because its hover capability allows it to operate from a small area while the power penalty reduces its long-range attractiveness, the V/STOL is the logical short-haul aircraft. The V/STOL is flexible in short-range operations, reducing total journey time significantly. For military purposes use of the V/STOL eliminates the need for prepared landing surfaces, thereby significantly improving battlefield mobility, responsiveness, flexibility of operation, and the ability to survive combat.

Unfortunately, because of its additional complexity and need for greater power, the costs of V/STOL aircraft are higher, and start-up costs are a drawback, even though total system costs are probably lower for many vital operations. It has therefore taken several generations for the helicopter-type V/STOLs to really take off. After three decades of progress, the future for the next generation of rotary-wing V/STOLS looks bright.

The history of the rotary-wing V/STOL really begins in the early 1930s with Gerard P. Herrick and E. Burke Wilford, both of whom worked in the Philadelphia area. The Herrick HV-2A was the culmination of about six years of development by Herrick, who is sometimes called the father of the convertiplane (see figure 5). Ralph McClarren, his chief engineer, designed the HV-2A to fly as an airplane, then to start the upper wing turning as a rotor for a vertical landing.

Wilford's gyroplane, while not strictly a V/STOL, is included here as an early example of a compound helicopter—a craft that has a powered rotor for lift but has another means of propulsion as well—and because it led Wilford, who greatly influenced the later development of V/STOL aircraft, into the V/STOL field.

The Focke-Achgelis Fa-61 lateral twin helicopter spawned a number of developments in V/STOL, as will be seen later. In 1937, this helicopter was flown sixty-seven miles between Bremen and Berlin, piloted by Hanna Reitsch, the twenty-six-year-old aviatrix who made the famous flights inside Berlin's Deutschland-Halle in 1938.

It is impossible to leave 1937 without a look at the Baynes Heliplane—a tilt-rotor craft patented but never built (see figure 6). From a British design that evolved in the course of several years, this aircraft was to be powered by a gas-generator turbine, with two Pescara-type gas generators in the mid

fuselage that were to supply high-pressure gases through a pipe in the wing to the turbines in the nacelles.

Another person of importance during the late 1930s was a man who never built an aircraft of any type. The influence of Alexander Klemin and the courses he taught at the Guggenheim School of Aeronautics of New York University are still being felt today. The list of students who attended his helicopter engineering courses and later made significant advances in the field of rotary-wing and V/STOL aircraft is too long to be included here.

Meanwhile, developments in the autogiro world and military testing of their capabilities culminated in the 1938 Dorsey bill of the U.S. House of Representatives, which appropriated $2 million for the development of a modern rotary-wing aircraft for the U.S. Army.

In the competition only two helicopter designs, the Platt-LePage XR-1 (see figure 7) and the Sikorsky VS-300, were submitted. All the others were autogiro designs. The XR-1, which was similar to the Focke-Achgelis helicopter, was selected over the Sikor-

Figure 5.
Herrick HV-2A stopped-rotor convertiplane

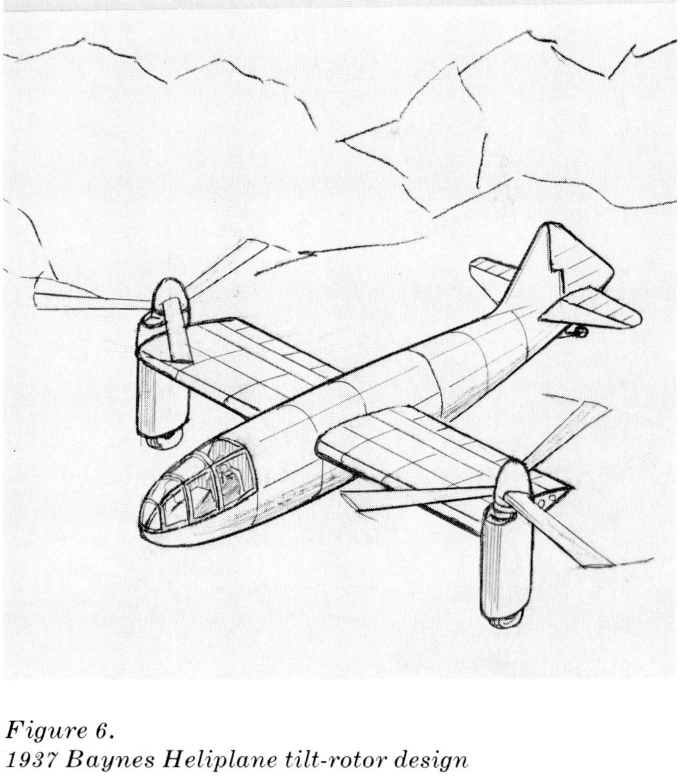

Figure 6.
1937 Baynes Heliplane tilt-rotor design

Figure 7.
The Platt-LePage XR-1 helicopter

sky design. The XR-1 had a fuselage similar to that of a normal airplane, with the engine located in approximately the middle of the fuselage. Extending from the fuselage were two identical pylons with rotors at the end that rotated in opposite directions to counteract the torque.

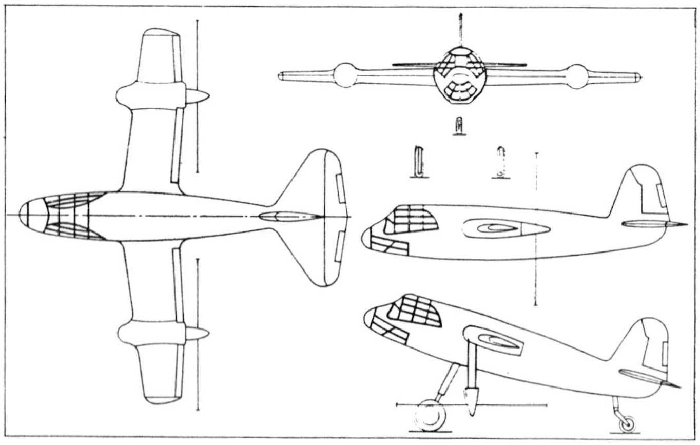

Figure 8.
The Focke-Achgelis Fa-269 pusher tilt-rotor design

Not to be outdone, however, Igor Sikorsky continued to develop his VS-300 and made successful flights early in 1941. He then made an unsolicited proposal to the army and was awarded the 1941 XR-4 contract, which used about $50,000 that remained from the Dorsey bill appropriation.

Sikorsky had first attempted to construct a helicopter in 1909, but was unsuccessful and gave it up. In 1913, he went on to design and build the world's largest airplane in Russia. He emigrated to the United States and continued to design and produce large airplanes and flying boats. He did not forget his first love—the helicopter—however, and luckily for all of us he continued his design studies, which led to the VS-300 and subsequent Sikorsky models.

The technically prolific Germans of the early 1940s exerted a great influence on the later, peaceful development of V/STOL aircraft. Professor Henrich Focke had been associated with the Focke-Wulf Aircraft Company since 1923, building transport airplanes; by 1938, however, in disfavor with the Nazis, he was forced out, and he established the Focke-Achgelis Company, which went on, from the Fa-61 lateral twin helicopter, to develop helicopters further during the war, while the Focke-Wulf Company concentrated on producing fighter planes.

Perhaps the most interesting V/STOL design developed by Focke was that of the Fa-269, a tilt rotor, but of the pusher variety (see figure 8). Because of his pressing helicopter developments, however, very little work was done on this project.

Incidentally, Focke joined the South Eastern French Helicopter Group after the war, where his lateral twin helicopters were further developed. Later he went under contract to Brazil, where he designed a tandem tilt-propeller V/STOL. A ground-test stand was constructed, but the aircraft was never flown.

Helicopters were gradually coming along as the United States emerged from World War II, and some forward thinkers began V/STOL-type rumblings. W. Laurence LePage, during the last days of the XR-1 development, suggested a tilt-rotor design based on the XR-1 (see figure 9). The proposed design consisted of a conventional airplane fuselage and wings, with a rotor mounted at each wing tip—very similar to the XR-1 and the Fa-61. As the aircraft accelerated, however, the rotors could be tilted to operate as propellers. Although it was an advanced design, the proposed 92-foot rotors and the 53,000-pound gross weight were far beyond the state of the art in 1946.

One of LePage's engineers, Robert Lichten, had earlier gone to Kellett Aircraft Company and had met an aero engineer by the name of Mario Guerierri. Lichten and Guerierri formed Transcendental Aircraft in 1945 and began development of a single-place tilt rotor using rotors seventeen feet in diameter and having a gross weight of 1,750 pounds. Lichten later ended his association with Guerierri and headed the tilt-rotor programs at Bell Helicopter.

Development of the Transcendental Model 1-G was financed entirely with private funds and, worked on by moonlighting engineers from Bellanca and elsewhere, took nearly six years to complete. The first ground test runs were plagued by dynamic rotor and

Figure 9.
LePage's Tilt-Rotor design

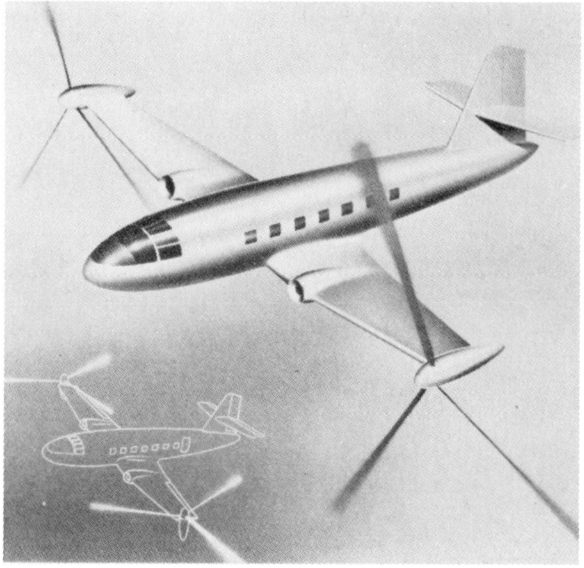

wing problems, and an accident in 1951 led to a series of U.S. Air Force contracts to investigate tilt-rotor test operations and gather data on such things as mechanical instabilities. After repair of the Model 1-G and further ground tests, free flight was achieved on July 6, 1954. During the following year, more than a hundred flights were made and twenty-three hours of flight time were accumulated. On July 20, 1955, however, in a flight over the Delaware River, the friction lock on the collective slipped and the aircraft went into a steep dive. Recovery was nearly complete when the landing gear hit the water, flipping the aircraft on its back for a complete washout.

By this time, Guerierri had been bought out by William E. Cobey, a well-known Kellett vibrations expert, and he managed to build an improved version, the Model 2 (see figure 10). Significant changes were an increase in horsepower from 160 to 250 and a one-foot increase in the diameter of the rotor, allowing gross weight to approach 4,000 pounds. First flown in 1956, the model was too late to compete with other advanced V/STOL aircraft, such as the Bell XV-3, which will be described later, and the program was closed down in late 1957.

Figure 10.
The Transcendental Model 2 tilt rotor

In 1949, E. Burke Wilford organized and presided over the historic First Convertible Aircraft Congress, which was held in Philadelphia. It was cosponsored by the Institute of Aeronautical Sciences and the American Helicopter Society and was attended by 200 V/STOL enthusiasts. The outcome of the meeting was sponsorship of the 1950 Convertiplane Competition by the U.S. Army.

That first congress and the Second Convertible Aircraft Congress, held in Philadelphia in 1952, were the high points of a total of seven congresses. The 1952 congress led to the Air Coordinating Committee Report by Colonel William B. Bunker, which seemed to kick off the U.S. Army's test-bed program of the late 1950s.

The 1949 Convertible Aircraft Congress was the catalyst that set the army and air force in motion. Two men, Colonel Dave Cogswell and Colonel Chet DeGarvre, led the way to the industrywide competition of the early 1950s for an observation and reconnaissance convertiplane. Nineteen designs were submitted by seventeen companies. Virtually all of them could be classified in three groups, so three designs were selected as the most logical approaches for the initial design studies, wind-tunnel tests, and construction of a mock-up.

McDonnell's XV-1 was a compound helicopter based on Fred Doblhoff's pressure jet plus a tip-burning rotor. The Sikorsky XV-2 composite aircraft with a retractable rotor was a single blader with a counterbalanced weight. This design was subjected to considerable wind-tunnel testing but was not selected for the follow-on prototype program. The Bell XV-3 proposal was, of course, a continuation of the LePage-Guerierri-Lichten tilt-rotor design. Both the McDonnell XV-1 and the Bell XV-3 were later selected for prototype development. The McDonnell XV-1 (see figure 11) was a two-place convertiplane incorporating a three-blade pressure-jet-driven rotor, a wing to unload the rotor at high speeds, and a pusher propeller in a twin-boom configuration.

Even though the McDonnell XV-1 made successful conversions in early 1955 and speeds of 200 miles an hour were reached during U.S. Air Force evaluations, configuration-induced aerodynamic problems and the excessive noise of the tip jet burning prompted the phaseout of the XV-1.

The first Bell XV-3 prototype tilt rotor was rolled out on February 10, 1955, as seen in figure 12 with Robert Lichten describing the tilting process. After completion of the usual structural-proof tests, rotor-whirl tests, and ground run-ups, the initial hovering tests were made on August 11, 1955, with Floyd Carlson of Bell at the controls. Powered by a single reciprocating engine driving twenty-three-foot rotors, the XV-3 initially had three-blade rotors mounted on long masts (see figure 13).

Following two months of hover and low-speed testing and attempts to convert from hover to forward flight in the first aircraft, a violent whirl-mode instability caused the crash and washout of that aircraft. After critical analysis of the cause and a decision to build and test a short-shaft two-blade rotor system on the second XV-3, the modified aircraft was tested in the National Aeronautics and Space Administration (NASA) Ames Research Center's forty-by-eighty full-scale tunnel in late 1957. This aircraft is shown in figure 14, with the modified rotor system,

Figure 11.
The McDonnell XV-1 compound helicopter convertiplane

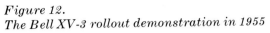

Figure 12.
The Bell XV-3 rollout demonstration in 1955

Figure 13.
Early hover tests of the Bell XV-3 with three-blade rotors

Figure 14.
The XV-3 hovering, with short-shaft two-blade rotors

in hover tests with Floyd Carlson again at the controls.

After another series of tests in the tunnel for further exploration of whirl-mode instabilities, the XV-3 made its first complete conversion from helicopter to airplane flight on December 17, 1958, with pilot Bill Quinlon in the cockpit (see figure 15).

During the next seven years, further full-scale wind-tunnel tests, U.S. Air Force tests at Edwards Air Force Base, and NASA flight-test programs, along with Bell's testing, established the feasibility of the tilt rotor. The XV-3 had operated for 375 wind-tunnel and ground-test hours, had made more than 110 full conversions and 250 test flights, and had flown for 125 hours. At least three army, two air force, two NASA, and four Bell pilots were indoctrinated into the tilt rotor's flight regime. Although there were detail problems inherent in the XV-3, the technology was near-at-hand for initiation of the follow-on tilt-rotor demonstrator program—the Bell XV-15 turbine-powered tilt rotor.

Figure 15.
The first full conversion of the Bell XV-3

Following the initiation of the army's convertiplane development with McDonnell, Sikorsky, and Bell, other developments of the rotary-wing V/STOL were begun. The Jacobs Aircraft Engine Company, for instance, built a small compound helicopter, the J-104, with intermeshing tail rotor and pusher propeller. A rather crude tilt-rotor test bed was built by C. H. York (see figure 16). In England, Fairey began the development of the gyrodyne that led to the large Fairey Rotodyne civil transport. The Rotodyne was similar in concept to the McDonnell XV-1 but was powered by two turboprop engines (see figure 17). The Russians followed suit with their Kamov Ka-22 compound convertiplane.

Throughout the 1950s and 1960s there were many attempts to find the practical, efficient, high-speed rotary-wing V/STOL,

Figure 16.
The Yorkopter convertiplane

whether in the form of a compound helicopter, a stoppable rotor aircraft, or a craft with a retractable stowed rotor. The list is nearly endless; coupled with concurrent developments in propeller, ducted-fan, and jet-lift V/STOLs, the result was a proliferation of V/STOL studies, proposals, and test-bed aircraft during this period.

In the meantime, development of the tilt rotor continued after completion, in 1966, of the XV-3 test programs. It was for the most part a dual effort for the next five years—financed by two companies, Bell and Boeing, and several government agencies—NASA, the U.S. Army, and the U.S. Air Force.

During the next five years, Boeing Vertol completed more than 3,500 hours of testing of tilt-rotor models. Since so much of the testing was of the dynamics, the program also required development of the technology of building and testing dynamically scaled models. Seven models were built and tested, principal among them the one-tenth

Figure 17.
The Fairey Rotodyne compound helicopter V/STOL

scale aeroelastic model, the thirteen-foot performance rotor with full-scale tip speeds, and then, with funds from the army and NASA, the twenty-six-foot full-scale demonstrator rotor. In addition, a full-scale wing with download alleviation devices on the leading and trailing edges was tested under rotor downwash. During this period a number of studies were made for NASA to evaluate the tilt-rotor concept in several commercial applications.

Bell had initiated a comprehensive small-scale model test and analytical program during the early 1960s in order to understand the technology questions coming from the wind-tunnel and flight testing of the XV-3 aircraft. Several different approaches for dynamic stability evolved and were studied in detail. Bell was one of three winners in the army's 1965 Composite Aircraft Program, and the design-definition phase was completed in 1967. This aircraft of 30,000 pounds gross weight was similar to today's JVX concept, and the army planned a major research program around it. Timely financial support did not materialize, however, and the Bell management decided to initiate a further company-financed program to develop a technology-demonstrator aircraft. A full-scale mock-up was constructed of the 9,000-pound Bell Model 300, and a twenty-five-foot rotor and drive system were developed. Rotor testing was performed at the NASA Ames Research Center's forty-by-eighty full-scale wind tunnel with funds from the army and NASA.

During 1969 and 1970, the air force sponsored model tests and design studies of a tilt rotor aimed at higher speeds, in which the rotors were feathered, stopped, then folded around the nacelle with high-speed thrust obtained from turbofan convertible engines.

As a result of the work on the XV-3 and all the model testing described, the army and NASA were ready by 1972 to offer a development contract for two technology-demonstrator aircraft. After a design competition between Bell and Boeing, Bell was selected to design and manufacture two tilt-rotor research aircraft having a maximum gross weight of 15,000 pounds, twenty-five-foot rotors, and two Lycoming LTC1K-4K engines of 1,550 shaft horsepower (shp) each—the XV-15 (Bell Model 301).

Bell's offering, the product of project engineer Ken Wernicke and his superb engineering staff, was a significantly improved Model 300 now having a gross weight of 12,400 pounds and a redesigned H-type tail, which offered greater directional stability. NASA requirements released during this period produced additional changes, not the least of which were replacement of the 1,150-shp Pratt & Whitney engines with 1,550-shp Lycoming engines, incorporation of dual-wheel Canadair CL-84 landing gear in place of single-wheel units, a change from Douglas ESCAPAC 1-E ejection seats to Rockwell-Columbus LW-3B ejection seats, the addition of crashworthy fuel tanks, the addition of boosted rudder and elevator controls, and a third hydraulic system for redundancy. The eventual result was an almost totally new aircraft. In fact, the revisions and redesigns were so numerous that Bell eventually elected to redesignate the vehicle as the Model 301.

On July 31, a contract for Phase IIA studies of the new tilt-rotor program was officially awarded to Bell Helicopter Textron. On September 26, 1973, Phase IIB officially got under way. This included the final design, the beginning of fabrication, and preliminary testing of two Model 301 tilt-rotor research aircraft.

The following is a chronology of the events that took place between the signing of the Phase IIB contract and the first hover flight of the number 1 XV-15 prototype:

- Engineering design completed—March 1975.
- Canopy-jettison and ejection-seat tests—July 1975.
- Transfer of Aircraft no. 1 fuselage from Rockwell to Bell Helicopter Textron—October 7, 1975.
- Final assembly of Aircraft no. 1—October 1975 to May 1976.

- Transfer of fuselage of Aircraft no. 2 from Rockwell to Bell Helicopter Textron—December 22, 1975.
- Transfer of Aircraft no. 1 to plant 6—May 15, 1976.
- Tests of checkout and integrated systems of Aircraft no. 1—May through December 1976.
- Official rollout of Aircraft no. 1 from plant 6—October 22, 1976.
- Beginning of ground run of Aircraft no. 1—January 21, 1977.
- Ground run of Aircraft no. 1.
- First conversion, 75 degrees—March 22, 1977.
- First full conversion—March 31, 1977 (see figure 18).

By the first of May, the XV-15 had completed more than thirty-two successful ground runs. Problems encountered were minor. Finally, on May 3, a free hover was accomplished for the first time (see figure 19). Because of the conservative attitude of everyone concerned, a decision had been made by NASA to limit the flight-test time of the number 1 XV-15 to three hours. NASA felt that it would be best to limit flight-envelope exploration until full-scale wind-tunnel tests had been completed. A time limit was placed not only on actual flight testing, but also on attainable speed. This consisted of 40 knots forward, 10 knots rearward, and 25 knots sidewise. The forward speed, incidentally, was mandated by the fact that the full-scale tunnel at the Ames Research Center had a usable low speed of no less than 60 knots.

From the end of the short three-hour test program on May 31, 1977, and its delivery to NASA Ames Research Center by Lockheed C-5A on March 23, 1978, the first prototype XV-15 was ground-run qualified, inspected, and modified for the coming wind-tunnel tests. Modifications included removal of the Rockwell ejection seats and their replacement by data-recording instruments and remote-control devices. The XV-15 was not to be manned during any of the Ames tests.

Figure 18.
The Bell XV-15 ground-run conversion test sequence

Figure 19.
The first flight of the Bell XV-15

Almost two months after its arrival at Ames Research Center, the number 1 XV-15A was mounted in the full-scale tunnel. The first test took place on May 18, the entire series lasting through June 23. Airspeeds of 60 to 180 knots were fully explored and all modes of helicopter and airplane flight were investigated. Extensive testing was done in the conversion corridor.

Significant quantities of data were accumulated during the twenty hours of tunnel tests, analysis of which revealed that the XV-15A was unquestionably a good aircraft, with few significant problems, if any. It was now cleared for further expansion of the actual flight envelope, while further exploration of the XV-15 envelope was scheduled to be undertaken by the second prototype.

While wind-tunnel tests with XV-15 number 1 were under way, number 2 was nearing completion. By the end of July, rollout had taken place, and on August 2, ground runs were initiated.

Ground testing continued throughout the rest of the year and into the spring of 1979. Finally, on April 23, the first successful hover flight was made—but not without difficulty; a number of minor problems plagued the airplane during the many months of its ground-test program. Among these was a stress-corrosion crack in the left engine gearbox, a clutch misengagement, and damage from foreign objects within the transmission.

The first in-flight partial conversion, from 90 degrees to 85 degrees, took place on May 5, 1979. This was followed by an 80-degree conversion on May 10, a 75-degree conversion on May 15, a 70-degree conversion on June 13, a 65-degree conversion on June 15, a 60-degree conversion on June 20, a 45-degree conversion on July 17, a 30-degree conversion on July 19, and finally, on July 24, a full conversion (to 0 degrees).

The full conversion was, of course, an event of tremendous import to the XV-15 program. Of equal significance was the ease with which it was accomplished (see figure 20). The entire mission had proved virtually trouble-free and the test crew, Dorman Cannon and Ron Erhart, had few, if any, complaints. Conversion had gone exactly as expected and almost exactly like those flown in the simulator at Ames Research Center.

By this time, Bell, the flight-test crews,

Figure 20.
Conversion sequence of the Bell XV-15

and NASA were confident enough to approve a fairly rapid exploration of the XV-15's flight envelope. Following the first full conversion, the procedure became almost commonplace during the weeks following.

In the contractor flight test phase at Bell, which concluded in August 1980, the basic conversion corridor and airspeed-altitude envelope up to 16,000 feet was demonstrated at one gross weight and center of gravity. Approximately a hundred full conversions were made from the helicopter mode to the airplane mode and back.

As is usual in any helicopter development program, some resonance and the resultant load problems were uncovered. When these had been identified, several possible solutions to relocate frequencies and reduce loadings were evaluated analytically, and some of the modifications were flight tested. These and aircraft operating techniques produced a large and virtually fatigue-damage-free envelope for proof of concept testing.

Handling qualities have been judged good to excellent. The quickness with which the pilots began to use the conversion system as an extra flight control was surprising. Some refinements were made in the in-ground-effect hover handling qualities by changes in the stabilization control augmentation system (SCAS).

The design criteria of the XV-15 systems demanded that a single failure would not prevent the completion of normal flight operations. The aircraft was therefore designed to be flown without the use of a system or component wherever possible. Systems that are essential for flight were designed to be fail-operate after the second failure. During the contractor test program, all potential failures were simulated in flight tests or on ground-tiedown tests. No hazardous effects on handling qualities or aircraft performance were noted during these tests, which inadvertently included an actual engine failure, dramatically demonstrating the benefits of the interconnected transmission system.

After the contractor test phase and the delivery of the two aircraft to the government, operation at gross weights up to the 15,000-pound short takeoff and landing (STOL) weight were demonstrated.

The aeroelastic stability of the wing-pylon-rotor system was one of the primary points of interest in the XV-15 flight-test program and has been one of the most successful phases of the program. Aeroelastic stability data that had been taken during level and windmilling flight agreed well with predictions. Additional testing up to a 360-knot design dive speed is planned, to determine whether any trends toward instability exist within the flight envelope and for correlation of actual flutter with the predictions.

The performance demonstration was equally gratifying. The predicted cruise speed of 300 knots was achieved with normal rated power at 16,000 feet in June 1980. This was particularly noteworthy in that the usual drag-reduction program had not yet been performed on the XV-15.

Sensitivity to gusts in the airplane mode flight, caused by the lightly loaded rotors, was predicted as a potential shortcoming of the tilt-rotor concept. It had been noted in the government flight test report of the XV-3 that,

though the response of the XV-3 to gusts was not an unacceptable deficiency, the unusual and annoying response characteristics should be included in this discussion of the principle. The XV-3 behaved peculiarly in gusts in that the aircraft responded with abrupt longitudinal accelerations and generally, with a yawing motion. . . . The seriousness of this peculiar response to gusts in future prop-rotor aircraft is unknown. The longitudinal response due to a gust will decrease as prop-rotor rpm decreases, airspeed increases, blade angle increases, and blade area decreases. Many of these factors would, by necessity, be incorporated in a future design having more performance.

The XV-15 demonstrated excellent ride qualities over all. Because of its high wing loading, its vertical response was noticeably lower than that of the turboprop chase airplane. Occasional forward surging and yawing in turbulence was noticeable, but the pilots preferred this motion to the hard ride of the chase airplane under the same conditions. None of the guest pilots of the XV-15 commented on gust sensitivity, even though some of these flights involved operation at high speed and low altitude in gusty twenty-knot winds. In fact, many have remarked on the good ride quality of the XV-15.

In January 1981, a series of hover, downwash, and noise tests were made by the Ames Research Center flight operations group, managed by the NASA-Army XV-15 Project Office and personnel from the Naval Air Test Center. The aircraft was hovered at various heights in addition to being operated on a tiedown facility at various rotor speeds and power settings. Data were obtained for hover performance both in and out of ground effect, downwash phenomena, handling characteristics as a function of hover height, and acoustics around the hovering aircraft. The results showed that the XV-15 is efficient in hover and that increased control activity is required as the aircraft approaches the ground. Downwash velocities are moderate at the sides of the aircraft and relatively high fore and aft. The acoustics evaluation revealed moderate noise levels with an acceptable sound quality.

In addition to these tests, an informal demonstration was conducted at Bell by a guest pilot, a lieutenant colonel in the Marine Corps, who requested permission to walk under the hovering XV-15 to evaluate the downwash. He reported no difficulty except in the fore and aft portion of the flow field where the outflow is deeper than at the sides of the aircraft. Even at the worst location, however, he was able to maintain position and move about as desired.

One potential benefit of the somewhat higher disc loading of the XV-15 was noted in a hover test conducted at Bell with a light coating of snow on the ramp. The downwash pushed the snow away from the aircraft, as expected, but there was virtually none of the recirculation that creates a white-out effect for a helicopter pilot. The XV-15 pilot reported that he had more than adequate visibility to hover, particularly since the outwash flow field tended to clear a path forward of the nose.

The results so far have supported a high degree of confidence that the projected benefits of the design—fast and efficient cruise, helicopterlike hover efficiency and handling qualities—have been demonstrated and that there are no potential problems to limit the capability of the aircraft.

Aircraft number 2 was flown by the NASA Ames Research Center Flight Operations Branch in the ongoing proof-of-concept program to document the performance and handling qualities of the XV-15 throughout its airspeed and altitude envelope at various gross weights, including evaluation of center-of-gravity effects. Modifications are planned that will improve the handling qualities of the aircraft, reduce gust sensitivity, and improve performance.

Meanwhile suitability testing for military missions was being done by Bell Helicopter with Aircraft number 1, under contract to the NASA-Army XV-15 Project Office. As part of this kind of testing, a guest-pilot program was initiated in late 1981 to familiarize high-level military pilots and selected civilian pilots with the unique capability of the tilt rotor to operate as either a helicopter or an airplane and make a smooth transition between the two. More than fifty guest pilots have flown the aircraft, including Senator Barry Goldwater, the Secretary of the Navy, and many admirals and generals.

Each flight by a guest pilot consisted of a brief demonstration of helicopter, conversion, and airplane modes by Dorman Cannon, Bell's XV-15 project pilot. The guest pilot then took the controls and flew the aircraft. After a few minutes of familiarization maneuvering, he was usually talked through an airplane mode stall, single-engine operation, and reconversion and conversion at altitude. After returning to the airport each pilot made several takeoffs and landings, usually converting to airplane mode and back on each circuit.

There was remarkable consensus in the post-flight debriefings of the guest pilots. They judged it to be as easy to hover in the aircraft as in a helicopter, if not easier. Conversion was unanimously considered to be a straightforward, low-workload process. Handling qualities in airplane mode, particularly during single-engine operations, were praised. Many commented on the low level of interior noise and the smooth ride. All were favorably impressed with the potential capability of the tilt rotor to perform a wide variety of military missions.

Another phase of the effort to demonstrate the capabilities of the XV-15 tilt rotor to a cross-section of operational, technical, and decisionmaking personnel in the military services took place in March 1982. An XV-15 flight demonstration was requested as part of the Army Aviation Systems Program Review to be held at Fort Rucker, Alabama. An East Coast demonstration tour was therefore arranged, which included seven flight demonstrations at six different locations in eight days.

The first demonstration was at Fort Rucker. The following morning the aircraft was on static display and was flown in a flight demonstration at NASA Langley Research Center for personnel from Lan-

gley Research Center, Langley Air Force Base, Norfolk Naval Air Station, Fort Eustis, and Fort Monroe. The following day it was demonstrated at the Marine Corps Air Station, Quantico, Virginia. Two demonstrations were provided at Fort Belvoir for Washington area personnel, followed by a visit to the Pentagon helipad. On its way back to Fort Worth, Texas, the XV-15 was demonstrated at Fort Campbell, Kentucky, and in Saint Louis, the latter to personnel from the Army Aviation Research and Development Command and from Scott Air Force Base.

The XV-15 was flown 2,600 nautical miles during this tour, routinely cruising at 275 knots true airspeed. A Cessna Citation jet is used to accompany the XV-15 on these trips. Only the routine daily preflight maintenance was required.

Following the East Coast tour, XV-15 number 1 was modified at Bell's Arlington, Texas, Flight Research Facility for participation in the Army Special Electronics Mission Aircraft (SEMA) evaluation. This included installation of an APR-39 radar warning system, a chaff-dispenser system, and a government-furnished video panel package, all in addition to the 1,100-plus pounds of research instrumentation system that the XV-15 normally carries.

The XV-15 departed the Fort Worth area for the Fort Huachuca, Arizona, area in early May. Less than three weeks later it was back, having completed the first phase of the SEMA evaluation at Fort Huachuca, radar cross-section measurements at the China Lake Naval Air Station, California, and another 2,100 miles cross country. After a scheduled inspection at Bell, the aircraft departed in late June for the second phase of the SEMA evaluation at Fort Huachuca, shipboard trials at sea aboard the *Tripoli*, an amphibious warfare ship, and the third and final phase of the SEMA evaluation at Nellis Air Force Base (see figure 21).

Figure 21.
Sea trials of the Bell XV-15 on the LPH-10 Tripoli

While the XV-15 program is not complete at this writing, the primary goals have been attained and can be summarized as follows:

Helicopter Mode

- Angle of Bank—60 degrees
- Autorotative descents
- Speeds of 100 knots forward
  —35 knots sideward
  —30 knots rearward
- Insensitive to wind direction
- Low downwash
- Excellent handling qualities
- Vertical takeoffs and landings at 4,500-foot density altitude

Conversion Mode

- Low workload–twelve-second conversion
- 70-knot-wide corridor
- Angle of bank—60 degrees
- Rolling takeoffs and landings on single-engine power
- 2g maneuvers

Airplane Mode

- True airspeed 100–300 knots
- Angle of bank—110 degrees
- 0 to 2.7g operation
- Climbs of 3,000 feet per minute
- Descents of 6,000 feet per minute
- 21,000-foot cruise
- Low noise and vibration
- Good ride quality

The XV-15 flight envelope is seen in figure 22.

So, after more than 350 hours of flight testing, and more than 400 conversions and reconversions, the XV-15 has proved the tilt-rotor concept. Combining this with the technology programs of Bell and Boeing—27 wind-tunnel models, 9,000 hours of wind-tunnel occupation, and more than 1,000 hours of flight-simulator development—the stage was set for the Joint Vertical Lift Aircraft

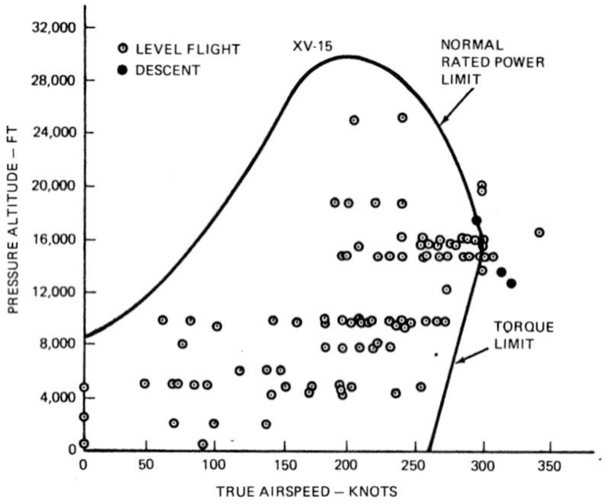

Figure 22.
The flight envelope of the XV-15

(JVX) program to provide tilt-rotor V/STOL for the marines, the navy, and others of the 1990s.

As World War II drew to a close and the terrible loss of human life during amphibious assaults by the marines was analyzed, the possibility of using helicopter V/STOLs as part of a combined sea and airborne troop assault was born. Beginning in 1946, a dedicated group of officers of the U.S. Marine Corps began to develop the vertical envelopment concept—initiated by Marine Helicopter Squadron HMX-1. Using HRP-1 helicopters, externally hung howitzers and supplies, and assault troops as well, were delivered from ship to shore.

With the addition of the HRP-2s, the marines were able to prove that the employment of helicopters in large numbers was feasible and desirable. Eventually, dedicated assault ships were developed, then in the early 1960s the marines bought the CH-46 and CH-53, the mainstays of the delivery side of the assault forces for the next twenty years.

The marines have been trying to replace these aircraft for the fifteen years beginning in 1968 with the Medium Assault Study. Actually the CH-53 was transformed during this period from a troop transport for assault into a heavy-equipment transport; the newly developed CH-53E will transport heavy equipment and perform related assignments for several years to come. Still, the marines have continued to appreciate the advantage of the higher speed V/STOLs, and they, and their navy partners, have continually examined V/STOL concepts for applicability across the board—antisubmarine warfare, airborne early warning, carrier onboard delivery, and assault.

For the past eight years or so the function of V/STOL aircraft has been vigorously studied under programs such as the medium VTOL study, V/STOL A, SBAMS, and initial V/STOL. Tilt rotors, advancing blades, helicopters, and tilt fans have been evaluated. Then finally, along came the XV-15 and its highly successful flight-test program. With the development of the XV-15 by the Bell-NASA-army team the potential of the tilt rotor was finally fully realized and the JVX program was launched.

The JVX tilt rotor is essentially a scaled-up XV-15 with components that represent many advances in technology. Figure 23 illustrates the 37,000-pound Marine Assault variant powered by two General Electric T-64 engines that drive thirty-eight-foot rotors. Its basic mission is to transport twenty-four marines over a radius of 200 nautical miles. Other missions include internal and external cargo load-carrying operations. For the navy and the air force, search-and-rescue missions are contemplated.

In retrospect, the ultimate medium subsonic-speed V/STOL solution is probably that of the tilting thrustor (see figure 3). The other approaches—tilting aircraft, vectored thrust, and separate thrustors—have been shown to be either too slow, too complex, fuel hungry, or aerodynamically and structurally inefficient, except for the special case of a single- or two-place combat aircraft, in which the vectored turbofan AV-8 Harrier has demonstrated its capability. During the V/STOL test-bed proliferation period—the 1950s and 1960s—the tilting propeller and ducted fan systems were eliminated from contention for various reasons, leaving the tilt rotor as the representative rotary-wing V/STOL concept of the future.

Figure 23.
The Bell-Boeing JVX tilt rotor

JOHN J. SCHNEIDER received the B.S. degree in aeronautical engineering from Ohio State University in 1948. He is now assistant project engineer for the Bell-Boeing JVX program. For many years, he was manager of configuration development at Boeing Vertol, where he directed exploratory studies of advanced vertical-lift aircraft. He has been responsible for configuration development of new aircraft in programs such as the army's Heavy Lift Helicopter System (HLH), Utility Tactical Transport Aircraft System (UTTAS), and the Advanced Attack Helicopter (AAH). In addition to these assignments, Mr. Schneider has been responsible for many advanced design projects in the VTOL field, ranging from compound helicopters, fan-in-wing, tilt-wing, and tilt-rotor aircraft to advanced LTA/helicopter configurations. Mr. Schneider has written numerous technical papers, holds a number of patents in aircraft designs, and has been active in the AIAA and the American Helicopter Society.

EDWARD F. KATZENBERGER AND EDWARD S. CARTER

The Technical Evolution of Sikorsky Helicopters, 1950–83

The evolution of helicopter technology from the early pioneering period of the 1940s through the introduction of the current generation of helicopters in the 1980s embodies the contributions of many individuals and many organizations. The earliest helicopters, to be considered a success, needed only sufficient lifting capability to get off the ground and the means to remain controllable both in hover and through a reasonable range of forward flight speeds.

But new challenges quickly arose. Each of the major developers exploited essentially the same sequence of technological building blocks as they became available to solve these problems and those that followed. The configuration possibilities; the basic understanding of rotor aeroelastic characteristics; the gas turbine engine; hydraulic-powered controls; electronic stability augmentation; materials technology in aluminum, magnesium, titanium and composites; and, most recently, the advent of microelectronics have all affected the evolution of all helicopters. The story of the technical evolution of Sikorsky designs can serve to illustrate the whole evolutionary story, because of the broad spectrum of sizes and missions of helicopters developed at Sikorsky Aircraft. More than twenty-five different designs and virtually every type of mission have been addressed in models ranging in size from 2,000 pounds to 70,000 pounds. Figure 1 illustrates these designs and their lineage as they evolved during the first forty years of Sikorsky's history.

Four periods can be identified. First, there was the period of the early pioneers, extending to approximately the end of World War II, in which the configuration possibilities and the solutions to the most fundamental problems were explored. The VS-300 (see figure 2), the R-4 (see figure 3), the R-5 (see figure 4), and the R-6 were the Sikorsky contributions during this period. The story of the early pioneers is told in other chapters of this book.

After the period of the pioneers came the period of initial development, during which the design teams took over from the pioneers and began to make specific designs for specific missions. As was true of all the early development, the initial period of development of Sikorsky helicopters was characterized largely by experimentation. It began at Sikorsky with the S-51 (HO2S) in 1945 (see figure 5) and extended to the coming of age of the helicopter, largely through the impetus of the Korean War, in the mid 1950s. The Korean War demonstrated the technical soundness of the helicopters that were under development during this period. It also demonstrated the capabilities of the helicopter for military operations, though these had only begun to be exploited when the war ended.

The Korean War thus established a basis upon which the armed services could define

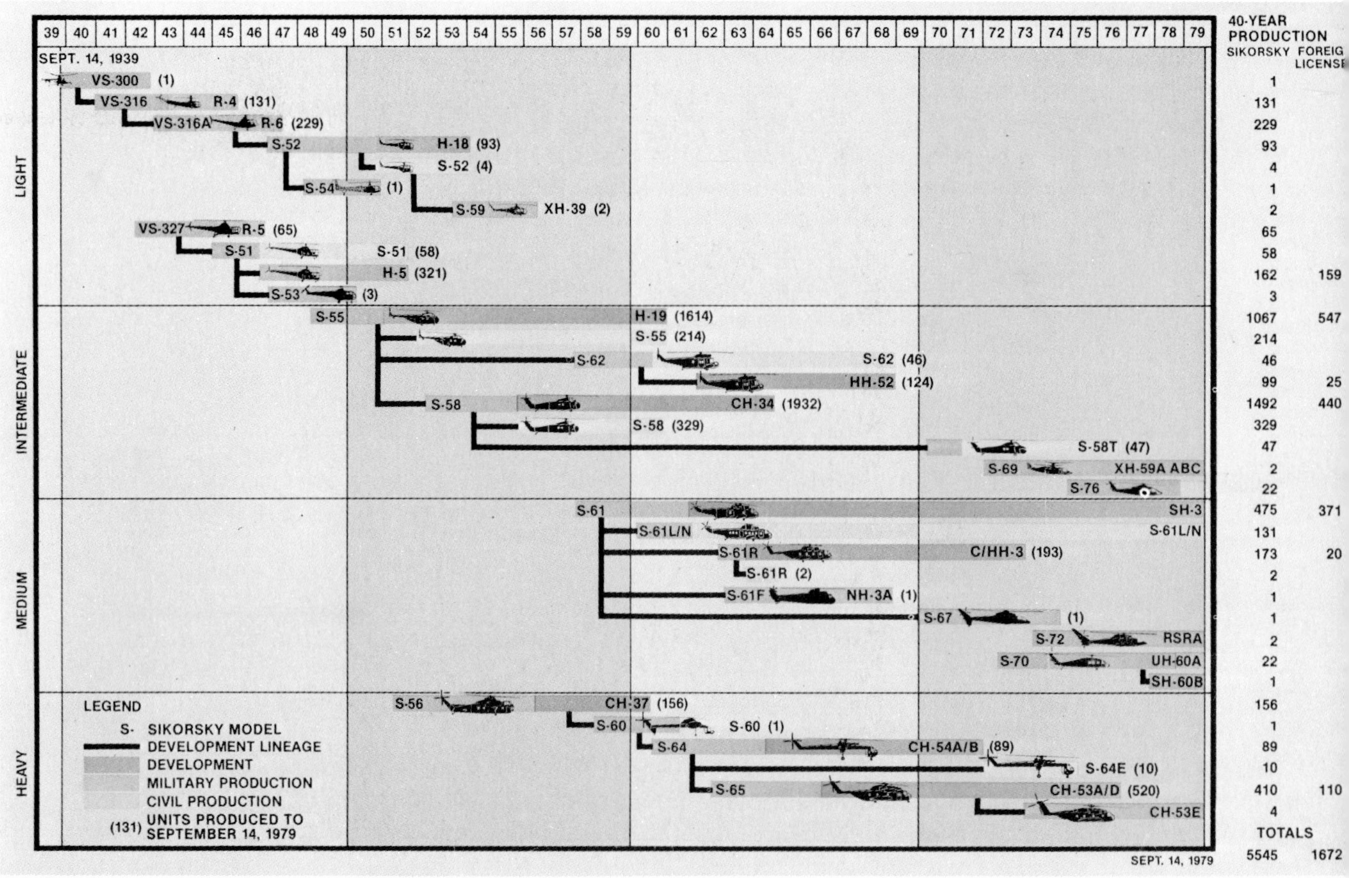

Figure 1. Sikorsky—Forty years of helicopter progress

Figure 2. The VS-300

Figure 3.
The VS-316 (R-4)

Figure 4.
The VS-325 (R-5)

Figure 5.
The S-51

technical and functional requirements, relating them for the first time to extensive operational experience. The first results of such definitions were the S-55 helicopter, which had made its first flight just before the outbreak of the Korean War, and the S-56 and S-58 helicopters, which emerged in the early 1950s.

The next period was one of maturation and technological development. It extended from the mid 1950s to the early 1970s and marks the end of significant reliance on trial and error. In contrast to the initial period, this period is marked by a great acceleration of research that began late in the 1950s and expanded dramatically from the mid 1960s onward. The technology of the aircraft developed during this period, however, was derived mainly from what had been learned during the initial period, since the designs from mid 1950 to the early 1970s had been laid down too early to benefit in any fundamental way from the new research.

During the latest period, the beneficiaries of the technology explosion of the 1960s and early 1970s have come into being. They are the contemporary aircraft—the S-69 (XH-59) Advancing Blade Concept Feasibility Demonstrator, the S-70 (UH-60), the civil S-76, and the three-engine version of the S-65, the CH-53E.

This chapter is concerned with the story of the last three periods as it unfolded at Sikorsky Aircraft.

The Initial Period of Development

Once technology had provided, primarily in the form of reasonably efficient power, the potential for helicopter configurations with significant disposable payload, a number of problems became apparent. Some of the most obvious problems were an adequate center-of-gravity range and the control power to accommodate it, management of control loads as helicopters got larger, designs for blades that could be manufactured with repeatable characteristics and that would stand up in service, and stability characteristics adequate for instrument flight. For the single-rotor helicopter, the center-of-gravity range was critical. While the R-5 had been stretched to a four-passenger version called the S-51 and had had moderate success as a passenger-carrying vehicle, and an all-new two-place helicopter, the S-52, was being designed, the utility helicopter with a significant payload variation had yet to be addressed.

Designers of the XHJS-1 (S-53), initiated for a U.S. Navy utility helicopter competition, were the first to attack the utility problem. Unfortunately, they merely extrapolated R-4 and R-5 concepts; the engine was mounted directly beneath the rotor to achieve the simplest and lightest transmission. They also used the zero-offset flapping hinge, which, while simplifying certain dynamic considerations, limited the control moment available for trim and maneuvers to that provided by tilting the thrust vector. As a consequence, the center-of-gravity limitations of this aircraft were severe and it lost out in a navy competition to a tandem-rotor design that eventually evolved into the HUP. For a time, it appeared that the single-main-rotor helicopter configuration might be limited to small vehicles for which variations in payload were insignificant.

In fact, the Sikorsky team even experimented briefly with a sesquitandem alternative to the single rotor, and the little-known S-54 was built and flown to evaluate this variation of the tandem concept, in which about 20 percent of the lift was carried on the rear horizontal rotor. After brief flight tests that exposed difficult handling qualities, however, all efforts were directed back to the single rotor. The S-55 quickly eradicated any concern for the future of the single rotor.

The S-55 (see figure 6) departed from earlier single-rotor practice in a number of critical ways. First, by locating the engine forward of the rotor instead of directly beneath it, a clear payload space directly beneath the rotor was obtained, thus achieving minimum center-of-gravity excursions for the range of loads required. Also, as it turned out, the S-55 achieved a more efficient struc-

Figure 6.
The S-55 (UH-19)

ture and better engine access for maintenance and replacement than could be obtained with a centrally located engine—an early example of the serendipity frequently noted in the evolution of the helicopter. The S-55 and S-56 designs might well have been only marginally successful without this innovation. For the four-passenger stretched version of the S-52, the S-52-3 (HO5S-1), a slightly different variation on the same approach was used: the engine was tilted aft to make the volume of space beneath the rotor available for disposable payload.

The S-55 configuration was almost immediately imitated by the Russians in the Mil Mi-4 design—including adoption of the S-55 quadricycle landing-gear configuration!

The S-55, and shortly thereafter the S-58, embodied many other technical innovations and departures from precedent. Technical developments up to the onset of the Korean War were carried out largely without the benefit of the direction and emphasis provided by extensive operational experience and, indeed, with little in the way of adequately supported research. Nevertheless, these developments had provided the basis for the significant advances in system design—principally in payload capacity, speed, and range—represented by the S-56 and S-58. This was true particularly with respect to the rotor and the control system, the basic configuration of which, first flown experimentally on late-model S-51 aircraft in 1947 and applied to the S-55 in 1949, remained substantially unaltered in their fundamentals through the S-65 model begun sixteen years later.

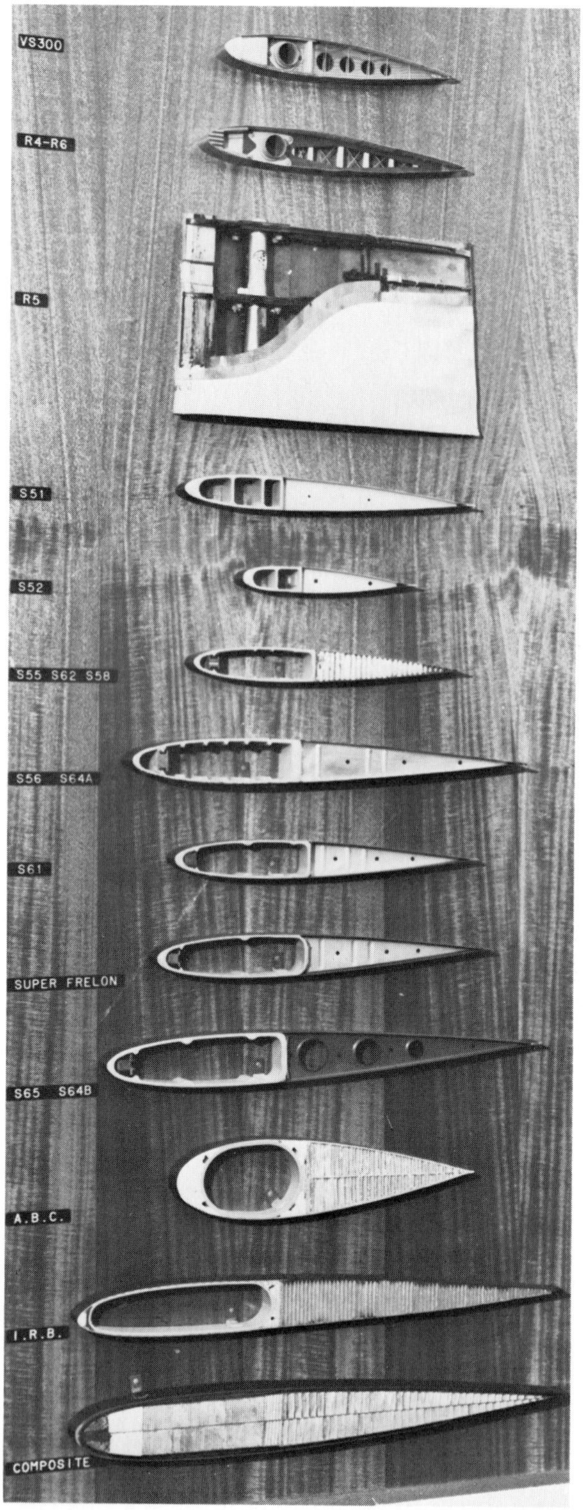

Figure 7.
Cross sections of main rotor blades

These significant developments were:

- The aluminum blade, the basic design of which remained through all Sikorsky models until the titanium-spar blade was developed for the S-70 and the three-engine version of the S-65 (CH-53E) in 1974. This evolution is shown in figure 7.
- The offset flapping hinge, which permitted the optimum selection of control power and damping and further extended the center-of-gravity range for single-rotor helicopters.
- The development of hydraulic servo-boosted controls.
- The initial development of an electronic autostabilization system.

The selection of the fully articulated rotor in the form adopted—that is, with coincident offset lag and flapping hinges inboard of the feathering (pitch) hinge—involves minimum pitch-flap and pitch-lag coupling and the minimum gyroscopic moment response to motions of the aircraft. It was a fortunate choice at the time, not only because it proved its soundness for the pure helicopter, but also because, for the period under discussion, the understanding of the dynamics of the helicopter had not progressed sufficiently for the influence of such coupling effects on handling qualities, control loads, blade stresses, and blade aeroelastic behavior to be assessed adequately.

It was learned during the late 1940s, however, from the S-52 and late-model S-51s, that the offset flapping hinge greatly reduced the lag in fuselage attitude response to a control input, and with this innovation it was found possible to provide an adequate platform for flight by instrument flight rules (IFR), especially when combined with electronic stabilization.

Hydraulic servos, like offset flapping hinges, were first used in prototype on the S-51. They were quickly recognized as necessary devices to solve the control-load problems of all but the smallest helicopters. All Sikorsky designs since the S-55 have incorporated four-channel hydraulic irre-

Figure 8.
The S-56 (CH-37)

versible controls. The S-55 had single stages and could be flown in an emergency with servos off, but all subsequent designs have had dual or triple redundancy.

Through the late 1940s and early 1950s, other pioneers worked extensively on irreversible mechanical controls or servo tabs and gyromechanical stabilizing devices, but Sikorsky made the commitment early to irreversible hydraulic servos, the offset flapping hinge, modest horizontal tails, and electronic stabilization for optimization of control. A prototype of this combination as a solution to the IFR flight problem was flown on the S-55, and a four-channel stick-command series stabilization system was designed into the S-58 as part of the initial design. The stabilization equipment was used in all development flying beginning with the first flight in 1954. With this aircraft, the concept of an integrated electronic stabilization system, which remained engaged at all times and was used for all modes of flight, was introduced. It became an inherent part of every subsequent helicopter built by Sikorsky for the U.S. Navy. The 100 percent commitment to electronic stabilization lagged a few years in army and civil application, but by the 1960s it was standard on all Sikorsky helicopters.

During the early stages of the Korean War, when the services issued the requirements for what was to become the HR2S-1 (S-56) (see figure 8) and HSS-1 (H-34/S-58) helicopters, it immediately became evident to the designers that the state of knowledge at the time, given sufficient design ingenuity, could accommodate the requirements of the S-58. This aircraft was largely an extrapolation of the S-55 at a little less than twice the gross weight, but it was only a marginal improvement when compared to the S-56, which had five times the gross weight of the S-55 and was 40 percent faster. The situation was reflected clearly in the contrasting histories of the development of the two aircraft: the S-58 had few serious problems in development, whereas the S-56 had several fundamental problems, particularly with respect to rotor-control loads, rotor elastic response, and weight growth. The solution to these problems turned out to demand fundamental changes in the design.

The original S-56 design, for example, specified a blade twist of 16 degrees to achieve the required hover performance within the constraint on rotor diameter imposed by the requirement for aircraft-carrier operations with a helicopter of about 30,000 pounds gross weight. Little was known at that time about the effect of twist on blade stresses in forward flight. Design cruise speed was 140 knots, about 40 percent greater than cruise speeds that had been achieved earlier. Not until the aircraft was flown, therefore, did it become apparent that a trade-off would have to be made between stress-limited speed and hover capability. Twist was reduced from 16 degrees to 8 degrees, but still the rotor diameter had to be increased by four feet to achieve a satisfactory compromise between hover performance and forward flight performance and to compensate for growth in the empty weight.

At that time, the integrated result at the hub of periodic forces and moments caused by blade response could not be determined for forces and moments beyond the second order. One result of this lack of knowledge was that both the frequency and magnitude of significant higher-harmonic control loads was not predictable. In both the S-58 and S-56, for example, the significant vibratory contribution in the rotating system above one per rev happened to be the sixth harmonic. This posed no problem in the S-58, which had a four-blade system, but produced a predominant five-per-rev vibration in the stationary portion of the S-56 control system. Fortunately, this frequency was well above resonance for the system, but the fact that it was relatively high—56 million cycles per 100 hours—forced redesign of the system in detail to meet the flight-safety requirement of infinite life for this portion of it.

In short, it became clear during the S-56 design cycle that the designers were scraping the bottom of the barrel with respect to relevant knowledge and experience. If further significant advances in system design were to be achieved, a better research base specifically related to the helicopter would be required. This realization was reflected in the creation in 1952 by the National Advisory Committee for Aeronautics—later the National Aeronautics and Space Administration (NASA)—of the Subcommittee on Helicopters, and the organization by Sikorsky in 1953 of a research section in the engineering department.

Nevertheless, these models did demonstrate progress on many fronts. One was the design and fabrication techniques for building magnesium-alloy airframes, which were developed to a high degree of sophistication. Magnesium skins and hot-formed magnesium frames, for example, were employed successfully in the S-56 and S-58 and in the afterbody fairing of the S-55. Significant savings in weight were realized.

Figure 9.
Blade Inspection Method (BIM) of the main rotor blade

A significant development later in this period was the flight-safety improvement achieved by greatly increased blade inspectability. The extruded D-section monolithic spar was pressurized with nitrogen. An indicator was installed near the blade root from which, with the blade stationary, it was possible to detect an indicated drop in pressure readily (see figure 9). Such an indication would mean either a gauge failure, a spar-seal failure, or—more significant—a spar crack.

Given that known crack-propagation rates are multiples of elapsed flight times, such a system could be used to determine blade removal "on condition," thus not only enhancing flight safety, but extending average blade use beyond conservatively determined safe-life retirement times. This system came to be known as the Blade Inspection Method (BIM).

Another important technique developed during this period was that of using the increased number of already developed blades to provide greater rotor capacity. The S-58 rotor was derived from the S-55, for example, and the S-61 rotor from the S-58. This technique did not eliminate blade development for the new model, since changes at least in diameter and tip speed were required, but it did reduce development time and cost.

In the parametric studies in 1950 that led to development of the S-56 (HR2S-1, H-37) the significance of rotor-disc loading as an independent variable, the choice of which largely determined the available payload fraction as a function of size and weight-empty power loading—pounds over horsepower—was recognized for the first time. This significance, which later became more or less obvious, was a difficult perception at the time, since the prevailing convention called for limiting disc loading to about three pounds per square foot.

The S-56 as finally proposed had a disc loading of 7.5 pounds per square foot, simply because this yielded the smallest and lightest aircraft for the job. On examination without the constraint of convention, there was no apparent reason why a disc loading of 3.0 pounds per square foot should not be exceeded. The designers drew an analogy with span-and-wing area loading in fixed-wing aircraft as a function of scale; though not exact, the analogy was instructive.

Toward the end of this early period—in 1953—Sikorsky initiated the use of digital computers for these parametrics studies, since the time or manpower required for the mass of calculations that it would take to cover an adequate range of design variables would otherwise be prohibitive. Before the computer, the problem was "solved" only by placing an excessive burden on the designer's judgment and intuition, with a large possibility of error as a result. At the same time, the digital computer began to assist the technical analyst in the complex aeromechanic disciplines of the helicopter, giving hope that eventually it might actually be possible to predict rotor phenomena on other than an empirical basis.

A parallel development in this early period of exploration of the technology base was the initial use of rotor models to explore the complex aerodynamic and aeroelastic behavior of rotors. During the mid 1950s, tests of a nine-foot generic main rotor model initiated what was to become a long series of rotor model tests in the eighteen-foot tunnel of the United Aircraft (now United Technologies) Research Laboratory. These tests, eventually combined with flow-visualization techniques, not only provided an insight into the way rotors operate, but also yielded a data base, taken under more controlled conditions than was possible in flight, for correlation of the analytical tools as they were developed with the advent of digital computers.

The scope of the design effort during this period also included early studies of dramatically different solutions to vertical lift missions. Studies ranged from single-rotor and multirotor crane helicopters to hybrid fixed-wing and helicopter configurations such as compound and tilt-rotor aircraft. One concept that received particular attention was the stowed-rotor convertiplane (S-57). These studies included a 1/20-scale-model wind-tunnel test as early as 1951 and 1/5-scale tests in 1953. The latter tests demonstrated the complete conversion cycle.

The S-57 incorporated a cold-cycle tip-jet, with a blade-tip nozzle through which was expanded the efflux of a compressor located in the fuselage without the transfer of additional energy to the stream by burning fuel upstream of the nozzle. This was one of a variety of tip-jet schemes studied toward the end of the period, with a view to possible application to the convertiplane and to very large crane helicopters. For crane applications it was argued that the saving in transmission weight would substantially exceed the sum of the additional weight of the larger gas producers required plus the additional

Figure 10.
The S-58

fuel weight, because of short-mission endurance requirements. Tip-ram and pulse jets were also studied, but these studies yielded unsatisfactory results largely because of the excessive noise of the pulse jet, the gross inefficiency at helicopter tip speeds of the ram jet, and structural problems of the blades.

Finally, the initial development period also saw the exploration of a host of missions as the reality of a vertical lift capability and a recognition of what this could mean began to dawn on military planners. Rescue, minesweeping, Medevac, antisubmarine warfare (ASW), and scheduled commercial operations were all initiated during this period. The uses of this helicopter were proliferating. The S-58 (see figure 10) was certified for civil use, and experimental configurations such as the HR2S-1W (see figure 11), built to evaluate the advanced early warning (AEW) radar potential of the helicopter, began to receive attention.

Figure 11.
The S-56 (HR2S-1W)

The Period of Technological Development

While all divisions into historical periods are to some extent arbitrary, the choice of the early 1950s to mark the completion of the initial development period and the beginning of the maturity of the helicopter seems justified largely because it marked the departure from trial-and-error experimentation. Henceforth, the knowledge gained through research would, as in fixed-wing aircraft, be of increasing importance in the advancement of helicopter technology. Also beginning with this period, extensive commercial and military experience began to help define and emphasize necessary and desirable attributes of systems.

These two facts were recognized by Sikorsky, first in the creation in 1953 of a research organization, and second, in participation with potential customers in studies of, for example, antisubmarine warfare (ASW), commercial operations, and army transport, observation, and Medevac. With the onset of the Vietnam conflict, counterinsurgency and the use of the helicopter to provide air mobility and firepower on the battlefield were studied. These studies were undertaken with the idea that only with the most thorough understanding of operations would it be possible, given a set of requirements, to identify and design systems with the best mix of attributes. To facilitate such studies and coordinate them closely with the design effort, a systems-and-operations analysis group was formed in 1960 as an integral part of the design organization.

The advent of the gas turbine in the early 1950s also marked the departure from the initial development period. This immediately broadened the range of possibilities for helicopter design, perhaps more than for fixed-wing aircraft, in which the propulsion system is not so intimately interrelated with the design of the total system. But the size of the turbine engine, its efficiency at high speed, and its lack of a clutch between engine and transmission recommended it particularly to the helicopter. In addition, the turbine engine provided power at a small fraction of the weight of the reciprocating engine—0.22 pound per horsepower for the early T58 turbine, for example, rather than 1.31 pound per horsepower for the Pratt & Whitney R-1820, the lightest reciprocating engine.

The first production application of the gas turbine was realized with the flight of the S-59 (YH-39) (see figure 12), in 1954. This aircraft, a derivative of the S-52, had only a modest production run. But experience with the Artouste II "fixed" turbine—an engine in which the output-power turbine is fixed to the shaft of the gas-generator section—proved valuable to the design of turbine engines specifically for use in the helicopter. It confirmed the choice of the "free" turbine configuration—that is, one in which the power turbine is only aerodynamically coupled to the gas generator.

The second application was realized by the first flight, in 1957, of the HSS-1F, which was the S-58 with two T58 turbines installed in the nose in place of the R-1820 reciprocating engine. Two aircraft were built, largely to provide a test bed for General

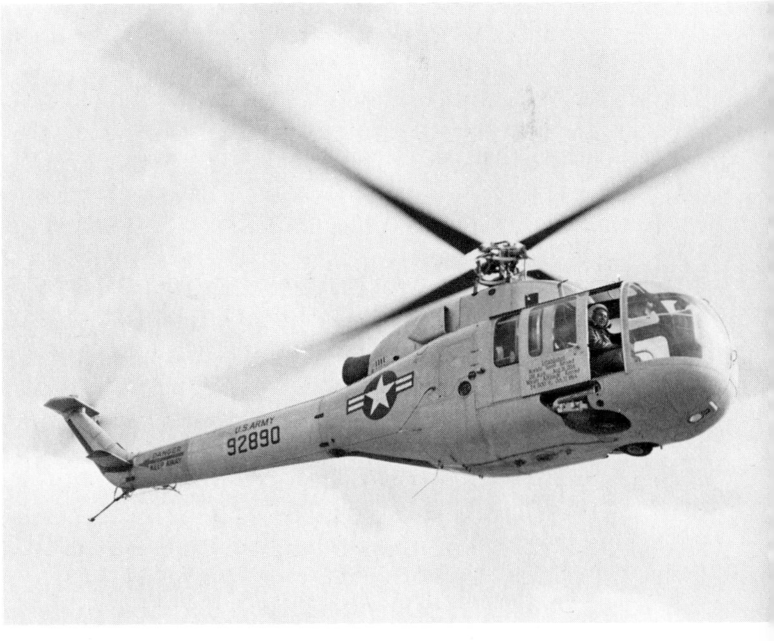

Figure 12.
The S-59 (YH-39)

Figure 13.
The S-61R (CH-3C)

Electric, the engine manufacturer, before the engine was committed to a development program aimed at volume production. No serious problems were encountered.

Concurrent with this program, studies were made of derivatives of the S-58 that employed two of these engines. Design effort centered about ASW requirements beyond the capacity of the HSS-1 (S-58), since such requirements were being developed by the navy.

Figure 14.
The S-61L

The system best matched to these requirements employed five blades not significantly different from the four blades of the S-58 except in diameter, which was increased six feet. The engines were located above and aft of the cockpit rather than forward and below as in the HSS-1F; this eliminated one bevel-gear train in the transmission. The helicopter, designated the HSS-2, had a seaworthy hull, sponsons for emergency water landing, and a gross weight of approximately 16,000 pounds; the gross weight of the HSS-1 was 11,500 pounds.

First flown in 1959, this aircraft was the prototype of the S-61 series, embodying fifteen military and commercial variants plus the Presidential Flight—a series that remained in production for almost twenty years, from 1961 to 1980. Among the most prominent variants were the CH-3C version for the U.S. Air Force (see figure 13) and subsequently the Coast Guard, which incorporated for the first time on a Sikorsky helicopter a rear loading ramp, and the S-61 civil version (see figure 14), which, with a five-foot airframe insert, provided a thirty-passenger transport helicopter destined eventually to become the backbone of longer-range offshore oil exploration. Another turbine-powered aircraft derived at about the same time from previous reciprocating-engine-powered aircraft was the S-62 (see figure 15), a single T58-powered derivative of the S-55 that employed the S-55 rotor system essentially unchanged and initiated the HH-52 series.

The advantages of turbine power were so pervasive that it even became economical to retrofit the S-58 helicopters with PT-6 Twin-Pacs, a conversion program initiated much later in the 1970s (see figure 16).

At the time, the basic configuration of large helicopters was also being reexamined. Sikorsky Aircraft, led by Igor Sikorsky personally, studied the concept of the crane helicopter intensively as a prime mover. The concept envisioned a basic helicopter mechanical system installed on a minimum airframe composed of nothing but the pilots' stations and the backbone of the propulsion system itself. The basic crane was optimized to handle external loads with a high-capacity winch, but it also had provisions for a variety of special pods. An early demonstrator, the S-60, was built around the S-56 drive system, and the six-blade S-64 was subsequently developed around twin JFTD-12 gas turbines (see figure 17), carrying still further the idea of minimizing the degree to which rotor technology was stretched by adding additional blades. Ini-

Figure 15.
The S-62 (HH-52A)

Figure 16.
The S-58T

Figure 17.
The S-64 (CH-54)

tial development of the S-64 was supported solely by Sikorsky and the Federal Republic of Germany, but eventually the interest of the U.S. Army was aroused, and some eighty-nine S-64s were bought by the army as the CH-54. Subsequently, the S-64 was certified and sold to commercial operators as the S-64F. Civilian demand, however, was not great enough to support a production line, and only ten civil versions were built.

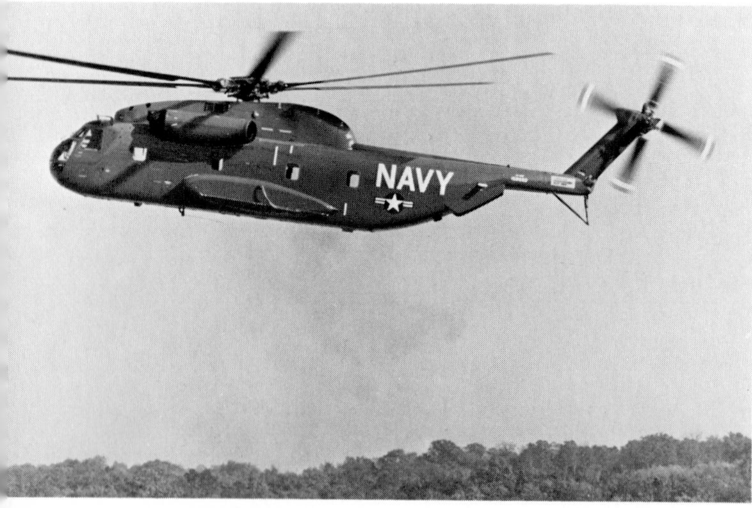

Figure 18.
The CH-53

The lesson of the S-64 appears to have been that, efficient as the crane concept was, the basic aircraft was too specialized and the markets for heavy lift were too few and far between to support a prime mover having only external heavy-lift capability. Except in certain special cases, the cost of ferrying the aircraft from mission to mission tended to offset the economies that might otherwise be realized by use of the crane. In the meantime, development had begun on the S-65 (CH-53A) (see figure 18), which drew on the dynamic components of the S-64 but combined its external lift capacity with significant internal load capacity and a rear door.

Late in the technological development period another novel approach to this problem of economical heavy lift was explored. Under the sponsorship of the army the idea of harnessing two helicopters to the same payload by means of a spreader bar was demonstrated using two CH-54s (see figure 19). With only conventional flight-control provisions, an air taxi capable of carrying a total load of twenty tons was demonstrated. But further work on automatic control to minimize the pilots' workload was terminated when the army decided to put all its heavy-lift resources into development of the HLH. The idea has since been put into practice by civil operators using smaller helicopters.

Initially, advances in technology realized during this period had the purpose of minimizing risk and cost and embodied relatively small extrapolations of the basic technology of the aircraft from which they were derived. It was realized that radical departures from earlier technology could be prudently undertaken only when a sufficient research base, in many instances including full-scale demonstration, had been achieved. By the end of the period, however, it was recognized that a growing base of knowledge not only permitted the design of advanced new aircraft with reasonable risk,

Figure 19.
The S-64s (CH-54s) in twin lift

Figure 20.
The S-61 bifilar

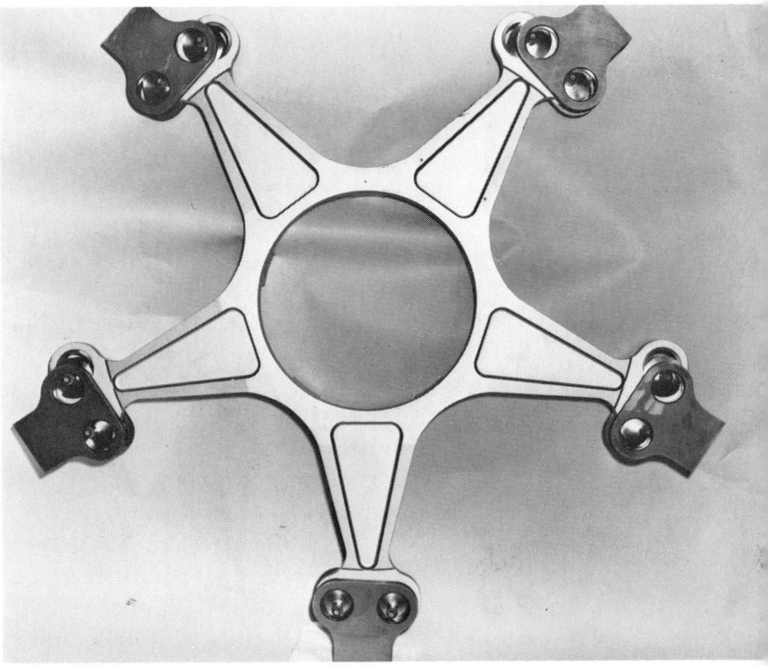

such as the contemporary XH-59, UH-60, S-72 RSRA, and S-76, but that much of the hardware made possible by this knowledge could be incorporated in derivative models of earlier aircraft. In some instances the hardware even could be retrofitted, as demonstrated by the turbinized version of the S-58, the S-58T.

Another example of retrofitting is the 1967 incorporation after several years of research, of bifilar rotorhead vibration absorbers in the S-61, thus improving the vibration environment for the crew and reducing vibratory stress levels, in turn improving structural reliability (see figure 20). These had the particular virtue of reacting to the vibratory excitations at their source and also of staying in tune with the excitation when rotor speed was varied. A better structural design for the tail rotor blades for both the S-61 and the S-65 was also developed. Research into structural configurations, materials, and materials processing continued, particularly into metal fatigue, research that made possible modifications in detail for greater structural reliability.

Development and use of very large titanium forgings, in which Sikorsky was among the leaders in the aircraft industry, made it possible in 1963, early in the S-65 program, to switch from steel to titanium rotor-hub components and thus to save about 300 pounds. This was done with a high degree of confidence that structural reliability would not be compromised.

Throughout the 1950s and 1960s, development of autostabilization systems continued, and the IFR capabilities of helicopters were extended for ever more demanding military missions. The breakthrough program had been the HSS-1N, which was designed to address the problem of the ASW mission conducted at night under IFR. In spite of four-axis body-attitude stabilization, pilots had found this mission far too demanding for normal operations. After many unsuccessful evaluations of various flight directors, a fully automatic approach-and-hover system, working off Doppler ground-speed sensors, was designed and immediately achieved positive results. Introduced into production in the HSS-1N variant of the navy ASW version of the S-58, this system was followed shortly by an improved system for the twin-engine HSS-2 (SH-3), which could be coupled to the navigation system as well. Autostabilization was subsequently extended to stabilization of sling loads, particularly for the S-64, and to towing operations for the minesweeping mission.

The decade of the 1960s was also noteworthy as a period in which both helicopter and fixed-wing aircraft industries undertook intensive studies of alternatives to rotorcraft as a means of providing vertical lift without the speed limitations of the lifting rotor. Gas turbine technology had reached the point at which engine specific weights could allow consideration of higher disc-loading rotors or even direct jet lift for vertical takeoff. The event that may have had the greatest influence in determining the direction and emphasis of helicopter technology during this period was the establishment in the mid 1950s of Army Aviation. The interest of the army in exploiting vertical flight to increase battlefield mobility led initially to a broadening of the scope of configuration studies to embrace a wide variety of vertical takeoff and landing (VTOL) aircraft, such as tilt-rotor, tilt-wing, tilt-fan, propeller-deflected-thrust, and ducted and unducted stand-on helicopters. Supplementary studies of the possibilities of wing-lift augmentation and jet deflection were conducted.

Toward the mid 1960s, the division of vertical or short takeoff and landing (V/STOL) effort among the services produced nonrotor types that were supported largely by the air force and the navy. For the navy, Sikorsky proposed a carrier-based tilt-wing transport. For the air force, Sikorsky studied wing-mounted lift-fan configurations. Sikorsky's S-57 stowed-rotor convertiplane, though a rotor-type VTOL, continued to be of interest to the air force, since it provided the possibility of high-speed rescue aircraft with the capability of extended hover.

In 1967, this interest culminated in a proposal by Sikorsky in response to an air force request for proposal for a 450-knot, long-range rescue aircraft—the Combat Aircrew Recovery Aircraft (CARA) program—incorporating a shaft-driven, two-blade stowable rotor. Sikorsky had conducted wind-tunnel studies of a shaft-driven, two-blade system that demonstrated the starting, stopping, and stowing ability of such a system and considered the scheme feasible, though it would have required a sizable development effort. No contract awards were made, however, and by the end of the 1960s Sikorsky and most of the rest of the industry had redirected research on high-speed vertical-lift aircraft back onto low disc-loading compounds and tilt rotors. Meanwhile, work had continued on stowed rotors, compound helicopter configurations, and supporting research into the problems of the high-speed rotor.

Various means of retracting the rotor in flight were investigated. One that received significant analytical treatment and a certain amount of model testing in 1964 was

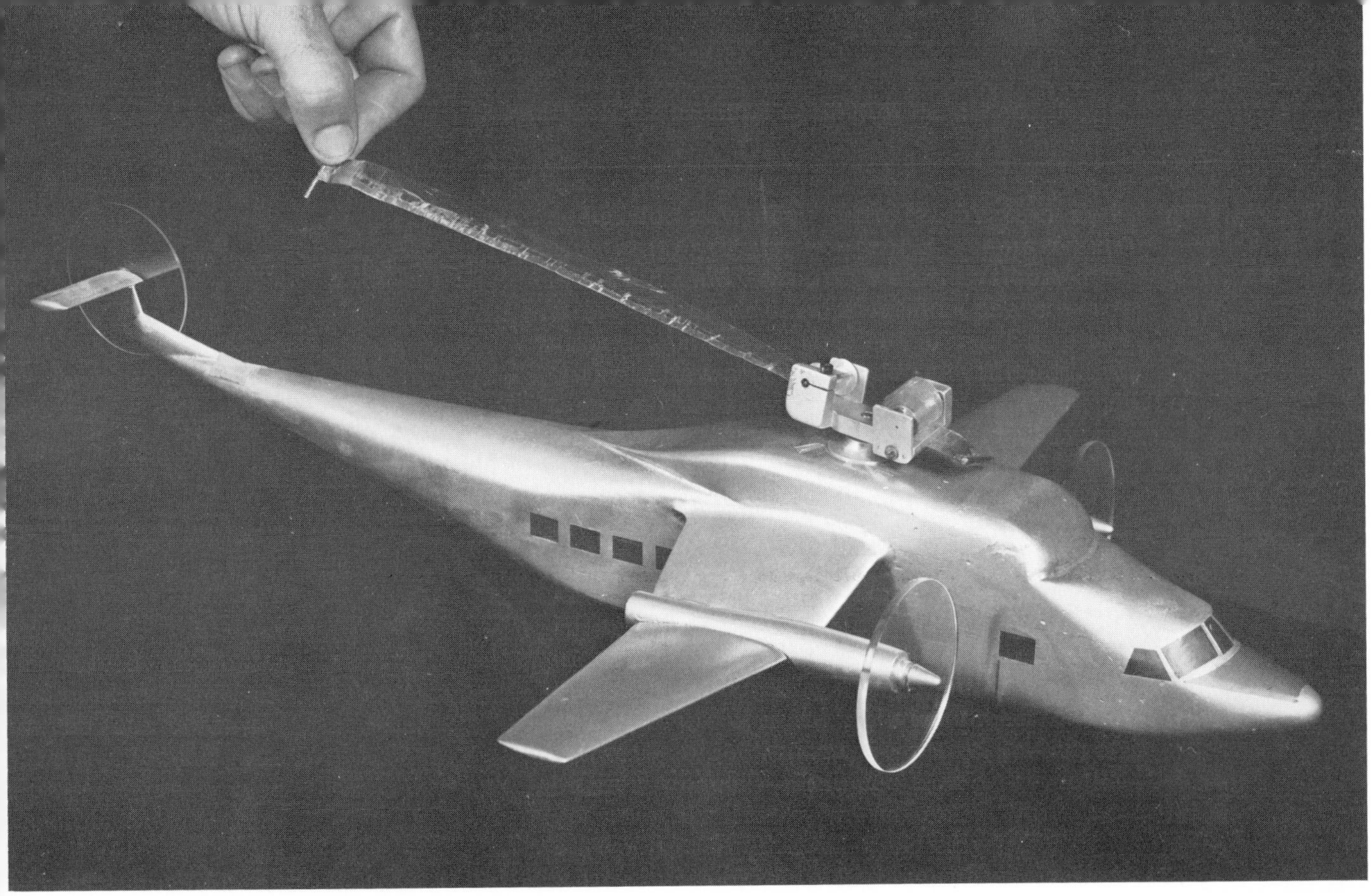

the roll-up rotor (see figure 21), composed of a very thin ribbon blade that depended on articulated tip weights to control the pitch. Although selected as late as 1970 in a study for the air force as the most practical means of retracting a rotor, it was never pursued beyond the model stage, because other, lower-risk nonretracting rotor approaches to higher speed seemed more promising.

During the period, and in fact going back to the early 1950s, system studies of the design parameters of maximum commercial profitability had emphasized the need for a cruise speed of not less than 200 knots for the short-haul markets of 100 to 200 miles that civil transport helicopters were expected to serve.

The compound helicopter appeared to offer this possibility. Feasibility had been demonstrated by the McDonnell XV-1 and the Fairey Rotodyne, though neither had reached a speed of 200 knots, for reasons not fundamentally associated with the concept. (The XV-1 achieved 174 knots, and the Rotodyne 166 knots.)

Numerous design studies of the compound configuration had been made, and the

Figure 21.
The roll-up rotor

problems of parasite and interference drag of hub-pylon configuration and of the behavior of rotors up to 340 knots had been investigated in NASA and United Technologies wind tunnels. Sufficient knowledge had been gained by the early 1960s to make it evident that an experimental compound could readily be derived from the S-61 by installing a wing for rotor unloading and two J-60 engines for propulsion; refairing the fuselage, rotor head, and rotor pylon; and modifying the horizontal tail surfaces and controls. These modifications were accomplished in 1965 in the S-61F, and a limited, low-cost demonstration program was undertaken. A speed of 210 knots was reached, and no significant problems were encountered. Various configurations were investigated, including five- and six-blade configurations with and without a wing. Rotor-twist and tip configurations were explored; the maximum speeds achieved were 215 knots in level flight and 230 knots in a descent, with no significant problems.

In was during the same period that military helicopters began to be considered explicitly as weapons systems. This led to systematic consideration in the design stage of all aspects of the systems that influenced operational effectiveness and cost. The development of systems analysis led to more detailed and accurate modeling of systems and the ability to determine the absolute and relative effectiveness and life-cycle cost of the possible attributes of systems. The capacity to make such analyses and to relate them explicitly to operational effectiveness had begun to be developed on a quantitative basis by the establishment, as noted earlier, of Sikorsky's systems and operations analysis group in 1960. Thus such capacity was well in hand for the advent of the Advanced Aerial Fire Support System (AAFSS) in 1965.

The technology therefore also appeared to be well in hand for the straightforward development of compound aircraft for a variety of possible applications. The AAFSS was one such application, and both Sikorsky and the other principal manufacturers proposed compound helicopters to meet this requirement. The winning entry, a compound produced by Lockheed, failed to achieve production status because of problems basically unrelated to the compound as a type. The technology is available but, for a number of reasons, no requirements have emerged since AAFSS for which the compound has appeared to be a prime contender. Nevertheless, opportunities such as a civilian compound derivative of the CH-53 have been given careful study.

One interesting by-product of the Sikorsky effort on AAFSS was the swing-tail concept, since the compound flying in the helicopter mode requires a tail rotor or its equivalent and, in high-speed flight, a propeller. Rather than use two separate units, as in the Lockheed design. Sikorsky proposed a "swing tail"—that is, a tail-mounted propeller that swiveled through 90 degrees and served as a tail rotor for low-speed flight and hover. During the competitive phase an experimental swing tail was built and was flown on an S-61, demonstrating the feasibility of transition from one flight regime to the other (see figure 22).

During this period of technological development, emphasis continued to be placed on speed in the pure helicopter. Investigation showed that closer study of aerodynamic efficiency potentials—concerning parasite drag, hub-fuselage interference drag, and propulsion-section momentum losses—could double the lift-to-drag ratio at cruise speeds. Many of these potentials were eventually to be achieved in the S-76, which made its first flight in 1977.

The immediate focus of this effort was the S-67 of the late 1960s and early 1970s. Responding to a growing interest on the part of the army in an antitank helicopter, Sikorsky and others in the industry began to study the optimum configuration for such missions. Sikorsky built a tandem-cockpit gunship aircraft using the S-61 dynamic components. Although never put into production, it served to demonstrate the agility potential of the articulated offset flapping-hinge rotor, including the ability to loop and roll.

At that time, the S-52 was the only articulated rotor helicopter to have executed a full loop, and none had rolled. Shortly thereafter, however, the S-65 repeated both maneuvers to demonstrate that size was no barrier to the agility potential of the offset flapping-hinge rotor. It is interesting to note that although the U.S. Department of Defense did not proceed with a gunship version of the S-61, the Soviets did in fact produce just such a craft in the Hind D.

In addition to a very low-drag airframe and rotor-head fairing, the S-67 incorporated swept blade tips and reduced blade twist to optimize the structural and aeroelastic stability of the S-61 rotor in high-speed flight. In 1970 it set a world speed record of 191.8 knots over the standard Fédération Aéronautique Internationale (FAI) 15–25-kilometer course. It also served as a test bed for an investigation of the ducted countertorque tail fan—the fenestron concept originally developed by the French—as shown in figure 23.

Figure 22.
The S-61 swing-tail rotor

Concurrently with the investigation of body drag, research in the mid and late 1960s pursued more detailed investigation than before of the flow conditions of the high-speed rotor and the significance of three-dimensional flow on assumed two-dimensional airfoil characteristics. It began with the availability of the first comprehensive data bank of rotary airloads under controlled conditions with the test of an instrumented H-34 (S-52) rotor in the forty-by-eighty-foot full-scale tunnel at the NASA Ames Research Center in California. An experimental reassessment was made of the concept of blade stall and lift stall coupling with blade dynamic response and of the

Figure 23.
The S-67 with Fenestron

assumption that drag and pitching-moment divergence was not related to blade and control-system stiffness. This reassessment made possible development of the airfoil in such a way as to avoid adverse elastic response and the definition of optimum twist distribution. Both are employed in the high-efficiency S-70 (UH-60A and its variants), the S-76, and the CH-53E version of the S-65.

The investigation of compressibility effects showed that the two-dimensional airfoil data yielded unduly conservative predictions of behavior. Blade-tip aerodynamics was investigated experimentally in more detail than before, yielding valuable data on planform, profile, and twist distribution that were employed later in the redesigned S-61 tip and the tip designs for the S-70, the S-76, and the CH-53E version of the S-65. More detailed studies were made of rotor flow patterns, and improvements were achieved in high-speed rotor-performance correlation. Two-dimensional oscillating airfoil data were obtained using a unique tunnel-spanning test facility developed by Sikorsky Aircraft and the United Aircraft Research Laboratories in further pursuit of a more useful definition of dynamic stall. Refinements continued to be made in hover performance analysis as a function of wake description. The induced-flow field was studied in detail with the use of schlieren, smoke (see figure 24), and, more recently, laser velocimeter techniques.

Paralleling these developments in rotor-aerodynamics research was accelerated investigation of stability and control and handling qualities, spurred by the requirements of high-speed and nap-of-the-earth operations—terrain following and terrain avoidance—precision hover, gun-platform tasks, and the handling of external loads. Further problems of control were specific to very large helicopters. Continued study of the compound helicopter required more precise understanding of wing-rotor lift sharing.

Renewed investigations into the effects of blade flexibility, particularly torsional, on stability and handling qualities were undertaken. With the emphasis on high speeds, a more precise determination was made of the effects of pitch-flap coupling on stability at very high advance ratios—that is, the ratio of flight speed to tip speed. To further these efforts, fixed and moving-base simulators were developed early in the period, using the facilities of the United Aircraft Research Laboratories.

In research into structures and materials, slow but steady progress was made in the development of the state of knowledge of structural fatigue in metals. There were no significant breakthroughs, except in successful application of this knowledge to development and use of very large titanium forgings, as noted earlier with respect to the S-65 rotor-head components.

The use of titanium forgings was quickly extended beyond that initial application. This was not without problems in control of titanium manufacturing processes for consistency of material strength, and new techniques and procedures had to be developed.

The theoretical basis of fatigue analysis was developed, particularly in handling combined high- and low-cycle fatigue loading and in interpreting constant- and variable-amplitude loading tests. Work was done to improve the definition of the limitations and the advantages of the alternative reliability concepts of "safe life" and "fail safe." The latter culminated in 1966 in the introduction of fail-safe concepts into the Civil Rotorcraft Fatigue Requirements of the Federal Aviation Administration.

As the need for increased performance grew, greater emphasis was placed on problems of dynamics: load prediction, vibration isolation or attenuation, definition of fully coupled elastic response of the rotor blade and of blade-motion stability, pitch-flap coupling, and self-excited blade oscillations at high subsonic Mach numbers. The interactions between control loads and fuselage vibration were investigated, as was fuselage response to wake turbulence.

Extensive use of glass-fiber composites was introduced with the S-65 (CH-53A) in the early 1960s in cockpit secondary structure and in pylon fairings. Work on advanced composites for primary structure did not begin until the late 1960s and was initially concentrated on the use of boron epoxy. A boron-epoxy tail-rotor shaft was fabricated and was tested with favorable results. The bending response of the S-64 (CH-54) tail cone to rotor-induced vibration was reduced by the application of boron-epoxy longeron stiffeners. Other applications of boron appeared promising, for example in the modification of rotor-swashplate stiffness.

But the cost of boron filament was high and it was not readily suited to applications such as main-rotor spars, which required the use of relatively small-bend radii. At about this time low-cost, high-quality graphite-epoxy filamentary composites became readily available. During the late 1960s and early 1970s, therefore, emphasis shifted decisively to graphite-epoxy. Boron remained a contender as late as 1974, but then an extensive study of airframe structural arrangements and producibility using fiberglass, Kevlar, boron, and graphite appeared to rule out any special use for boron, at least with current technology and at current prices.

In using composites, the designer is, in effect, capable of designing the material by varying the mix of filament orientations. This permits a great variety of structural configurations—in such contrasting applications, for example, as the cross-beam rotor, the composite bearingless tail rotor used on the S-70 and S-76—in which the principal structural member must be flexible in torsion and flapwise bending while the blade of the same rotor must be torsionally rigid and stiff in-plane. An even greater contrast in properties might be noted between rotor and static-airframe applications.

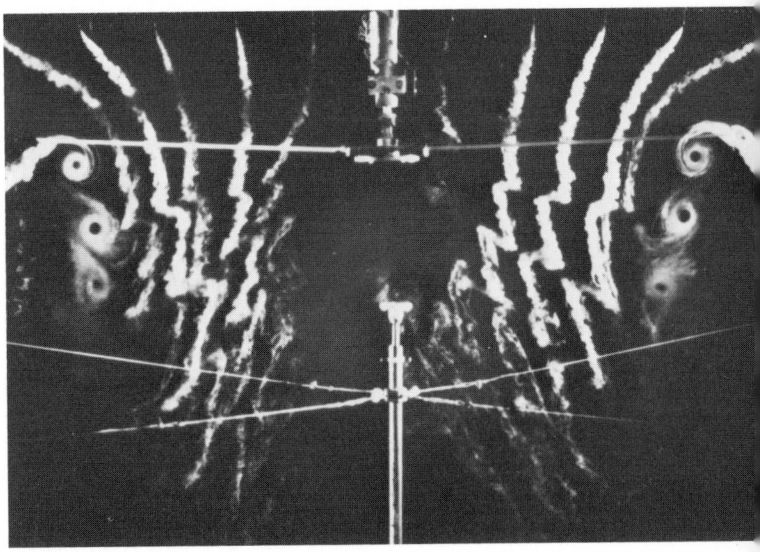

Figure 24.
The rotor-wake smoke test (United Technologies Research Center)

During the fatigue test program for experimental graphite-epoxy S-61 main rotor blades built and tested under navy contract in the mid 1970s, it was also learned that such structures are essentially free of the problems of fatigue. This navy program marked the beginning at Sikorsky of the development of the manufacturing technology for graphite-epoxy composite blades. Such blades can now be offered in production of all Sikorsky models.

The first step in the departure from the aluminum spar blade, however, was made with the decision to employ production titanium spars on the S-70, the CH-53E version of the S-65, and the S-76. (The first flights of the S-70 and S-65E were made in 1974, and of the S-76 in 1977.) The use of titanium and the later use of composites embodied a considerable advantage over aluminum, in that blade twist for optimum hover could be employed without inhibiting forward flight performance as a function of the blade stress levels associated with high twist. This is because the titanium spar has a considerably higher endurance limit than the aluminum spar, and the composite spar is essentially fatigue-free. This made it possible to increase both hover efficiency and forward flight speed.

A major effort was launched to develop the necessary manufacturing technology for the timely production of titanium spars within the limitations of the budget. Essentially, every step in the process involved some degree of innovation: hot and cold forming of sheets tapered in thickness; obtaining clean, high fatigue-strength welds; meeting close dimensional tolerances of cross-section and twist; and developing new methods of inspection.

The ability to survive hostile environments through structurally redundant control-system design and the development of damage-tolerant structures became central considerations with the advent of AAFSS. They received even greater emphasis with the Utility Tactical Transport Aircraft System (UTTAS) (S-70/UH-60A). Accordingly, considerable development effort was expended in investigating configurations and selecting materials. Specimens were subjected to ballistics tests and development proceeded largely by trial and error in the evolution of battleworthy components that would survive combat. Unique designs that would make possible continued functioning of a cable-control system after severance of half the system were developed.

Work also continued on the design of high-speed helicopters. Studies of the Advancing Blade Concept (ABC) had begun as early as 1965. When rigid counterrotating coaxial rotors are employed, rotor lift and maneuver capability are retained at high speeds, since equilibrium requirements do not dictate that lift be limited by the stall of the retreating blade. Thus, a wing is not required for high-speed flight as it is in the compound helicopter. No elastic or mechanical lag or flapping hinges are required, thus greatly simplifying the hub design. Nor, of course, is there any need for a tail rotor. An experimental forty-foot ABC rotor was tested in the Ames Research Center tunnel in 1970 under army sponsorship; from this a feasibility demonstrator aircraft, the S-69 (XH-59A) was build with Sikorsky funds and tested with support from the army, the navy, and NASA (see figure 25). This aircraft has been flying since 1973, generating valuable data both as a pure helicopter and as a compound using two J-60 engines for propulsion at high speed. The ABC rotor was found to be more efficient in hover and to generate less noise than a conventional rotor. While not as efficient in high-speed cruise as the tilt rotor, it combines the ultimate in low-speed agility and maneuverability with a straightforward unconstrained transition to very high dash speeds. It is particularly suited to missions demanding both a nap-of-the-earth capability and intermittent high-speed operation.

Other approaches to high speed continue to be investigated. During the early 1970s further investigations of the tilt-rotor concept, including model tests of its aeroelastic stability problems, were conducted by Sikorsky with air force sponsorship. During

the last half of the 1970s, Sikorsky built and developed the RSRA (S-72) for NASA (see figure 26). This aircraft, although basically a flying wind tunnel for rotor research, can also serve as a demonstrator for compound and high-speed rotor technology.

Other types of high-speed convertible rotor designs also continued to be investigated. During the early 1970s, Sikorsky demonstrated, in large-scale-model tests with army sponsorship, the feasibility of the Telescoping Rotor Aircraft (TRAC) concept—a rotor that is telescoped to approximately 60 percent of its hovering dimension during high-speed flight. The concept envisions either operation at high speed in the retracted position—the compound helicopter configuration—or stopping and retracting the rotor for the ultimate in high-speed drag reduction—the stowed-rotor configuration (see figure 27). Work on this concept was shelved when the army adjusted its priorities and moved away from high-speed concepts to allow for more emphasis on technology incorporating reduced maintenance.

Figure 25.
The S-69 Advancing Blade Concept (ABC)

The Latest Generation

With the advent of the S-70, the S-76, the S-69 (ABC) and the CH-53E, a new period was entered—"new" in that it is characterized largely by the fullest possible exploitation of a long period of intensive research. This research, while benefiting to some degree aircraft produced during the preceding period, matured long after these aircraft had entered production. The S-56, S-58, S-62, S-61, S-64, and S-65—their first flight dates were 1953, 1954, 1958, 1959, 1962, and 1964, respectively—are all essentially derivative of helicopter technology developed during the early period of trial-and-error experimentation.

Of course, much had been learned. Improvements in detail were made, the gas turbine engine became available, large titanium forgings could be produced, lighter and more efficient transmission systems were

Figure 26. The S-72 (RSRA)

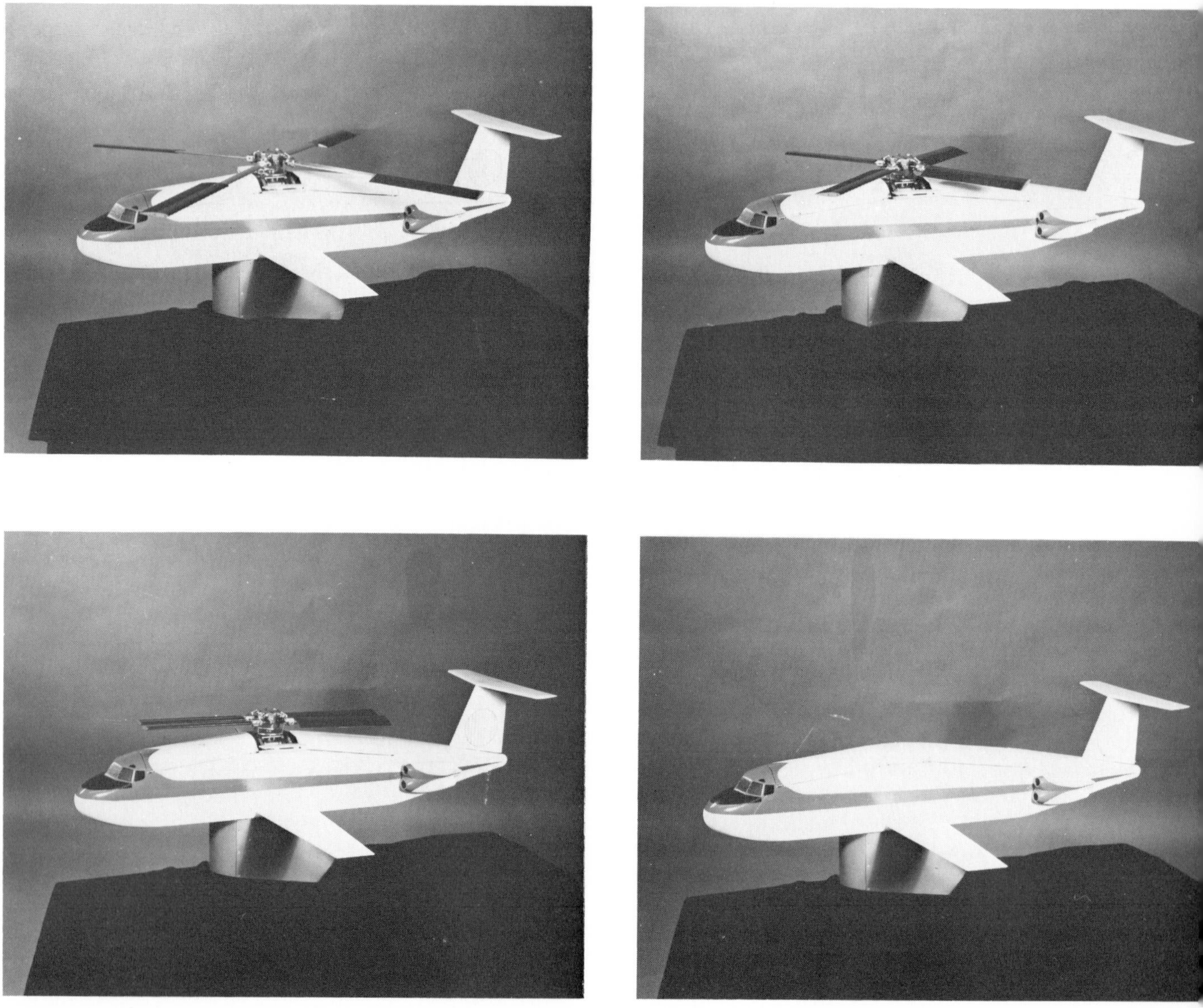

Figure 27. TRAC rotor configurations

designed, advanced autostabilization and automatic flight control systems were installed, and variants were developed for a large number of applications; there were fifteen variants of the S-61 alone. But only entirely new aircraft could take full advantage of the considerable augmentation of knowledge that had begun in a modest way during the early 1950s.

These are the latest models: the production S-70, S-76 (see figure 28), and S-65E (see figure 29), and the experimental S-69 (ABC) and RSRA (built for and operated by NASA). In aerodynamic and structural efficiency, in levels of noise and vibration, in handling qualities, reliability, maintainability, and suitability to operating environments, these aircraft embody significant advances over earlier models—advances that were made possible by the research base built up between the mid 1950s and early 1970s.

In more concrete terms, these aircraft incorporate the following principal improvements over previous models that would not have been possible without the extensive research summarized above:

Figure 28. The S-76

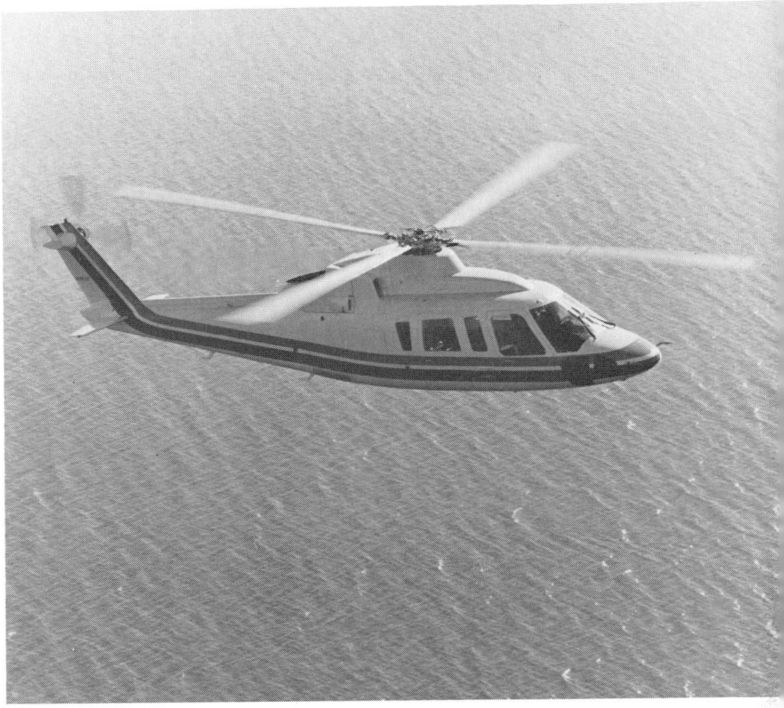

Figure 29. The S-65E (CH-53E)

1. The elastomeric-bearing main rotor hub on the S-70 and S-76. This hub eliminates the need for bearing lubrication, has a smaller drag coefficient, has a smaller envelope, and is lighter than previous hubs. Significantly, the primary geometry of previous hubs is retained; namely, coincident offset lag and flapping hinges with the feathering hinge outboard.

2. The cross-beam (graphite composite bearingless) tail rotor on the S-70 and S-76. This configuration eliminates not only all bearings but the hub hardware as well for sustaining centrifugal loads. It is substantially lighter than previous hubs.

3. Titanium-spar main rotor blades (see figure 30) using (a) compound twist—in contrast to linear twist used heretofore—optimized for hover efficiency without compromise of forward-flight capability; (b) an advanced swept-tip configuration for maximum forward-flight efficiency, minimum noise, and certain aeroelastic benefits; (c) a new series of Sikorsky-developed cambered airfoils—in contrast to the NASA 0012 used heretofore—which not only provide higher angle of attack and lift coefficients and lower drag at high subsonic Mach numbers, but, perhaps more important, achieve this with a thinner airfoil. The airfoil in particular illustrates an interesting situation: spar thinness, and hence airfoil thinness, is important as a means of reducing the stresses caused by the use of high blade twist in high-speed flight. This is just one more illustration of the synergistic manner in which all the design elements must be combined to achieve an indirect result—in this case to increase hover efficiency while simultaneously increasing high-speed capabilities.

4. Greater structural efficiencies than had been achievable before, in part the result of the use of more precise load determination and analysis in the design stage and in part of the use of composites for both primary and secondary structure.

5. The canted tail-rotor concept, which made it possible to achieve satisfactory trim in a configuration with a longer main rotor blade mounted farther forward on the fuse-

Figure 30.
The S-70 improved rotor blade

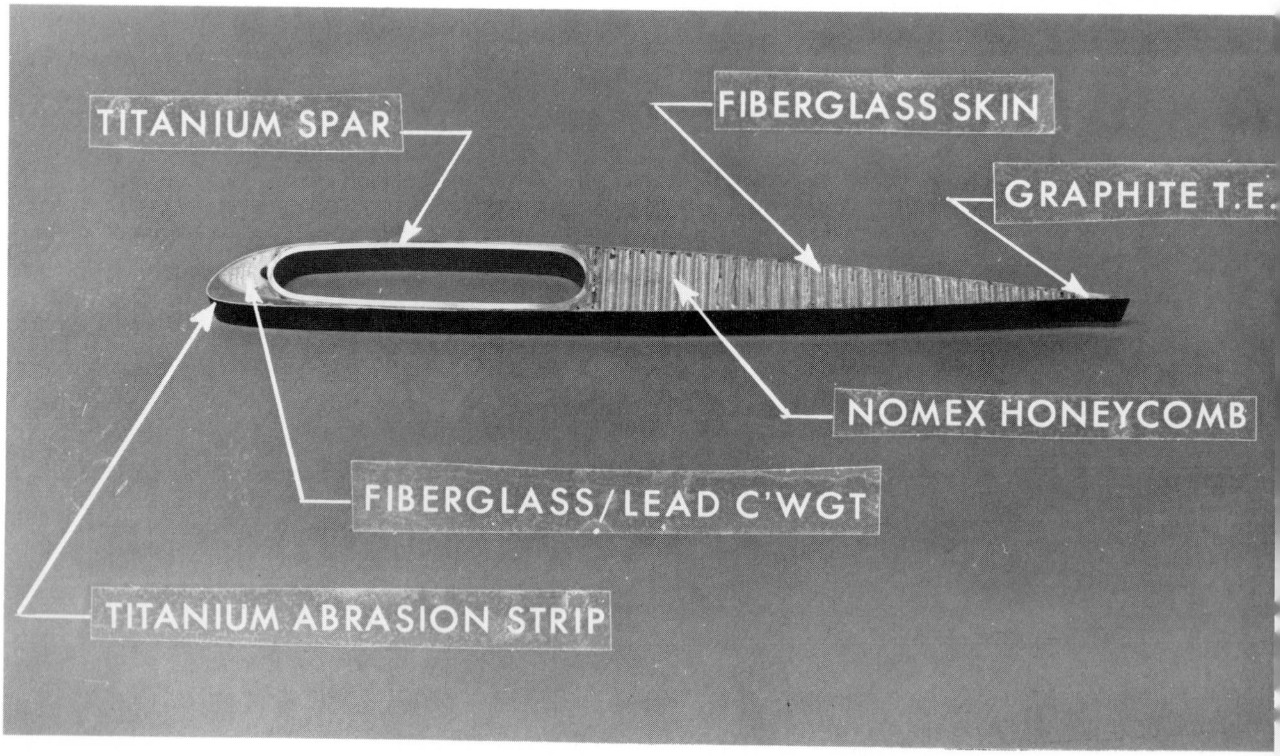

lage. This, in turn, allowed a larger main rotor diameter, and hence a significantly larger payload with the same engine power, while staying within physical size constraints imposed by air transportability (in the case of the UH-60) and by the limitations of aircraft-carrier elevators (in the case of the CH-53E).

6. The use of composite materials, which reduce weight and cost of fabrication while allowing aerodynamically cleaner structures and removing a large part of the fatigue problem.

7. In the ABC, the use of a rotor whose lift capability is not limited at high speed by retreating blade stall, producing a helicopter in the compound mode capable of achieving lift to speeds as high as 300 knots.

The record of the new generation of helicopters speaks for itself, but the effect of each new piece of technology is not easy to trace. It is part of the essential nature of the helicopter design problem that the synergistic effects of many small advances combine to provide large improvements, sometimes in an indirect manner. While much of the new technology, such as lighter-weight structures and more efficient use of power, would appear to be for the purpose of improving performance, the most dramatic improvements in the new generation of aircraft have been the result of the way in which the increase in useful load margins, made possible by advances in aerodynamics and structures, has been plowed back into improved provisions for safety, reliability, maintainability, crashworthiness, and ability to survive combat. Each of these attributes has drawn on advances in its own discipline but has similarly benefited from the whole.

Conclusion

A look to the future suggests that this evolutionary trend is the route by which rotorcraft will continue to advance. But the field is by no means static. New technologies and new configuration possibilities continue to receive attention, the most prominent current example being the application of circulation control technology to the X-Wing concept. This concept, scheduled for testing on the RSRA, involves stopping a very rigid rotor mounted on a thrust-augmented wingless compound helicopter and using the stopped rotor as a lifting wing.

The principal question today is whether the basic technological advances in aerodynamics, structural efficiency, and electronics have reached the point at which a significant departure in configuration such as the tilt rotor, the advancing blade concept, or the X-Wing can provide adequate payload-carrying capability with acceptable initial cost and maintenance burden. This is what is required to capitalize on the potential of these configuration options for higher speeds and greater productivity. The decade of the 1980s should provide the answer.

Edward F. Katzenberger was chief engineer at United Technologies Corporation when he retired in 1976. He joined Sikorsky Aircraft in 1942 as a project engineer, and he was chief of design there from 1947 until 1967. Mr. Katzenberger is a fellow of the Royal Aeronautical Society, associate fellow of the American Institute of Aeronautics and Astronautics, and a founding member and honorary fellow of the American Helicopter Society. He has served on a number of government committees and association committees and holds sixteen patents, fourteen of which are related to helicopters.

Edward S. Carter has been with the Sikorsky Division of United Technologies since 1946. At present he is director of technology. His helicopter activities have ranged from the design and development of the first rotary-wing aircraft automatic control systems to supervision of Sikorsky's aeronautical technology activities. Mr. Carter received the B.S. degree in aeronautical engineering from Princeton University in 1943 and the M.S. degree in aeronautical engineering (automatic controls option) from MIT in 1951. He holds a number of patents on rotary-wing control and automatic stabilization and was awarded the 1958 United Aircraft George Mead Gold Medal for Outstanding Engineering Achievement for his efforts in the successful achievement of helicopter instrument flight. He is an honorary fellow of the American Helicopter Society and a fellow of the American Institute of Aeronautics and Astronautics. He has served on a number of advisory committees of NASA and is chairman of the Rotorcraft Subcommittee of the NASA Aeronautics Advisory Council. He also serves on the Princeton University Department of Aerospace and Mechanical Sciences Advisory Council.

JOHN F. WARD

The Future of Rotorcraft: Embarking on the Second Forty Years

The growth of all sectors of aviation during the past half century has been dramatic. The growth in the rotary-wing or rotorcraft sector of aviation during this period has generally lagged behind that of conventional or fixed-wing aircraft by approximately thirty-five years, primarily because of the greater initial difficulty of achieving controlled vertical flight. Reliance on design evolution by experimenting with modest incremental departures from proven designs also slowed the early development of the rotary-wing sector. During the last decade, significant improvements have been made in the helicopter as a result of substantial investments in research and development by both industry and government. As a result, the state-of-the-art rotorcraft design has matured significantly, as is evident in today's third-generation designs for military and civil vehicles.

Perhaps the best general perspective of the rotorcraft industry is given by figure 1, which shows comparisons with other segments of the aircraft industry, general aviation, and commercial transport, through aircraft sales in the United States, plotted as a function of year of first significant use. This figure gives a graphic perspective on the state of the rotorcraft industry in almost all areas—technology, market development, and sales—and gives an indication of the direction the industry may take during the next forty years.

The future vehicles and their applications evolve from the research and development now under way in industry and government. This effort is addressing the unique needs and challenges of the rotary-wing sector of aviation. The technology needed for a rotary-wing market takeoff must be focused primarily on the achievement of well-defined and proven design and analytical capability in a number of areas, including

- Noise reduction
- Vibration reduction
- Development of all-weather capability
- Reduction of fuel consumption
- Improvement of flying and ride quality
- Improvements in safety
- Improvement of reliability and maintainability
- Improvement of productivity

Meeting these needs will provide the basis for creating a wider market.

The challenges faced by the scientists and engineers in this industry are as great as those in any other field. One challenge is that of complicated flow fields, shown in figure 2. These fields include unsteady transonic flow, yawed flow, dynamic stall, and blade-vortex interaction. In one revolution of the rotor, which takes about two-tenths

Figure 1.
Trends in U.S. aircraft sales

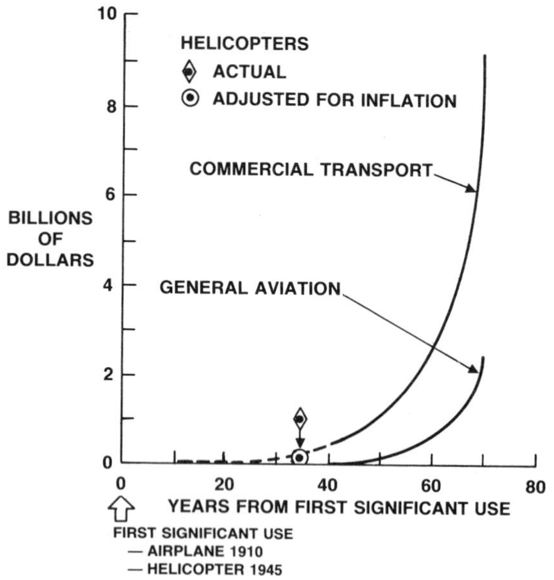

Figure 2.
Rotor-transient aerodynamics

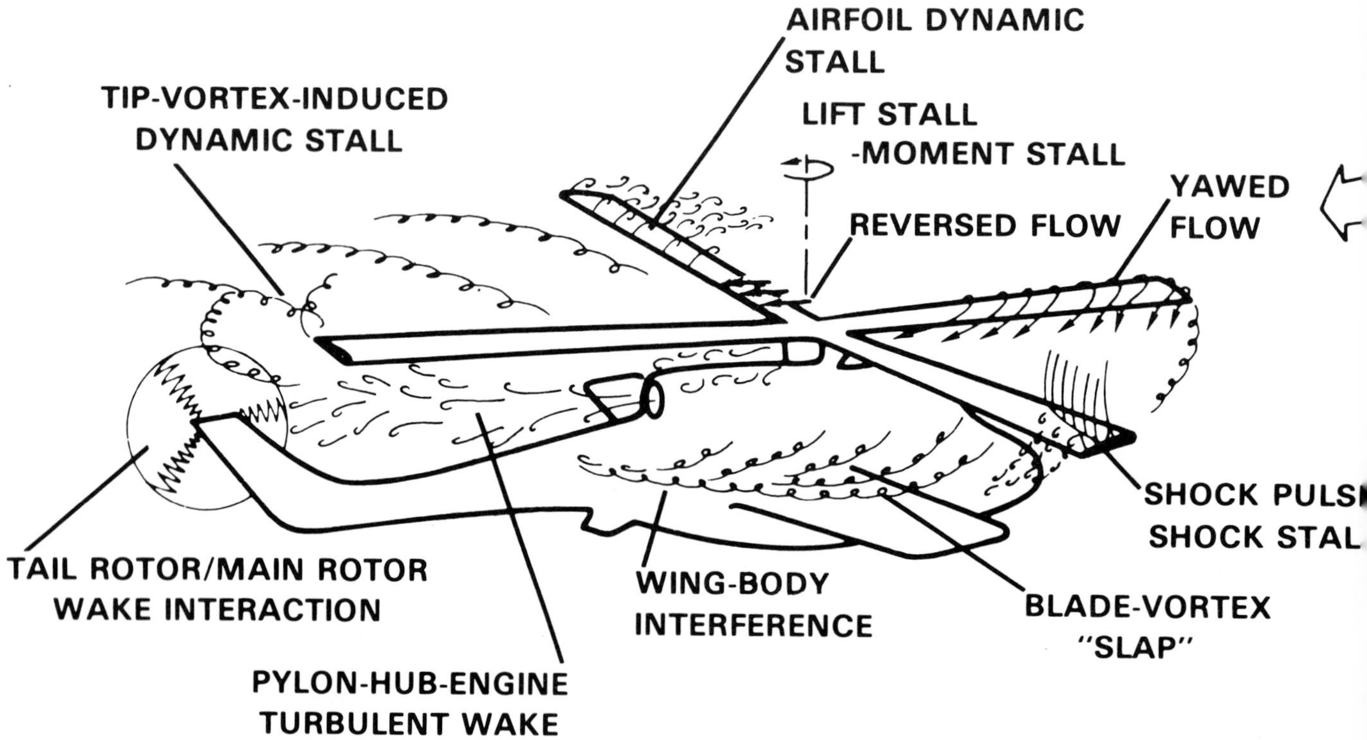

of a second, each blade of the main rotor is subjected to more aerodynamic events than a fixed wing encounters during an entire flight mission from takeoff to landing. This has made rotorcraft design as much an art as a science and has contributed to the high costs and risks associated with its development. While improvements in prediction capability are under way, rotorcraft design will continue to involve significant testing to substantiate new designs.

Technological Challenges

The overall technological needs for developing advanced rotorcraft run the full gamut of aeronautical disciplines, including aerodynamics, acoustics, structures and materials, flight control and avionics, propulsion, and vehicle configuration. Careful attention to these enabling technologies by the industry will assure the effectiveness and acceptance of rotorcraft in a growing number of applications. Although some aspects of rotorcraft technology are common to other aeronautics technologies, the differences are great. In the development of rotorcraft technology many unique, extremely complex, and interrelated requirements in dynamics, aerodynamics, flight control, and structural design must be addressed and integrated into a single design.

Aerodynamics

Despite the continued strong growth potential in the use of rotorcraft, limitations in payload, range, and forward speed frequently pose serious shortcomings in economics and utility for the operator. Improvements in both hover and cruise efficiency are clearly called for, and progress is being made. Cruise efficiency is increasing because of improved aerodynamic designs. An important ingredient in cruise performance is fuselage or airframe drag reduction. The trend in airframe drag force per ton of vehicle gross weight has been a reduction by half every fifteen years.

The challenge for the future in aerodynamics is to achieve advanced rotorcraft designs that take into account the many aerodynamic interaction effects that may influence the performance and dynamic loading of the total vehicle. Aerodynamic interactions among the rotor, airframe, fixed control surfaces in the rotor wake, auxiliary propulsion systems operating in and out of the rotor wake in proximity to the ground, and variations in these interactions with forward speed have been difficult to model during the design process. With the enormous capacity of modern computers, however, these aerodynamic interactions are being addressed with increasing success. In the future, theoretical approaches to rotorcraft design will benefit tremendously from the rapid growth in the capabilities of Computational Fluid Dynamics (CFD). The supercomputers envisioned for the early twenty-first century will have the capacity and speed to deal adequately with the complex aerodynamic flow of an entire vehicle.

Acoustics

A critical technological challenge is presented by the growing need to use helicopters in proximity to residential and business communities. For the manufacturer this means the ability to predict external noise accurately before launching a new vehicle program and assurance that the noise certification requirements can be met within the budget of the program.

In response to this need for advancing the ability to predict external noise, government and industry have joined together in a cooperative five-year research program to develop and validate prediction methods. The participation of the industry is coordinated by the American Helicopter Society in conjunction with the National Aeronautics and Space Administration (NASA). The Federal Aviation Administration (FAA) and the Helicopter Association International are also participants in the program. Beyond accurate prediction methods, technology that will make possible much quieter designs will ultimately be needed. These designs will require lower tip speeds and detailed aerodynamic refinements. The problem is extremely complex and will require an integrated approach involving advanced rotor aerodynamics, new transmission systems, energy-storage devices to maintain autorotation capability at low tip speeds, vibration suppression to allow operational rotor speeds to cross rotor resonance frequencies during variations in rotor speed, and advanced turbine engines that can operate efficiently across a broad range of rotational speed. These technical challenges must be met if quieter rotorcraft are to be achieved. Research efforts are being devoted to the problem, however, and substantial progress can be expected.

Vibration

The reduction of vehicle vibration levels, which will improve the ride quality of modern rotorcraft, has received considerable attention in recent years. Operating electronic equipment amid sustained vibration has led to early deterioration of the equipment. Apart from its effects on the comfort and fatigue of the crew and passengers, therefore, vibration also takes a heavy toll in maintenance costs and downtime. Vibration is highly complex in a vehicle in which large rotor systems and other rotating elements interact dynamically with the flexible airframe. Both industry and government have invested heavily in structural modeling, dynamic methods of computation, and sophisticated vibration-suppression mechanisms. Commendable low levels of vibration have been achieved in the latest generation of helicopters, though with a significant investment in vibration-control devices that have added to the weight and cost of the vehicles. The challenge is to take the next step to a truly jet-smooth ride in a far more efficient manner.

The key to meeting the next challenge is both an understanding of rotor dynamics, aeroelasticity, and coupling between rotor and fuselage and an accurate representation of the dynamic response of the fuselage. Again, the power of the computer is opening the way to a fully integrated analysis of this complex dynamic system during the design of new rotorcraft. Just as in aerodynamics, the characterization of the entire vehicle with the emerging supercomputers will have a significant effect on the ability to design jet-smooth vehicles without penalties in weight and cost.

All-Weather Capability

The ability to perform better in instrument meteorological conditions (IMC) is a key to continued growth in the use of rotorcraft. The ultimate goal is IMC performance that is comparable to performance under visual meteorological conditions (VMC). The vertical lift and control characteristics of rotorcraft are advantages only when these unique characteristics can be used under instrument flight conditions as effectively as under visual flight conditions. Rapid progress in avionics and microelectronics has led to significant progress in instrument flight capabilities. The technology is emerging for routine steep-gradient, zero-zero automatic landing capability. Here, the challenge is to develop these automatic systems at costs that are within the practical reach of the operators of medium to light helicopters. Studies have revealed an apparent limit of 7 percent on the share of acquisition costs that operators are willing to invest in instrumentation for IMC. This precludes economic use of the more sophisticated systems required for all-weather operation in any but the largest helicopters.

Advanced Systems Technology

Research and development programs being conducted by the Department of Defense, the helicopter and engine manufacturers, NASA, and the FAA will offer significant opportunities for growth in future markets for civil and military rotorcraft. These organizations in the United States are part of a worldwide network of government and industry groups with expanding programs in rotorcraft technology. Foreign countries that have increasingly effective technology-development programs include France, the United Kingdom, Italy, West Germany, Japan, and the Soviet Union. A few examples of the advanced rotorcraft systems under investigation in the United States serve to illustrate worldwide trends in rotorcraft technology. As usual, market competition among industries in the free world and military competition between the free world and the Soviet bloc are the primary stimulants to the development of rotorcraft technology.

Advanced Airframes

The helicopter industry is aggressively pursuing the application of advanced composite materials to fuselage structures, which will make it possible to reduce parts count and manufacturing costs substantially and to design helicopters that are lighter in weight and are fail-safe. The use of composite materials in rotor blades and in secondary airframe structures is well established, and research is moving to demonstrate the technology for their use in primary fuselage structures.

An important program in this area is the U.S. Army Advanced Composite Airframe Program (ACAP). Bell Helicopter Textron and Sikorsky Aircraft are each building and testing three composite fuselages to demonstrate the potential benefits of extensive use of composite materials. The two airframe designs will be fabricated and the rotor and propulsion systems from the Bell Model 222 and the Sikorsky S-76 will be installed in their respective airframes in preparation for flight testing. The results of this program are expected to advance the technology of airframe design and to yield benefits that include a reduction of 20 to 30 percent in weight. A 15 to 20 percent reduction in cost is possible because of reduced scrappage, reduced parts count, and automated fabrication techniques made possible by the tailored use of composite materials such as Fiberglas/epoxy, graphite, and Kevlar. Additional benefits in improved aerodynamic performance and dynamic response characteristics may be achieved, since the new technology offers the freedom to fabricate complex contours and the ability to tailor the properties of the composite materials. Better field repairs and lower maintenance costs are also benefits that may come out of this program.

Rotor Systems

As noted earlier, the use of composite materials in rotor blades is well established; extensive production of composite blades has been under way for several years. Now, emphasis is shifting to the design of composite rotor hubs, which represent a greater challenge because of the complexities inherent in integrating blade articulation, control kinematics, highly loaded attachments between blade root and rotor shaft and in tailoring complex aeroelastic features in a hub that is aerodynamically efficient. The design of such a rotor system is

Figure 3.
Integrated Technology Rotor program—the conceptual approach

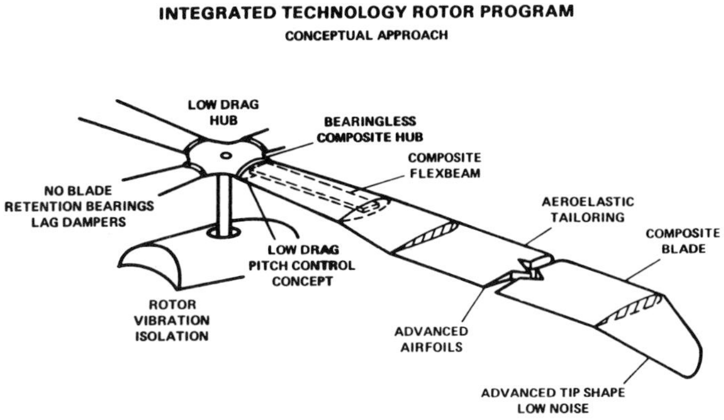

of potential benefit for many of the same reasons that have been identified for advanced airframes—reduced weight, reduced part count, ease of fabrication, tailored aeroelastic characteristics, and the possibility of making them fail-safe.

The U.S. Army and NASA have embarked on a joint Integrated Technology Rotor/Flight Research Rotor (ITR/FRR) program to assess the benefits to be realized by incorporating the many advances in technology of recent years into one rotor design and to provide the research capability that will sustain the next generation of rotorcraft technology. The ITR project will demonstrate a significant advance in rotor systems technology by integrating the disciplines of rotor design, aerodynamics, structures and materials, dynamics, and acoustics. The conceptual approach is illustrated in figure 3. The FRR derivative of the project may provide an advanced flight-research rotor that would make possible significant variation in selected rotor properties, thereby further advancing rotor technology.

Industry-supported development of advanced rotor systems is also under way. The Bell Helicopter Textron Model 680 bearingless main rotor system was first flown in 1982. The advanced multiblade bearingless rotor is illustrated in figure 4. The term *bearingless* indicates that, rather than

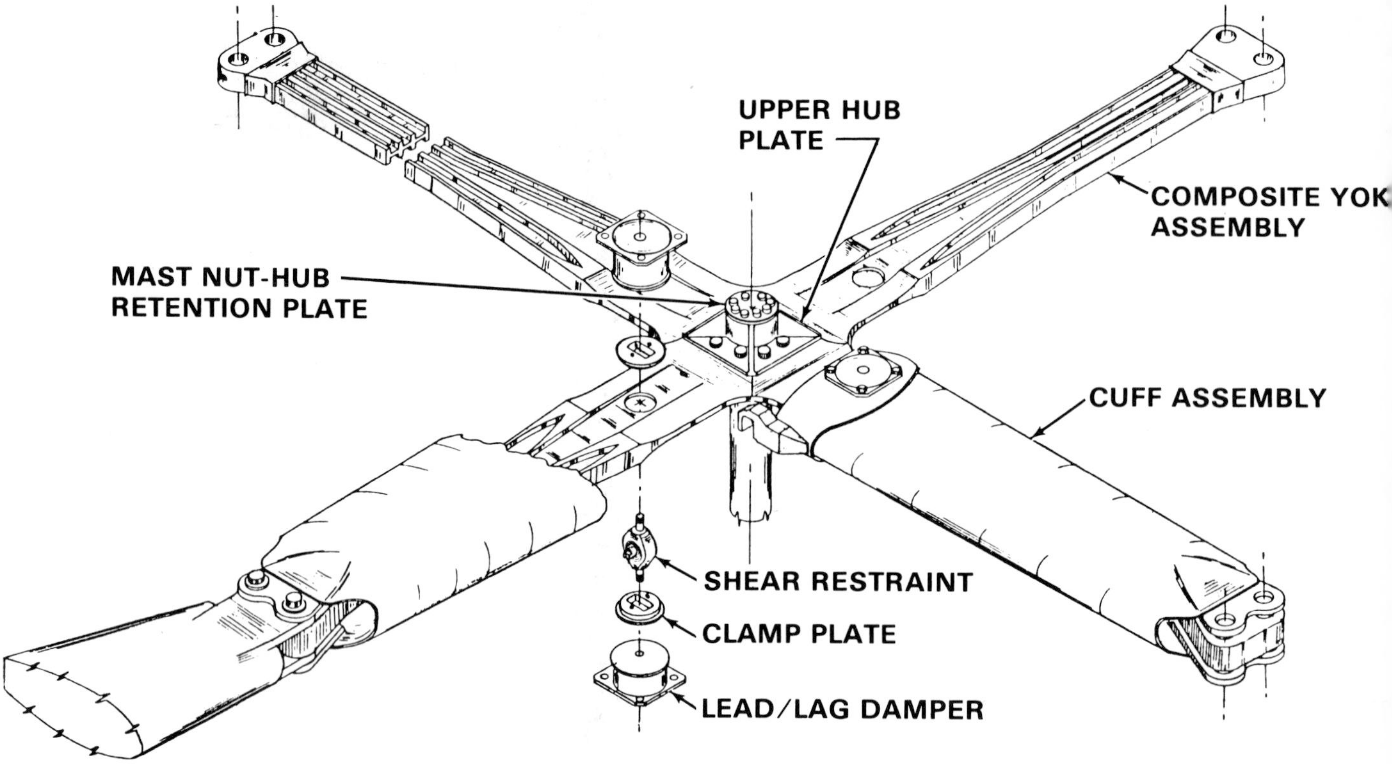

Figure 4.
Advanced multiblade bearingless rotor—Bell Helicopter Model 680

through mechanical bearings, blade articulation is achieved through deflection of composite flexures identified as the composite yoke assembly in figure 4. This flexure concept is generic to bearingless rotor hubs. The details of the flexure design and the use of elastomeric bearings, however, vary between one design and another. The growing data base concerning bearingless rotors from government and industry programs demonstrates a strong potential for simple, efficient designs suitable for a growing number of future production rotors.

Propulsion Systems

The development of propulsion technology for rotorcraft depends on engine-design methodology, power-transfer technology, and systems integration. Advanced engine-design methodology will yield component analytical prediction methods and improvements in technology, including engine diagnostics and control, that will lead to improvements in the life, maintainability, and efficiency of future components of small gas turbine engines, such as compressors, turbines, and combusters. Improvements in engine performance will come primarily in the form of improved thermodynamic cycles—that is, higher pressure ratios, efficiencies, and temperatures. Much of this will be the result of improvements in CFD that permit the design of components that depend on higher technology. Turbine cooling is a prime candidate for improvement. Benefits in engine performance will also be derived from advanced seal and coating technologies.

The trend in small gas turbines has been to use superalloy integral castings, which eliminate the cost and structural problems associated with individual blade attachments. Cast turbine wheels, however, are not amenable to air cooling and have limited life. An attractive monolithic substitution for an integral wheel casting in a small turbine engine is a dual-property turbine wheel, which eliminates problems of conventional mechanical attachment by diffusion bonding of high-fatigue-strength discs to creep-resistant airfoils that have properties tailored to their respective functions. The use of ceramic components in hot sections of engines is expected to yield long-range benefits. Among the advancements needed for future rotorcraft that these materials offer are

- increased temperature capability without cooling,
- reduced weight, and
- minimization of dependence on the import of strategic materials.

Ceramic technology has been advanced during the last decade in programs sponsored by NASA and the U.S. Department of Energy for vehicular engines. A note of caution is in order concerning ceramics. The properties of a material are determined by the flaws it contains. The larger the volume of a part the greater the probability of flaws. This means that ceramics should be tried in small engines first. Of course, a number of questions must be answered before ceramics are applied in flight engines. The returns in better engine performance and reduced weight, however, are so significant that pursuit of successful ceramics applications is clearly warranted.

The propulsion technology programs now under way promise significant improvements in fuel consumption per shaft horsepower that will be attained in production engines in about ten years. The 800-hp Advanced Technology Demonstrator Engine

Figure 5.
Convertible fan-shaft engine propulsion X-Wing concept

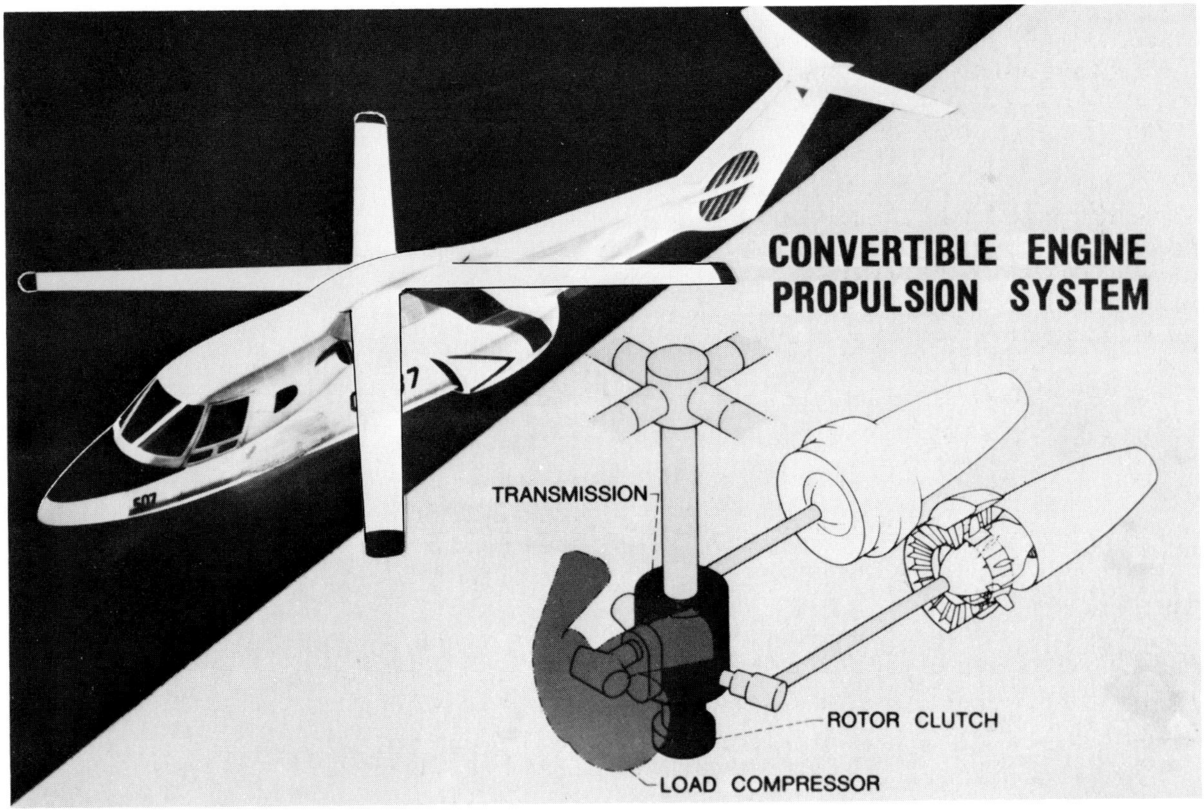

(ATDE) promises impressive gains should full-scale development of it be required for light helicopters. The ATDE program was launched in 1977, when both Avco-Lycoming and Detroit Diesel Allison were selected competitively by the U.S. Army to conduct the advanced-development program. The most recent series of demonstrators is the 5,000-hp Modern Technology Demonstrator Engine (MTDE), which may well find a home in many applications—in the CH-47, P-3, and JVX, for example. Competitive advanced-development contracts for the MTDE program were let by the U.S. Army to Pratt & Whitney and General Electric. Each of these demonstrator programs represents a significant step forward, making available power-plant choices that are second to none.

Two other advanced-engine designs worth noting are the convertible engine and the Compound Cycle Turbine-Diesel Engine (CCTDE) concept. The interest in the convertible engine has been stimulated by high-speed rotorcraft concepts such as Advancing Blade Concept (ABC) aircraft, Folding Tilt Rotor (FTR) aircraft, and the X-Wing concept shown in figure 5. In application, the convertible engine provides shaft power to the rotors in hover and low speed, then the same engine converts to a turbofan mode for high-speed cruising. NASA and the Defense Advanced Research Projects Agency (DARPA) are funding a joint Convertible Engine Systems Technology program at the Lewis Research Center of NASA in Cleveland, Ohio, to investigate the concept, using a modified General Electric TF-34 turbofan engine. Other studies and exploratory testing are under way to assess the benefits of this fan-shaft engine that would supplant the separate rotor-drive and cruise engines on high-speed rotorcraft and other VTOL aircraft. A number of systems are being studied for converting from shaft to fan drive. These include variable inlet and exit guide vanes for the turbofan and variable-pitch fans, clutches, and fluidic couplings.

The compound-cycle turbine-diesel engine has many potential applications, including future rotorcraft designs that will require 500 to 1,500 hp. The basic design combines a turbine engine compressor and turbine with a diesel engine core for better specific fuel consumption, low exhaust-gas temperature (750°F), low weight, and power density greater than 4.8 hp per cubic inch, which is five times what has been realized with current diesel technology. Research must be focused on advanced diesel-engine propulsion technology to provide a technology base for long-life, high-speed diesel core designs. Assuming that a technology base and demonstrator engine are ready in the mid 1980s, the test results for the CCTDE demonstrator could be available in the early 1990s. Such a program is now being reviewed and discussed among interested parties within the Department of Defense and NASA.

New transmission systems, such as split-torque, hybrid, and variable-speed drives, are being evaluated, and feasibility demonstrations are being planned. The hybrid concept combines advanced gear designs with traction drive. Traction drive incorporates rollers, without gear teeth, under high contact pressure with a special traction lubricant to achieve 100 to 1 reductions in speed between the engine output shaft and the main rotor shaft of a helicopter. This activity also includes NASA and Army research which indicates that technology can lead to new transmission designs that will represent a considerable step forward, particularly in materials, structures, and lubrication. The goals of advanced drive systems are to achieve a reduction in weight, noise, and cost while improving reliability and maintainability and achieving longer life. This combined effort should bring a 20 to 50 percent increase in mean time between removal.

Avionics and Control

The benefits that can accrue from application of advanced avionics and control concepts to new rotorcraft designs include improvements in fuel efficiency, maneuver-

Figure 6.
Future helicopter command and control center by Sikorsky Aircraft

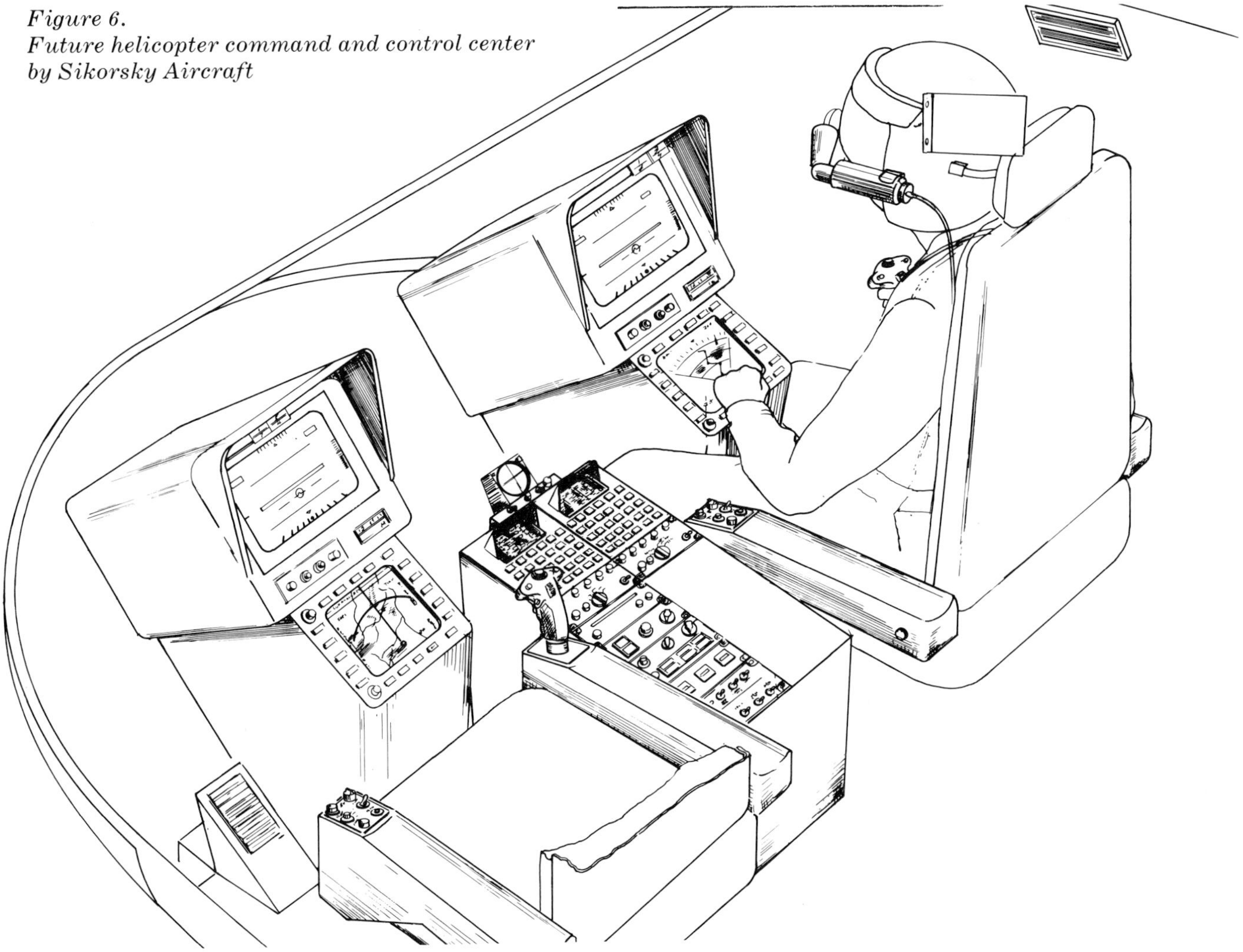

ability, flying and ride qualities, and precision flight-path control and decreases in pilots' workload. Additional benefits are the potential reduction of control surfaces and reduction of vehicle weight by the substitution of fly-by-wire or fly-by-light systems for complex mechanical control systems.

The greatest effect on the rotorcraft of the twenty-first century, however, will come from the continuing revolution in microelectronics. It is projected that the size, cost, weight, and power of computers will be improved at least 100 times over what they are today. Speed of computation will approach that of light, and memory density will nearly equal that of the human brain. This means that multiple, identical electronic subsystems that can switch between components automatically will make self-healing possible. In addition, the application of automatic recording of flight problems and ground trouble-shooting capability, now being introduced, will increase. As a result, the pilot's workload can be reduced dramatically, freeing him to devote more attention outside the cockpit.

The use of digital electronics in rotary-wing control systems will make it possible, through the use of complex mathematical laws, to ensure full control of the helicopter under any adverse flight conditions. The control systems will be self-adaptive, eliminating compromises in flying qualities with changes in gross weight, altitude, and center of gravity. Low-cost miniaturization will permit the installation of backup systems and failure-management features that eliminate any loss of control following an electronic failure. Flight tests for certification will be much simpler than they are today, since there will be no degraded flight modes and failure transients to demonstrate in flight. The validation of software by analysis and simulation, however, will grow to be an important element of future certification programs.

The cockpit in the next generation of rotorcraft may look like the one illustrated in figure 6. Pulleys, cables, bellcranks, and pushrods will give way completely to actuators controlled by electrical or optical sensors. Large-motion flight control will be replaced by limited-motion force controls. Other manual controls will be replaced by voice-controlled computer actuation. High-resolution, full-color flat panel displays, with depths one-tenth that of existing instruments, will enable behind-the-panel integration of an entire avionic system. Mission reconfiguration of the cockpit will require nothing more than changing a replaceable "crew station module." With aircraft performance data monitored and stored in the on-board computer core, flight planning will be as simple as dropping a disc into the home computer.

One of the programs that is beginning to establish the technology base for future flight-control systems is the U.S. Army Advanced Digital/Optical Control System (ADOCS) flight demonstrator program. Under this program, Boeing Vertol is designing, is developing, and will flight test a new computerized helicopter flight-control system that is linked together by fiber optics. The ADOCS system will be flight tested on a UH-60 Blackhawk.

The new control system technologies offer a potential for better ride quality through suppression of gusts and vibrations. Ride quality may have a substantial effect on both the reliability of aircraft equipment and the comfort or fatigue of crew and passengers. Using gust-suppression techniques, by automatic feedback of vehicle body motions into the control system, rotorcraft that operate in the turbulent low-altitude range can be made to have ride qualities more nearly competitive with those of fixed-wing transports that spend most of their time above 30,000 feet. Using higher-harmonic control (HHC) for vibration suppression is another opportunity for improving ride quality. The primary elements of this active vibration-suppression system are: acceleration transducers that sense the vibratory response of the fuselage; a higher-harmonic blade-pitch actuator system that will drive the blade pitch at n times the normal rotational speed of the rotor, where n is usually the number of blades in the rotor system and the predominant frequency of the unsuppressed vibratory loads transmitted to the fuselage; a flightworthy microcomputer that incorporates a mathematical model for reducing vibrations; and a signal-conditioning system, the electronic control unit, which interfaces between the sensors, the microcomputer, and the HHC actuators. These and other components of the system, installed in the OH-6A helicopter, are shown in figure 7. The feasibility of the concept has been demonstrated with the OH-6A in a program involving the U.S. Army, NASA, and Hughes Helicopters. The OH-6A configured with the HHC system flew closed loop in 1983. The results of this initial flight testing and of NASA research on multicyclic control technology indicate that this technology offers significant opportunity to improve the ride quality of the helicopter dramatically.

The new control technologies and the electronic cockpit will have profound effects in meeting the needs of future rotorcraft operators, including more productive and safer missions and greater acceptance by passengers and the community. Linking the new rotorcraft to advanced guidance and navigation systems, such as the Navigation System using Time and Ranging (NAVSTAR), through the electronic cockpit will

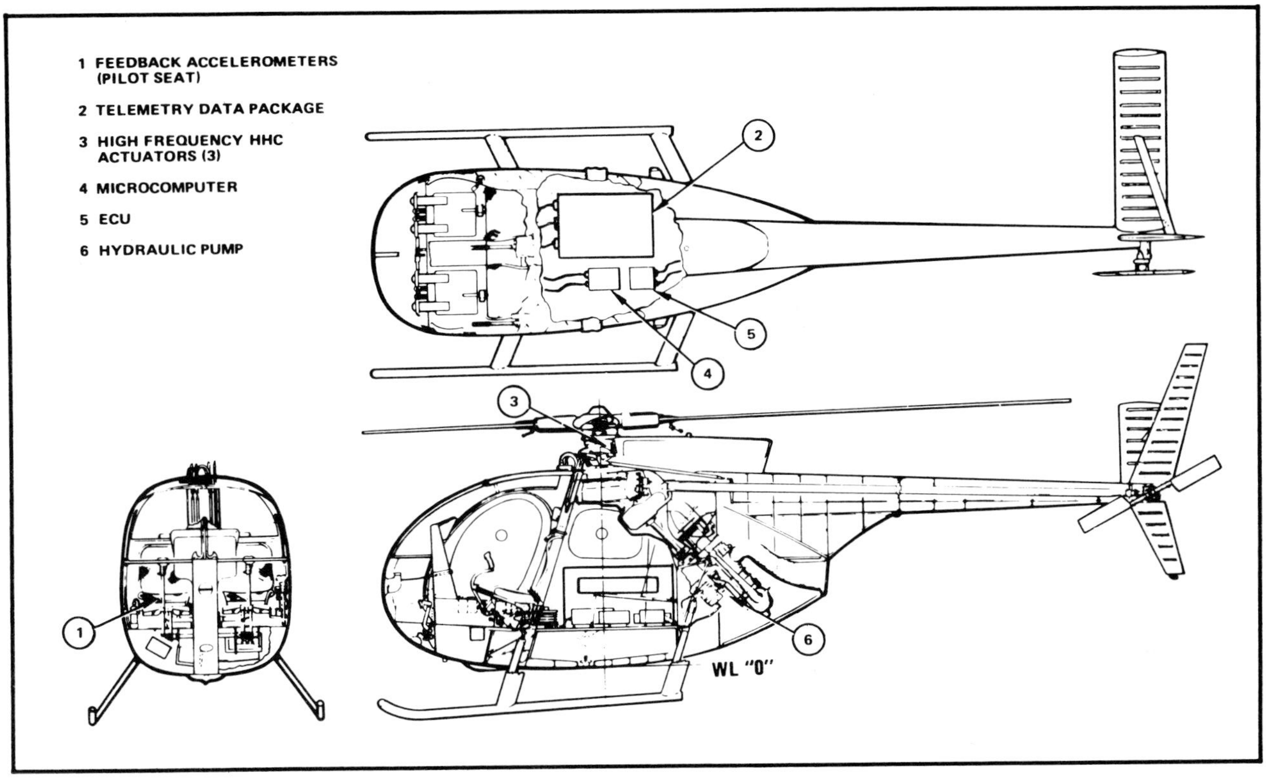

Figure 7.
OH-6A installation of Higher Harmonic Control System

allow much more effective use of the airspace, particularly in congested terminal areas. Increased frequency of operation by separation from airplane traffic with discrete approaches to and departures from heliports and airports will be made possible by low speed-control and guidance systems. The FAA's CH-53 research-and-development helicopter has demonstrated inflight helicopter navigation using NAVSTAR in a 100-mile round-trip flight from Atlantic City to Cape May, New Jersey. NASA is also exploring low-cost civil guidance systems that can use degraded signal inputs from the military global positioning system satellites now being put into operation.

Advanced Rotorcraft Configurations

The ultimate demonstration of the viability of advanced technology developed at the systems level is integration of these technologies into a proof-of-concept or demonstration vehicle, which makes it possible to investigate the correlation between actual and predicted characteristics at full scale in flight. As an indication of what the future may hold in new operational configurations, there are four active research-and-development rotorcraft flight programs with primary emphasis on advanced vehicle technology:

- The Model 360 Advanced Technology Helicopter
- The Advancing Blade Concept
- The Tilt-Rotor Research Aircraft
- The RSRA/X-Wing Rotor programs

A wide variety of advanced technology flight-test activities is under way within the rotorcraft industry. The four programs selected here are considered to indicate the

Figure 8.
Advanced-technology tandem helicopter—Boeing Vertol Model 360

principal advances in fundamental vehicle concepts that offer opportunity for new mission applications. It is expected that the late 1980s and 1990s will present needs and opportunities for application of these advanced vehicle configurations.

Boeing Vertol is at work on the development of the Model 360 composite aircraft (see figure 8) that will feature a number of advanced systems. Efforts to develop a more efficient rotor system for the advanced-technology helicopter have been under way at Boeing Vertol since 1977. The goal of the program is to develop a system that will provide improved hover and forward-flight performance with fixed-wing cruise speed in excess of 200 knots coupled with noise levels low enough to assure community acceptance. Composites are used extensively in the Model 360 medium-lift helicopter. The four-blade rotor incorporates composite blades. The mixed-modulus composite rotor hub is fail-safe and is equipped with elastomeric bearings. Rotor shafts and interconnecting shafts, also of mixed-modules composite construction, are therefore fail-safe, are lower in weight, and require less maintenance. The upper transmission housings that carry the flight loads from the rotor into the airframe are also composite. A composite fuselage is being constructed, as shown in figure 9. The longerons and frames are constructed of graphite composites, and the skin panels are Kevlar and Nomex honeycomb. Reinforcing members around cutouts in these panels are graphite. The goal of integrating these and other improvements in technology is to increase payload capacity 25 percent over that of current metal-technology aircraft. The objective of the Model 360 flight program will be to confirm the payload benefits of composites and the achievement of improved rotor hover performance and greater cruise efficiency to speeds greater than 200 knots.

Another candidate for higher speed missions is the Sikorsky Advancing Blade Concept aircraft shown in figure 10. This vehicle has successfully demonstrated forward speeds of more than 250 knots in a research program sponsored by the U.S. Army and participated in by the U.S. Navy and NASA. By avoiding retreating blade stall, which is a key limiting factor in the speed and maneuver capability of a pure helicopter, the ABC has been made faster and more maneuverable. It has two counterrotating, coaxial, rigid rotors. At high speed the retreating blades of both rotors are unloaded, and the majority of the rotor load is carried on the advancing blades of both rotors. The system eliminates the need for an antitorque tail rotor and its related gearboxes, drive shafts, and other components. In its compound configuration, the demonstration aircraft is equipped with two outboard-mounted Pratt & Whitney J-60 turbojet engines for auxiliary thrust. This aircraft has reached a service ceiling of 35,500 feet and a maximum speed of more than 260 knots. The ABC aircraft may have potential as a small, compact, quiet, public-service rotorcraft for operations in proximity to communities. The special advantage of eliminating the tail-rotor safety hazards is of particular interest.

The next rotorcraft in the high-speed category is the tilt-rotor aircraft, which has been demonstrated successfully in a proof-of-concept program using the Bell Helicopter Textron XV-15 Tilt Rotor Research Aircraft. Two of these aircraft were built and flown under a joint NASA-Army program. The XV-15 program demonstrated the viability of a vehicle that combines the features of an efficient hover and low-speed helicopter with the high-speed cruise efficiency of a fixed-wing turboprop aircraft. The wingtip-mounted engines, transmissions, and twenty-five-foot rotors tilt from a vertical position for hover and vertical takeoffs and landings, to a horizontal position for forward flight. The transition between these two extremes is accomplished through a broad speed corridor with minimum pilot workload. Full conversion from hover to fixed-wing mode at 180 knots can be made in approximately twelve sec-

Figure 9.
Model 360 composite fuselage

Figure 10.
Advancing Blade Concept—Sikorsky Aircraft XH-59A

onds. The potential benefits of the tilt-rotor concept include the ability to conduct missions of twice the speed and range of the helicopter using a given quantity of fuel. In addition, the cruise configuration is more akin to a turboprop airplane with low vibration levels and high-altitude capability. The implications for future military and civil application are significant. Recent military suitability tests with the XV-15 demonstrated advantages in agility, handling qualities, precise control in nap-of-the-earth flying, shipboard operations, and simulated search-and-rescue missions. The civil potential is equally significant in support of offshore oil exploration at ranges well beyond that of the helicopter. Also, the tilt rotor's terminal area flight path control capability will allow the use of helicopter terminal area flight rules on dedicated instrument approach systems so that they will pose no additional burden to crowded terminal airspace. Significant hub airport relief could be obtained by using tilt-rotor vehicles on regional routes of up to 400 nautical miles. Using tilt-rotor aircraft to extend air transportation to remote regions is also a potential application that would reduce the investments in land and the environmental effects of large airfield installations.

The most recent rotorcraft concept to evolve is the X-Wing configuration, which has a design speed goal of 450 to 500 knots. An artist's conception of this vehicle is shown in figure 11. The primary enabling technology in this concept is the X-Wing rotor, which functions much like a helicopter rotor in hover and low-speed flight, then converts to a stopped-rotor mode at a speed of approximately 200 knots. The vehicle then flies as a fixed-wing aircraft while accelerating to high speed with an auxiliary propulsion system. The design incorporates circulation-control rotor (CCR) technology that enables the rotor to perform the dual function of a helicopter mode when rotating and fixed-wing mode when stopped. In the CCR rotor blade, air supplied by a compressor system is ejected out of a thin slot that runs the full length of the rotor blade on both the leading and trailing edges of an elliptical airfoil. Blowing air out of either the trailing or leading edge augments the lift capability of the airfoil and also delays airflow separation from the airfoil, which improves its stall characteristics. By cyclically modulating the amount of ejected airflow, cyclic rotor control is obtained. Also, by collectively controlling the ejected airflow, collective lift control is obtained. The rotor blades operate with fixed mechanical pitch and are shaft-driven in a conventional manner in the helicopter mode of operation. During conversion from helicopter operation to fixed-wing mode, the circulation-control system is used to maintain aircraft trim and to minimize vibratory rotor loads as the rotor is stopped. In the fixed-wing mode, the ejected airflow from the blades is modulated to achieve aircraft control.

Figure 11.
Artist's conception of the X-Wing high-speed rotorcraft

The X-Wing rotor will be investigated in a joint NASA/DARPA proof-of-concept flight program using the Rotor Systems Research Aircraft (RSRA), shown in figure 12. The RSRA is a unique flight-test facility procured by NASA and the U.S. Army for flight investigation of advanced rotor systems. Two of these research vehicles are available with special instrumentation and measurement systems. The primary objective of the joint NASA/DARPA RSRA/X-Wing rotor program is to investigate conversion from rotary-wing flight to fixed-wing, stopped-rotor flight and back to rotary-wing flight. This is the most challenging flight mode for the X-Wing concept. The RSRA will be used to investigate the dynamic stability, performance, and rotor-control characteristics of the X-Wing rotor system during the testing.

Military Developments

As in the past, the engineering development of new military rotorcraft leads to the introduction of new capabilities into the civil arena as well. This has been the single most important catalyst in the development of the rotorcraft industry. The experience and trained manpower produced by military rotorcraft programs directly supports and influences future civil developments. Government investments in helicopters such as the UH-1, OH-58, OH-6, and CH-47 have been essential to their civil market applications. Similar opportunities can be expected to stem eventually from current military production programs, such as the UH-60 and CH-53.

The emerging program for the development of the Joint Services Advanced Vertical Lift Aircraft (JVX) program has important implications for future civil applications. The JVX is a multimission vertical-takeoff-and-landing tilt-rotor aircraft. The design uses advanced, mature technology proven in the Bell Helicopter Textron XV-15 Tilt Rotor Research Aircraft program supported and managed jointly by the Army and NASA. Bell is teamed with Boeing

Figure 12.
NASA-Army Rotor Systems Research Aircraft

Vertol for the preliminary design phase of JVX. The new vehicle is expected to go into operation in 1992 with a production of well over 500 aircraft. The vehicle will have a gross weight in the range of 40,000 pounds and a maximum cruise speed of 350 knots at an altitude of 17,000 feet. The JVX will have a capacity to move thirty assault troops on missions with up to a 250-mile radius. This joint-services program will provide a common aircraft for amphibious assault, combat search and rescue, and special operations. The new rotory-wing vehicle will have twice the speed, range, and altitude of today's helicopters and will be self-deployable throughout the world. Its performance is expected to provide an important new tactical force multiplier and many new mission capabilities. The design of the JVX incorporates a number of advanced technologies, including extensive use of composite materials, advanced digital flight controls, and aerodynamic, aeroelastic, and crashworthiness design methods demonstrated in other government and industry research and development programs. The timely movement from the successful XV-15 Tilt Rotor Research Aircraft proof-of-concept and mission suitability program to the JVX engineering development program is a notable example of the effective transfer of new technology to meet existing mission requirements. The development of the JVX will also be a vital stimulant to the development of civil transport configurations that could be in operation in the late 1990s. The civil counterpart of the JVX would transport thirty passengers 300 nautical miles in one hour, execute a vertical landing and takeoff, and return with thirty passengers without refueling. This capability creates numerous opportunities for application, including offshore oil transportation systems, where new fields are beyond the range of helicopters. The applications to intercity and regional transportation are also of interest as airport congestion grows.

Another important military development effort that will have a significant effect on the evolution of modern rotorcraft is the U.S. Army aircraft system known as the Light Helicopter Family (LHX). The initial configuration for the LHX will be an armed reconnaissance–light attack helicopter, with a utility variant to be developed later. It is expected to be in use by the late 1990s. A family of small helicopters that would use an affordable design developed around a common set of dynamic components—engines, transmissions, rotors, and the like—to be produced in large numbers, is desired. A requirement of up to 7,000 vehicles is currently projected.

Initial studies, based on the postulated mission requirements and the desired aircraft characteristics, have been focused on the feasibility of a one-man crew. An important feature of the LHX design likely to affect all future rotorcraft significantly is the emphasis placed upon avionics architecture and the integration of subsystems. Preliminary studies show the potential for saving up to a third of the weight that the LHX would have if present state-of-the-art technology were used. The LHX would be able to perform scout and attack missions with a one-man crew by automating communications; navigation and target acquisition; identification, radar warning, and missile detection; fire control; and flight control. As an example, many control functions performed by the pilot can be effected through a voice-actuated control system. An Advanced Rotorcraft Technology Integration (ARTI) program initiated in 1983 is addressed to the many issues related to integration of the available technologies into an efficient and cost-effective aviation weapons system.

Meeting the challenges of the ARTI program and successfully developing the LHX vehicle will advance the sophistication of rotorcraft dramatically. The availability of this advanced technology base will foster other military and civil developments and applications. As an example, derivatives of the LHX would be promising candidates for meeting a wide variety of public-service rotorcraft requirements of the future. Many police, fire, and emergency medical needs

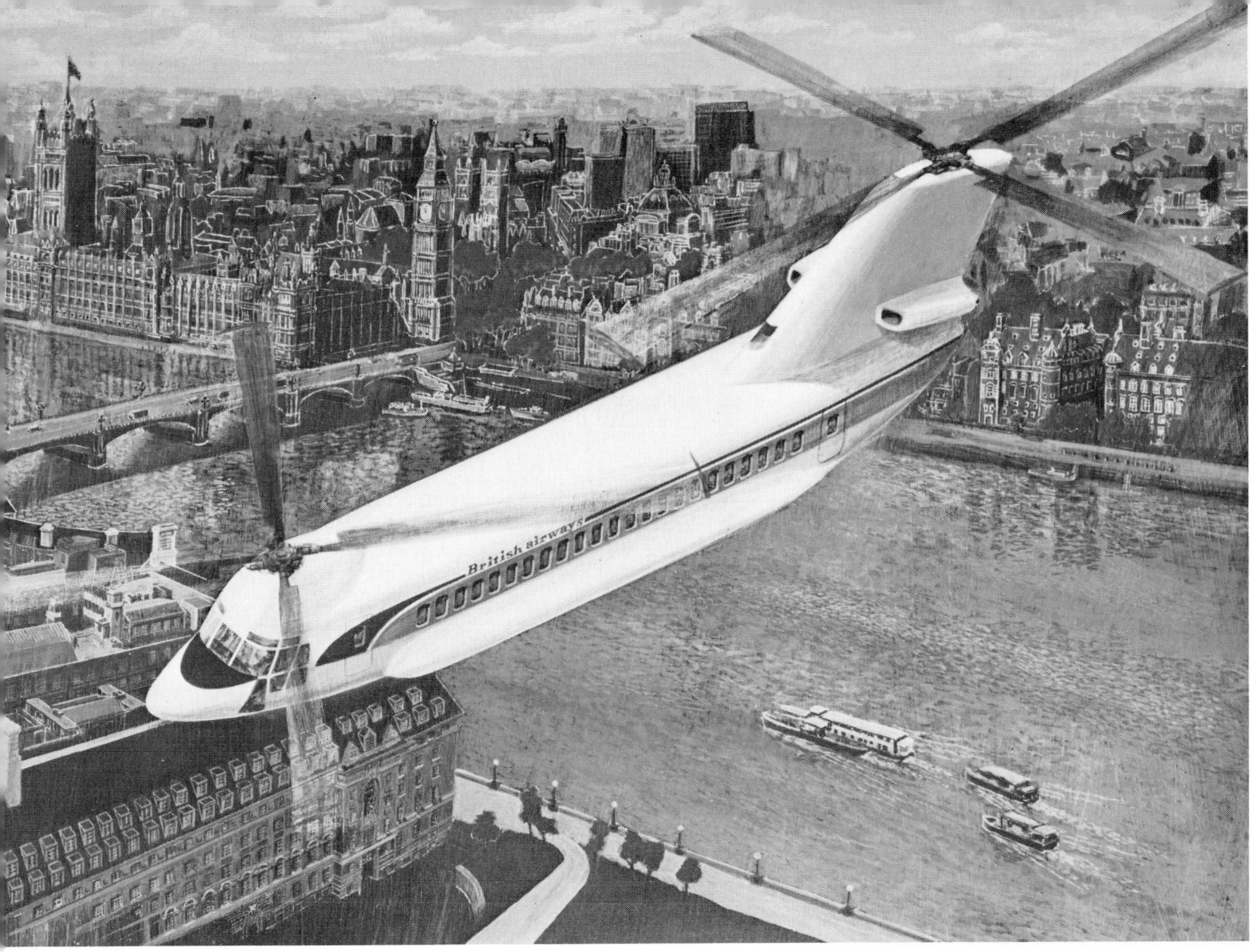

for rotorcraft could be met by highly integrated systems of the type envisioned for the LHX. Rapid guidance, navigation, communication, and control functions that can be handled by a one-man crew in all-weather and night operations would be valuable contributions to public service.

The third military rotorcraft, the Advanced Cargo Helicopter, ACH-XX, is just beginning concept definition and is envisioned both as a follow-on to the CH-47 and as a possible alternative to the XCH-62 Heavy Lift Helicopter. The ultimate size of the ACH-XX and the design payload could be significantly larger than that of the CH-47 Chinook. Another important parameter will be its required radius of operation, which might dictate a configuration other than that of a conventional helicopter. Whatever the configuration or payload capacity of the ACH-XX, the need for such a system to increase the surface mobility of ground combat forces is evident.

Figure 13.
Large transport helicopter for intercity transportation (200 knots)

Federal Aviation Administration

A solid indication of the growth potential of the rotorcraft sector of aviation is the significantly increased attention to rotorcraft matters within the FAA. While the southwest region has been designated the principal place for rotorcraft certification, a Rotorcraft Program Office has been established at FAA headquarters in Washington, D.C. In addition, a recently issued Rotorcraft Master Plan outlines the many tasks being performed by the FAA in its effort to achieve full acceptance of rotorcraft as an essential part of civil aviation. These efforts are of three sorts:

- To improve the National Airspace System so as to permit rotorcraft to employ their

Figure 14.
Advancing Blade Concept medium transport (250 knots)

unique operating capabilities to the greatest extent possible

- To provide for an adequate system of public VFR/IFR heliports to accommodate rotorcraft

- To improve safety by means of more exacting criteria and application of advanced technology in the airworthiness and certification process

The Rotorcraft Master Plan is focused on the tasks required to move from the mid 1980s into the early twenty-first century with a fully capable rotorcraft airspace system, public heliports, and an effective certification process. The objective of the National Airspace System is to move from an environment designed for fixed-wing aircraft, in which rotorcraft are merely accommodated, to a nationwide all-weather rotorcraft system comparable to, and integrated with, fixed-wing operations, including those at low altitudes and in remote areas. The objective in heliports is to move from a limited system of public-use VFR heliports to a fully adequate system of public-use urban VFR and IFR heliports. With respect to certification the goal is to move to procedures that, without undue constraints, improve rules, guidance materials, and resources to assure safe and efficient certification, maintenance, and operation of rotorcraft.

The National Prototype Demonstration Heliport program has been launched with the initial selection of four large cities that will build prototype heliports in their central business districts. These cities are New Orleans, New York, Los Angeles, and Indianapolis. The prototype heliports will serve as models in the development of procedures and equipment to demonstrate the feasibility and desirability of urban area all-weather heliports. The plan envisions all-weather heliports with supporting route structures in twenty-five major cities by the year 2000. The general advocacy and acceptance of this program is based on the recognition of the following point stated by Fred Fine, the chairman and chief executive officer of Island Helicopters, following two and a half years of operation by New York Helicopters: "Unless an acceptable heliport network is established in city centers with good interface with surface transport, the helicopter will never reach its potential as a prime mover of people."

Civil Applications

The civil uses of rotorcraft are perhaps more varied than their military uses. Besides their value in transport, their use in forestry and agriculture, in the exploration and development of natural resources, in construction, in police surveillance, and in emergency medical service is expanding and is expected to continue growing through the 1990s.

Air Transportation

In air transportation, corporate and business rotorcraft represent a growing segment. Here the primary consideration is the value placed on the traveler's time. In the current transportation market, ground transportation performs adequately for ranges of 10 to 30 miles, and fixed-wing aircraft do an excellent job for trips of 200 to 400 miles, but there is an ill-defined middle range in which neither is entirely satisfactory. Rotorcraft is growing as the appropriate mode of transport in this range. When the traveler's time has quantifiable value, such as that of a corporate executive, the helicopter is proving to be extremely successful. It is anticipated that air taxi operations, as well as air carrier operations, will grow significantly during the next twenty years. In addition, the ranges over which rotorcraft will be able to compete successfully will extend well beyond the present 200-nautical-mile stage length. Some of the potential configurations for air transport rotorcraft are shown in figures 13 through 16.

In the future, rotorcraft will grow in value as a tool that will help industry move out of high-cost locations into areas in which the costs of buildings, overhead, and land are lower and management and customer services can still be maintained. Air taxi operations will be able to serve these special transportation needs. The development of scheduled rotorcraft service will depend, however, on aggressive operators, the availability of reliable equipment, and a substantial reduction in the cost of operation and ownership. Continued development of quiet, economical, all-weather, extended-range vehicles should cause civil rotorcraft air transportation to grow significantly during the next two decades. Benefits in time savings, congestion relief, improved urban transportation, and more efficient use of real estate can be realized from shifting toward the use of public heliports and away from more land-intensive transportation systems.

Forestry and Agriculture

Helicopters have made a substantial contribution to forest management in recent years. As timber costs have risen, it has become more cost-effective for owners and managers of timberland to invest in complete forest-management technology and techniques, from seeding new crops to protecting young trees from insects and disease. Helicopters perform these tasks more efficiently than ground equipment and more precisely than their fixed-wing counterparts. The Forest Service alone employs more than 140 helicopters to assist in fight-

Figure 15.
Tilt-Rotor commuter transport (350 knots)

ing forest fires, often because there is no other effective way.

Because of their ability to turn around more quickly than fixed-wing aircraft and to land on top of support trucks or on site for reloading and refueling, helicopters are also expected to make significant inroads into the agricultural aviation market.

Resource Exploration and Development

Most of the world's reserves of natural resources are in remote areas to which access by ground transportation is generally difficult if not impossible. This is equally true of a coal field in the Appalachians, an oil field in a South American jungle, and a drill rig in the Gulf of Mexico or off the coast of Alaska. Without the helicopter, recovery of these reserves would be much more difficult.

The helicopter is a vital link in the search for and production of oil. It is used for delivering men and equipment to offshore rigs, constructing and servicing pipelines in remote areas, and moving entire drill rigs in otherwise inaccessible areas. During periods of peak operation, more than 230,000 passengers are transported each month in the Gulf of Mexico. Similar scheduled transport operations are in place in the North Sea, which now includes the routine use of large transport helicopters over stage lengths in excess of 200 nautical miles. All aspects of the multibillion-dollar oil industry are expensive, and every hour saved by means of the helicopter means savings of thousands of dollars in rig costs and manhours. While so far it has been used primarily for transporting crews, large helicopters that could move whole drilling towers would save more than $40,000 a day in crane-rental costs alone. Regardless of their acquisition and operating costs, the use of rotorcraft will continue to grow in the exploration and development of natural resources.

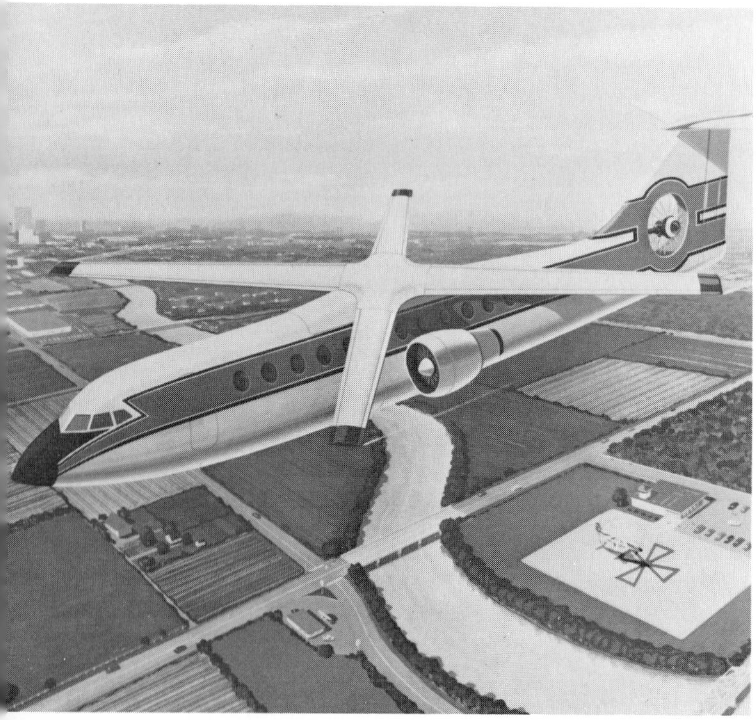

Figure 16.
The X-Wing transport (450 knots)

Construction

Helicopters are used in half the power-line construction in Canada and about 10 percent of that in the United States. The potential for reducing the costs of installing heavy equipment is significant. Where mobile cranes are required, the cost of using helicopters is half that of conventional methods and takes one-twentieth of the time.

Conventional methods of construction will be around for a long time, but more and more contractors are turning to helicopters for special one-shot tasks because they save both time and money. If a task is repetitive, the chances are that the set-up time and costs of a conventional crane are cost-effective. When a task is of limited duration or involves movement of materials from a remote staging area, however, the helicopter is the more cost-effective choice. At the same time, requests are often received by operators to move loads as large as 60,000 pounds, which is not within the present capability of rotorcraft.

The technology for large rotorcraft is not yet well established in the free world. Sig-

Figure 17.
Heavy-Lift Helicopter for cargo (Boeing Vertol XCH-62A derivative)

nificant progress was made in the Army's XCH-62A Heavy Lift Helicopter program, however, which was terminated in the mid 1970s for lack of funds. This program produced the primary components for a prototype vehicle and contributed significantly to the technology for large transmissions, large airframes, flight control, rotor systems, and propulsion systems. Figure 17 illustrates the XCH-62A configuration in use in construction of an oil rig.

A near-term opportunity to meet the need to lift much heavier external loads than is now possible is the use of multilift techniques to extend the productivity of helicopters of all sizes. This use of two helicopters coupled together by a suspended spreader bar was explored some years ago by Sikorsky Aircraft using two S-64 helicopters. Civil operators have now begun using this technique, and at least two operators have experimented successfully with twin-lift of rigid loads. Such operations have been somewhat limited by concerns about the pilots' workloads. Opportunities now exist, however, with the use of active control technology, to deal effectively with this workload problem.

Use of the hybrid airship offers another opportunity to deal with very heavy external loads. The hybrid airship is a joining of four lifting rotors with an airship hull, a combination that provides a vertical lift capability ten times that of any helicopter at present. Various hybrid types are envisioned, and the configurations investigated most recently include rotors and drive components modified from current helicopters. Forward and reverse propulsion is achieved

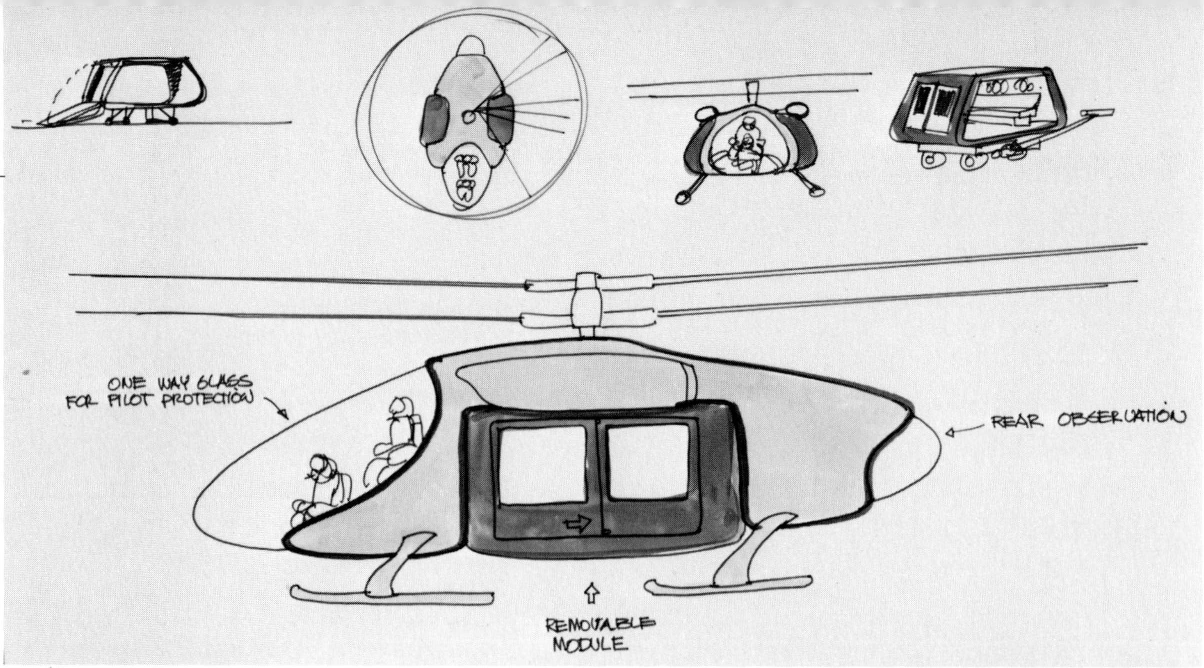

Figure 18.
User-defined, idealized, public service rotorcraft design

with separate propellers. The airship hull supports the empty weight of the vehicle, leaving the lifting rotors available for control and for lifting the external payload. The U.S. Forest Service has awarded a contract, administered by the U.S. Navy, to the Piasecki Corporation for the development and operation of a Heli-stat to demonstrate aerial logging of federal forests.

Public Service

The first public service helicopter mercy mission was flown in 1945. Since that time, countless lives have been saved; the Aerospace Industries Association has estimated that for every helicopter built in the free world seven lives have been saved.

More than sixty-five cities and twenty states use helicopters for police work because their response time is less and their surveillance capabilities are greater than those of ground units. In addition, more and more communities are using helicopter ambulance service in connection with emergency medical care. One of the most serious problems that confronts the medical profession today is inefficient delivery of emergency health care that would minimize trauma—life-threating injuries and attendant shock—from accidents of all types. Trauma is the fourth largest cause of death in the United States. Helicopter teams with heliports at trauma centers are now being supported by many communities. As a consequence, the number of heliports at hospitals is growing rapidly.

Growing attention is being given to the contributions that advanced technology can make to the improvement of public service rotorcraft. Assessment studies, workshops, and symposia have recently been sponsored by NASA. The objectives have included the definition of needs, problem areas, and desired vehicle characteristics and the assessment of research options. One achievement of the workshops was a defintion of the vehicle needed by the public service sector (see figure 18). The potential users specified high speed, long endurance, modular design, and low levels of noise and vibration among the many attributes desired in a public service vehicle. While this definition reflects an unconstrained approach to specifications, it will serve as a starting point in determining the extent to which the application of modern technology may be able to respond to public service needs.

The Future Market

The long-term projection of rotorcraft production in the free world remains optimistic despite some short-term slowdown in the civil sector caused by world economic conditions. This optimism is based on the recognition that rotorcraft are now an integral part of the world military scene and that, while civil uses of rotorcraft have increased dramatically during the past decade, the potential market is far from being fully developed.

As indicated in figure 19, rotorcraft production for the military forces of the free world was approximately $200 million in 1960. The annual investment approached $2 billion by 1968, largely because of the deployment of U.S. Army air mobile forces to Vietnam. Unit production in 1968 was more than 3,000. By 1980 the unit production had declined to fewer than 700 a year, but the dollar investment remained proportionately higher, at about $1.5 billion a year. This reflected both the influence of increased vehicle size and complexity and the effect of inflation on the cost per vehicle. This trend in complexity and sophistication of installed weapon systems will dominate the level of investment in military rotorcraft in the future. The indications are that by 1990 $7 billion a year will be invested in producing about 1,000 units a year for the free world military rotorcraft market.

The production of civil rotorcraft in the free world has increased steadily in each decade since 1960 and is forecast to more than double again during the 1980s to a level of approximately 3,000 units a year. The financial investment in civil rotorcraft through the years has increased much faster than unit sales, again because of the growth in vehicle size and complexity and the effect of inflation. Figure 20 illustrates the market growth and indicates that during the 1970s the market increased more than twelve times to a level of $350 million a year. By the 1990s sales are forecast to increase approximately seven and a half times to $4 billion a year. Fulfillment of this projection may be delayed somewhat by the slowdown in the world economy, but the long-term projection of continued market growth remains valid.

Without constant improvement in the technology of rotorcraft, such as can be expected in other modes of transportation,

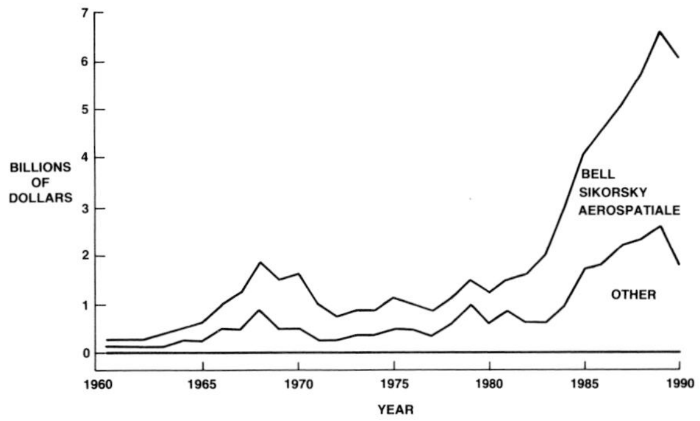

Figure 19.
Free-world military rotorcraft production forecast

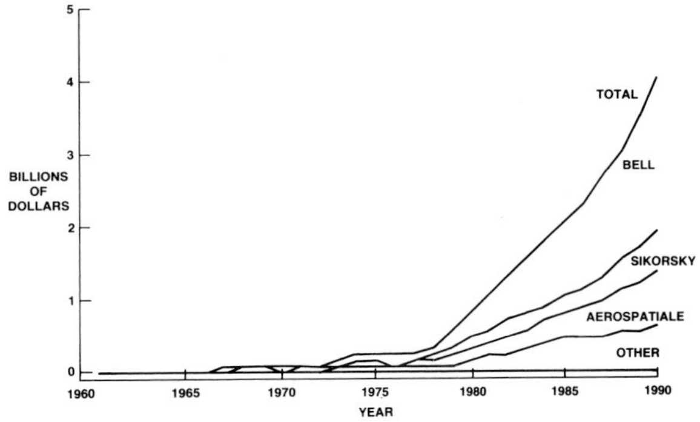

Figure 20.
Free-world civil rotorcraft production forecast

a baseline of market penetration would tend to decline during the 1990s. In order to indicate the sensitivity of the civilian market forecast to new technology, an assessment was made under NASA sponsorship on the basis of the following projections of technological capability:

- By 1985, a market baseline, represented by the Bell Model 222, the Sikorsky S-76, the Boeing Vertol 234, and the Hughes 500, is projected to show several improvements.

- By 1985, there will be a 15 percent improvement in speed, range, payload, quietness, reduced vibration, and direct operating cost (DOC) over the best that has been realized with present technology.

- By 1990, a 225-passenger rotorcraft having a cruise speed of 180 knots, a range of 600 nautical miles, and a DOC per seat per nautical mile of $0.04 will be in operation.

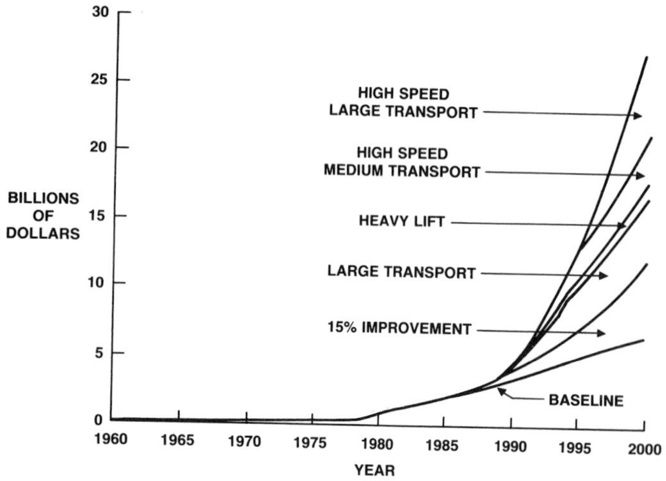

Figure 21.
Free-world civil rotorcraft market sensitivity to new technology

- By 1990, a heavy-lift rotorcraft having an external lift capability of thrity-five tons with a cruise speed of 100 knots will be in operation. In a thirty-ton internal-payload configuration the cruise speed would be 180 knots, with a range of 600 nautical miles and a DOC of $0.04 a ton per mile.

- By 1990, a 50-passenger rotorcraft having a cruise speed of 300 knots, a range of 800 nautical miles and a DOC of $0.04 a seat per nautical mile will be in operation.

- By 1995, a 150-passenger rotorcraft having a cruise speed of 350 knots, a range of 800 nautical miles, and a DOC of $0.04 a seat per nautical mile will be in operation.

These projections are considered to be technically feasible on the basis of research and technology programs under way or planned. The timing of introduction of the various vehicles into service is quite optimistic, however, because of the restraints of world economic factors. Figure 21 illustrates the effects of these technological projections on the potential world market for civil rotorcraft. It is interesting to note that the potential growth trend resembles the takeoff of the fixed-wing markets in the sixty-to-seventy-year period that followed their first significant use, as illustrated in figure 1.

The Long-Term Overview

Although some aspects of rotorcraft technology are common to other aeronautical technologies, the differences are great. Rotorcraft technologies must address many unique, highly complex, and interrelated requirements in dynamics, aerodynamics, flight control, and structural design. Developed to their full potential, rotorcraft will have broader functions in military tactics, surveillance, rescue, logistics, and special missions. With improved passenger and community acceptance, commercial operators will be able to exploit lower operating costs, higher speeds, and greater range in civil operations, including all-weather zero-zero operations.

The general trends in technology will lead to opportunities for reducing costs through the use of new materials, more elegant designs based on more sophisticated engineering techniques, and simple construction techniques made possible by robotics, which will stress high quality in volume production. Also, through the use of computer-guided manufacturing, limited production runs can be made at lower cost. Significantly lower operating costs should be possible with the use of new propulsion systems with increased fuel efficiency, on-condition maintenance procedures aided by on-board monitoring systems, and the opportunity to achieve full operation in all weather conditions. With the improvements in rotorcraft design, public acceptance will grow as reliability is increased, noise is reduced, and ride quality is improved in the next generation of rotorcraft. The productivity of future rotorcraft is assured by technological developments, such as the tilt rotor and the Advancing Blade Concept, that are under way. The economies of size can also be achieved with the introduction of large transport and cargo rotorcraft.

The underpinnings of the new technologies are dominated by the revolution in electronics and materials. The availability of more large, high-speed computers will make possible significant advances in integrated design techniques. Complex, interactive analyses of aerodynamics, aeromechanics, acoustics, and structural designs will be possible as a matter of routine. These analyses will be capable of dealing with detailed flow interactions throughout the vehicle. Automated design optimization will be a key to efficient design by replacing laborious and time-consuming design iterations and tradeoffs made on the basis of trend curves. Specialized computers and displays that will evolve from today's computer-aided design and computer-aided manufacturing techniques will expand to include record tracking, specification compliance, and certification procedures. High-fidelity ground-based simulation will be used extensively for crew training and design development and evolution. High-speed microcomputers will also provide the opportunity for voice control, satellite navigation and communication, terrain following, and automatic flight-manual call-up.

The materials revolution foreshadows important benefits for the rotorcraft industry, in which structural efficiency is essential if the full potential of future designs is to be realized. Composites, hybrid materials, ceramics, and advanced metals coupled with new fabrication techniques will produce higher strength capabilities, lower weight, longer service life, greater damage tolerances, and more efficient production and repair capabilities. New geometries are already emerging in rotor-blade planform, tip shapes, and varying airfoil shapes along the blade radius. These design techniques are being applied now to rotor hubs and fuselages. In the long term even more striking concepts may emerge, such as polymers that "heal" themselves, biocomputer chips, tailor-made molecules, and bistable materials.

It appears that the underlying theme of the next forty years of rotorcraft design and use will be integration. This will begin with integration of the many subsystems of the vehicle into an efficient operational system. Integration of the operational system will go hand in hand with integration of the new designs into the civil airspace and transportation system. Likewise, new military rotorcraft will continue to be integrated more extensively into modern offensive and defensive mission plans. As a result, by the year 2024, the majority of the jobs that the helicopter does will be jobs that are not being done today.

ACKNOWLEDGMENT

The following government and industry organizations contributed resource material for use in preparing this chapter: American Helicopter Society; Bell Helicopter Textron; Boeing Vertol Company; Detroit Diesel Allison, Gas Turbine Operations; Federal Aviation Administration; Helicopter Association International; Hughes Helicopters, Inc; Island Helicopter; National Aeronautics and Space Administration; Naval Air Systems Command; Sikorsky Aircraft Division of United Technologies; U.S. Army Aviation Research and Development Command.

The views and opinions expressed in this chapter are those of the author and not necessarily those of the National Aeronautics and Space Administration or any of the other contributing organizations.

JOHN F. WARD, at present NASA Manager, Rotorcraft Office, Office of Aeronautics and Space Technology (OAST), at NASA Headquarters in Washington, D.C., and executive secretary of the NASA Aeronautical Advisory Committee Informal Subcommittee on Rotorcraft Technology, was born in Watertown, New York, and received the B.S. degree in civil engineering from Clarkson College of Technology in Potsdam, New York, in 1952. Mr. Ward joined the National Advisory Committee for Aeronautics in 1952 as an aerospace research scientist. His research activities have been devoted exclusively to rotary-wing aircraft since 1959. The recipient of a NASA Langley Special Achievement Award in 1972 for his work in rotorcraft research, Mr. Ward is the author of numerous technical papers dealing with aircraft structures, loads, and aerodynamics. He was the first recipient of the American Helicopter Society Howard Hughes Award (1978) for his contributions to helicopter research and technology. He is a member of the Helicopter Association International and he has served as editor of the *Journal of the American Helicopter Society* and technical chairman of the 40th Annual Forum.

RUSSELL E. LEE

Famous Firsts in Helicopter History

400 B.C.—A flying Chinese rotary-wing top appears to be the first man-made object of any kind to fly under its own power.

1325—A Flemish manuscript shows the first known illustration of a helicopter, this one powered by pulling a string.

1480s—A drawing by Leonardo da Vinci shows a lifting, spiral airscrew, illustrating the world's first proposal for a full-size rotary-wing device.

1784—Flying mechanical models made by the French naturalist Launoy and his assistant, the mechanic Bienvenu, proved that rotary-wing flight was possible.

1810—Sir George Cayley published his remarkable paper on aerodynamics that contained the foundation for all future helicopter development.

September 29, 1907—A rotary-wing aircraft first lifted a man above the earth and held him for a sustained period. Built by Louis Breguet and an engineer named Volumard, the *Gyroplane No. 1,* steadied from the ground by four men with poles, rose approximately two feet above the ground and remained airborne for almost a minute.

November 13, 1907—On this date, free flight, without assistance from the ground, was achieved by Paul Cornu. Flying near Lisieux, France, Cornu's aircraft was powered by a 24-hp Antoinette engine that furnished enough power to hover about one foot above the ground.

1912—Cyclic pitch control of the rotor blades for precise, stabilized flight was used successfully for the first time by the Danish aviator J. H. C. Ellehammer.

May 17, 1918—Flight-tested with three 120-hp Le Rhone engines, the Austro-Hungarian PKZ 2 was the first helicopter intended for military use to fly successfully. In unmanned tests the craft could rise on tethering cables to 164 feet (50 meters) and remain there for up to thirty minutes. Wilhelm Zurovec, the designer, saw the PKZ 2 as a replacement for flammable hydrogen observation balloons.

January 9, 1923—The autogiro, a craft that used an unpowered, free-turning rotor for lift with a conventional, tractor/propeller engine for propulsion, made its first successful flight from Getafe, Spain. The machine was designed and built by Juan de la Cierva, who designated his machine the C-4.

April 14, 1923—The first Fédération Aéronautique Internationale (FAI) distance record for helicopters was established when Etienne Oehmichen flew his type no. 2 a distance of 1,181 feet (358 meters).

April 18, 1924—Marquis Raul Pateras Pescara flew his *Pescara No. 3* for a distance of 2,429 feet (736 meters) using collective and cyclic pitch control successfully for the first time. Before Pescara's flight, rotary-wing aircraft had used the conventional tractor engine for forward motion.

September 28, 1928—An autogiro was the first rotary-wing aircraft to fly across the English Channel. Juan de la Cierva piloted one of his own aircraft, a C8L Mk. II, across the channel, carrying a passenger from Croydon, England, to Le Bourget, France.

August 1930—Tethered flight trials of the TsAGI 1-EA, the Soviet Union's first helicopter, began on this date.

June 26, 1936—Making its maiden flight, the Focke-Achgelis Fa-61 was the first true, successful helicopter to carry out repeated, sustained flights. Built by Henrich Karl Johann Focke, the aircraft had controllable cyclic pitch and featured a wingless fuselage with the two main rotors mounted on cumbersome outriggers.

1937—The first helicopter to remain airborne for more than an hour was the Focke-Achgelis Fa-61.

1938—Hanna Reitsch, the world's first female helicopter pilot, flew the Fa-61 inside the Berlin Deutschland-Halle, a large meeting hall, before thousands of spectators.

July 6, 1939—This date marks the first scheduled airmail service by rotary-wing aircraft. A Kellett KD-1A, adorned with the colors and markings of Eastern Airlines, carried mail from the Philadelphia Post Office to the Camden, New Jersey, airport.

December 8, 1941—On this day, Igor Sikorsky flew the definitive version of his VS-300 helicopter. Incorporating the predominant features used in modern helicopters—collective pitch control with single main and tail rotors—it was the first helicopter in the world to incorporate these ideas in a single airframe.

January 13, 1942—This date marks the first flight of the Sikorsky XR-4, an improved VS-300 and forerunner of the R-4, the first production helicopter outside Germany and the only helicopter used in U.S. military operations during World War II. Designated the Hoverfly I, the R-4 was also the first helicopter used by British armed forces.

1943—Flown in the spring, the German Doblhoff WNF 342 was the world's first helicopter to be powered by rotor blade tip-jets. Supplied by tanks in the fuselage, the fuel mixture was directed through the hollow rotor blades and ignited at the tips.

October 16, 1943—The U.S. Navy's first helicopter, a Sikorsky R-4 (HNX-1), was accepted.

1944—The German World War II Ministry of Defense placed a production order for 1,000 of Anton Flettner's Fl 282 Kolibri helicopters, making it the first military rotary-wing craft to be ordered into mass production.

January 3, 1944—The first recorded helicopter mission of mercy was performed by a Sikorsky R-4 of the U.S. Coast Guard. A cargo of blood plasma was transported to more than 100 crewmen of a U.S. Navy destroyer who were injured in an explosion aboard ship.

September 1945—Flown by a German crew to the Airborne Forces Experimental Establishment in southern England, a Focke-Achgelis Fa 223 Drache (Dragon) became the first true helicopter to fly across the English Channel. This large utility vehicle featured an engine in the fuselage that drove two outrigger-mounted rotors.

May 1946—The Bell Model 47 received CAA Type Certificate H-1, making it the first American commercial helicopter. The Model 47, which made its maiden flight on December 8, 1945, has been produced by more countries than any other helicopter in the world.

April 24, 1947—The Kellett XR-10, the first all-metal helicopter in the world and the first twin-engine rotorcraft in the inventory of the U.S. Air Force, made its initial flight.

June 12, 1947—America's first woman helicopter pilot, Anne Shaw Carter, received her license. She later made sightseeing flights over New York.

August 20, 1947—Making its maiden flight, McDonnell's XH-20 *Little Henry* was the first ram-jet-powered helicopter in the world.

High fuel consumption and excessive noise kept the XH-20 from production.

1948—A Sikorsky S-52 was the first helicopter to loop. This agile flyer was equipped with all-metal rotor blades, the first ever fitted to a helicopter.

September 1948—Designed by Mikhail Leontyevich Mil, the Mil Mi-1 (NATO code name Hare) was the first mass-produced Soviet helicopter.

1949—A Hiller Model 12 made the first transcontinental flight across the United States by a commercial helicopter.

April 25, 1949—A commercial certificate of airworthiness was awarded to the Bristol Type 171 Sycamore, making it the first British commercial helicopter.

June 1, 1950—The world's first scheduled helicopter passenger service was initiated by British European Airways using Sikorsky S-51s.

December 10, 1951—Making its maiden flight the Kaman K-225 was the first helicopter powered by a turbine engine to fly.

December 18, 1953—This date marks the maiden flight of Sikorsky's first twin-engine helicopter, the S-56, and the first production rotary-wing aircraft in the world to have retractable landing gear.

March 1954—Kaman's modified Huskie HTK-1 made its inaugural flight and became the first twin-turbine-engine helicopter in the world.

1957—The Soviet Union's first production turbine-powered helicopter, the Mil Mi-6 (NATO code name Hook), flew for the first time.

1962—A Sikorsky S-61 was the first helicopter to exceed 200 miles an hour in level flight officially.

1963—The first commercial turbine-powered helicopter to operate in the United States was the Aérospatiale Alouette.

1965—Helicopter flight instructor and mother of three, Gay Maher was the first person to fly solo from coast to coast. Flying a Hughes 300, she made thirty-three fuel stops during the ten-day flight across the United States.

September 7, 1965—Making its maiden flight on this date, the Bell AH-1 Cobra was the U.S. military's first dedicated attack helicopter.

1967—Sikorsky's S-61 became the first helicopter to cross the Atlantic nonstop.

September 30, 1982—Flying a Bell 206L-1 LongRanger, H. Ross Perot, Jr., and Jay Coburn accomplished the first circumnavigation of the earth by helicopter.

July 22, 1983—The first solo helicopter flight around the world was flown by Dick Smith in a Bell JetRanger III.

RUSSELL E. LEE is a research assistant with the National Air and Space Museum. He began working for the museum in 1981, after his graduation from Southwest Texas State University with a degree in history. In his research he has concentrated on rotorcraft, and he assisted in redesigning the museum's *Spirit of Texas* helicopter exhibit.

DOMINICK A. PISANO

The Helicopter: A Selective Bibliography and Research Guide

The scope of the published literature on the helicopter and rotary-wing aircraft is vast. Here the intention is to offer a selection of works that will illuminate the history, technology, and practical use of the helicopter and its predecessors. Underlying the organization of the bibliography was an effort to provide information for anyone and everyone with an interest in rotorcraft and, rather than presenting an exhaustive list of titles, to direct the reader to especially fruitful sources of information.

In the historical section of part one, the reader will find a sampling of references to the origins of the helicopter, its development, and its application, both civil and military. In the general section will be found a number of popular books on the subject, including references to handbooks and illustrated guides. The third section of part one is a list of works that cover such technical aspects of the helicopter as aerodynamics, flight characteristics, and design theory. In the section on practical uses, sources of information on the use of the helicopter in municipal affairs, medical emergencies, and law enforcement are listed.

Part two is a survey of some of the general reference sources available to the researcher who is interested in more specific information concerning particular types of helicopters, rotary-wing aircraft, and propulsion systems.

Part One: Books and Articles Concerning Helicopters and Rotary-Wing Aircraft

Historical

Autogiro Company of America. *The Autogiro.* Philadelphia: Pitcairn-Cierva Autogiro Company of America, 1930.

Besser, Rolf. *Technik und Geschichte der Hubschrauber.* 2 vols. Munich: Bernard & Graefe, 1982.

Bracke, Albert. *Les Helicopteres Paul Cornu.* Paris: F. L. Vivien, 1908.

Cierva, Juan de la, and Don Rose. *Wings of Tomorrow: The Story of the Autogiro.* New York: Brewer, Warren & Putnam, 1931.

de Bothezat, George. "The Actual State of the Helicopter Problem." Paper delivered to the War Department, Engineering Division, Air Service, McCook Field, Dayton, Ohio, April 22, 1921.

Delear, Frank J. *Igor Sikorsky: His Three Careers in Aviation.* New York: Dodd, Mead, 1976. Originally published in 1969 with a foreword by James H. Doolittle.

Erickson, Frank. *Fishers of Men: The Story of the Development of Seagoing Helicopters.* Introduction by Igor I. Sikorsky, n.p., n.d. A microfilm of a manuscript copy in the Naval Historical Center of the Department of the Navy is available in the National Air and Space Museum Library, Washington, D.C.

Everett-Heath, John. *Soviet Helicopters: Design, Development and Tactics.* Boston: Jane's Publishing, 1983.

Fails, William R. *Marines and Helicopters, 1962–1973.* Washington, D.C.: U.S. Marine Corps, 1978. See also the entry in this section for Rawlins, Eugene W.

Faure, Pierre. *Trente ans au service de l'aviation; Louis Breguet*. Paris: Blondel La Rougery, 1938.

Focke, Henrich. "German Thinking on Rotary-Wing Development." *Journal of the Royal Aeronautical Society*, May 1965, pp. 293–305.

Francis, Devon E. *The Story of the Helicopter*. New York: Coward-McCann, 1946.

Free, F. W. "Russian Helicopters." *Aeronautical Journal*, September 1970, pp. 767–85.

Gablehouse, Charles. *Helicopters and Autogiros: A History of Rotating-Wing and V/STOL Aviation*. Rev. ed. Philadelphia: Lippincott, 1969. Previous edition published as *Helicopters and Autogiros: A Chronicle of Rotating-Wing Aircraft* (Philadelphia: Lippincott, 1967).

Gibbs-Smith, Charles H. *Sir George Cayley's Aeronautics: 1796–1855*. London: Her Majesty's Stationery Office, 1962.

———. *Leonardo da Vinci's Aeronautics*. London: HMSO, 1967.

———. *Aviation: An Historical Survey from Its Origins to the End of World War II*. London: HMSO, 1970.

Gregory, Hollingsworth Franklin. *Anything a Horse Can Do: The Story of the Helicopter*. Introduction by Igor Sikorsky. New York: Reynal & Hitchcock, 1944.
Revised editions were subsequently published under the titles *The Helicopter; or, Anything a Horse Can Do* (New York: Reynal and Hitchcock, 1948) and *The Helicopter* (South Brunswick, New Jersey: A. S. Barnes, 1976).

Grose, Parlee C. *The Problem of Vertical Flight*. McComb, Ohio: General Publishing Company, 1931.

Grosz, Peter. "Helicopter Pioneers of World War I." *Air Enthusiast*, March-June 1978, pp. 154–59.

Hubler, Richard G. *Straight Up: The Story of Vertical Flight*. New York: Duell, Sloan and Pearce, 1961.

Hurren, Bernard J. *Helicopters of Tomorrow*. London: Staples Press, 1947.

Jackson, Robert. *The Dragonflies: The Story of Helicopters and Autogiros*. London: Barker, 1971.

Klemin, Alexander. "Principles of Rotary Aircraft." *Journal of the Franklin Institute*, March 1939, pp. 393–94.

———. *The Helicopter Adventure*. New York: Coward-McCann, 1947.

Lambermont, Paul M., and Anthony Pirie. *Helicopters and Autogyros of the World*. Rev. ed. New York: A. S. Barnes, 1970.
Original edition published in 1959 with foreword by Igor Sikorsky.

Liptrot, R. N. "Historical Development of Helicopters." *American Helicopter*, March 1947, pp. 12–14; 24–27.

Loening, Grover. "The Helicopter's Limited Future." Lecture given at the Brooklyn Institute of Arts and Sciences, December 3, 1943.

Macauley, C. B. F. *The Helicopters Are Coming*. New York: McGraw-Hill, 1944.

Montross, Lynn. *Cavalry of the Sky: The Story of U.S. Marine Combat Helicopters*. New York: Harper, 1954.

Morris, Charles Lester. *Pioneering the Helicopter*. New York: McGraw-Hill, 1945.

Peters, A. Gerald, and Donald F. Wood. "Helicopter Airlines in the United States, 1945–75." *Journal of Transport History*, February 1977, pp. 1–16.

Ponton d'Amecourt, Gustave. *La Conquête de l'air par l'hélice: exposé d'un nouveau système d'aviation*. Paris: E. Sausset, 1863.

Porter, James Robertson. *The Helicopter Flying-Machine: An Account of Previous Experiments, Including an Analysis of the Author's Turbine Machine, with Theory and Deductions*. London: "Aeronautics," 1911.

Rawlins, Eugene W. *Marines and Helicopters, 1946–1962*. Washington, D.C.: U.S. Marine Corps, 1976.
See also the entry in this section for Fails, William R.

Sanders, C. J., and A. H. Rawson. *The Book of the C.19 Autogiro*. London: Sir Isaac Pitman & Sons, 1931.

Sikorsky, Igor. "Commercial and Military Uses of Rotating Wing Aircraft." Proceedings of the Second Annual Rotating Wing Aircraft Meeting, Institute of the Aeronautical Sciences, 1939.

———. *The Story of the Winged-S: Late Developments and Recent Photographs of the Helicopter, An Autobiography*. New York: Dodd, Mead, 1958.

Smith, Frank Kingston. *Legacy of Wings: The Story of Harold F. Pitcairn*. New York: Jason Aronson, 1981.

Stewart, Paul W., et al. *Survey of Travel in 1941 and Potential Market for Helicopter Service*. Prepared for the Greyhound Corporation, August 1943.

Tolson, John J. *Airmobility, 1961–1971*. Washington, D.C.: U.S. Department of the Army, 1973.

Turner, John F. *Hovering Angels: The Record of the Royal Navy's Helicopters*. London: Harrap, 1957.

[U.S. Army] Far East Command. *Helicopters in Korea, 1 July 1951–31 August 1953.* Fort Eustis, Virginia: [Army] Transportation School, 1955.

Warleta, Jose. *Autogyro.* Madrid: Instituto de Espana, 1977.

Westland Helicopters. *A History of British Rotorcraft, 1866–1965.* Yeovil, England, 1968.

Young, Warren R. *The Helicopters.* Epic of Flight Series. Alexandria, Virginia: Time-Life Books, 1982.

General

Adwill, James. *Helicopters in Action.* New York: Meredith Press, 1969.

Ahnstrom, D. N. *The Complete Book of Helicopters.* Rev. ed. New York: World Publishing Co., 1968.

Brown, Joseph M. *Helicopter Directory.* New York: Hippocrene Books, 1976.

Butterworth, William E. *Air Evac.* New York: W. W. Norton, 1967.

———. *Helicopter Pilot.* New York: W. W. Norton, 1967.

Campbell, John Paul. *Vertical Takeoff and Landing Aircraft.* New York: Macmillan, 1962.

Cooke, David C. *How Helicopters Are Made.* New York: Dodd, Mead, 1968.

Coombs, Charles I. *Skyhooks: The Story of Helicopters.* New York: William Morrow, 1967.

Croome, Angela. *Hover Craft.* Leicester, England: Brockhampton Press, 1960.

Delear, Frank J. *The New World of Helicopters.* New York: Dodd, Mead, 1967.

———. *Helicopters and Airplanes of the U.S. Army.* New York: Dodd, Mead, 1977.

Floherty, John J. *Whirling Wings: The Story of the Helicopter.* Philadelphia: Lippincott, 1961.

Gunston, Bill. *An Illustrated Guide to Military Helicopters.* New York: Arco, 1981.

———. *Helicopters of the World.* New York: Crescent Books, 1983.

Hellman, Harold. *Helicopters and Other VTOLs.* Garden City, New York: Doubleday, 1970.

Howard, Jean Ross. *All about Helicopters.* New York: Sports Car Press, 1969.

Keating, Bern. *Chopper: The Illustrated Story of Helicopters in Action.* Chicago: Rand McNally, 1976.

Lent, Henry B. *The Helicopter Book.* New York: Macmillan, 1956.

Munson, Kenneth G. *Helicopters and Other Rotorcraft since 1907.* New York: Macmillan, 1969.

Polmar, Norman, and Floyd Kennedy. *Military Helicopters of the World: Military Rotary-Wing Aircraft since 1917.* Annapolis: Naval Institute Press, 1981.

Swanborough, Frederick G. *Vertical Flight Aircraft of the World.* Los Angeles: Aero Publishers, 1965.

Taylor, John W. R. *Helicopters and VTOL Aircraft.* Garden City, New York: Doubleday, 1968.

Taylor, Michael J. H. *Helicopters of the World.* 3d ed. London: Ian Allan, 1981.

Taylor, Michael J. H., and John W. R. Taylor. *Jane's Pocket Book of Helicopters.* New York: Collier Books, 1981.

Young, Arthur S. *The Bell Notes: Journey from Physics to Metaphysics.* Mill Valley, California: Robert Briggs Associates, 1984.

Design, Engineering, and Flight

Bramwell, A. R. S. *Helicopter Dynamics.* New York: Wiley, 1976.

Collier, Larry. *How to Fly Helicopters.* Blue Ridge Summit, Pennsylvania: Tab Books, 1979.

Dommasch, Daniel O. *Elements of Propeller and Helicopter Dynamics.* New York: Pitman Publishing Corp., 1953.

Dzik, Stanley J. *Helicopter Design and Data Manual.* Appleton, Wisconsin: Aviation Publications, 1974.

Fay, John. *The Helicopter: History, Piloting, and How It Flies.* North Pomfret, Vermont: David & Charles, 1976.

Gessow, Alfred, and Garry C. Myers, Jr. *Aerodynamics of the Helicopter.* New York: F. Ungar, 1967.

Johnson, Wayne. *Helicopter Theory.* Princeton, New Jersey: Princeton University Press, 1980.

Liptrot, Roger N., and J. D. Woods. *Rotorcraft.* London: Butterworths Scientific Publications, 1955.

McDonald, John J. *Flying the Helicopter.* Blue Ridge Summit, Pennsylvania: Tab Books, 1981.

Nikolsky, Alexander A. *Notes on Helicopter Design Theory.* Princeton, New Jersey: Princeton University Press, 1944.
A series of lectures delivered in March and April 1944 at Princeton University.

———. *Helicopter Analysis.* New York: Wiley, 1951.

Payne, Peter R. *Helicopter Dynamics and Aerodynamics.* New York: Macmillan, 1959.

Prouty, R. W. *Practical Helicopter Aerodynamics.* Peoria, Illinois: PJS Publications, 1982.

Saunders, George H. *Dynamics of Helicopter Flight.* New York: Wiley, 1975.

Schafer, Joseph. *Fundamentals of Helicopter Maintenance.* Basin, Wyoming: Aviation Maintenance Publications, 1980.

———. *Helicopter Fundamentals.* Aviation Technician Training Course Series. Basin, Wyoming: Aviation Maintenance Publications, 1980.

Two Decades of Helicopter Design. London: Temple Press, 1953.

Young, Raymond A. *Helicopter Engineering.* New York: Ronald Press Co., 1949.

Zweng, Charles A. *Helicopter Rating: A Practical Guide to the CAA Helicopter Pilot Ratings.* North Hollywood, California: Pan American Navigation Service, 1954.

Practical Uses

Beall, James R., and Robert E. Downing. *Helicopter Utilization in Municipal Law Enforcement: Administrative Considerations.* Springfield, Illinois: Thomas, 1972.

Brown, Eric M. *The Helicopter in Civil Operations.* New York: Van Nostrand Reinhold, 1981.

Chartres, John. *Helicopter Rescue.* London: Ian Allan, 1980.

Davis, Ann, and Robert A. Richardson. *The Helicopter: Its Importance to Commerce and to the Public.* Washington, D.C.: Helicopter Association of America, 1978.

Kinnard, Harry W. *Vertical Airlift.* Edwin A. Link Lecture Series. Smithsonian Publication 4761. Washington, D.C.: Smithsonian Institution Press, 1968.

Lavalla, Rick. *Helirescue Manual: Personal Safety and SAR Operations around Helicopters.* Tacoma, Washington: Survival Education Association, n.d.

National Institute of Law Enforcement and Criminal Justice. Center for Criminal Justice Operations and Management. *The Utilization of Helicopters for Police Air Mobility.* Washington, D.C.: U.S. Law Enforcement Assistance Administration, 1971.

North Atlantic Treaty Organization. Advisory Group for Aerospace Research and Development. Aerospace Medical Panel. *Aeromedical Aspects of Helicopter Operations in the Tactical Situation.* Paris, 1967.

Port of New York Authority. Aviation Department. *Transportation by Helicopter, 1955–1975: A Study of Its Potential in the New Jersey-New York Metropolitan Area.* New York, 1952.

United Aircraft Corporation. Sikorsky Aircraft Division. *The Employment of Helicopters and V/STOL Aircraft in Counter-Insurgency.* Stratford, Connecticut, 1963.

Part Two: Bibliographic Note

The references listed in the following paragraphs represent a selection of some readily accessible and useful books that will provide additional information concerning technical reports, periodical articles, aircraft and aero engine yearbooks, photographs, motion pictures, and miscellaneous sources having to do with the helicopter and other rotary-wing aircraft.

Technical Reports

The amount of technical report material on rotary-wing aircraft is indeed vast, but the researcher will be glad to know that such material can be found in National Aeronautics and Space Administration (NASA), *Scientific and Technical Aerospace Reports* (Washington, D.C., 1963–). *STAR*, as it is popularly known, is a comprehensive abstracting and indexing journal that covers current worldwide reports in space science and technology and is also an important source of technical data on rotary-wing aircraft design and aerodynamics. Pre-1963 technical material can be found in NASA, *Index of NACA Technical Publications, 1915–1960* (Washington, D.C., 1949–60), which indexes the reports of NASA's predecessor, the National Advisory Committee for Aeronautics (NACA). The gap between 1960 and 1963 is filled by various annual indexes published by NASA. NASA has also published a thirteen-year compilation of technical reports on rotorcraft called *Rotary Wing Aircraft: Scientific and Technical Publications of NASA, 1970–1982* (1982), compiled by John D. Hiemstra.

Another invaluable source of information concerning technical literature on rotary-wing aircraft is *International Aerospace Abstracts* (Phillipsburg, New Jersey, 1961–). Published semimonthly, *IAA* covers published literature, not only in periodicals and books, but also in meeting papers and proceedings issued by professional and academic organizations; it also abstracts translations of foreign-language journal articles.

In addition, since the end of World War II, the American Helicopter Society has published each year compilations of the papers presented at its annual conferences. References to these papers will be found in *Engineering Index* (New York, 1934–).

Periodical Literature

Researchers who are interested in locating historical literature concerning the helicopter and its predecessors in periodicals should consult *Bibliography of Aeronautics* (Washington, D.C.: Smithsonian Institution, 1910–37). First compiled by Paul Brockett and continued by the National Advisory Committee for Aeronautics (NACA), the *Bibliography of Aeronautics* is arranged alphabetically by author or title and includes books and pamphlets. The primary value of Brockett's, as it is familiarly known, is that it indexes articles in nearly 200 aviation periodicals from the early period of practical rotary-wing development to the late 1930s.

The *Bibliography of Aeronautics* should be supplemented by the *Readers' Guide to Periodical Literature*, which contains a surprising number of references to articles on helicopters that have appeared in popular magazines. The *Readers' Guide* is also useful for contemporary articles on the autogiro during the late 1920s and throughout the 1930s and is especially helpful for a researcher who wishes to trace, in the periodical literature, the vision of the autogiro's future as an air vehicle for popular use. Also, parts 8, 9, and 10 of U.S. Works Progress Administration, *Bibliography of Aeronautics* (New York: Institute of the Aeronautical Sciences, 1938), contain a great deal of information concerning periodical articles and technical reports on helicopters, autogiros, cyclogiros, and gyroplanes published during the 1930s.

Researchers interested in periodical literature concerning specific helicopters should find August Hanniball's *Aircraft, Engines and Airmen: A Selective Review of the Periodical Literature, 1930–1969* (Metuchen, New Jersey, 1972) of great value. One of the most compact and comprehensive aviation history reference books ever published, Hanniball's includes references to articles on helicopters that have appeared in specialized periodicals such as *American Helicopter* and in more general sources such as *Aviation Week and Space Technology*.

Unfortunately, Hanniball's covers only a forty-year period, and no published reference source takes up the slack from 1969 to the present. The National Air and Space Museum Library, however, does maintain an unpublished index to periodical literature on aviation that covers the years from about 1973 to the present and that also contains a good many references to popular articles on helicopters. For additional information, write to the National Air and Space Museum Library, Smithsonian Institution, Washington, D.C., 20560.

Another important source of information concerning periodical literature on helicopters is the *Air University Library Index to Military Periodicals* (Maxwell Air Force Base, Alabama, 1949–). The index is arranged in such a way that it not only covers individual helicopter types but also lists articles on helicopters in warfare, rescue work, and business.

Although it is not actually a periodical index, Library of Congress, *Aeronautical and Space Publications: A World List* (Washington, D.C.: 1962), contains brief descriptions of many periodicals published throughout the world that specialize in aviation, and it covers a great many magazines and journals that specialize in helicopters and rotary-wing aircraft.

Finally, many articles on the development, technology, and use of helicopters will be found in these specialized journals and magazines: *American Helicopter* (New York); *Approach: Naval Aviation Safety Review* (Norfolk, Virginia); *Army Aviation* (Westport, Connecticut); *Aviation Week and Space Technology* (New York); *Helicopter Annual* (Washington, D.C.); *Helicopter International Magazine* (Avon, England); *Journal of the American Helicopter Society* (Alexandria, Virginia); *Rotor and Wing International* (Peoria, Illinois); *United States Army Aviation Digest* (Washington, D.C.); *Vertica: The International Journal of Rotorcraft and Power Lift Aircraft* (Elmsford, New York); and *Vertiflite* (Alexandria, Virginia).

Aircraft and Engine Yearbooks.

Published continuously since early in the century, *Jane's All the World's Aircraft* (London: 1909–) is one of the most important sources of information on helicopters and rotorcraft, past and present. Arranged alphabetically by country and manufacturer, *Jane's* contains descriptions, specifications, illustrations, and photographs of every important military and commercial rotary-wing aircraft produced internationally since the advent of vertical flight. *Jane's* is also useful in that it offers comprehensive coverage of rotary-wing propulsion systems manufactured throughout the world.

Supplementing *Jane's* in rotary-wing propulsion is Paul H. Wilkinson's *Aircraft Engines of the World* (Washington, D.C., 1941–70, irreg.).

Photographs

Since a comprehensive index of the sources of aerospace photography is not available, researchers must rely on general photographic reference books for information. One of the most valuable of these for the aviation historian or researcher is *Picture Sources 3: Collections of Prints and Photographs in the U.S. and Canada*, edited by Ann Novotny and Rosemary Eakins (New York, 1975). Although sadly out of date, *Picture Sources 3* provides references to some of the most important collections of aeronautical photographs in the United States, including some that contain rotary-wing aircraft. *Picture Sources 3*, however, cannot be substituted for a badly needed guide to aerospace photography.

Picture Sources 3 does contain a brief and on the whole accurate description of the photographic collection of the National Air and Space Museum. This collection, one of the largest of its kind in the world, contains photographs of virtually every kind of rotorcraft manufactured internationally since the advent of practical rotary-wing flight. Since 1982, most of the collection of photographs, indexed by aircraft manufacturer, is now available on videodisc, which means that thousands of photographic images are immediately accessible. Additional information concerning the NASM photograph collection and the Archival Videodisc Program may be obtained by writing to Pete Suthard, Chief, Records Management Division, National Air and Space Museum, Smithsonian Institution, Washington, D.C., 20560.

Since *Picture Sources 3* was last published, the contemporary photographic collections of the army, the navy, the Marine Corps, and the air force, which had been separately maintained and which contain a wealth of photographic material on rotary-wing aircraft, have been reorganized into the Defense Audiovisual Agency (DAVA). Fortunately, the description of these valuable collections in *Picture Sources 3* is still largely accurate despite the reorganization. Additional information on these military photographic collections may be obtained by writing to the Defense Audiovisual Agency (DAVA-W), Building 168, NDW, Washington, D.C., 20374.

For information on the photographic collection of the National Archives and Records Service, one of the richest sources of historical aviation photography, including rotary-wing aircraft, researchers should consult *Guide to the National Archives of the United States* (Washington, D.C.: National Archives and Records Service, General Services Administration, 1974). The National Archives houses the Wright Air Development Center Collection, which contains official photographs of helicopters and autogiros in service with the U.S. Air Force and its predecessors from 1917 to 1959. Also in the collection of the National Archives are the official photographs of the U.S. Navy from 1932 to 1957, and the historical photographic collections of the U.S. Marine Corps and the U.S. Coast Guard, all of which contain photographic material on rotary-wing aircraft. Official air force photographs of helicopters after 1959 and of navy helicopters after 1957 will be found at DAVA (see above). Photographs of helicopters in service with the U.S. Coast Guard are available through the Commandant, United States Coast Guard (C-BPA-1), Washington, D.C., 20593.

Motion Pictures

Researchers also suffer from the lack of a comprehensive index or guide to aviation motion picture films. Nevertheless, stock film footage of post–World War II helicopter operations in the armed forces, particularly during the Korean and Vietnam war eras, will be found in the central film repository at DAVA. Additional information may be obtained by writing to the Defense Audiovisual Agency (DAVA-NLGDA), Building 248, Norton Air Force Base, California, 92409.

Miscellaneous Reference Sources

Because there are hundreds of books that contain information concerning rotary-wing aircraft of every country, type, and vintage, a detailed listing here is impossible. The following selection of titles should provide the researcher with sources of quick and ready reference as well as basic facts at a glance. Titles of books in print on helicopters and autogiros will be found in the most recent edition of *Subject Guide to Books in Print* (New York: R. R. Bowker), which is available in libraries and most bookstores.

Three books by Charles H. Gibbs-Smith are fine sources of information on helicopter prehistory: *Aviation: An Historical Survey from Its Origins to the End of World War II* (London: Her Majesty's Stationery Office, 1970), *Leonardo da Vinci's Aeronautics* (HMSO, 1967), and *Sir George Cayley's Aeronautics: 1796–1855* (HMSO, 1962). Gibbs-Smith, the dean of the historians of early aeronautics, is undoubtedly the best source of information on the precursors of practical rotary-wing development. His *Aviation: An Historical Survey*, for example, includes text, photographs, and illustrations pertaining to the work of such experimenters as Launoy and Bienvenu, Sir George Cayley, Ponton d'Amecourt, and Forlanini.

Unfortunately, Paul Lambermont and Anthony Pirie's *Helicopters and Autogyros of the World* (New York: A. S. Barnes, 1970), one of the best and most comprehensive collections of information on rotary-wing aircraft, is out of date and no longer in print. Lambermont and Pirie's book has a valuable historical introduction that sketches the precursors of the modern helicopter. The remainder of the book is arranged by country and includes very good commentary on a number of historically significant prewar and postwar rotary-wing developments up to 1970.

Another fine all-around source is Kenneth Munson's colorfully illustrated *Helicopters and Other Rotorcraft since 1907* (New York: Macmillan, 1969).

Researchers seeking information on present-day rotary-wing aircraft will find Joseph Mill Brown's *Helicopter Directory* (New York: Hippocrene Books, 1976) very useful. Brown's book contains photographs, specifications, and brief descriptions and is arranged by country of manufacture.

Still more recent material will be found in Michael J. H. Taylor's *Helicopters of the World* (London: Ian Allan, 1981). Now in its third edition, Taylor's book includes the principal helicopter types in service and under development and is arranged by country. Part three of the book is especially interesting for its international coverage of home-built rotary aircraft. Another source of up-to-date information is Michael J. H. Taylor and John W. R. Taylor's *Jane's Pocket Book of Helicopters* (New York: Collier Books, 1981). Like *Jane's All the World's Aircraft*, this book is arranged by country of manufacture and is well illustrated with photographs and three-view drawings.

Up-to-date sources of information concerning military helicopters are Bill Gunston's *An Illustrated Guide to Military Helicopters* (New York: Arco, 1981), and Norman Polmar and Floyd Kennedy's *Military Helicopters of the World: Military Rotary-Wing Aircraft Since 1917* (Annapolis: Naval Institute Press, 1981). Both of these books contain many illustrations and a great deal of factual material.

Also of interest are *The Helicopter Blue Book: A Complete Helicopter Price and Performance Guide*, (Skokie, Illinois: Helicopter Financial Services, 1984), which is revised quarterly, and Jean Ross Howard's updated edition of the *Directory of Heliports/Helistops in the United States, Canada, Mexico and Puerto Rico* (Washington, D.C.: Aerospace Industries Association, 1984).

DOMINICK A. PISANO is an associate curator in the Aeronautics Department of the National Air and Space Museum. A graduate of both the Pennsylvania State University and the Catholic University of America, he is the author of similar bibliographic and reference guides for *Charles A. Lindbergh: An American Life* (1977), *The Wright Brothers: Heirs of Prometheus* (1978), *Apollo: Ten Years since Tranquillity Base* (1979), and *The Jet Age: Forty Years of Jet Aviation* (1979), all published for the National Air and Space Museum by the Smithsonian Institution Press.

WALTER J. BOYNE is director of the National Air and Space Museum. He was formerly curator of aeronautics and chief of preservation and restoration at the museum's Silver Hill Facility.

Mr. Boyne joined the museum in June 1974 and was assigned curatorial duties for the Gallery of Air Transportation. Subsequently, it was his task to schedule and supervise the assembly, installation, and suspension of all of the artifacts in the museum.

He was born in East Saint Louis, Illinois, in 1929, and obtained his first taste of flying at the Parks Air College Field. Having entered the U.S. Air Force in 1951, he retired as a colonel in 1974, with more than 5,000 flying hours in a score of different aircraft. Mr. Boyne graduated with honors from both the University of California—Berkeley (B.S., B.A.) and the University of Pittsburgh (M.B.A.).

At present he is an associate editor of *Wings and Airpower* magazine. He has had five books published, has two others ready for publication, and has written more than 250 articles on subjects in aviation. He writes monthly columns for two national aviation magazines.

DONALD S. LOPEZ is deputy director for curatorial sciences of the National Air and Space Museum. His responsibilities include the supervision of the curatorial staff and the curatorial support staff. Before his appointment as deputy director, Mr. Lopez was chairman of the Aeronautics Department.

Mr. Lopez holds the B.S. degree in aeronautical engineering from the Air Force Institute of Technology and the M.S. in aeronautics from the California Institute of Technology, and he is a graduate of the U.S. Air Force Test Pilot School.

During World War II, Mr. Lopez served in China, flying P-40s under General Claire L. Chennault, where he became an ace. His other assignments included five years as a fighter test pilot, a combat tour flying F-86s in Korea, and five years at the U.S. Air Force Academy as an associate professor of aeronautics and chief of academic counseling. Following his retirement from the air force in 1964, Mr. Lopez worked as a systems engineer on the Apollo/Saturn Launch Vehicle and the SKYLAB Orbital Workshop. He joined the Smithsonian Institution in 1972.

Mr. Lopez is a member of the American Fighter Aces Association, the American Institute of Aeronautics and Astronautics, and the Society for the History of Technology.